John DOS PASSOS

a reference guide

A
Reference
Guide
to
Literature

Ronald Gottesman
Editor

John DOS PASSOS

a reference guide

JOHN ROHRKEMPER

G.K.HALL&CO.

70 LINCOLN STREET, BOSTON, MASS.

Library of Congress Cataloging in Publication Data

Rohrkemper, John.
  John Dos Passos, a reference guide.

  (A Reference guide to literature)
  Includes index.
  1. Dos Passos, John, 1896-1970—Bibliography.
I. Title. II. Series: Reference guides to
literature.
Z8237.89.R63 [PS3507.O743]   016.813'52   80-17591
ISBN 0-8161-8105-5

This publication is printed on permanent/durable acid-free paper
MANUFACTURED IN THE UNITED STATES OF AMERICA

Contents

Introduction

Critical attention came early to Dos Passos, both the acclaim and the
criticism loud and emotional. Barely twenty-five when he published
Three Soldiers, Dos Passos soon found his novel embroiled in a controversy which would be typical of reactions to his later books, a
controversy both literary and extra-literary. This novel, the first
major treatment of World War I by an American participant, earned the
highest praise from many reviewers. One critic characterized the
novel as "an absorbing, powerful, brutally frank view of the A.E.F.
and its war life" (Booklist, 1921). Another admired Dos Passos'
rigorous honesty and thought the book "the harmonious expression of a
well-chewed rage" (Blum, 1921). Heywood Broun thought that "nothing
which has come out of the school of American realists has seemed to
us so entirely honest. There is not an atom of pose in this book.
It represents deep convictions and impressions eloquently expressed"
(Broun, 1921). H. L. Mencken admired Dos Passos' "passion for the
truth" and his "imagination that makes the truth live" (Mencken,
1921). Mencken felt that the novel set the standard for future war
novels and "changed the whole tone of American opinion about the war"
(Mencken, 1922).

At the same time, other critics were literally scandalized by the
book. One thought it portrayed "the most unreal of reality" and
would appeal to only "a few who came out of the army a grouch . . .
or who gloat over goddamns" (Outlook, 1921). H. N. Fairchild thought
Three Soldiers a "piece of sordid, narrow-minded realism" (Fairchild,
1921). Coningsby Dawson, in an article entitled "Insulting the Army"
in the New York Times Book Review, could not contain his repulsion
for the novel which he felt was "a nationwide insult . . . a dastardly
denial of the splendid chivalry which carried many a youth to a soldier's death with the sure knowledge in his soul that he was a
liberator" (Dawson, 1921). One thing is certain about the critics'
reaction to Three Soldiers: no clear consensus on the novel's merits
was reached. The only common characteristic of the reviews--and it
is an important one--was that hardly any of the reviewers addressed
themselves in any detail to the art of the novel; their reactions
were almost entirely to the content.

Introduction

Such an omission would be hardly possible with Dos Passos' next major novel, Manhattan Transfer, again a harshly critical analysis of modern society, but this time with more obvious stylistic bravado and inventiveness. Some of Dos Passos' most sympathetic critics plainly did not like the stylistic innovations. Mencken was disappointed that his new novel did not seem to fulfill the promise of Three Soldiers: "It is incoherent and not infrequently very dull. It staggers all over the lot" (Mencken, 1926). Upton Sinclair made a "plea" to Dos Passos to avoid the trickery and write a "straightaway novel with the same emotional power and radical insight" (Sinclair, 1927).

Others, however, thought that Manhattan Transfer's technique was precisely what gave it its power. One critic, who felt the portrayal of New York "too crude and materialistic," nevertheless felt that in the style and structure of the novel "Dos Passos displays his power, his architectonic ability, and a poetic sense of rhythms, colors, sounds and smells" (C., N.R., 1925). Allan Angoff thought the novel "a vivid and masterly impression of chaos" (Angoff, 1927). Unquestionably, the most ecstatic praise for Manhattan Transfer came from Sinclair Lewis. In a review which was later published as a pamphlet by Dos Passos' publisher, Lewis wondered if the book might not be "a novel of the very first importance," and thought it "more important in every way than anything written by Gertrude Stein or Marcel Proust or even . . . Mr. James Joyce's Ulysses," because Dos Passos makes use of "all their experimental psychology and style," yet has created a book that is interesting (Lewis, 1925).

Still other reviewers were mixed in their evaluation of the novel. Mary Ross thought it had an exciting, kaleidoscope effect, but thought that Dos Passos failed to show any real sensitivity to or affection for the characters (Ross, 1925). Others admired the book's energy, but thought that that energy lacked focus. Negative reviews of Manhattan Transfer were few, but when they did appear they were vigourously negative. Paul Elmer More argued that the life represented in Dos Passos' work "is about the lowest we have produced," that Manhattan Transfer was nothing more than "an explosion in a cesspool" (More, 1928). More's view, however, was becoming the exception as Dos Passos' critical reputation continued to rise throughout the twenties, so much so that, by 1926, Joseph Warren Beach could call him "the most promising" of experimental writers, the "indubitable superior" of Virginia Woolf (Beach, 1926). By 1930 even Dos Passos' harshest critics had to concede that he had established himself as a major figure in modern American writing. It was during this next decade, in which he produced his masterpiece, the U.S.A. trilogy, that Dos Passos achieved his greatest critical acclaim. The impact of U.S.A. was so great that Jean-Paul Sartre was moved to proclaim Dos Passos "the greatest writer of our time" (Sartre, 1955). The critics praised Dos Passos for his portrayal of America's sociopolitical environment in the twentieth century and also for his structural and stylistic innovations. Here was a writer with the ambition to choose an entire continent and an entire generation for his subject, and the virtuosity to maintain control--even to impose order--over such a broad and potentially unruly expanse.

The reaction to the first volume of the U.S.A. trilogy, The 42nd Parallel, was not so universally positive, however, for some critics, not realizing that this was the first volume of an extended work, were disappointed by its apparent lack of scheme and its open-endedness. One reviewer felt that this lack of order was merely an example of "the naturalistic pessimism and spiritual anarchy which mask our age" (Bookman, 1930). Fanny Butcher, who had praised Manhattan Transfer's "perfect marriage of material and manner," was disappointed with this novel's lack of cohesion (Butcher, 1930). Other critics saw the novel's technique as a virtue, one particularly admiring the excitement of directly observing Dos Passos "groping toward some new approach" (Ross, 1930). Edmund Wilson was wholly positive. Undaunted by the concerns of other critics, admiring The 42nd Parallel virtually without reservation, he called it "the most remarkable, the most encouraging American novel . . . since the War" (Wilson, 1930).

The critics seemed better prepared for 1919, the second volume of U.S.A., when it appeared two years later, in 1932. This time their reaction was overwhelmingly positive. Fanny Butcher thought Dos Passos' method particularly appropriate for 1919 for that year "was one of utter restlessness, morally and spiritually, as well as physically" (Butcher, 1932). Another critic called the book "a vast surging drama" of American life and speculated that "Dos Passos is experimenting with a novelistic technique that in the future may develop into the most important literary contribution of the century" (H., E. 1932). Henry Hazlitt, writing in The Nation, felt that with 1919 Dos Passos clearly surpassed Hemingway in language, in range of sympathy, and in social implications (Hazlitt, 1932). The critics were more nearly unanimous in their praise of 1919 than of any other book Dos Passos had written or would write.

The reviews of The Big Money, the novel which concluded the trilogy, have the feel of a summation, possibly because the trilogy had established its own credibility and its value no longer needed to be argued. Max Lerner's review might best represent this view. He felt that, with The Big Money, Dos Passos emerged as

> the most considerable and serious of our American
> writers . . . His talent is expansive rather than
> concentrated. . . . There is a massiveness about
> Dos Passos' work . . . that places it squarely in
> the path of our attention (Lerner, 1936).

Other critics, however, were not entirely satisfied with the trilogy's conclusion. Malcolm Cowley, who admired The Big Money as "a furious and somber poem" (Cowley, 1936), was nevertheless dismayed at Dos Passos' pessimism which, he felt, precluded the writer's ability to

> express one side of contemporary life--the will to
> struggle ahead, the comradeship in struggle, the
> consciousness of new men and new forces continually
> rising" (Cowley, 1936).

What Cowley had begun to sense, and what would become increasingly
apparent in Dos Passos' next several works, was that he was coming to
reject the social panacea prescribed by many concerned Americans in
those troubled times; he was coming to reject the revolutionary struggle of the left. Nevertheless, by the late thirties, with U.S.A.
just behind him, Dos Passos occupied an esteemed place in the American literary world on the basis of his radical critique of American
life, expressed through startling and breathtaking innovations in
style and structure.

In fact, as the thirties neared an end, Dos Passos may have
seemed to stand alone among contemporary American novelists. Fitzgerald seemingly had been all but forgotten; Faulkner was a decade
away from receiving the recognition he deserved; Hemingway appeared
to be floundering, seemingly unable to duplicate the artistic success
of his novels of the twenties. The critics were still not unanimous
in their assessment of Dos Passos, but there could be no doubt about
the vitality of his art, no question of his productivity. The doubts
and questions were to emerge, however--before the decade was out.

1939 was a watershed year for Dos Passos. The twenties had been
a decade of experimentation: he had worked in many genres and ex-
plored the possibilities of the novel; with each work he seemed to
change, to learn, to grow. As flawed as any particular novel may
have been, taken together they seemed to mark the emergence of a
gifted and serious novelist who could eloquently explore the dark
side of the American dream and at the same time help to reshape our
notions about the possibilities of form and style in the novel.
U.S.A. seemed to fulfill that early promise, but the 1939 publication
of Adventures of a Young Man, his first novel since The Big Money,
signalled in the minds of many of his critics an abrupt shift in both
his social and artistic thought.

While perceptive critics, such as Cowley, had begun to realize,
at least as early as The Big Money, that Dos Passos' assessment of
modern America's ills was not Marxist, few were prepared for Adventures of a Young Man's broadside against the Communists. Not so much
an attack against Marxist theory as against its practice by unscrupu-
lous manipulators, Adventures of a Young Man portrayed Communist
leaders as parallel in their tactics to the capitalist manipulators
of U.S.A.. To many, this portrayal represented an inexplicable
about-face for Dos Passos. Furthermore, not only had Dos Passos
apparently turned his back on the political left, he also seemed to
be turning away from his experiments in fictional technique. Adventures of a Young Man is relatively conventional in form, an episodic
novel, with a chronological narrative focusing on the life of one
character, from youth to early manhood.

Introduction

The reviewers were surprised, unpleasantly so. Leftist critics were particularly savage. Samuel Sillen, writing in New Masses, called the novel "a crude piece of Trotskyist agit-prop" and was convinced that Dos Passos' "literary failure is very definitely related to his reactionary political orientation" (Sillen, 1939). A more moderate leftist, Malcolm Cowley, was disappointed by the novel's conservatism, but equally dismayed by the narrative technique which made the book read "more like other people's novels" (Cowley, 1939). R. J. Conklin, writing in the Springfield Republican, did not object to Dos Passos' politics per se, but called Adventures of a Young Man a "futilitarian" novel because Dos Passos seemed "moved principally by a disgust with life" (Conklin, 1939).

A few reviewers admired the novel. Philip Rahv called it "perhaps the most thoughtful and realistic portrait of the radical movement" yet produced by an American (Rahv, 1939). Wilbur Schramm praised Dos Passos for his courage in being able to change both in theme and form (Schramm, 1939). Still another reviewer, who had admired Dos Passos' earlier style, found the technique of Adventures of a Young Man even more successful than that of his previous work (O'Brien, 1939). Despite the occasional favorable review, however, most of Dos Passos' most thoughtful and influential critics reacted negatively to Adventures of a Young Man, their responses ranging from cool disdain to heated condemnation of the novel.

While the reviewers freely expressed their disappointment with Adventures of a Young Man, they seemed incapable of sympathetically perceiving Dos Passos' dilemma as the thirties drew to a close. The two things which they valued most about him--his social criticism and his concern with technique--were precisely the things that Dos Passos, himself, also valued most dearly. He never lost his fascination with the way social systems, particularly the American system, worked. This concern is an unbroken thread throughout his writing. And, despite his later attention to non-fiction and history, Dos Passos could not--and presumably would not want to--forget young Dos Passos the Harvard Aesthete, the imagist poet of A Pushcart at the Curb and portions of One Man's Initiation--1917, the painter who painted sets for Les Noces. Dos Passos never really forgot what the best writers of his generation knew so well--that in his craft was his integrity.

Dos Passos really faced two dilemmas: one concerned his growing reservations about the politics of the left, a politics that he had grown closer to throughout the twenties and early thirties; the second dilemma concerned his stylistic and structural direction now that the massive experiment of U.S.A. had been completed. Dos Passos' political dilemma was the result of his awareness of the increasing Stalinization of the left, both in America and abroad, and was influenced particularly by two events. The first was the violent disruption by the Communists of a Socialist rally held in Madison Square Garden in 1934. In response to the incident, Dos Passos signed a letter of protest which was published in New Masses, which, he later explained, was meant to express his fear of

> the growth of unintelligent fanaticism that, in my
> opinion, can only end in the division of the con-
> scious elements of the exploited classes into im-
> potent brawling sects, and in the ruin for our time
> of the effort toward a sanely organized society
> (Landsberg, 1972).

Dos Passos was, however, severely chastised for what was seen as a
break from orthodoxy, an orthodoxy, ironically, to which he had never
adhered. This incident raised questions about the motives of the
left which were to trouble Dos Passos throughout the rest of the
decade.

The second and most important event which hastened Dos Passos'
disillusionment with revolutionary politics was the apparent execution of his friend Jose Robles by the Soviet Secret Police. Robles,
a professor at Johns Hopkins University, had volunteered to fight for
the Loyalist cause during the Spanish Civil War, but was apparently
executed for counter-revolutionary fascism. Dos Passos, in Spain to
film the movie, The Spanish Earth, heard of Robles' arrest and rumors
of his execution and tried to gain information about his friend, but
to no avail. Returning to America, shaken by the brutal and arbi-
trary tactics of the Soviet Secret Police, Dos Passos felt that he
had seen the future and that it most assuredly did not work. This
event, so personal and dramatic, more than any other convinced Dos
Passos to look to his own American heritage rather than to the leftist
ideologies that he had come to see as foreign for his inspiration.
Temperamentally an anarchist, Dos Passos was to find a more embrace-
able philosophy in the American libertarian tradition than he had
found in Marxism. Adventures of a Young Man is an exorcism, a casting out of the old beliefs before turning to an examination of the
new.

Of course, those most attuned to the delicate shifting of political
opinion on the left were aware of Dos Passos' disenchantment before
the publication of Adventures of a Young Man. Michael Gold, who had
praised Dos Passos as a militant collectivist in 1933, savaged him in
a 1937 Daily Worker article in which he bitterly denounced Dos Passos
and his writing as full of "merde," and claimed that "organically he
seems to hate the human race." Dos Passos was learning that there
was little room for him on the left as long as he persisted in maintaining his intellectual independence. He was also learning first
hand, as the Socialists in Madison Square Garden and Jose Robles in
Spain had learned, that the penalty for deviation can be swift and
harsh.

Dos Passos' second dilemma, the artistic one, was also trouble-
some. All the experimentation and innovation of the twenties had
culminated in U.S.A. and much of the power of that culmination was
the result of the compatible marriage of content and technique. What
would he do next, now that his political views were shifting and his

trilogy completed? He could have laid personal claim to the style and structure of U.S.A. and continued to mine it, continuing his narrative to chronicle the thirties. That might have seemed a reasonable thing to do. Instead he wrote Adventures of a Young Man which, in fact, was a continuation of the narrative voice of U.S.A., stripped of its elaborate structure, for Dos Passos now wished to focus in greater detail on the life of an individual who, like his friend Jose Robles, and like himself, had become swept up in the treacherous currents of the modern world.

Many critics accused Dos Passos of losing interest in technique upon completing U.S.A., but a close look at his subsequent novels proves otherwise. Throughout his career, Dos Passos continued to experiment with form and style, seeking to match subject matter with appropriate technique. In the novels following U.S.A., he experimented with the picaresque, the panoramic, the Bildungsroman, and the family chronicle; he revamped and revised the radical techniques which he had used in Manhattan Transfer and U.S.A., and he attempted to expand the possibilities of more conventional narrative. Dos Passos never ceased to experiment with fictional technique, although he was never again to duplicate the success of his thirties trilogy. Some of the later novels are dreadful; others are interesting failures; still others are, in fact, fine novels which, if they at times seem pale, appear so only in comparison with U.S.A.

Dos Passos' 1943 novel, Number One, which was loosely based on the career of Huey Long, was met with more enthusiasm than it probably deserved. Most reviewers admired the portrayal of Chuck Crawford, the night school educated lawyer from the backwoods, intent on achieving political success whatever the costs. Many reviewers agreed with Horace Gregory that Number One offered a warning to all thinking Americans about the delicate balance between leadership and despotism (Gregory, 1943). Stephen Vincent Benet thought it important for its portrayal of "the particular kind of fascism we could breed in the United States" (Benet, 1943). Readers today might be inclined to feel such praise unwarranted: the novel's plot is lackadaisical, its language--particularly the dialogue--seems hackneyed and dated. Given the grim situation of the war-time world, however, and with the spectre of Huey Long still fresh in people's memories, it is not surprising that readers valued the novel as a document which spoke to their world and their concerns.

Howard Mumford Jones understood the difference between the novel's message and its art, however, calling Number One a "vivid, adroit, and disturbing" social document, but a seriously flawed novel, "naive in structure and without express conflict" (Jones, 1943). Today's reader is probably less likely to find the novel's documentation sufficient to justify overlooking its obvious flaws.

With The Grand Design, in 1949, it became apparent to some that this and the two novels which immediately preceded it were related.

Each focused on a member of the Spotswood family and each portrayed a particular manifestation of contemporary American politics: communism in Adventures of a Young Man, right wing demagoguery in Number One, and New Deal politics in The Grand Design. Indeed, the three novels were later to be published together as District of Columbia. The reviews of The Grand Design were mixed. Few considered it an unqualified success. Maxwell Geismar thought it an outstanding stylistic performance, but also found it "entirely superficial" in its presentation of the "modern collapse of values" (Geismar, 1949). Cowley called the work "a political or religious tract" in which Dos Passos sacrificed his art to argument (Cowley, 1949). Cowley was particularly disappointed because he felt that Dos Passos had never been a particularly astute social reporter and now it seemed that he had willfully sacrificed his artistic talents (Cowley, 1949). Others agreed, some incensed at what they thought to be a political hatchet job on the New Deal, many believing that Dos Passos had lost control of his art. By the end of the forties, Dos Passos' critical reputation had been seriously eroded. Because he had written three overtly political novels, Dos Passos' critics reacted politically as well, for the most part finding his politics bitter and misguided. Only a few critics were able to penetrate the novels' content in order to examine the continued stylistic concerns of Dos Passos' second trilogy.

If Dos Passos' critical reputation declined in the forties, it collapsed in the fifties. His first novel of the decade, Chosen Country, received greatly varying reviews. Arthur Mizener thought it "may well be John Dos Passos' best novel" (Mizener, 1951). Milton Rugoff thought it read "more like a major novel than any Dos Passos had undertaken in a long time" (Rugoff, 1951). Both felt that Dos Passos had shown more warmth toward his characters than ever before. Others, however, thought Chosen Country "abysmally boring" (Kirkus, 1951). Harrison Smith found the novel's ending particularly embarrassing, "as slick and as artificially embroidered as a banal love story in a mass circulation magazine" (Smith, 1951). Other critics, however, welcomed the new warmth and even sentimentality, hoping it might foretell more successful and more optimistic novels from Dos Passos in the future.

They were to be disappointed, for Most Likely to Succeed (1954) garnered Dos Passos' most consistently negative reviews. Harold Clurman called the novel "a wretched piece of work" whose central character was "a phony, a mental incompetent, and a moral castrate" (Clurman, 1954). George D. Murphy thought the book represented "the tragic exhaustion of a once formidable talent" (Murphy, 1954). The reviewers' revulsion was partially a result of the novel's strongly autobiographical elements. Most Likely to Succeed--the title itself bitterly ironic--seemed to be a savage rejection of all that Dos Passos had believed in and worked for. Some critics suggested that the characters were so thinly disguised that the book was libelous, indulging in the "worst kind of assassination" in its tired stereotypes (Barron, 1954). The only reactions which were even partially positive were from those who, caught up in the spirit and rhetoric of the Cold War, saw Most Likely to Succeed as an unmasking of the deviousness of "the disciplined disciples of the Marxist conspiracy" (Engle, 1954).

Dos Passos' last novel of the fifties, The Great Days (1958), fared no better with the critics. Daniel Aaron called it "a sad book, the weakest of Dos Passos' novels" (Aaron, 1958). Phoebe Adams thought it "no more than a querulous wail that old men grow old and Utopia does not arrive" (Adams, 1958). Malcolm Cowley could not contain his exasperation with his old friend, indignantly maintaining that his "is not the novel we have the right to expect" from a novelist of Dos Passos' stature (Cowley, 1958).

Yet, while his stature as a novelist plummeted, his acclaim as an historian rose. At the same time that he was producing his worst novels, he was also writing three creditable studies of the revolutionary era: The Head and Heart of Thomas Jefferson (1954), The Men Who Made the Nation (1957), and Prospects of a Golden Age (1959). For the most part, these histories received favorable reviews and were particularly valued for Dos Passos' ability to bring character and event alive. Perhaps his fiction suffered during the fifties because this was the one time in his career when it was clearly subordinated to other writing interests. Even so, Dos Passos had not totally abandoned his craft since, in the histories, he was applying all his novelistic skills and experience to create history that lived and breathed. Unfortunately, his novels suffered for want of that breath of life.

In the sixties, Dos Passos enjoyed something of a critical renaissance. The publication of Midcentury, in 1961, was considered a major literary event and the reactions to it were almost evenly divided among those who viewed it favorably, those who viewed it unfavorably, and those who considered the novel significant but flawed. Almost all the critics noted the structural and stylistic similarities between Midcentury and U.S.A. One thought it a refinement of the technique of the trilogy (Granklin, 1961). Most, however, felt that it did not match the mastery of U.S.A. Nevertheless, Granville Hicks was impressed with Dos Passos' solid integrity and thought that Midcentury revealed the sure hand of an accomplished craftsman (Hicks, 1961). Harry T. Moore thought the novel "retrieve[d] a long-lost reputation with a single stroke" due to Dos Passos' skillful handling of his materials (Moore, 1961). Dos Passos ever provoked controversy, however, and for each favorable view there was a negative one. Robert Stilwell called the novel "an almost complete fiasco . . . a dismal hodgepodge of specious thought and outrageously bad craftsmanship" (Stilwell, 1961). And Gore Vidal lambasted both the book, which he found "oddly disgusting," and the author who "has mistaken the decline of his own flesh and talent for the world's decline" (Vidal, 1961). Most of the reviews fell somewhere between these extremes. Most praised Dos Passos' effort, but thought either that the style was weak or the goal of debunking post-war American society misguided. Whether or not they found the novel successful, most critics applauded Dos Passos for his return, in <u>Midcentury</u>, to the panoramic novel of social criticism. Dos Passos was again back to the task of taking the nation's pulse, and, although the reading may not have been entirely accurate, he was back at least to the work that he knew best.

Dos Passos remained busy throughout the sixties: 1966 was a particularly eventful year. In his seventieth year, two of his books from the fifties--<u>District of Columbia</u> and <u>Most Likely to Succeed</u>--were reissued; Kenneth Lynn published <u>World in a Glass</u>, a collection of Dos Passos' writing selected from the novels; and Dos Passos, himself, published two new books: <u>The Shackles of Power: Three Jeffersonian Decades</u>, and his memoir, <u>The Best Times</u>. The reissues were passed over quickly, although some reviewers appreciated the reappearance of Dos Passos' second trilogy. Dos Passos' study of Jefferson and his times received a generally favorable reception, valued, as his earlier studies of the period had been, for his idiosyncratic and lively approach to history. And <u>World in a Glass</u> functioned to remind the critics of the breadth and depth of Dos Passos' achievement.

One reviewer thought the anthology an excellent exposition of Dos Passos' "mammoth lifetime work," and felt it reaffirmed Dos Passos' "essential sincerity, indignation; and 'formidable independence.'" Paul Showers, in the <u>New York Times Book Review</u>, wrote that the collection offered an "impressive picture" of the world made vivid through Dos Passos' work. Oscar Handlin thought the book of special significance because it clearly showed the essential consistency of Dos Passos' thought: "From beginning to end, Dos Passos conveys a sense of the strivings for dignity of the people in all their variety" (Handlin, 1966).

<u>The Best Times</u> received primarily favorable reviews. Many reviewers commented on the way Dos Passos' basic goodness and kindness suffused the book, especially when compared to Hemingway's gossipy memoir, <u>A Moveable Feast</u>. Granville Hicks, for instance, felt that the book left him with a renewed interest in the man (Hicks, 1966). Melvin Maddocks thought <u>The Best Times</u> was as important for what it implied about the "lost generation" as for what it showed of Dos Passos himself. He found particularly fascinating the account of Dos Passos' father which begins the book: "He has quite deliberately grafted his autobiography onto the memory of his father," thus, by implication, building "a good case for the Lost Generation being a continuing chapter in the tradition of the American artist rather than a break with it" (Maddocks, 1966). Still others appreciated the book simply as an entertaining account of an interesting man and his fascinating generation.

Taken together, <u>World in a Glass</u> and <u>The Best Times</u> offered the critics a chance to reassess Dos Passos and his career with a long view. From this perspective, and on the additional basis of the qualified success of Midcentury, Dos Passos' stock rose. When he died in 1970, Dos Passos could feel that his reputation was in ascendence.

For one thing, critics began, in the seventies, to take a more careful look at Dos Passos and his writings. Until this decade there had been only five general studies of Dos Passos. One of those was a pamphlet; three of the five were published abroad; all were parts of larger comprehensive series of studies in American literature. In the seventies there were eight book-length studies of Dos Passos: Allen Belkind's Dos Passos, the Critics, and the Writer's Intention (1971), Melvin Landsberg's John Dos Passos' Path to U.S.A. (1972), David Sanders' The Merrill Studies in U.S.A. (1972), Townsend Ludington's The Fourteenth Chronicle: Letters and Diaries of John Dos Passos (1973), Andrew Hook's Dos Passos, A Collection of Critical Essays (1974), George Becker's John Dos Passos (1974), Iain Colley's Dos Passos and the Fiction of Despair (1978), and Linda Wagner's Dos Passos, Artist as American (1979).

The collections of Belkind, Sanders, and Hook are particularly valuable because they bring together much of the best Dos Passos criticism of the past and provide an historical perspective on the writer's critical reputation. Belkind's book is especially helpful for it suggests the possible breadth of Dos Passos studies by including essays on the relationship between Dos Passos' fiction and the other arts. The biographical studies of Melvin Landsberg and Townsend Ludington are also significant. While the definitive Dos Passos biography has not yet appeared, taken together, Landsberg and Ludington offer a fascinating, if still incomplete, picture of the artist's life. Landsberg's biography stresses the development of Dos Passos as a social critic, while Ludington primarily focuses on his development as an artist. Linda W. Wagner examines the interrelationship between Dos Passos' political and artistic thought in Dos Passos: Artist as American. Wagner also offers the most comprehensive discussion to date of Dos Passos' nonfiction writing.

In addition to these book-length studies, a number of impressive shorter studies and portions of books which discuss Dos Passos have appeared in the seventies. Particularly notable is Claude-Edmonde Magny's treatment of Dos Passos' writing in The Age of the American Novel: The Film Aesthetic of the Fiction Between the Two Wars (1972). Barbara Foley's "From U.S.A. to Ragtime: Notes on the Forms of Historical Consciousness in Modern Fiction" (1978) and Jonathan's Morse's "Dos Passos' U.S.A. and the Illusions of Memory" (1977) offer insights into the writer's historical imagination. Lois Hughson's "In Search of the True America: Dos Passos' Debt to Whitman in U.S.A." (1973) and John D. Baker's "Whitman and Dos Passos: A Sense of Communion" (1974) attempt to place Dos Passos in the mainstream of the American literary tradition. The continuing interest in Dos Passos' political thought is well represented by David Sanders' "John

Introduction

Dos Passos as Conservative" (1976) and Richard F. Hill's "Dos Passos:
A Reassessment" (1976). Two articles by David L. Vanderwerken,
"Manhattan Transfer: Dos Passos' Babel Story" (1977) and "U.S.A.:
Dos Passos and the 'Old Words'" (1977) offer particularly insightful
analyses of Dos Passos' inventive use of language.

If we are in the beginnings of a Dos Passos renaissance, as the
appearance of these books and articles might suggest, it might be because these scholars and critics are, for the most part, of a new
generation, a generation which did not experience first-hand the turbulent artistic and political world of Dos Passos' formative and
mature years. This new generation can more easily maintain its objectivity as it evaluates Dos Passos and his work. We should not
underestimate Dos Passos' effect on his generation. We should not
forget how passionately his generation praised and disdained his
work, and honored and reviled the man. Such passion might attract us
to the writing of our contemporaries, but it does not necessarily
make for the most balanced and reasoned criticism. This new generation can, to a certain extent, escape the strict confines of chrono-
logy, moving quickly, for instance, through the dreary fifties and
savor the best of the more fruitful periods. This generation has
greater opportunity than previous ones had to turn the kaleidoscope
in order to see new patterns in Dos Passos' writing.

Another advantage for this generation is that it can begin its
scrutiny of Dos Passos, if it chooses, in the sixties, a decade which
should lay to rest the idea that Dos Passos was either merely a social
activist who retreated from the contemporary world to an idealized
past, or simply a literary innovator who lost interest in his craft.
For in his last decade, Dos Passos energetically reaffirmed his commitment to the world in which he lived and to the craft which he
practiced. This is evidenced in his literary activity during the
sixties.

He began the decade with Midcentury, a panoramic assessment of
his nation midway through its most difficult century. He ended the
decade working on Century's Ebb, the last of his contemporary chronicles, published posthumously in 1975. Malcolm Cowley thought this
last book left one "with more admiration for the series as a whole,
including the later books which have been too easily rejected"
(Cowley, 1975). Owing much to U.S.A., Midcentury and Century's Ebb
are nevertheless books of their times, books of a man whose concern
for his country and his art remain unabated. Between his last two
fictions, Dos Passos returned to his historical studies, producing a
book on the glory days of the Portuguese empire and another on the
glory days of the early American republic, but he also looked forward,
in Brazil on the Move, to a new world that was yet just emerging. He
wrote of a new interest in Easter Island, Island of Enigmas, and of
an old interest which was ever new for him in Mr. Wilson's War. He
published a record of his convictions in his collection of essays,
Occasions and Protests, and he published a record of his life in his
memoir, The Best Times.

Introduction

In surveying the intellectual curiosity, integrity, and vigor of these last years, critics and scholars might find the true Dos Passos. In a career spanning a half century, Dos Passos inevitably slumped at times; he wrote books which did not do justice to his talent; he struggled with his own doubts and fears, sometimes unsuccessfully. Future critics cannot ignore this unevenness, but neither should they ignore Dos Passos' essential consistency in his commitment to art and to the world. In his best work theme and form are inseparable—and for this he deserves our attention and admiration.

This bibliography lists materials in the year during which they appear as either "A. Books" or "B. Shorter Writings," which also includes parts of books not exclusively about Dos Passos. Materials are arranged alphabetically by author within each year. All entries are annotated except those preceded by an asterisk (*), which indicates that the material for some reason was not available for reading. In such a case, the source of its listing is given instead of an annotation. Some entries, particularly some from the fifties and sixties, were found in the Dos Passos collection of the University of Virginia. In most cases, these were clippings without page numbers. Where possible, I have identified the page numbers; where not possible, I have included the entry without them. A bibliographer must be realistic. While I have attempted to locate and include all but the most incidental references to Dos Passos written in English, as well as the most important non-English treatments, I am aware that I have probably overlooked some references which could be included. For this, I apologize.

I would like to acknowledge the many people and institutions which have assisted in this project. Special thanks to my dissertation director, Linda W. Wagner, and the members of my doctoral committee, Russel B. Nye, Barry Gross, and William Johnsen. Their example and advice have been invaluable. Thanks also to the staffs of the libraries of Michigan State University, The University of Virginia, and The University of Michigan for their assistance while I learned the bibliographer's trade. I also owe a debt to the College of Arts and Letters of Michigan State University for a graduate research scholarship which defrayed part of the cost of my research. And thanks to Jo Cornell for her typing and editorial advice. Finally, a very special thanks to Elizabeth Kella, who so greatly assisted in this project by performing much of the least attractive work of compiling a bibliography, but did it always with grace and good humor. For her concerned efforts and thoughtful advice I am deeply indebted.

Writings by John Dos Passos

1920   One Man's Initiation--1917. London: Allen & Unwin; reprinted
       as First Encounter. New York: Philosophical Library, 1945,
       and as One Man's Initiation--1917. Ithaca, N.Y.: Cornell
       University Press, 1969.

1921   Three Soldiers. New York: George H. Doran Company.

1922   A Pushcart at the Curb. New York: George H. Doran Company.

1922   Rosinante to the Road Again. New York: George H. Doran
       Company.

1923   Streets of Night. New York: George H. Doran Company.

1925   Manhattan Transfer. Boston: Houghton Mifflin Company.

1926   The Garbage Man: A Parade with Shouting. New York: Harper
       and Brothers.

1927   Facing the Chair: Story of the Americanization of Two Foreign-
       born Workmen. Boston: Sacco-Vanzetti Defense Committee; re-
       printed, New York: Da Capo Press, 1970.

1927   Orient Express. New York: Harper & Brothers.

1928   Airways, Inc. New York: Macaulay Company.

1930   The 42nd Parallel. New York: Harper and Brothers.

1932   1919. New York: Harcourt, Brace and Company.

1934   In All Countries. New York: Harcourt, Brace and Company.

1934   Three Plays (includes Fortune Heights). New York: Harcourt,
       Brace and Company.

1936   The Big Money. New York: Harcourt, Brace and Company.

Writings by John Dos Passos

1937–38 U.S.A. (The 42nd Parallel, 1919, and Big Money). New York: Harcourt, Brace and Company.

1937 The Villagers Are the Heart of Spain. New York: Esquire-Coronet.

1938 Journeys Between Wars. New York: Harcourt, Brace and Company.

1939 Adventures of a Young Man. Boston: Houghton Mifflin Company.

1940 The Living Thoughts of Tom Paine. New York: Longmans, Green.

1941 The Ground We Stand On: Some Examples from the History of a Political Creed. New York: Harcourt, Brace and Company.

1943 Number One. Boston: Houghton Mifflin Company.

1944 State of the Nation. Boston: Houghton Mifflin Company.

1946 Tour of Duty. Boston: Houghton Mifflin Company.

1949 The Grand Design. Boston: Houghton Mifflin Company.

1950 The Prospect Before Us. Boston: Houghton Mifflin Company.

1951 Chosen Country. Boston: Houghton Mifflin Company.

1952 District of Columbia. Boston: Houghton Mifflin Company.

1954 The Head and Heart of Thomas Jefferson. Garden City, N.Y.: Doubleday and Company.

1954 Most Likely to Succeed. New York: Prentice-Hall.

1956 The Theme Is Freedom. New York: Dodd, Mead and Company.

1957 The Men Who Made the Nation. Garden City, N.Y.: Doubleday and Company.

1958 The Great Days. New York: Sagamore Press.

1959 Prospects of a Golden Age. Englewood Cliffs, N.J.: Prentice-Hall.

1961 Midcentury. Boston: Houghton Mifflin Company.

1962 Mr. Wilson's War. Garden City, N.Y.: Doubleday and Company.

1963 Brazil on the Move. Garden City, N.Y.: Doubleday and Company.

1964 Occasions and Protests. Chicago: Henry Regnery Company.

Writings by John Dos Passos

1966   The Shackles of Power, Three Jeffersonian Decades.   Garden City, N.Y.: Doubleday and Company.

1966   The Best Times: An Informal Memoir.   New York: New American Library.

1969   The Portugal Story: Three Centuries of Exploration and Discovery.   Garden City, N.Y.: Doubleday and Company.

1971   Easter Island, Island of Enigmas.   Garden City, N.Y.: Doubleday and Company.

1975   Century's Ebb: The Thirteenth Chronicle.   Boston: Gambit.

Writings about John Dos Passos

1921 B   SHORTER WRITINGS

1   ANON. Review of Three Soldiers. Booklist, 18 (December), 83.
        Calls Three Soldiers "an absorbing, powerful, brutally
    frank view of the A.E.F. and its war life." Mentions the
    incredible controversy about its portrayal of that life.

2   ANON. Review of Three Soldiers. Outlook, 129 (26 October),
        306.
        Calls Three Soldiers "so-called realism" which might re-
    cord faithfully actual events, but which, taken together,
    add up to "the most unreal of unreality." Feels it will
    only please "a few who came out of the army a grouch . . .
    or who gloat over goddams."

3   ANON. "Three Other Soldiers." Nation, 113 (26 October), 480-
        481.
        Applauds Three Soldiers for its realism in dialogue and
    characterization, but finds the description at times too
    precious. Feels Dos Passos is correct in downplaying the
    conventional "chamber of horrors" of war novels and stress-
    ing the dehumanizing effects of the "crazing monotony behind
    the front." Credits Dos Passos with creating John Andrews,
    a believably flawed yet admirable character.

4   B., E. "The Same War." The Nation and The Athenaeum, 30
        (22 October), 148.
        Considers Three Soldiers to be "written with fiery ardor
    and almost savage energy," but feels that Dos Passos
    stretches his credibility in his portrayal of the officers
    and "Y" men.

1921

*5   BESTON, H.   Bookshelf.   <u>Atlantic</u>, 128 (December).
        Unlocatable.   Cited in "John Dos Passos and His Re-
     viewers," by William White, <u>Bulletin of Bibliography</u>, 20
     (May-August 1950), 45-47.

  6   BISHOP, JOHN PEALE.   "Three Brilliant Young Novelists."
     <u>Vanity Fair</u> (October).
        Review of Fitzgerald's <u>The Beautiful and the Damned</u>,
     Benet's <u>The Beginning of Wisdom</u>, and Dos Passos' <u>Three
     Soldiers</u>, the last of which Bishop thinks is so good that
     "I am tempted to topple from my critical perch and go up
     and down the street with banners and drums."   Calls it "the
     stuff and breath" of the A.E.F., a magnificent portrayal of
     the American soldier, with "the firm structure of steel."
     Concludes that "John Dos Passos is a genius."   Reprinted:
     1948.B1.

  7   BLUM, W.C.   "A Moralist in the Army."   <u>Dial</u>, 71 (21 November),
     606-608.
        Admires Dos Passos' honesty in portraying the repressive
     aspects of military life in <u>Three Soldiers</u>, a novel charac-
     terized as "the harmonious expression of a well-chewed
     rage."

  8   BROUN, HEYWOOD.   "A Group of Books Worth Reading."   [Am.]
     <u>Bookman</u>, 54 (December), 393-394.
        Scorns the politically based criticism of <u>Three Soldiers</u>.
     Feels that "nothing which has come out of the school of
     American realists has seemed to us so entirely honest.
     There is not an atom of pose in this book.   It represents
     deep convictions and impressions eloquently expressed."   If
     anything, the impressions are sometimes too eloquent for a
     realistic study of army life.

  9   CANBY, HENRY SEIDEL.   "Human Nature Under Fire."   <u>New York
     Evening Post Book Review</u> (8 October), p. 67.
        Calls <u>Three Soldiers</u> a passionate work of sincere litera-
     ture.   Thinks it to be "by no means a perfect book, but it
     is a very engrossing one, a first-hand study, finely imagined
     and powerfully created . . . It is convincing, even though
     partial."

 10   DAWSON, CONINGSBY.   "Insulting the Army."   <u>New York Times Book
     Review</u> (2 October), pp. 1, 16-17.
        Questions the veracity of <u>Three Soldiers</u>, calling it "a
     dastardly denial of the splendid chivalry which carried
     many a youth to a soldier's death with the sure knowledge
     in his soul that he was a liberator."   Thinks that "the

book fails because of its unmanly intemperance both in
language and in plot. The voice of righteousness is never
sounded," and concludes that Three Soldiers is "a nationwide
insult."

11 FAIRCHILD, H. N. "Three Soldiers from Greenwich Village."
    Independent, 107 (29 October), 97.
        Objects to the one-sidedness of Three Soldiers which
    portrays the army as "a monstrous Juggernaut of oppression
    which crushes the bodies and souls of men." Concludes that
    it "must be set down as a rather brilliantly written piece
    of sordid, narrow-minded realism . . . [which] . . . is
    less the cry of young America than the cry of Greenwich
    Village." Calls Andrews "an essentially ignoble character"
    whose fate does not produce catharsis because he is
    unlikeable.

12 GIBBS, A. HAMILTON. "Men in Khaki." Freeman, 4 (30 November),
    282-283.
        Calls One Man's Initiation--1917 "impressionstic, vivid
    [but] disjointed," a rehearsal for Three Soldiers. Thinks
    the latter a stunning book: "The vividness of his picture
    bewilders, sometimes terrifies, so that one forgets the
    technique and responds to the tremendous call which it
    makes upon one's emotions."

13 HACKETT, FRANCIS. "Doughboys." New Republic, 28 (5 October),
    162-163.
        Finds Three Soldiers brilliantly expressive and admires
    Dos Passos for his candor in presenting the war.

14 HOWARD, SIDNEY. Review of Three Soldiers. Survey, 47
    (5 November), 221-222.
        Feels Three Soldiers is a personal and bitter work, one
    which is, despite omissions, basically accurate: "much of
    what he wrote is dreadful, all the more because it is also
    irrefutable."

15 MENCKEN, H. L. "Variations on a Familiar Theme." Smart Set,
    66 (December), 138-144.
        Calls Three Soldiers a daring novel, an attempt to por-
    tray the war as it really was: "a passion for the truth is
    plainly there, and with it an imagination that makes the
    truth live."

16 PEARSON, EDMUND LESTER. "New Books and Old." Independent,
    107 (1 October), 16.

1922

> Strongly objects to the critical tone of Three Soldiers.
> Argues that 95% of enlisted men willingly accepted the
> discipline of military life. Finds disagreeable the empha-
> sis on the sordid aspects of the military.

1922 A BOOKS - NONE

1922 B SHORTER WRITINGS

1 ANON. "Pushcarts and Other Poetic Things." New York Times
   Book Review (17 December), p. 2.
       Finds the poems of A Pushcart at the Curb to possess the
   same "virility, passionate and unyielding realism, and sear-
   ing expression of thought" as Three Soldiers. Feels there
   is a rhythmic harmony within the best of these sensuous
   poems, a construction best called "architectonic."

2 ANON. "Recent Books in Brief Review." [Am.] Bookman, 55
   (July), 538.
       Feels that "Dos Passos excels in painting vivid pic-
   tures rich with color; he is sensuous and sensitive . . .
   aesthetic in his tastes."

3 ANON. "Recent Books in Brief Review." [Am.] Bookman, 55
   (August), 648.
       Sees One Man's Initiation as a memoir, a trial run for
   Three Soldiers. Despite the book's unpleasantness--espec-
   ially in its portrait of mental devastation--feels the
   literary workmanship is remarkably skillful as war is
   forced "to parade in nakedness--robbed of its chauvinistic
   romance-embroidered clothing."

*4 ANON. Review of One Man's Initiation--1917. Literary Review
    of the New York Evening Post (17 June), p. 747.
        Cited in "John Dos Passos and His Reviewers" by William
    White, Bulletin of Bibliography, 20 (May - August 1950),
    45-47.

5 ANON. Review of One Man's Initiation--1917. Pittsburgh
   Monthly Bulletin, 27 (November), 460.
       Very brief review.

6 ANON. Review of Rosinante to the Road Again. Booklist, 19
   (November), 49.
       Brief summary of the book. Thinks it will surprise
   readers who only know Dos Passos from Three Soldiers.

7   ANON. Review of <u>Rosinante to the Road Again</u>. <u>Boston Transcript</u>
        (1 April), sec. 4, p. 9.
          Calls the book "charmingly discussive and full of
        quaint moods and reflections." Calls <u>Rosinante</u> "unlike as
        it can be from <u>Three Soldiers</u>," and feels it enhances Dos
        Passos' reputation as "one of the most gifted of the younger
        American authors."

8   ANON. Review of <u>Rosinante to the Road Again</u>. <u>Nation</u>, 114
        (7 June), 698.
          Remarks on Dos Passos' appreciation of Spain's unchange-
        able, old ways. Does not find him adept at social diagnosis
        but finds the style clearly professional. Considers Dos
        Passos' discussion of the writers Azorin, Unamuno, Machado,
        and Baroja the "most competent pages."

9   ANON. Review of <u>Rosinante to the Road Again</u>. <u>Pittsburgh</u>
        <u>Monthly Bulletin</u>, 27 (June), 298.
          Very brief review.

10 ANON. Review of <u>Rosinante to the Road Again</u>. <u>Wisconsin</u>
        <u>Library Bulletin</u>, 18 (June), 155.
          Brief review.

11 ANON. "Verse by Dos Passos." <u>Springfield Republican</u>,
        (19 November), sec. A, p. 7.
          Feels there is, in <u>A Pushcart at the Curb</u> a "raw,
        crude, almost animal sensibility to color, and hunger for
        it." Thinks Dos Passos needs to "discipline and refine his
        medium," but feels there is great potential in his verse if
        he can temper his pervasive cynicism, can "recover from the
        war."

12 BLACK, CONSTANCE. Review of <u>One Man's Initiation--1917</u>. <u>New</u>
        <u>York Tribune</u> (13 August), p. 5.
          Admires Dos Passos' ability to capture "in large bold
        strokes" the essence of a scene and thinks he "should be
        the logical man to achieve the still unwritten great novel
        of modern America," but thinks both this book and <u>Three</u>
        <u>Soldiers</u> are "artistically injured by the fact that the
        iron of army futilities and war futilities have eaten into
        the soul of the writer . . . making him too biased."

13 CANBY, HENRY SEIDEL. "The Young Romantics." In <u>Definitions:</u>
        <u>Essays in Contemporary Criticism</u>. New York: Harcourt,
        Brace & Co., pp. 149-163.
          Cites <u>Three Soldiers</u> as an example of the autobiographi-
        cal novel of the early twenties.

1922

14   CARVER, GEORGE. "The Enormous Room: A Review." Midland, 8
          (November), 302-313.
              Calls Three Soldiers and The Enormous Room "expositions
          of stupidity," the stupidity that lay behind the war.
          Feels that Dos Passos ignored the gayety of army life
          which allowed most of the participants to return with
          "some slight degree of wholesomeness." Admires Cummings'
          use of "gayety" which is taken as a sign of "a clean sane-
          ness that can do no less than carry conviction."

15   F., A.E. "Three Soldiers Protests Too Much." Springfield
          Republican (8 January), p. 13a.
              Thinks that Three Soldiers, "despite pictures drawn with
          much amazing skill and despite the wonderful accuracy in
          its descriptions of little things, is not fair," because it
          exaggerates the reactions of soldiers to war and military
          life.

16   GORMAN, HERBERT S. "Spain and the Spaniard." New Republic,
          31 (23 August), 366.
              Views Rosinante to the Road Again as "a series of margi-
          nal notes, some of them sound, others rather tentative, and
          still others the unconscious self-revelation of Dos Passos
          himself." Especially dislikes this self-analysis, feeling
          that it obscures any truths which might be revealed about
          Spain.

17   MENCKEN, H. L. "Portrait of an American Citizen." Smart Set,
          67 (October), 138-144.
              Review of Willa Cather's war novel One of Ours in which
          Mencken offers high praise for Dos Passos: "What spoils the
          story is simply the fact that a year or so ago a young
          soldier named John Dos Passos printed a novel called Three
          Soldiers . . . no story that is less meticulously true will
          stand up to it. . . . It changed the whole tone of American
          opinion about the war."

18   MITCHELL, STEWART. "Spain From the Air." Dial, 72 (June),
          640-641.
              Despite the shortcomings of Rosinante to the Road Again
          --the occasional lapses in language, especially when Dos
          Passos "tries the splurge and somersaults of poetry"--
          finds the book fresh and original and "a work of unusually
          good journalism."

19   MORRIS, LLOYD R. "John Dos Passos in Perspective." New York
          Times Book Review (18 June), pp. 17, 22.

Considers Dos Passos to possess primarily a "lyric temperment" and calls One Man's Initiation--1917, "essentially a lyric interlude, poetic in feeling and conception." Feels few American writers possess such a vivid command of sensory perception. Feels Rosinante to the Road Again emphasizes Dos Passos' "essentially impressionistic method." Concludes that Dos Passos, more than any contemporary, seems to have adopted William Blake's doctrine that "the road of excess leads to the palace of wisdom."

20 PEARSON, EDMUND LESTER. "New Books and Old." Independent, 108 (18 March), 283.
Brief mention of Rosinante to the Road Again with snipes at Three Soldiers, which was written "with the knitted brows and acid stomach of the Earnest Young Intellectual."

21 UNTERMEYER, LOUIS. "Four Poets." [Am.] Bookman, 56 (December), 495.
Finds some of the poems of A Pushcart at the Curb to "have the quality of a vivid improvisation . . . are seldom over-elaborate, always stimulating." Nevertheless, senses a damaging uncertainty as to "which tone to adopt, which gesture to use" and concludes that "Dos Passos is a poetic writer rather than a poet" who "attains in his prose a rigor and clarity absent from this volume."

22 VAN DOREN, CARL. Contemporary American Novelists: 1900-1920. New York: The Macmillan Company, p. 176.
Mentions Three Soldiers, "the most controverted novel of the year," which Van Doren feels "dealt brilliantly with the unheroic aspects of the American Expeditionary Force."

23 VAN DOREN, MARK. "In Line." Nation, 115 (15 November), 530.
Considers the poems of A Pushcart at the Curb "stale enough to startle." Despite the occasional sharp satire and vivid image, finds Dos Passos has adopted "the imagist stare--cold, sullen, eyeless contemplation of life in terms of aesthetic expression," which "for the most part . . . gets nowhere."

1923 A BOOKS - NONE

1923 B SHORTER WRITINGS

1923

    1 ANON. Review of <u>A Pushcart at the Curb</u>. <u>Booklist</u>, 19
       (February), 152.
           Calls <u>A Pushcart at the Curb</u> "vignettes of travel . . .
      in the form of free verse."

1924 A BOOKS - NONE

1924 B SHORTER WRITINGS

    1 COLLINS, JOSEPH. "Unpleasant Novels," in his <u>Taking the</u>
       <u>Literary Pulse</u>. New York: Doran, pp. 156-168.
           Feels that <u>Streets of Night</u> "leaves a decidedly bad
      taste," primarily for its "profane and vulgar words," and
      its casual treatment of bad manners.

    2 MENCKEN, H. L. "Rambles in Fiction." <u>American Mercury</u>, 2
       (July), 380-381.
           Characterizes <u>Streets of Night</u> as "simply a series of
      peurile and often improbable episodes in the lives of two
      silly boys and an even sillier girl."

1925 A BOOKS - NONE

1925 B SHORTER WRITINGS

    1 ANON. "Abby Presents <u>Moon Is a Gong</u>." <u>Boston Traveler</u>
       (18 May).
           Calls the play, performed by the Harvard Dramatic Club,
      "expressionistic drama bearing close relationship to such
      plays as <u>Begger on Horseback</u> . . . and <u>Processional</u>."
      Identifies the central theme as "the conflict between the
      individual and society."

  *2 BRICKELL, HERSCHEL. Review of <u>Manhattan Transfer</u>. <u>Literary</u>
       <u>Review of the New York Evening Post</u> (28 November), p. 5.
           Cited in "John Dos Passos and His Reviewers," by William
      White, <u>Bulletin of Bibliography</u>, 20 (May-August 1950), 45-
      49.

    3 C., N. R. Review of <u>Manhattan Transfer</u>. <u>Boston Evening</u>
       <u>Transcript</u> (30 December), sec. 2, p. 6.
           Feels that the portrayal of New York is "too crude and
      materialistic," but feels that in the structure and style

of <u>Manhattan Transfer</u> "Dos Passos displays his power, his
architectonic ability, and a poetic sense of rhythms,
colors, sounds and smells.

4 HARPER, MOSES. Review of <u>Manhattan Transfer</u>. <u>New Republic</u>,
     45 (16 December), 118-119.
        Feels Dos Passos was overly ambitious in choosing such
     a large canvas: there are too many scenes and they are
     "over-documented with facts." Claims the book is unfor-
     tunately influenced by the French naturalists.

5 LEWIS, SINCLAIR. "Manhattan at Last!" <u>The Saturday Review of
     Literature</u>, 2 (5 December), 361.
        Lewis wonders "whether it might not be true that <u>Manhattan
     Transfer</u> is a novel of the very first importance," if "Dos
     Passos <u>may</u> be more than Dreiser, Cather, Hergesheimer,
     Cabell, or Anderson the father of humanized and living fic-
     tion . . . not merely for America but for the world!"
     Rates <u>Manhattan Transfer</u> "more important in every way than
     anything by Gertrude Stein or Marcel Proust or even the
     great white boar, Mr. James Joyce's <u>Ulysses</u>," because Dos
     Passos makes use of "all their experimental psychology and
     style," yet has created a book that is <u>interesting</u>. Con-
     siders Dos Passos' "passion for the beauty and stir of
     life," even more impressive than the technique. Lewis
     feels that the novel may be "the first book to catch
     Manhattan." Reprinted: 1926.A1; 1926.B11.

6 MORRIS, LLOYD. "Skimming the Cream From Six Months' Fiction."
     <u>New York Times Book Review</u> (6 December), p. 2.
        Views <u>Manhattan Transfer</u> as "an attempt to achieve an
     expressionistic picture of New York . . . courageous but
     not impressive."

7 P., H. T. "A Tall Feather for the Cap of Harvard Players."
     <u>Boston Evening Transcript</u> (13 May).
        Review of <u>The Moon Is a Gong</u>. Of Dos Passos: "The
     quality by which he outshines his fellow-craftsmen in their
     new genre is the poetic impulse, the poetic vision, the
     poetic sense of spaced, rhythmed, worded speech . . . a
     new mood, manner, idiom fill and animate these episodes.
     All three are rooted in this American life of the hour, all
     three are made vital in the theatre." Also notes Dos
     Passos' "sardonic, satirical humor."

8 ROSS, MARY. "Beads in a Box." <u>New York Herald Tribune Books</u>
     (27 December), pp. 1-2.

1925

> Calls <u>Manhattan Transfer</u> "a novel with a rhythm, not a
> plot," and thinks that its authority is gained chiefly by
> "the solidity with which it is rooted in sensuous ex-
> perience." While the work has an exciting, kaleidoscope
> effect, Ross misses any real sensitivity to or affection
> for any of the characters.

9   STUART, HENRY LONGAN. "John Dos Passos Notes The Tragic Trivia
    of New York." <u>New York Times Book Review</u> (29 November),
    pp. 5, 10.
> Concedes that <u>Manhattan Transfer</u> is "a powerful and sus-
> tained piece of work," but finds the method itself flawed
> by its relentless impressionism and super-naturalism which
> allows Dos Passos to ignore "the immunity which the imagina-
> tion acquires when disheartening or bewildering impressions
> crowd upon it, the compensations that keep it sane and
> balanced under almost any circumstances."

1926 A   BOOKS

1   LEWIS, SINCLAIR. <u>John Dos Passos' "Manhattan Transfer."</u> New
    York: Harper & Brothers, 22pp.
> Expanded version of 1925.B5.

1926 B   SHORTER WRITINGS

1   ANON. "John Dos Passos." <u>Bowdoin Institute of Modern
    Literature</u>. Lewiston, Maine: Lewiston Journal Company,
    pp. 97-101.
> Account of Dos Passos' reading and discussion of drama.

2   ANON. Review of <u>The Garbage Man</u>. <u>Independent</u>, 117 (31 July),
    136.
> Considers <u>The Garbage Man</u> a dramatic application of the
> <u>Manhattan Transfer</u> formula. Concludes that "a good deal of
> the comment is shrewd, a good deal of the acid burlesque
> bites deep into the lump of our shams; but the author
> fails . . . to make his hero and heroine either real or
> interesting."

3   ANON. Review of <u>The Garbage Man</u>. <u>Saturday Review of
    Literature</u>, 3 (28 August), 75.
> Calls <u>The Garbage Man</u> "ebullient" and "athletic," a
> "swift and lyric" medley.

4   BEACH, JOSEPH WARREN. The Outlook for American Prose.
    Chicago: University of Chicago Press, pp. 16-18; 254.
        Calls Dos Passos "the most promising" novelist of what
    is called the "futuristic" style. Admires Dos Passos'
    material and his method of presentation: "his blocks of
    human experience wierdly juxtaposed, his strangely woven
    strands of fate and impulse." Considers him the "indubi-
    table superior" of Virginia Woolf.

5   CANBY, HENRY SEIDEL. "Thunder in Manhattan." Saturday Review
    of Literature, 2 (16 January), 489, 495.
        Compares Manhattan Transfer and Christopher Morley's
    Thunder on the Left. Thinks the "broken narrative of Dos
    Passos' book, its shake-up of figures shivering one against
    the other, its flashes which make no pattern, is tremendously
    convincing."

6   CHASE, STUART. "A Yell From the Gallery." New Masses, 1
    (June), 22.
        After viewing John Howard Lawson's Nirvana, Eugene
    O'Neill's The Great God Brown and Dos Passos' The Moon is
    a Gong, Chase complains that he is "getting fed up with
    poetry mixed in with half baked philosophy."

7   EASTON, WALTER PRICHARD. "From Garbage Man To Satan." New
    York Herald Tribune Books (29 August), p. 9.
        Finds The Garbage Man lacking in suspense and sympathetic
    characters. Objects to the "unreality" of the expressionist
    techniques and concludes that "as a dramatist or philosopher
    Dos Passos needs less of the moon and more of this real and
    inescapable earth."

8   GOLD, MICHAEL. "A Barbaric Poem of New York." New Masses, 1
    (August), 25-26.
        Calls Dos Passos "fiercely honest," a "propagandist of
    truth," and thinks Manhattan Transfer "is education; for it
    extends one's knowledge of America." Especially admires
    Dos Passos' ability to capture the spirit of the city and
    to know the various types that populate it. Feels the only
    flaw of this and Dos Passos' others books is his middle
    class idealism and urges the author to educate himself in
    "history, psychology, and economics and plunge himself into
    the labor movement."

9   KRUTCH, JOSEPH WOOD. Review of The Moon is a Gong. Nation,
    122 (31 March), 348.

1926

    Calls the play a failure and "doubly discouraging" be-
cause Dos Passos had shown such previous talent. Thinks
the play "only violent and noisy when it should be stirring."

10 LAWSON, JOHN HOWARD. "Debunking the Art Theatre." New Masses,
     1 (June), 22, 28, 30.
      Response to Stuart Chase's criticism of the new play-
     wrights which appeared in same issue. Brief mention and
     defense of Dos Passos and Manhattan Transfer.

11 LEWIS, SINCLAIR. Review of Manhattan Transfer, in Current
     Reviews. Edited by Lewis Worthington Smith. New York:
     Henry Holt and Co., pp. 216-227.
      Reprint of 1925.B5.

12 MANTLE, BURNS. The Best Plays of 1925-26. New York: Dodd,
     Mead, pp. 566-567.
      Characterizes The Moon is a Gong as "an episodical ex-
     posure of the things jazz is doing to the world."

13 MENCKEN, H. L. "Fiction Good and Bad." American Mercury, 7
     (April), 507-508.
      Doubts that "any human being will ever be able to read
     it [Manhattan Transfer] from end to end. It is incoherent
     and not infrequently very dull. It staggers all over the
     lot." Mencken does not feel that Dos Passos has proved
     "that the promise of Three Soldiers had any substance in it."

14 SEEBUR, H. "Writer Too Shy to Speak in Public." Brooklyn
     Daily Eagle (19 September), p. 6.
      Dos Passos discusses city life ("'New York is gloriously
     chaotic'"), experimental writing ("'go as you like'"),
     women ("'she is undoubtedly rapidly approaching equality
     with man'"), imperialism and war ("'the only remedy for
     overproduction is imperialism; the only remedy for imperial-
     ism is war'"). Notes Dos Passos' talent as a painter and
     playwright as well as a novelist. Dos Passos says that he
     feels the theatre is the "'best medium for expression.'"

15 TATE, ALLEN. "Good Prose." The Nation, 122 (10 February),
     160-162.
      Calls Manhattan Transfer "a breathless movie scenario"
     containing "a great deal of excellent prose," but feels it
     "lacks all unity of projection," is not focused, does not
     adequately discriminate the significant actions.

16 YOUNG, STARK. Review of The Moon is a Gong. New Republic, 46
     (31 May), 174.

Feels the play helps to "break the ground for more poetic
writing in our theatre," but that it lacks the passion,
vigor, and theatricality of John Howard Lawson's
Processional, a play which Young thinks it resembles.

1927 A BOOKS - NONE

1927 B SHORTER WRITINGS

1 ANGOFF, ALLAN. Review of Manhattan Transfer. The Times
   Literary Supplement (3 February).
        Calls Manhattan Transfer a "vivid and masterly impres-
   sion of chaos."

2 ANON. "Globe Trotting Through Books." [Am.] Bookman, 65
   (August), xxiv-xxvi.
        Finds Orient Express a welcome relief from conventional
   travel books, a kaleidoscopic style "joined to a genuine
   knack for evoking sights, sounds, and smells exotic with
   a realistic tang."

3 ANON. Review of Orient Express. Booklist, 23 (June), 379.
        Feels the bits, fragments and glimpses of Orient Express
   form "a colorful mosaic."

4 BOYNTON, PERCY H. "Sinclair Lewis," in his More Contemporary
   Americans. Chicago: The University of Chicago Press, pp.
   179-198.
        Mentions that Lewis' review of Manhattan Transfer in-
   spired Lewis to formulate his own definition of the "ideal
   novel."

5 CRAWFORD, JOHN W. "Mr. Dos Passos Makes a Sentimental Journey."
   New York Times Book Review (15 May), p. 14.
        Feels that "the only other travel book which fuses sub-
   ject and object and mode of conveyance as perfectly as
   Orient Express" is Sterne's Sentimental Journey. Calls it
   lavish and sumptious, the short sentences appropriately
   sounding as if they were "written between jerks of a
   train."

*6 GLEN, ISA. Review of Orient Express. Literary Review of the
   New York Evening Post (2 April), p. 1.
        Cited in "John Dos Passos and His Reviewers" by William
   White, Bulletin of Bibliography, 20 (May-August 1950),
   45-47.

1927

7   LAWRENCE, D. H.   Review of <u>Manhattan Transfer</u>.   <u>Calendar of</u>
       <u>Modern Letters</u> (April).
           Calls <u>Manhattan Transfer</u> "the best modern book about New
       York that I have read."   Notes the similarities of the nar-
       rative technique to film technique and also Dos Passos'
       thematic interest in the success ethic.   Reprinted:
       1936.B22.

8   RUHL, ARTHUR.   "Mr. Dos Passos on a Camel."   <u>Saturday Review</u>
       <u>of Literature</u>, 3 (26 March), 677.
           Calls <u>Orient Express</u> "clever . . . a sort of travel
       diary . . . a kind of ode or disordered dream on travel
       itself," as well as the state of the world and, especially,
       the author himself.

9   S., H.   "Dos Passos' <u>Orient Express</u>."   <u>New York World</u> (5 May),
       p. 11m.
           Finds <u>Orient Express</u> worthless as a guidebook, but
       interesting to read: "He has caught for us some of the
       sights and sounds and smells and tastes of dozens of Eastern
       cities and of countryside, of desert and of wharves."
       Critical of Dos Passos' negativism and "cussing."

10   SINCLAIR, UPTON.   <u>Money Writes!</u>   New York: Albert and Charles
       Boni, pp. 211, 214.
           Makes a "plea" to Dos Passos, after the publication of
       <u>Manhattan Transfer</u>, to "write a plain, straightaway novel
       with the same, emotional power and radical insight and thus
       join our best-sellers."

11   W[ILSON], E[DMUND].   "And the Red Gods Call for You."   <u>New</u>
       <u>Republic</u>, 51 (7 June), 52.
           Feels Dos Passos captures in <u>Orient Express</u> the
       "trembling spiritual moods under the awareness of the
       surface" in both his prose and his watercolors which
       illustrate.   Finds the major drawback to be that the
       material is somewhat dated: much has changed since the
       journey was undertaken, six years earlier.

12   WEIL, ELSIE.   "An Eastbound American."   <u>New York Herald</u>
       <u>Tribune Books</u> (1 May), p. 19.
           Calls <u>Orient Express</u> "a sparkling travel narrative" and
       Dos Passos "a philosopher in a boxcar" for his earthy
       analysis.

13   WRIGHT, CUTHBERT.   "Hadrian Liked to Travel."   <u>Dial</u>, 83
       (July), 60-62.

Finds Orient Express quite remarkable in its imagistic, photographic attention to detail but somewhat lacking in the "gift of contemplation."

1928 A   BOOKS - NONE

1928 B   SHORTER WRITINGS

1 MORE, PAUL ELMER. "Modern Currents," in The Demon of the Absolute. Princeton: Princeton University Press, p. 63.
    Notes that many left-wing American realists are from the Midwest and tend to have relatively little formal education. Dos Passos, as a Harvard graduate, has more education than most, but More feels the life represented in his works "is about the lowest we have yet produced." Characterizes Manhattan Transfer as "an explosion in a cesspool."

2 WATTS, RICHARD, Jr. "Applying the Pulmotor to Modernist Drama." New York Herald Tribune (23 September), sec. 7, pp. 1, 4.
    Believes that The Moon is a Gong and a number of other "expressionistic" plays gave "indication of the thrilling and imaginative qualities the freer form could bring to our stage."

1929 A   BOOKS - NONE

1929 B   SHORTER WRITINGS

1 COLUM, PADRIAC. "Airways, Inc." Dial, 86 (29 May), 442.
    Thinks Airways, Inc., despite being "sincerely written," to be a series of disasters rather than a tragedy because Dos Passos "has not found any spiritual background for the people of his play."

2 KREYMBORG, ALFRED. Our Singing Strength: An Outline of American Poetry (1620-1930). New York: Coward-McCann, p. 619.
    Feels that the ironies of Keene Wallis' radical poetry are "as savage as those of Michael Gold, John Dos Passos or John Howard Lawson, poets who write fiery novels and plays."

3 LEISY, ERNEST ERWIN. American Literature: An Interpretative Survey. New York: Thomas Y. Crowell Co., pp. 218, 259.
    Mentions Dos Passos.

1929

4 POSSELT, ERICK, ed. <u>On Parade: Caricatures by Eva Herrmann</u>.
   New York: Coward-McCann, pp. 42-45.
   Caricature of Dos Passos, along with a quote from him on
   writing and a listing of his books.

5 WATTS, RICHARD, JR. "<u>Airways, Inc</u>. Given by New Playwrights
   at the Grove Street." <u>New York Herald Tribune</u> (21 February),
   p. 19.
   Calls <u>Airways, Inc</u>., "uneven, garrulous, unco-ordinated
   and badly edited."

6 WILSON, EDMUND. "Dos Passos and the Social Revolution." <u>New
   Republic</u>, 58 (17 April), 256-257.
   Calls <u>Airways, Inc</u>. a "dramatic poem of modern America."
   Wilson criticizes Dos Passos for his tendency to sentiment-
   alize but praises him as "the only [member of his generation]
   who has tried seriously to study all aspects and forces of
   America, and to compose with them a picture which makes
   sense." Reprinted: 1952.B23.

<u>1930 A BOOKS - NONE</u>

<u>1930 B SHORTER WRITINGS</u>

1 ANON. "Books in Brief." <u>Christian Century</u>, 47 (30 April),
   562.
   Calls <u>The 42nd Parallel</u> a "worthy attempt to write 'the
   great American novel' in the modern mode." Comments favorably on various narrative sections, but finds the work too
   limited in its cross section of characters and the time
   covered. Wants Dos Passos to proceed through the war and
   the decade following.

2 ANON. "New Novels." <u>Saturday Review</u> (London), 150 (20
   September), 345.
   After admitting bias against "senseless" manipulation of
   technique, continues: "unlike certain would-be innovators in
   technique, he understands the art of narrative, he knows
   how to present characters convincingly, and he can write a
   prose of his own." Further, admires his plain, straightforward style, concluding that his "experiment in diction
   is . . . no less significant than the larger experiment of
   technique.

3 ANON. "New Novels." <u>Times Literary Supplement</u> (4 September),
   p. 648.

After asserting that many modern American writers "seem to be bent on ruling the aesthetic element out of their novels," argues that The 42nd Parallel "presents this problem in its starkest form." Finds both the style and subject matter unattractive, and chaotic--only in the biographies does the work come alive, in places, approaching poetry.

4 ANON. Review of The 42nd Parallel. Booklist, 27 (September), 28.
   Calls The 42nd Parallel "an achievement in form." Notes the kaleidoscope effect.

5 ANON. Review of The 42nd Parallel. [Am.] Bookman, 71 (April), 210-211.
   Finds The 42nd Parallel, like Manhattan Transfer, to be experimental, influenced by Stein and Joyce. Critical of the Camera's Eye, Newsreel, and biographies, but finds the main narrative sections to be "told in that carefully naive, condensed, colloquial style that Ernest Hemingway . . . has most successfully affected." Critical of the lack of apparent scheme and open-endedness of the novel, concluding that it seems merely a sample "of the naturalistic pessimism and spiritual anarchy which mark our age."

6 ANON. Review of The 42nd Parallel. Cleveland Open Shelf (July), p. 111.
   Calls the novel "a moving picture film of life."

*7 ANON. Review of The 42nd Parallel. New Statesman, 35 (23 August), 622.
   Cited in "John Dos Passos and His Reviewers," by William White, Bulletin of Bibliography, 20 (May-August 1950), 45-47.

8 ANON. Review of The 42nd Parallel. Springfield Republican (2 March), p. 7e.
   Feels that the "separate episodes have small interest for the critical reader . . . Mr. Dos Passos started with an interesting scheme, but the material to realize it is lacking."

9 BUTCHER, FANNY. "Movie Methods Feature Novel." Chicago Daily Tribune (1 March), p. 15.
   Finds a "perfect marriage of material and manner" in Manhattan Transfer, but finds the attempt at the same in The 42nd Parallel to be less satisfying, primarily because there seems to be little cohesion and almost no closure.

1930

10 CHAMBERLAIN, JOHN. "Drift and Mastery in Our Novelists," in
    The Critique of Humanism: A Symposium. Edited by Clinton
    Grutlan. Essay Index Reprint Series. New York: Books for
    Libraries Press, Inc., pp. 257-280.
        Admires The 42nd Parallel because "it is shaped with an
    idea towards making a philosophical judgment rise positively
    out of the record."

11 _____. "John Dos Passos Satirizes an America 'On the Make.'"
    New York Times Book Review (2 March), p. 5.
        Calls The 42nd Parallel, "very effective social castiga-
    tion . . . a satire on the tremendous haphazardness of life
    in expansionist America." Finds the book unsatisfyingly
    incomplete, hypothesizing that it is either merely part of
    a longer work or meant to suggest the chaos of modern
    American life. Whatever the causes, the effect is not
    satisfying for the novel does not coalesce. Notes the in-
    fluence of Joyce and John Howard Lawson, but applauds Dos
    Passos for his sensible "balance between expression and
    communication."

12 HANSEN, HARRY. Review of The 42nd Parallel. New York World
    (19 February), p. 11.
        Feels that Dos Passos, in The 42nd Parallel, "is again
    adopting the manner of Manhattan Transfer, but he is more
    aloof, resorting less to literary trickery . . . he pic-
    tures a man as he sees him, reports impartially on his
    acts, and lets it go at that."

13 HAZLITT, HENRY. "Kaleidoscope." Nation, 130 (12 March), 298.
        Cannot find any unity in The 42nd Parallel "except that
    supplied by the bindings." Finds the novel stylistically
    haphazard and thematically dreary. Only the newsreels hold
    fascination. Still, thinks the novel "shares the capital
    danger of all futilitarianism in fiction: the fiction is
    apt to seem as futile as the events it records."

14 PATTEE, FRED LEWIS. The New American Literature, 1890-1930.
    New York: The Century Co., pp. 387, 451, 461.
        Occasional mention of Dos Passos.

15 PRITCHETT, V. S. "The Age of Speed?" Spectator, 145
    (27 September), 421-422.
        Says that the author of The 42nd Parallel has incredible
    vitality, but "he is like a man who is trying to run in a
    dozen directions at once, succeeding thereby merely in
    standing still and making noise. Sometimes it is amusing
    noise and alive; often monotonous." Despite the novel's

"startling kaleidoscopic vividness," thinks Dos Passos "has no emotions, only moods: moods of revulsion, satire, lyricism, sensuality."

16 ROSS, MARY. "Where Storms Meet the Ocean." New York Herald Tribune Books (23 February), pp. 3-4.
  Calls The 42nd Parallel a brave experiment in dynamic fiction. Feels Dos Passos is "groping toward some new approach" which will eliminate the narrow frame of conventional narrative. Thinks Dos Passos' novel "becomes in the end a search for generalization, as a spectrum whirled on a dish shows solid white."

17 SINCLAIR, UPTON. "John Dos Passos: American Writer." New Masses, 5 (April), 18-19.
  Highly critical of the technical devices of The 42nd Parallel. Still, Sinclair feels that it is "the most interesting novel I have read in many a long day."

18 STRACHEY, RICHARD. "Mainly American." The Nation and The Athenaeum, 48 (1 November), 169-170.
  Finds The 42nd Parallel an "interesting experiment," largely successful, conveying "as much by his direct and harsh style as by the subject matter of his work, the restless energy of a great country."

19 WILSON, EDMUND. "Dahlberg, Dos Passos and Wilder." New Republic, 62 (26 March), 156-158.
  Finds The 42nd Parallel a considerable advance from earlier works as a result of Dos Passos' newly exhibited ability "to immerse himself in the minds and the lives of his middle-class characters." Wilson feels that it is "the most remarkable, the most encouraging American novel . . . since the War." Reprinted: 1952.B22.

1931 A BOOKS - NONE

1931 B SHORTER WRITINGS

 1 BEACH, JOSEPH WARREN. "The Novel from James to Joyce." The Nation, 132 (10 June), 634-636.
  Considers Dos Passos to be one of a number of novelists who "have more or less come under Joyce's influence." Beach feels that Dos Passos "suggests Joyce's use of themes which are symbols, that is, something superadded to the realism of character portrayal, and in the introductory

1931

prose poems of <u>Manhattan Transfer</u>, the camera eye and 'news reels' of <u>The 42nd Parallel</u>, he makes the most effective use of any of the school of that poetic symbolism which is the inimitable feature of <u>Ulysses</u>."

2 HICKS, GRANVILLE. "Dos Passos' Gifts." <u>New Republic</u>, 67 (24 June), 157-158.
   Considers Dos Passos one of the few writers to directly confront contemporary life and specifically the problem of industrialism. Hicks examines three characteristics of Dos Passos which he feels enables him to deal effectively with contemporary themes: his poetic imagination, his radical orientation, and his commitment to artistic experimentation.

3 JOHNSON, MERLE, ed. "American First Editions: John Dos Passos." <u>Publishers Weekly</u>, 120 (18 July), 259.
   List of Dos Passos' first editions to 1931.

4 TANTE, DILLY [Stanley Kunitz], ed. <u>Living Authors: A Book of Biographies</u>. New York: H. W. Wilson, pp. 105-106.
   Brief summary of Dos Passos' life and career.

1932 A BOOKS - NONE

1932 B SHORTER WRITINGS

1 ANON. "Blood and Carnival." <u>Review of Reviews</u>, 85 (June), 6.
   Calls <u>1919</u> a "mad epic of a mad era." Calls it "starkly, brutally realistic," smacking of revolt.

2 ANON. "Episodes in a Chain by John Dos Passos." <u>Springfield Republican</u> (13 March), p. 7e.
   Faults <u>1919</u> for its seemingly random construction and Dos Passos for "sophisticated exploitation" of his material: "These episodes seem oftener conceived for their daring than for their significance." Considers the chief merit to be one of style: "Mr. Dos Passos' fluid, almost rhythmical prose imparts the sense of first-hand reality to narration."

3 ANON. Review of <u>1919</u>. <u>Booklist</u>, 29 (September), 17.
   Feels that <u>1919</u> has "magnitude of conception, vitality, and verisimilitude." Finds the episodic structure "amazingly faithful to the hectic tempo of war-time existence."

4 ANON. Review of <u>1919</u>. <u>Commonweal</u>, 16 (11 May), 55.
   Calls Dos Passos "a brilliant practitioner of the unusual in fiction," but finds <u>1919</u> a victim of "the double bane

24

which vitiates all of Mr. Dos Passos' work: his lack of
tenderness or exaltation in characterization, and his shrill
finger pointing at the vices of capitalism as the single
cause of man's suffering."

*5 ANON. Review of 1919. Forum, 87 (April), iv.
     Cited in "John Dos Passos and His Reviewers," by William
     White, Bulletin of Bibliography, 20 (May-August 1950),
     45-47.

6 ANON. Review of 1919. Times Literary Supplement (23 June),
     p. 462.
     Crotchety review which concludes that 1919 is "a depres-
     sing and at times a revolting book," despite the author's
     seemingly wide experience, power of observation and gift
     for the pungent statement."

7 ANON. "War and Peace, and Revolution." New Statesman and
     Nation, 3 (11 June), 770.
     Calls 1919 (along with The 42nd Parallel) "a modern War
     and Peace," but one which does not focus on the public
     structure, but the cross section underneath: "he gives us,
     instead of the distant view, these glimpses of vivid swarm-
     ing units. Concludes that Dos Passos, like Hemingway, "is
     essentially master of a small art . . . but possessed of
     immense zest for life and an incomparable native vigour
     in expressing it."

8 BABBITT, IRVING. On Being Creative and Other Essays. Boston
     and New York: Houghton Mifflin Co., pp. 219-222.
     On Manhattan Transfer: "In the name of reality, Mr. Dos
     Passos has perpetrated a literary nightmare. Such a work
     would seem to have slight value even as a sociological
     document; unless, indeed, one is prepared to admit that
     contemporary Manhattan is inhabited chiefly by epileptic
     Bohemians. . . . The technique of Manhattan Transfer is as
     dubious as its underlying philosophy."

9 BAKER, HELEN CODY. "Mad Year." Survey, 68 (1 May), 152.
     Finds 1919 dazzling, not so much for the plot, but for
     the brilliant medley of heat and glare and color."

10 BEACH, JOSEPH WARREN. "Abstract Composition: Dos Passos," in
     his The Twentieth Century Novel: Studies in Technique.
     New York: Appleton-Century-Crofts, Inc., pp. 501-511.
     Admires Dos Passos' ability, in The 42nd Parallel and
     1919, to show the relationship among the seemingly unrelated
     elements of the society he portrays. Considers the first

1932

two volumes of <u>U.S.A.</u> a logical expansion upon the themes and technique of <u>Manhattan Transfer</u>.

11 _____. "Discontinuity: John Dos Passos," in his <u>The Twentieth Century Novel: Studies in Technique</u>. New York: Appleton-Century-Crofts, Inc., pp. 437-448.
    Compares <u>Manhattan Transfer</u> to Jacob Wasserman's <u>The World's Illusions</u> and <u>The Gooseman</u>, noting the similarities in their expressionistic manner which Beach describes as "cutting the slice lengthwise as well as breadthwise."

12 BROOKS, WALTER R. "The New Books," <u>Outlook</u>, 160 (April), 231.
    Finds Dos Passos' narrative technique in <u>1919</u> to "provide an accompaniment of the march of events without drawing out his individual themes." Feels the various narrative sections gain richness from one another.

13 BUTCHER, FANNY. "A Slice of Life, Describes Book of Dos Passos." <u>Chicago Daily Tribune</u> (12 March), p. 10.
    Feels Dos Passos' method is particularly appropriate in <u>1919</u> for that year "was one of utter restlessness, morally and spiritually as well as physically." Though the book is difficult, with "no surface calm whatever," it is valuable as the actual living, breathing record of a period in its most intense manifestation.

14 CALMER, ALAN. "John Dos Passos." <u>Sewanee Review</u>, 40 (July), 341-349.
    Emphasizes Dos Passos' effort "to bridge the gulf between bookish literature, designed only for the specialist, and a robust literature, embedded in social and political issues, written for the general reader."

15 CALVERTON, V. F. <u>The Liberation of American Literature</u>. New York: Charles Scribner's Sons, pp. 462-468, passim.
    Views Dos Passos as a Marxist revolutionary and feels his success "has been the most important event in the history of the American left-wing movement in literature." Feels that, unlike Upton Sinclair, Dos Passos creates characters who live by virtue of their own flesh and blood rather than by virtue of the ideas which they are supposed to convey.

16 CHAMBERLAIN, JOHN. "John Dos Passos' Experiment with the 'News' Novel." <u>New York Times Book Review</u> (13 March), p. 2.
    Calls <u>1919</u> a "news" novel and, as such, much like Frederick Allen's <u>Only Yesterday</u>. It is also more than that by virtue of the skillful interweaving of the public and the private, the non-fictional characters and events

26

with the fictional. Thinks this appropriate because "so
many Americans live in and by the news." Feels that, given
Dos Passos' plan of merging the public and the private, the
characters are necessarily flat. Nevertheless, after com-
paring Dos Passos with Wilder, Hemingway, and Fitzgerald,
concludes that he is "the most adventurous, the most widely
experienced, the man with the broadest sympathies among our
novelists."

17 COWLEY, MALCOLM. "The Poet and the World." New Republic, 70
(27 April), 303-305.
    Maintains that Dos Passos "is in reality two novelists":
one a late-Romantic, individualistic esthete; the other a
collectivist, a radical historian of the class struggle.
Cowley considers much of the earlier work that of the former
but finds 1919 a powerful example of the latter. Calls 1919
"a landmark in American fiction." Reprinted: 1971.A2;
1974.A3.

18 H., E. "A View of the American Scene." Boston Evening
Transcript (23 March), sec. 4, p. 2.
    Feels that in 1919, and its predecessor, The 42nd
Parallel, Dos Passos has created a "vast surging drama" of
America. Thinks that "Dos Passos is experimenting with a
novelistic technique that in the future may develop into
the most important literary contribution of the century."

19 HAZLITT, HENRY. "Panorama." The Nation, 134 (23 March), 344.
    Finds 1919 even better than The 42nd Parallel "which was
itself the outstanding American novel of 1930." Admires
the panoramic scope and the versatility of the third person
narratives which are, nevertheless, "from the standpoint of
the first person." Feels Dos Passos most closely approaches,
in tone, Hemingway, but in language, in range of sympathy,
and social implications, surpasses Hemingway. Finds the
weakness of the technique of both writers to be a certain
"shallowness of feeling" among their characters, but feels
it may be an appropriate reflection of the shortcoming of
American life itself.

20 HICKS, GRANVILLE. "John Dos Passos." [Am.] Bookman, 75 (April),
32-34.
    Places Dos Passos in the Realist tradition but feels he
is able to produce more successful novels for two reasons:
he has found a "revolutionary vision" which provides a
framework for understanding; he has developed a personal
style "which allows him to capture the breadth and depth of
the American experience. Hicks is particularly impressed

1932

with Dos Passos' narrative voice which shifts constantly to suit the character.

21 JOSEPHSON, MATTHEW. "A Sad 'Big Parade.'" Saturday Review of Literature, 8 (19 March), 600.
Sees Dos Passos as a pure Marxist. Believes 1919 to be a more effective, more cohesive novel than The 42nd Parallel despite the persistence of innovations in language and style which Josephson feels are unnecessary.

22 KNIGHT, GRANT C. American Literature and Culture. New York: Ray Long and Richard R. Smith, Inc., pp. 456-461.
Considers Dos Passos a member of a promising generation of fiction writers.

23 LEAVIS, F. R. "A Serious Artist." Scrutiny, 1 (Summer), 173-179.
Reviews Manhattan Transfer, The 42nd Parallel, and 1919. Discusses the difficulty of reconciling a collectivist approach with attention to individuals, of suggesting "the multitudinous impersonality of the ant-heap through individual cases that, without much development, interest us as such." Reprinted: 1974.A3.

24 LEIGHTON, LAWRENCE. "An Autopsy and a Prescription." Hound and Horn, 5 (July-September), 519-539.
Surveying the writing of Hemingway, Fitzgerald, and Dos Passos, finds their work adolescent and merely fashionable: "Their imaginations are banal, their sensibility is sick. . . . In Dos Passos' ant-like accumulation of detail and forlorn literalness there is a suggestion that he has come to be like the loathed object he looks upon. There is not discernible in his two later novels, Manhattan Transfer and The 42nd Parallel, any quality of imagination or divination other than the humdrum workings of the ordinary bourgeois mind."

25 LEWISOHN, LUDWIG. "The Naturalists," in his Expression in America. New York: Harper & Co., pp. 462-522.
Calls the stories of The 42nd Parallel "powerful examples of a harsh and desperate naturalism," but objects to the technique which is characterized as a "spurious imitation" of originality.

26 ROSS, MARY. "Dos Passos Writes a Symphony of War." New York Tribune Books (13 March), p. 5.
Compares 1919's structure with that of a symphony, each narrative section being like a different orchestral section.

Calls the writing "distinguished by a remarkable sensuous
perception . . . a directness, independence, and poignancy
of thought and emotion that seems . . . unexcelled in current fiction."

27 STRONG, L.A.G. "Fiction." Spectator, 148 (25 June), 910.
      Finds the form of 1919 unusual but thinks that only an
    initial and surmountable obstacle to an interesting and
    important novel.

28 ZELINSKI, C. and PIOTR PAVLENKO. "Russia to John Dos Passos."
      Living Age, 343 (October), 178-179.
      Letter to Dos Passos which mixes praise and a warning to
    avoid "ideological isolation from life," meaning the influ-
    ence of James Joyce's Ulysses. Asks Dos Passos to publicly
    support the Soviet Union against "the new tactics of
    imperialism."

1933 A BOOKS - NONE

1933 B SHORTER WRITINGS

1 ANON. "Soviet Literature and Dos Passos." International
      Literature, 4 (1933-1934), 103-112.
      Excerpts from papers presented at a symposium on Dos
    Passos by five Soviet scholars.

2 ASEYEV, N. "Song of the 42nd Parallel." International
      Literature, 4 (1933-1934), 68-69.
      A reaction, in verse, to The 42nd Parallel: "America of
    The Forty-Second Parallel/An America against the dollar
    kings/Glimpsed, seen and understood by Comrade John Dos
    Passos/Written not upon the wall/But in the hearts and
    brains/ O workers, punctured by their fists/Dictated to
    the arch stenographer, John Dos Passos."

3 BOWER-SHORE, CLIFFORD. "John Dos Passos." Bookman (London),
      85 (December), 198-199.
      Calls Dos Passos "the most significant figure in the
    younger school of American authors," and finds astonishing
    the "vigour and fecundity" of his imagination. Calls 1919
    "a great and terrible book," the work of a man of "abnormal
    energy and ultra-sensibility."

4 EDGAR, PELHAM. "Four American Writers: Anderson, Hemingway,
      Dos Passos, Faulkner," in his The Art of the Novel From
      1700 to the Present Time. New York: The Macmillan Co.,
      pp. 338-351.

1933

Finds Dos Passos a "brilliant and ambitious" writer who
can make use of the staccato style for an "even more biting
realistic effect" than Hemingway, but feels that his books
are not particularly memorable whether from a lack of poetic
instinct or a "desire to crowd too many aspects of life"
into his novels.

5 GOLD, MICHAEL. "The Education of John Dos Passos." The
English Journal, 22 (February), 87-97.
Marxist analysis of Dos Passos' career. Sees Dos Passos'
education as a struggle to purge the tendencies to be the
"passive aesthetic and individualist," to "ruthlessly destroy
the Jimmy Herf-Ernest Hemingway negativism" which "poisoned"
his early writing. Thinks the war and, especially, the
Sacco-Vanzetti case have been the most important factors in
his education. Believes that The 42nd Parallel and 1919
mark "the beginning of a new Dos Passos. He is winning a
struggle against himself. These novels are the first fruits
of a victory of the militant collectivist" over his aristo-
cratic past.

6 HICKS, GRANVILLE. The Great Tradition. New York: The
Macmillan Co., pp. 287-291, passim.
Marxist survey of American literature. Views Dos Passos
as a proletarian writer.

7 LEAVIS, F. R. "John Dos Passos," in For Continuity. Cambridge,
England: Minority Press, pp. 102-110.
Reprint of 1932.B23.

8 STEIN, GERTRUDE. The Autobiography of Alice B. Toklas. New
York: Harcourt, Brace and Company, p. 267.
Mentions Dos Passos' friendship with Hemingway.

1934 A BOOKS - NONE

1934 B SHORTER WRITINGS

1 ANON. "Books in Brief." Christian Century, 51 (9 May), 634.
While noting that much of the material of In All Countries
was written somewhat earlier, concludes that his lively
style and the persistence of the basic issues of the work
keep the book timely and interesting.

2 ANON. "Books in Brief." Christian Century, 51 (6 June), 771.
Review of Three Plays. Finds, in the plays, a style like
that of Dos Passos' fiction, "staccato and discontinuous,"

or like that of the pointillist painters. Wonders whether
they could be coherent in production, but thinks that, when
read, they are "profoundly impressive."

3 ANON. "A Disturbed World." Springfield Republican (20 April),
    p. 12.
        Feels that In All Countries fails because "the information
lacks weight and the impressions lack force." Thinks Dos
Passos botches most attempts at sensual description.

4 ANON. "In All Countries." Times Literary Supplement
    (23 August), p. 573.
        Finds In All Countries frequently obscure and misleading
although "his gift for hearing the moving or dramatic experience extends to a flow of words, phrases, images and
metaphors for describing it."

5 ANON. "Plays By Dos Passos." Springfield Republican
    (23 August), p. 8.
        Focuses on Dos Passos' preface to Three Plays, which is
called a "turgid and one-sided" diatribe against the
American theatre.

6 ANON. Review of In All Countries. Booklist, 30 (June), 311.
        Admires the impressionistic style of In All Countries.

7 ANON. Review of In All Countries. Cleveland Open Shelf
    (May), p. 11.
        Calls the book "vivid."

8 ANON. Review of In All Countries. New Outlook, 163 (May),
    60.
        Brief summary of In All Countries.

9 ANON. Review of In All Countries. Survey Graphic, 23 (August),
    396.
        Calls the travel sketches of In All Countries "the raw
material from which Dos Passos creates his exciting novels."

10 ANON. Review of Three Plays. Booklist, 30 (July), 345.
        Finds the three plays to "depict American life from the
point of view of a social revolutionary."

11 ANON. Review of Three Plays. Theatre Arts Monthly, 18
    (August), 648.
        Finds Dos Passos' views on the theatre invigorating and
necessary; concedes that Broadway should be more experimental. Concludes, however, that the plays of Three Plays are
just not good enough examples of experimental theatre, that

1934

the characters don't have the life of the characters in his
novels.

12 ANON. "A Travel Book By Dos Passos." New Statesman and
Nation, 8 (8 September), 300.
Finds the indignation of In All Countries powerful except
when it dissolves into "the slightly stereotyped pattern of
black and white." These lapses are seldom, however, and
his "sensitiveness to natural beauty" helps the reader forget them.

13 ASCH, NATHAN. "The Artist as Reporter." New Republic, 78
(9 may), 370-371.
Admires the stylistic intensity of In All Countries:
"writing a jaggedly contemporary prose, he drives the
sights and sounds and tastes and shudders into the reader's
bones."

14 CODMAN, FLORENCE. "The Camera Eye." Nation, 138 (9 May),
540.
Finds In All Countries like the Camera Eye of The 42nd
Parallel in that "both are impressionistic and highly
effective when convincing, formless and dull when badly
done."

15 COURNOS, JOHN. "The Art of Travel." Yale Review, N.S. 23
(June), 823-827.
Contains a review of In All Countries which is admired
for its sharp-eyed presentation of scenes of social upheaval.

16 COWLEY, MALCOLM. Exile's Return: A Literary Odyssey of the
1920's. New York: W. W. Norton Company, pp. 52-53, passim.
Many references to Dos Passos the expatriate.

17 _____. "Good Books That Almost Nobody Has Read." New Republic,
78 (18 April), 281-283.
Poll of a number of writers, including Dos Passos, asking
them to note recent works which have received undeservedly
small readerships. Dos Passos mentions Laugh and Lie Down
by Robert Cantwell, Woman of Earth by Agnes Smedley, Nobody
Starves by Catherine Brody, Forgotten Frontiers by Dorothy
Dudley, The American Jitters by Edmund Wilson, and The
Disinherited by Jack Conroy. Not surprisingly, most of
the books have proletarian themes.

18 DUFFUS, R. L. "The Peregrinations of John Dos Passos." New
York Times Book Review (6 May), pp. 3, 13.

Thinks In All Countries is marred by its simplified
treatment of social classes and Dos Passos' "disturbing
hatred for hyphens," his tendency to collapse words into
one. Calls the book "primarily radical propaganda . . . he
sees the world through doctrinal spectacles." As a result,
the book lacks objectivity and realism.

19 EATON, W. P. Review of Three Plays. New York Herald Tribune
    Books (1 July), p. 12.
       Thinks the plays of Three Plays seem "oddly old-
    fashioned." Doubts that "Fortune Heights" would be any
    more successful than its predecessors, for "valuable as a
    snapshot observation may be in drama," it does not neces-
    sarily make interesting theatre. Feels Dos Passos' chief
    faults are his deficiency in characterization and in build-
    ing suspense.

20 FLETCHER, JOHN GOULD. "Two Travellers." American Review, 3
    (September), 530-536.
       Compares In All Countries with Aldous Huxley's Beyond
    the Mexique Bay. Thinks the latter book is flawed by
    Huxley's own confused opinions, but admires the way Dos
    Passos "enlists our sympathy by simply giving us what he
    has seen without comment."

21 G., H. S. Review of Three Plays. Saturday Review of
    Literature, 10 (23 June), 771-772.
       Thinks "Fortune Heights" the strongest of the plays.
    It is "by turns, sardonic, cynical, tragic, pitiful."
    Finds Dos Passos' preface to the volume, despite occasional
    "well-armed and amusing critical barbs, to be intemperate
    in its blanket condemnation of Broadway."

22 H[UTCHINSON], P[ERCY]. "The Combative Plays of John Dos
    Passos." New York Times Book Review (20 May), p. 2.
       Finds Dos Passos shrill and unnecessarily combative in
    his condemnation of traditional theatre. Feels his plays
    are too much like his novels, particularly Manhattan
    Transfer, arguing that "a play . . . which does not clarify
    itself as it goes along blurs and defeats itself." Never-
    theless, finds a "sort of rough poetry, a Whitmanesque
    note . . . as well as a rugged honesty of purpose in the
    plays."

23 HARTWICK, HARRY. "The Anarchist," in his The Foreground of
    American Fiction. New York: American Book Company, pp.
    282-293, passim.

1934

In summarizing Dos Passos' intent in The 42nd Parallel and 1919, Hartwick mixes metaphors: They are, he writes, a "pair of enlarged tabloid papers, two wide futuristic canvasses in which the author has again employed his 'flicker' technique to reproduce by suggestive excerpts a vista that is much too spacious to be captured entire." Thinks Dos Passos an American Rousseau or Kropotkin, essentially a philosophical anarchist.

24 HICKS, GRANVILLE. "Notes of a Novelist." New Masses, 1 (24 April), 25-26.
    Feels that In All Countries reveals, in a lesser degree, the qualities of Dos Passos' moods: "the vivid, authentic reproduction of sights and sounds, the lively sense of the paradoxical and the symbolic, the honest sympathy with working men and women." Hicks also feels it exaggerates the weaknesses of the novels: "the absence of solid, inclusive, irrefutable knowledge of political and economic movements, and the absence of the kind of insight that only direct, disciplined participation in struggle can give." Reprinted in Granville Hicks in the New Masses, pp. 78-79.

25 KRUTCH, JOSEPH WOOD. "Hissing the Villains." Nation, 138 (27 June), 735.
    Critical of Three Plays both for the plays themselves and for Dos Passos' introduction which is critical of the theatre establishment. Krutch feels that these three plays and many other experimental works fail only as a result of their own dramatic ineptness.

26 L., T. S. "John Dos Passos Looks at The World About Him." Boston Transcript (28 April), book section, p. 1.
    Calls In All Countries "a graphic delineation of the world about us."

27 LUCCOCK, HALFORD E. Contemporary American Literature and Religion. Chicago: Willett, Clark and Company, pp. 148-150, passim.
    Calls Dos Passos "an historian of a lost generation." Luccock feels his novels "are filled with sharp criticism of the existing order, criticism that has far-reaching ethical and social significance. His work has more value as a stimulant and challenge to religiously inspired social idealism than has all the piously labeled 'religious fiction' of a generation." Thinks Three Soldiers, in 1921, "absent without leave from headquarters, walked across the stage of literature, and marked the advent of a new spirit in the treatment of war."

28 RUHL, ARTHUR. "Distance Lends Enchantment." <u>Saturday Review
      of Literature</u>, 10 (5 May), 675.
          Finds <u>In All Countries</u> uneven, best in those sections on
      Russia and Spain. Some parts of discussion of Mexico and
      Central America are "sound, some shaky." Finds the final
      section, which focuses on America, to be the worst, marred
      by a simplistic leftist perspective.

29 T., R. "Novelists as Travelers." <u>Current History</u>, 40 (July),
      vii.
          Calls the author of <u>In All Countries</u> an "excellent
      journalist, the maker of hard, impressionistic, fast moving
      phrases" who views the world through "Marxian spectacles."

30 THOMPSON, DOROTHY. "Dos Passos and His Bourgeois Conscience."
      <u>New York Herald Tribune Books</u> (29 April), p. 5.
          Finds the impressionistic sketches of <u>In All Countries</u>
      delightful but feels "a general impression of lameness"
      because it is sensed that the radical perspective which
      colors this and other Dos Passos books seems to be pri-
      marily a product of bourgeoise guilt rather than conviction
      to Marxist principles. As a result, there is a certain con-
      fusion in the tone of this work.

31 WALTON, EDITH H. Review of <u>In All Countries</u>. <u>Forum</u>, 91
      (June), v.
          Short review which concludes that "in Dos Passos humor
      and indignation combine. He is a wit as well as a crusader,
      and his vignettes of contemporary life have a biting vigor
      which few writers can match."

32 WAUGH, EVELYN. "Travellers." <u>Spectator</u>, 153 (28 September),
      448, 450.
          Says <u>In All Countries</u> "is not a travel book," but obser-
      vations on "the progress of communism." Finds the Russian
      section less successful, conveying "puzzled awe and the
      peevishness of the American tourist."

<u>1935 A BOOKS - NONE</u>

<u>1935 B SHORTER WRITINGS</u>

1 COWLEY, MALCOLM. "What the Revolutionary Movement Can Do for
      a Writer." <u>New Masses</u>, 15 (7 May), 20-22.
          Identifies, as a major theme between 1880 and 1930, "the
      conflict between the individual and society, between the

1935

Artist and the World." Cowley cites <u>Manhattan Transfer</u> as exemplifying the theme.

2 DAMON, S. FOSTER. <u>Amy Lowell: A Chronicle</u>. Boston and New York: Houghton Mifflin Company, pp. 574-575, 632.
Quotes Lowell's praise for <u>Three Soldiers</u>: "an extremely interesting book . . . a remarkable record of the attitude of a certain kind of soldier" despite the fact that "like all realistic books, the other side of realism, the side that makes life worth living, is left out." Also quotes Lowell's praise of <u>Rosinante to the Road Again</u>.

3 DEVOTO, BERNARD. "Classy Literature." <u>Saturday Review</u>, 12 (5 October), 26, 31.
Review of Joseph Freeman's <u>Proletarian Literature in the United States: An Anthology</u>. Devoto feels that, though often crude and mawkish, the proletarian literature represented may serve its primary function as class literature better than "the subtleties of Dos Passos which only sophisticates can appreciate."

4 DORAN, GEORGE H. <u>Chronicles of Barabbas</u>. New York: Harcourt, Brace & Co., pp. 285-286.
Gives rationale for censoring, before publication, <u>Three Soldiers</u> and explains why Doran refused to publish Dos Passos' next book: "He indignantly refused to be published by a coward, a coward being a man who would not wittingly offend the sensibilities of his mother, his sister, or his daughter. Dos Passos employed the common language of the degenerate."

5 HATCHER, HARLAN. <u>Creating the Modern American Novel</u>. New York: Farrar & Rinehart, pp. 130-139, passim.
Feels Dos Passos has the nature of a poet and the eye of a painter and uses these to explore his major theme: the disillusion of the post-war era. Considers him, as a novelist of protest, to be "somewhere between Upton Sinclair and Sinclair Lewis. He is too much an artist to, like Sinclair, use his novels as tracts and, unlike Lewis, his novels are more than satirical portraits due to his concern with "accuracy and a vision of a better life." Thinks Dos Passos is the only writer of his generation who "has fully arrived and is established beyond the stage of promise."

6 HICKS, GRANVILLE. <u>The Great Tradition</u>, Revised edition. New York: The Macmillan Company, pp. 287-292, passim.
Views Dos Passos as a leading proletarian writer.

Writings about John Dos Passos

1936 A   BOOKS - NONE

1936 B   SHORTER WRITINGS

1 ADAMS, J. DONALD. "John Dos Passos Pictures The Boom Years."
   New York Times Book Review (16 August), p. 2.
        Calls The Big Money "a forceful if inconclusive chapter
   to our social history." Finds perhaps Dos Passos' greatest
   asset to be his keen eye for so many different kinds of
   people: "his range of close acquaintance with American
   types, groups and classes is probably wider than that of
   any other well-known American novelist."

2 ANON. "Mr. Dos Passos' American Kaleidoscope." Springfield
   Republican (9 August), p. 7e.
        Notes that Dos Passos' narrative technique in The Big
   Money is not as radical as innovation as it seemed. He has
   simply eliminated the connecting links which hold together
   traditional episodic novels. Feels that such a technique
   is most effective in portraying "contrasting aspects of
   life with a casualness and lack of contact that are true
   in the actual scene." Thinks Dos Passos more effective in
   his rhetorical passages than in his tales.

3 ANON. "Private Historian." Time, 28 (10 August), 51-53.
        Brief overview of Dos Passos' life and career with
   special attention to The Big Money. Emphasizes the oblique
   commentary which results from the careful juxtapositions of
   the novel's narrative segments.

4 ANON. Review of The Big Money. Booklist, 33 (September), 22.
        Calls The Big Money "a serious and furious presentation
   of a slice of . . . American life."

5 ANON. Review of The Big Money. Christian Century, 53
   (26 August), 1135-1136.
        While acknowledging Dos Passos' gifts, wonders at his
   direction, particularly in The Big Money. Asserts that his
   focus on the corrupt and immoral, his "determined selection
   of the worst" is not true realism.

6 ANON. Review of The Big Money. Cleveland Open Shelf
   (October), p. 20.
        Very brief review.

7 ANON. Review of The Big Money. Current History, 44
   (September), 128.

1936

> Thinks that, in The Big Money, "conventionalities of
> sequence and theme fall before [Dos Passos'] seemingly
> spontaneous outbursts of ideas and observations of the
> world and its people."

8   ANON.   Review of The Big Money.   Times Literary Supplement
     (24 October), p. 859.
     Acclaims The Big Money and the trilogy it completes as
     "an outstanding contribution to modern American fiction."
     Considers this last novel "firmer, brisker, more masterly"
     than its predecessors, particularly in the biographies.
     Nevertheless, feels Dos Passos has been unable to eliminate
     three flaws which run through the trilogy: the "puppet-
     nature of the characters," the "distinct narrowness in the
     individual response and actions," the inability to synthe-
     size the various narrative sections.

9   ANON.   "Third Dos Passos Book on Modern Era is a Vivid One."
     Chicago Daily Tribune (5 September), p. 12.
     Summary of The Big Money which concludes that Dos Passos'
     premise is that "after the great war . . . America offered
     unparalleled opportunities for the golden rewards of human
     rottenness."

10   BOYNTON, PERCY H.   Literature and American Life: For Students
     of American Literature.   Boston: Ginn and Co., pp. 862–866.
     Notes the American Marxists' interest in Dos Passos and
     feels he "implies their doctrines . . . and fulfills their
     contention that revolutionary literature must be good as
     literature."

11   BRICKELL, HERSCHEL.   Review of The Big Money.   Review of
     Reviews, 94 (September), 12.
     Finds The Big Money disgusting and trivial, and hardly
     believable: "Mr. Dos Passos' America seems to me a figment
     of his own imagination, and I doubt the value of his
     reportage of our period."

12   CANBY, HENRY SEIDEL.   Seven Years' Harvest: Notes on
     Contemporary Literature.   New York: Farrar and Rinehart,
     pp. 106, 239, passim.
     Considers Dos Passos one of the experimentalists and
     mentions his contribution to the development of the modern
     city novel.

13   COWLEY, MALCOLM.   "Afterthoughts on Dos Passos."   New
     Republic, 88 (9 September), 134.

Feels that, in U.S.A., Dos Passos has successfully
merged techniques of the art novel and the collectivist
novel, using the Jocyean Camera Eye sections "to supply the
'inwardness'" that is lacking in his general narrative.
Does feel that Dos Passos' pessimism precludes his ability
"to express one side of contemporary life--the will to
struggle ahead, the comradeship in struggle, the consciousness of new men and new forces continually rising."
Reprinted: 1967.B7; revised: 1937.B5.

14 _____. "The End of a Trilogy." New Republic, 88 (12 August),
23-24.
Emphasizes Dos Passos' depiction, in The Big Money, of
the "two nations" of upper and lower class which merge in
twentieth-century America. Views the novel as "a furious
and somber poem, written in a mood of revulsion even more
powerful than that which T. S. Eliot expressed in 'The
Wasteland.'"

15 _____. "Hymn of Hate." New Republic, 89 (23 December),
249-250.
Review of George Grosz's Interregnum which contains an
introduction by Dos Passos.

16 DE VOTO, BERNARD. "John Dos Passos: Anatomist of Our Time."
Saturday Review of Literature, 14 (8 August), 3-4, 12-13.
Feels Dos Passos has developed more consistently than
his American contemporaries and that The Big Money is his
finest work. De Voto summarizes the novelist's career,
finding him a brilliantly perceptive observer of American
life whose writing, nevertheless, lacks the warmth of one
who has deeply experienced life.

17 _____. Review of Proletarian Literature in the United States,
in Forays and Rebuttals. Boston: Little, Brown, pp. 334-
339.
Reprint of 1935.B3.

18 FADIMAN, CLIFTON. "Mr. Dos Passos' Newsreel, Continued."
New Yorker, 12 (8 August), 52-53.
Considers Dos Passos one of the few serious American
writers even if he is not a great one or even, like
Hemingway, a brilliant one. Applauds his ambition and
breadth: when he fails, as he does on occasion, it is with
major material. Does not feel The Big Money has quite the
drive of the two preceding novels, "being looser and more
cluttered with pedestrian sketches." Still, "it represents

1936

the American social novel at its most serious and
conscientious."

19 GREGORY, HORACE. "Dos Passos Completes His Modern Trilogy."
    New York Herald Tribune Books (9 August), p. 1.
         Thinks The Big Money a fitting conclusion to the Dos
    Passos' trilogy. Says that Dos Passos, "more than any other
    living American writer, has exposed to public satire those
    peculiar contradictions of our poverty in the midst of
    plenty." Feels the narrative effectively conveys the
    "sense of speed and concentrated action" of his America.
    Finds the trilogy to improve as it progresses, except for
    the Camera Eye sections which seem "uncomfortably arty
    rather than artful." Calls Dos Passos the "most incisive
    and direct of American satirists."

20 HENDERSON, PHILIP. "America: Dos Passos," in his The Novel
    Today. London: John Lane, pp. 130-136.
         Calls Manhattan Transfer one of the technical triumphs of
    the age for its "vitality, scope and acuteness of visual
    and psychological impressionism." This technique owes much
    to Joyce's work, without which, "Dos Passos would be in-
    conceivable." Feels though that Dos Passos surpasses Joyce
    in at least one respect, in seeing modern capitalist civili-
    zation as the motive force of the degradation and banality
    of modern life.

21 HOPKINS, GORDON A. "The Bitter Tongue of John Dos Passos."
    Boston Transcript (8 August), sec. 6, p. 4.
         Feels that "The Big Money has reality and a boldness, it
    makes one realize suddenly that bold literature is being
    written in our times." Believes that Dos Passos' characters
    "represent the forces which the author believes are decaying
    the foundations of our immense structure and will someday
    bring it toppling down."

22 LAWRENCE, D. H. Phoenix, The Posthumous Papers (1936) of D. H.
    Lawrence. Edited by Edward D. McDonald. New York: Viking
    Press, pp. 363-365.
         Reprint of 1927.B7.

23 LEAVIS, Q. D. "Mr. Dos Passos Ends His Trilogy." Scrutiny,
    5 (December), 294-299.
         Feels that The Big Money forcefully portrays the moral
    as well as economic bankruptcy of American capitalistic
    society. While Dos Passos is not viewed as radically
    original, Leavis thinks that "he uses his predecessors
    [particularly Joyce] without being parasitic upon them."

Finds the objection that Dos Passos' work is not psychologically penetrating to be not wholly valid; considers
many of the portraits, particularly the account of Thorstein
Veblen, to be psychologically insightful.

24 LERNER, MAX. "The America of John Dos Passos." Nation, 143
    (15 August), 187-188.
        Feels that with The Big Money, Dos Passos emerges as "the
    most considerable and serious of our American writers . . .
    His talent is expansive rather than concentrated . . . there
    is a massiveness about Dos Passos' work . . . that places
    it squarely in the path of our attention." Concludes that
    as a writer Dos Passos "will keep moving. His social be-
    liefs are still fluid, his sense of innovation still has a
    sharp edge. But what will carry him farthest is his belief
    in American life."

25 QUENNELL, PETER. "New Novels." New Statesman and Nation, 12
    (31 October), 680, 682.
        In reviewing The Big Money, calls Dos Passos "one of the
    most interesting novelists of the second rank whom modern,
    post-war America has produced." Rejects that idea that he
    is profound: "I should have imagined that superficiality
    was to be included among his main assets" since it allows
    him to be broad in his interests. Nor does he feel that
    Dos Passos is original but that his technique "owes much to
    Hemingway, something to Joyce and, here and there, not a
    little to . . . Miss Gertrude Stein." Concludes that his
    books are worth reading because "he is thorough, honest,
    intelligent, and reports extremely well."

26 REES, GORONWY. "John Dos Passos." Spectator, 157
    (27 November), 960.
        Review of The Big Money. Thinks Dos Passos is even more
    an historian, sociologist, and reporter than a novelist and
    since he is "indeed more interested in telling the truth,
    in explaining a historical process, in expressing certain
    moral values, than in creating works of art," he is not
    always entirely successful in dramatization. Feels Dos
    Passos' "poetic gifts go into his descriptions of what is
    real; his patience and industry into what is imagined."
    Concludes that "he has a feeling comparable to Whitman's"
    in that America and American democracy are the real heroes
    of his work.

27 SCHNELL, JONATHAN. Review of The Big Money. Forum, 96
    (September), iv.
        Finds The Big Money flawed in its structure, for "the
    book might have been a masterpiece of its kind if the

1936

author had managed to show us how the goings on of the
characteristic outstanding characters had affected the
characteristic little figures of the day."

28 TAYLOR, WALTER F. "Variety and Eclecticism--The Novel," in
his A History of American Letters. Chicago: Henry Regnery
Co., pp. 451-463.
Brief summary of Dos Passos' career. Considers U.S.A.
neither propaganda nor tragedy, but a "serious and bitter
satire."

1937 A BOOKS - NONE

1937 B SHORTER WRITINGS

1 ANON. "Creator's Congress." Time, 29 (21 June), 79-81.
Report on the Second Writers' Conference, held in New
York, includes mention of the presentation of an unfinished
version of The Spanish Earth and notes that The Big Money
was chosen by the delegates as one of "the most valuable
works of the past year."

2 ANON. Review of The Big Money. Pratt Institute Quarterly
(Winter), p. 38.
Very brief review.

3 ANON. Review of the Film, The Spanish Earth. Time, 30
(23 August), 48-49.
Discusses the numerous well-known collaborators on the
film which is considered imaginative and moving.

4 CLEATON, IRENE and ALLEN. Books and Battles: American
Literature 1920-1930. Boston: Houghton Mifflin Co., pp.
10, 74, 146, 227.
Survey of official and unofficial literary censorship
which mentions Dos Passos' problems with Three Soldiers and
Streets of Night.

5 COWLEY, MALCOLM. "Dos Passos: Poet Against the World," in his
After the Genteel Tradition: American Writers Since 1910.
New York: W. W. Norton, pp. 134-146, passim.
Feels that Dos Passos offers no illuminating solution to
the "evil" world he presents in his novels other than to
maintain one's standards and "go under." Revised from
1932.B17 and 1936.B13.

6 FERGUSON, OTIS. "And There Were Giants on the Earth." <u>New Republic</u>, 92 (1 September), 103.
    Review of <u>The Spanish Earth</u> which concludes that, while there are flaws, "the picture is definitely on the side of the harsh truth."

7 LOGGINS, VERNON. "Revolution: Jack London, Upton Sinclair, Carl Sandburg and John Dos Passos," in his <u>I Hear America</u>. . . . New York: Thomas Y. Crowell, pp. 250-281, passim.
    Notes the influence of Whitman, Sandburg, Joyce, and the motion pictures on the fiction of Dos Passos. Notes the jazz feel of <u>Manhattan Transfer</u> and concludes that "the novel is the discordant harmony of New York." Calls the novels of <u>U.S.A.</u> "a moving panorama of impressions held together by one idea--greed, the passion for 'big money.'"

8 McCOLE, C. J. "John Dos Passos and the Modern Distemper," in his <u>Lucifer at Large</u>. New York: Longman, Green, pp. 175-200, passim.
    Examination of the prevalence of pessimistic determinism in American literature which includes an historical perspective, then focuses on Dos Passos, a writer who "has grappled with present-day problems . . . with a really vigorous and unyielding spirit" but who, in later writing, has "succumbed to cynicism, determinism, and despair."

9 McMANUS, JOHN T. "Down to Earth in Spain." <u>New York Times</u> (25 July), pp. x, 4.
    Background on the making and promotion of <u>The Spanish Earth</u>.

10 _____. "Realism Invades Gotham." <u>New York Times</u> (22 August), pp. x, 3.
    Calls <u>The Spanish Earth</u> "a great propaganda picture, bitter and hard and unrelenting in its hatred of Spain's enemies, and the most rational and compelling explanation of the need for a government victory that has thus far been presented on the screen."

11 M[cMANUS], J[OHN] T. Review of the Film, <u>The Spanish Earth</u>. <u>New York Times</u> (21 August), p. 7.
    Finds Joris Ivens' camera work eloquent and superior to Hemingway's commentary. Feels the film concentrates too much on the war and not enough on the Spanish people themselves.

12 MULLER, HERBERT. "Naturalism in America: Theodore Dreiser and Proletarian Fiction," in his <u>Modern Fiction: A Study of Values</u>. New York: Funk and Wagnalls, pp. 199-222.

1937

       Considers Dos Passos an overrated member of the prole-
tarian school of American naturalism. Feels that critics
make too much of his technical experiments. Finds them
"neither original . . . nor brilliantly effective." Considers his chief limitation to be in characterization.

13 REID, JOHN T. "Spain as Seen By Some Contemporary American
      Writers." Hispania, 20 (May), 139-150.
         Study of the significance of Spanish culture on several
writers, including Dos Passos. Feels Dos Passos was first
attracted to Spain as a kind of "delightful oasis in a
desert of sordid industrialism," and later came to see
Spain as a seat of radical action.

14 SCHWARTZ, HARRY W. This Book Collecting Racket. Revised
      edition. Chicago: Normandie House, pp. 75-77, passim.
         Discusses identifying marks and availability of Dos
Passos' first editions.

15 WADE, MASON. "Novelist of America: John Dos Passos." North
      American Review, 244 (Winter), 349-367.
         Presents Dos Passos as a master synthesizer who is able
to pull together the lessons of his youth, his reading, and
his own experiences to create a powerful literary character:
the mass man.

1938 A BOOKS - NONE

1938 B SHORTER WRITINGS

1 ANON. "Dos Passos." Springfield Republican (27 February),
      p. 7e.
         Calls the publication of U.S.A. in one novel "a bargain
for anyone with a live interest in American writers."

2 ANON. "Far and Wide on a Magic Carpet: Mr. John Dos Passos'
      Journey." Times Literary Supplement (10 September), p. 585.
         Asserts that the "brilliant American gift for descriptive
writing is a serious contribution to the literature of our
time" and that Journey Between Wars is a good example.
Finds "the novelist's power of characterization" superior
to the political analysis, and finds the organization anything but tight; instead, recommends the reader enter at
nearly any point "and wander fascinated with him [Dos
Passos]."

3   ANON. "Note on U.S.A." Times Literary Supplement (1 October),
      p. 630.
         Notes publication of 42nd Parallel, 1919, and The Big
      Money in one volume.

4   ANON. Review of Journeys Between Wars. Christian Century, 55
      (6 April), 438.
         Briefly summarizes Journeys Between Wars, marveling at
      Dos Passos' descriptive style.

5   ANON. Review of Journeys Between Wars. Cleveland Open Shelf
      (March), p. 6.
         Very brief review.

6   ANON. Review of Journeys Between Wars. Wisconsin Library
      Bulletin, 34 (June), 127.
         Brief review.

7   ANON. Review of U.S.A. Wisconsin Library Bulletin, 34 (March),
      47.
         Brief review.

8   ANON. "Roving Writer." Time, 31 (11 April), 73-74.
         Summary of Journeys Between Wars.

9   BLANCK, JACOB. "Exploding the Three Soldiers Myth."
      Publishers Weekly, 133 (18 June), 2377-2378.
         Examines the controversy over the authenticity of first
      editions of Three Soldiers.

10 BURNHAM, DAVID. Review of Journeys Between Wars. Commonweal,
      28 (6 May), 52-53.
         Considers Dos Passos' skepticism to be "both his advan-
      tage and disadvantage, "allowing him, as an independent
      leftist, to avoid propagandizing, but also causing a lack
      of positive direction." Finds that, in Journeys Between
      Wars, Dos Passos is less skeptical, more civilized and
      natural than in the novels which require "a certain sub-
      humanization." Considers the section on Spain "the most
      deep-felt and . . . the best of the book's four parts."

11 C[ONKLIN], R. J. "World Impressions." Springfield Republican
      (2 June), p. 8.
         Calls Journeys Between Wars "authentic Dos Passos": "it
      has the spasmodic disjointed episodic writing, the pessimism
      and earthiness and clarity which mark all the work of this
      author."

1938

12   COUSINS, N. B. "The Traveling Novelist." <u>Current History</u>, 48
(May), 70.
     Admires Dos Passos' versatility in dealing with diverse
forms and subjects in <u>Journeys Between Wars</u>. Notes the
relationship of places and incidents in this book and his
novels.

13   COWLEY, MALCOLM. "Reviewers on Parade." <u>New Republic</u>, 93
(2 February), 371-372.
     On the occasion of the publication of <u>U.S.A.</u>, Cowley
criticizes the reviewers of <u>The Big Money</u>, most of whom he
believes badly misread the book.

14   _____. "Reviewers on Parade: II." <u>New Republic</u>, 94
(9 February), 23-24.
     Continues the review of Dos Passos' reviewers, concen-
trating on Bernard De Voto's review of <u>The Big Money</u> in
<u>The Saturday Review</u>.

15   CUMMINS, E. A. Review of <u>Journeys Between Wars</u>. <u>Churchman</u>,
152 (15 May), 5.
     Calls Dos Passos "an expert with the candid camera of
the written page." Thinks the "most charming, most full of
imagination, starkest of all these stories are those devoted to . . . Spain."

16   DAVIS, HASSOLDT. "John Dos Passos Retraces His Journeys Between Wars." <u>New York Times Book Review</u> (24 April), p. 9.
     Feels that <u>Journeys Between Wars</u>, "considered simply as
a travel book, or as a sociological odyssey . . . has not
recently been surpassed." Feels that Dos Passos combines
"the dramatic impetus of a novelist, the perception of a
remarkable correspondent and the vigorous, independent
curiosity of the great travelers of the past."

17   GOLD, MICHAEL. "The Keynote to Dos Passos' Works." <u>Daily
Worker</u> (26 February), p. 7.
     After outlining Dos Passos' disengagement with the left,
Gold concludes that Dos Passos' writing is and always has
been full of "merde." Thinks that his hatred of communism
occurs because "organically he seems to hate the human
race."

18   HICKS, GRANVILLE. "The Moods and Tenses of John Dos Passos."
<u>New Masses</u>, 27 (26 April), 22-23.
     Marxist critique of Dos Passos' writing on the occasion
of the publication of <u>Journeys Between Wars</u> and <u>U.S.A.</u>
Feels that the travel book fails because it is merely

perceptions, because Dos Passos never analyzes those perceptions, because he does not take a stand. Hicks feels
that this is symptomatic of the flaws in his fiction, particularly The Big Money. Feels that his best work was
written in the early thirties when he was most closely
aligned with the Communists. Reprinted: 1974.B14.

19 IRWIN-CARRUTHERS, G. "Mr. Dos Passos." Manchester Guardian
(6 September), p. 5.
Admires the "unforgettable pictures" of Journeys Between
Wars.

20 JOSEPHSON, MATTHEW. "Grim Interlude." New Republic, 94
(27 April), 365.
Praises Journeys Between Wars because Dos Passos, the
traveler, is always himself, in love with people, with a
taste for history and a sharp eye for detail. Sees a
growing pessimism in Dos Passos and wonders about its implications for the writer and as a possible prophesy. Calls
Dos Passos' novels "more significant than those of his contemporaries," even those who write better, because of his
natural cultivation, his character, his sense of history."

21 LYALL, ARCHIBALD. "Journeys Between Wars." Spectator, 161
(16 December), 1060.
Feels that Journeys Between Wars, although a collection
of various past and recent travel essays, is given a unity
by Dos Passos' "own vivid and all-pervading sense of the
unity of the world." Finds the writing "always sensuous
and sensitive, leaving a trail of unforgettable images on
the mental retina."

22 MAIR, JOHN. "New Novels." New Statesman and Nation, 16
(1 October), 495-496.
Finds the Newsreel and Camera Eye sections of U.S.A.
already to seem dated, yet much of the rest to possess an
"engaging reality." Concludes that U.S.A. cannot justly
be compared to War and Peace as some have tried: "Mr. Dos
Passos is not the Tolstoy, or even the Jane Austin of the
post-war purgatory; he has not the breadth or superior
cynicism required of a social historian."

23 MANTLE, BURNS. "John Dos Passos," in Contemporary American
Playwrights. New York: Dodd, Mead, and Company, p. 221.
Mentions Dos Passos among other novelists and poets who
have experimented in drama.

24 PARSONS, GEOFFREY. "A Writer, A Hiker and A Bicyclist." New
Statesman and Nation, 16 (22 October), 628-629.

1938

>   Calls Journeys Between Wars, despite being "distressingly
> topical," a "real excitement to read . . . if you want to
> know what the wake of war is like." Notes Dos Passos'
> growing pessimism.

25 POORE, CHARLES. "Books of the Times." New York Times
    (28 January), p. 19.
>   Calls the novels of U.S.A. "among the most forceful,
> the truest of our post-war time," and Dos Passos a brilliant
> experimentalist. Notes the influences on him and his own
> influence on contemporary novelists.

26 SCHWARTZ, DELMORE. "John Dos Passos and the Whole Truth."
    Southern Review, 4 (October), 351-367.
>   Thinks that, in Dos Passos' obsession with the "curious
> mixture of the private worlds and the public worlds," U.S.A.
> is very much, in form, like a newspaper. Comments on Dos
> Passos' tendency "to get documents, to record facts, and to
> swallow the whole rich chaos of modern life." Despite the
> excitement of such a technique, despite his great talents
> as a craftsman, and despite his passion for the truth,
> Dos Passos is unable to represent the "whole truth" because
> of his naturalistic method which focuses on the "what"
> without the "ought," which is obsessed with recording how
> things are without showing how they might be. U.S.A., he
> feels, does not capture the "whole truth" because it lacks
> a transcendent imagination which can represent both the
> "actual and the potential." Reprinted: 1970.B30.

27 SLOCOMBE, GEORGE. "On the Battlefields." Saturday Review of
    Literature, 17 (9 April), 5-6.
>   Brief review of the travel book, Journeys Between Wars,
> which Slocombe finds "curiously inconsequential," a series
> of pictures which appear "out of focus, like photographs
> taken with a distorting lens."

28 SOLOW, HERBERT. "Substitution at Left Tackle: Hemingway for
    Dos Passos." Partisan Review, 4 (April), 62-64.
>   Humorous charting of Hemingway's move to the left and
> Dos Passos' move to the right during the 1930s.

29 TRILLING, LIONEL. "The America of John Dos Passos." Partisan
    Review, 4 (April), 26-32.
>   Sees U.S.A. as "the important novel of the decade," but
> feels it fails to fulfill the promise of the original plan.
> Trilling disagrees with those who find it startlingly
> original: "it confirms but does not advance and it sum-
> marizes but does not suggest." Feels the work is informed

by a rather traditional romantic morality. Reprinted:
1974.A3.

30 WELLER, GEORGE. "Poet-Reporter." Nation, 146 (9 April),
418-419.
Finds the various sketches of Journeys Between Wars to
possess the detail of good reporting and the lyricism of
poetry but, together, they do not provide a unified effect
or a comprehensive view of the contemporary European scene.

31 WHIPPLE, T. K. "Dos Passos and the U.S.A.." Nation, 146
(19 February), 210-212.
Marvels at the technical brilliance of U.S.A., comment-
ing in some detail about the use of vivid sensory detail.
Whipple argues that Dos Passos' pessimism, which leads to
the conclusion "that human beings and human life are banal,"
is convincingly undercut by the vitality of the characters
portrayed in the biographies. Reprinted: 1974.A3.

1939 A BOOKS

1 CHAMBERLAIN, JOHN. John Dos Passos: A Biographical and
Critical Study. New York: Harcourt, Brace, and Company,
20pp.
Pamphlet, slightly enlarged from 1939.B12.

1939 B SHORTER WRITINGS

1 ADAMS, J. DONALD. "A New Novel by John Dos Passos." New York
Times Book Review (4 June), p. 6.
Feels Adventures of A Young Man to be written "out of a
mood of disillusionment" as have all Dos Passos' novels.
Thinks the novel has "bite, point, and substance," that it
is clear-cut, conclusive in its negation. Considers it to
be no advance in Dos Passos' career as a novelist, except,
perhaps, in its focus on the individual, although the
characterization is not very imaginative or perceptive.

2 ANON. "Dos Passos and Communism." Springfield Republican
(30 July), p. 7e.
Brief discussion of the portrayal of communism in
Adventures of a Young Man.

3 ANON. "Heresy." Time, 33 (5 June), 86, 88.
Summarizes Adventures of A Young Man which "cooks his
goose for good, as far as the communists are concerned."

1939

> Concludes that the story is racy, his views are sincere,
> but that the characters are one-dimensional, making the
> novel "read like a minor pamphlet."

4 ANON. Review of Adventures of a Young Man. Booklist, 35
       (1 June), 332.
>   Finds Adventures of a Young Man's story stereotypic and
> the characters unreal.

5 ANON. Review of Adventures of a Young Man. North American
       Review, 248 (Autumn), 204.
>   Brief review which concludes that "Mr. Dos Passos is
> fairly successful with Glen's early years, but becomes
> somewhat too angry at the end to be artistically convincing.

6 ANON. Review of Adventures of a Young Man. Pratt Institute
       Quarterly (Autumn), p. 27.
>   Very brief review.

7 ANON. Review of Adventures of a Young Man. Times Literary
       Supplement (17 June), p. 355.
>   Admires Dos Passos as "truthful, humane and unaffectedly
> idealistic, enterprising in craftsmanship," but feels that
> Adventures of a Young Man is not one of his better books
> for "in concentrating upon left-wing quarrels and contro-
> versies he has bleached the story of colour."

8 ANON. Review of Journey Between Wars. Pratt Institute
       Quarterly (Winter), p. 26.
>   Very brief review.

9 ANZOFF, CHARLES. "Bewilderment on the Left." Living Age, 357
       (September), 96.
>   Feels that "the hidden tear in a friend's eye apparently
> affects him more than the anguish of the masses." Thus the
> early novels are successful while "a recent book like The
> Big Money already seems mannered." Warns that Adventures
> of a Young Man should be read for its artistic merit,
> rather than as a political tract as the critics of both
> the left and right are apt to do. Finds it in artistic
> terms, "an indifferent book, in parts good and in parts
> extremely bad."

10 BEARD, CHARLES A. and MARY R. America in Midpassage. New
        York: Macmillan and Company, pp. 691-695.
>   Considers the social criticism inherent in Dos Passos'
> fiction. Finds it powerful despite the necessarily limited
> perspective it provides.

11 BRIGHOUSE, HAROLD. "Novels of Past and Present." <u>Manchester
    Guardian</u> (20 June), p. 7.
        Calls <u>Adventures of a Young Man</u> "a tragedy of universal
    liberalism," and Dos Passos a "great American stylist."

12 CHAMBERLAIN, JOHN. "John Dos Passos." <u>Saturday Review of
    Literature</u>, 20 (3 June), 3-4, 14-15.
        Finds <u>Adventures of a Young Man</u> to be slim compared to
    <u>U.S.A.</u> but is not surprised by Dos Passos' seemingly more
    conservative point of view. Traces the author's social
    and political attitudes and concludes that Dos Passos was
    never a leftist ideologue; he has always been a Jeffersonian
    libertarian. Revised: 1939.A1.

13 CONKLIN, R. J. "John Dos Passos' Futile Young Man."
    <u>Springfield Republican</u> (11 June), p. 7e.
        Calls <u>Adventures of a Young Man</u> a "futilitarian" novel:
    "The older novelists give an impression of writing from
    sheer enjoyment of and interest in life--Dos Passos seems
    moved principally by a disgust with life." Thinks the
    book is "marred by several pornographic and scatological
    passages."

14 COWLEY, MALCOLM. "Disillusionment." <u>New Republic</u>, 99
    (14 June), 163.
        Cowley is disappointed with the conservativism of
    <u>Adventures of a Young Man</u>. Feels that Dos Passos is over-
    reacting to strong-arm tactics he witnessed the communists
    employ in the Spanish Civil War. He is equally dismayed
    about the conventional narrative technique which makes the
    book read "more like other people's novels."

15 FADIMAN, CLIFTON. "Rebels and Ants." <u>New Yorker</u>, 15
    (3 June), 74-75.
        Finds <u>Adventures of a Young Man</u> a rather uninspired
    example of the Sensitive Young Man novel. Finds the moral
    to be that "official communism and a genuine revolutionary
    impulse are at the moment irreconcilable," but wishes, if
    that is the case, that Dos Passos had condensed and focused
    his attention more directly on this theme.

16 FARRELL, JAMES T. "Dos Passos and the Critics." <u>American
    Mercury</u>, 47 (August), 489-494.
        Critical of the reviews of <u>Adventures of a Young Man</u>,
    many of which dismissed the novel for primarily political
    reasons. Thinks this novel is more like <u>U.S.A.</u> than most
    critics would admit: Dos Passos' theme in both is the
    problem of maintaining one's integrity in modern America.

1939

In this sense, Farrell thinks the novel is similar to Ignazio Silone's Bread and Wine.

17 FOOTMAN, R. H. "John Dos Passos." Sewanee Review, 47 (July), 365-382.
    Argues that Dos Passos is a second-rate novelist as a result of a mistaken sense of the nature of art: a belief that history is more important than fiction, which results in an emphasis of thesis over characterization. Feels the only real value of the novels is as contemporary advocacy for the dispossessed, as "a kind of liberal weekly in volume form."

18 GARSIDE, E. B. "Dos Passos and the Lost Generation." Boston Transcript (3 June), sec. 4, p. 1.
    Feels that the devices of U.S.A. are skillfully refined in Adventures of a Young Man. Feels that Dos Passos' narrower focus in this novel results from a desire to create moral fiction which not only shows a panorama but tries to explain why we are as we are. Feels that Dos Passos' pessimism makes the total effect of the novel "profoundly dispiriting and sterile."

19 KAZIN, ALFRED. "American History in the Life of One Man." New York Herald Tribune Books (4 June), p. 3.
    Says that Adventures of a Young Man "trembles with an internal disgust," most notably revealed in Dos Passos' obvious hatred of his characters. Considers it to be a retreat for Dos Passos from the "expansive sagas of the machine age to the rank of folksy satire."

20 KRONENBERGER, LOUIS. "Politics and Fiction." Nation, 148 (3 June), 648.
    Calls Adventures of a Young Man a novel in the form of "those innumerable young-men stories that flourished in the twenties"; in content, it is "of those numerous studies of social awareness that have dominated the thirties." Considers the observation rich, the scenes vivid, and the hero interesting, but bemoans the narrow scope and lack of objectivity which preclude "a true disinterestedness" necessary for good fiction.

21 KRUTCH, JOSEPH WOOD. The American Drama Since 1918: An Informal History. New York: Random House, pp. 36, 244.
    Mentions Dos Passos as a practitioner of "the drama of social criticism," which, Krutch feels, "soon hardened into a very monotonous convention [for] . . . one cross section is bound to look very much like another."

1939

22 MAIR, JOHN. "New Novels." New Statesman and Nation, 17
     (24 June), 984.
           Thinks that, while U.S.A. was comparable, in the intent
     of its effect, to Dante's Inferno, Adventures of a Young
     Man is more like Pilgrim's Progress in which the hero "is
     not whirled through chaos, but seeks the truth as doggedly
     as Christian, and the enemies who beset him are as clear-
     cut and single minded as figures in allegory." Finds that
     "Mr. Dos Passos is in the unhappy position of hating the
     enemy for his intolerance, distrusting his friends for
     their incompetence, and despising the neutrals for their
     neutrality." Notes that Dos Passos does not provide an-
     swers to the social problems he raises, that he is as con-
     fused as his protagonist.

23 MERSAND, JOSEPH. Traditions in American Literature: A Study
     of Jewish Characters and Authors. New York: Modern
     Chapbooks, pp. 94, 161.
           Mentions Dos Passos' Harvard friendship with Robert
     Nathan and notes his generally favorable portraits of Jewish
     characters, including Ben Compton who is "one of the few
     characters in [U.S.A.] who preserve their integrity in an
     opportunistic post-war world."

24 O'BRIEN, KATE. "Fiction." Spectator, 163 (7 July), 27.
           Characterizes Dos Passos as "a sound, observant re-
     porter . . . a camera-man who happens to shoot from a sym-
     pathetic angle." Considers the technique of Adventures of
     a Young Man preferable to the "former jerky and journalis-
     tic method." Feels, however, that the novel "lacks pace
     and passion, whereas as a character study it could positively
     be described as lackadaisical."

25 RAHV, PHILIP. "Bookshelf." The Atlantic Monthly (July).
           Calls Adventures of a Young Man "perhaps the most
     thoughtful and realistic portrait of the radical movement"
     yet produced by an American. Despite the title, Dos Passos
     is still more historian than biographer for his character
     is more a social type than a fully developed character.
     Applauds the brisk, idiomatic style and the blending of
     private and political scenes.

26 SCHRAMM, WILBUR L. "Careers At Crossroads." Virginia
     Quarterly Review, 15 (Autumn), 627-632.
           Sees Adventures of a Young Man as an important transi-
     tionary work, turning from U.S.A., "the most substantial
     monument of proletarian literature this country has pro-
     duced." Not only does Dos Passos turn his back on statesmen

1939

but he shifts his focus from society at large to the problems of an individual within that society. Applauds Dos
Passos' courage for being willing to change both in theme
and form.

27 SILLEN, SAMUEL. "Misadventures of John Dos Passos." New
Masses, 32 (4 July), 21-22.
Calls Adventures of a Young Man "a crude piece of
Trotskyist agit-prop," and argues that Dos Passos' "literary
failure is very definitely related to his reactionary
political orientation." Sillen concludes that "the man,
in short, has succumbed to the 'philosophy' of Trotskyism,
which professionally breeds despair and confusion and
division."

28 SMITH, BERNARD. Forces in American Criticism: A Study in the
History of American Literary Thought. New York: Harcourt,
Brace and Company, pp. 159, 308, 369.
Occasional mention of Dos Passos.

29 SYLVESTER, HARRY. Review of Adventures of a Young Man.
Commonweal, 30 (2 June), 163-164.
Considers Adventures of a Young Man Dos Passos' best
book to date. Notes the growing disillusionment with the
sectarian left. Especially praises Dos Passos' rigorously
honest objectivity.

30 UNTERMEYER, LOUIS. From Another World: The Autobiography of
Louis Untermeyer. New York: Harcourt, Brace and Company,
pp. 84, 314.
Mentions Dos Passos.

1940 A BOOKS - NONE

1940 B SHORTER WRITINGS

1 BOYNTON, PERCY HOLMES. America in Contemporary Fiction.
Chicago: University of Chicago Press, pp. 185-203, passim.
Critical of Dos Passos' portrayal of the sordid life,
of over-indulgence in alcohol and sex. Finds, in U.S.A.,
that the non-fictional characters overwhelm the fictional
because they can dream, because they have purpose, because
"their pleasures are not confined to the senses." Finds
Dos Passos at his best when most romantic and prophetic.

1940

2 BROOKS, VAN WYCK. <u>New England: Indian Summer, 1865-1915</u>. New
York: E. P. Dutton and Co., Inc., pp. 511, 517.
Cites Dos Passos as a member of Harvard's pre-war generation and one of those who turned to the "low life" for
literary inspiration.

3 DUPEE, FRANK W. "William Carlos Williams as Novelist." <u>New
Republic</u>, 103 (18 November), p. 700.
Notes that Williams had been accused of merely "rewriting
Dos Passos according to imagist principles," in <u>The White
Mule</u>.

4 LUCCOCK, HALFORD E. <u>American Mirror: Social, Ethical and
Religious Aspects of American Literature: 1930-1940</u>. New
York: Macmillan and Co., pp. 154-160, passim.
Admires the "realism, sympathy, poetry and hot moral
indignation over waste of valuable human material," in the
works of Dos Passos. Finds "a truly Elizabethan quality
about him" in that, like the great Elizabethan dramatists,
he possesses the capacity "of visualization, of making ab-
stractions and symbols come to life as concrete things."

5 MacLEISH, ARCHIBALD. "Post-War Writers and Pre-War Readers."
<u>New Republic</u>, 102 (10 June), 789-790.
Maintains that the novels of World War I, including Dos
Passos' were attacks not only on the military, but also the
principles for which the war was fought and have led to the
conclusion held by many "that not only the war and the war
issues but all issues, all moral issues were false--were
fraudulent--were intended to deceive." MacLeish considers
this view potentially disastrous in the face of fascism.

6 MARSHALL, MARGARET. "Writers in the Wilderness: John Dos
Passos." <u>Nation</u>, 160 (6 January), 15-18.
Summarizes Dos Passos' career. Feels that, in his fiction, Dos Passos has confronted America "with a tough faith
in the vague but undeniable promise of American life" and a
determined "disillusion with its specific broken promises."
<u>U.S.A.</u>, in particular, "reflects both the unflinching dis-
illusion and the persistent renewal." Finds Dos Passos to
possess an "extraordinary capacity for observation," but is
"unable to create in his fictional characters the illusion
of life which is already there to be reported in his real
characters." Thinks <u>Adventures of a Young Man</u> to be
"refreshingly free of devices . . . a move in the direction
of integration of both style and content, which seems . . .
to be Dos Passos' primary problem as a novelist."

1940

7 ORIANS, HARRISON G. <u>A Short History of American Literature:</u>
<u>Analyzed by Decades</u>. New York: F. S. Crofts and Company,
pp. 280, 301, 302, 303.
Occasional references to Dos Passos' publications.

8 VAN DOREN, CARL. <u>The American Novel, 1789-1939</u>. New York:
The Macmillan Company, pp. 334-338, passim.
Revised and enlarged from 1921 edition. Briefly summarizes Dos Passos' career and concludes that he is "a
novelist who could not always write with dispassion but
must now and then escape into irony or rise to poetry."

9 WILSON, EDMUND. "Archibald MacLeish and the Word." <u>New</u>
<u>Republic</u>, 103 (1 July), 30-32.
Rebuttal of criticism by MacLeish (in <u>New Republic</u>, 102,
June 10, 1940) that the war novels of Dos Passos and
Hemingway are an attack on all moral causes and could influence readers not to oppose fascism. Considers such a
view "obviously absurd": "Moral principles play a more
serious part in Dos Passos' work than in that of almost any
other important American novelist." Reprinted: 1950.B93.

1941 A BOOKS - NONE

1941 B SHORTER WRITINGS

1 ALSBERG, HENRY G. "Dos Passos Asks America To Follow Founding
Fathers." <u>PM's Weekly</u> (14 September).
Quarrels with certain of Dos Passos' basic assumptions
in <u>The Ground We Stand On</u>, but, in general, finds the book
lively and interesting.

2 ANON. "Ancestors." <u>New Republic</u>, 17 (1 September), 282-283.
Feels that, in <u>The Ground We Stand On</u>, Dos Passos "reveals a new attitude" toward the United States and "a new
direction" for his writing career: "It is interested in
patterns of behavior rather than social theories, and in
the art of politics . . . rather than the science of
economics." While the book, for a variety of reasons, is
not one of Dos Passos' best, it "succeeds in its aim of
casting a new light on the present. And it gives one the
feeling that Dos Passos, after some sort of moral crisis,
is perhaps beginning a new career."

3 ANON. "Bookshelf." <u>Atlantic Monthly</u>, 168 (November).
Admires, in <u>The Ground We Stand On</u>, the fair and intense
interest in and treatment of the progressive and

56

reactionary, the major and minor characters that have
shaped American history.

4   ANON. "Dos Passos And Our Past." Philadelphia Inquirer
    (3 September).
         Feels The Ground We Stand On is "afire with zeal for
    democracy." Notes Dos Passos' "breezy, almost slangy"
    style.

5   ANON. Review of The Ground We Stand On. Booklist, 38
    (15 October), 49.
         Brief summary of The Ground We Stand On.

6   ANON. Review of The Ground We Stand On. Commonweal, 35
    (5 December), 172.
         Calls the book "principally a study of the Protestant
    aspect of the divorce between Church and State."

7   ANON. Review of The Ground We Stand On. The Jewish Spectator
    (October).
         Calls The Ground We Stand On "an integrated presentation
    of the idea of freedom in its practical and theoretical
    implications."

8   ANON. Review of The Ground We Stand On. Pratt Institute
    Quarterly (December), p. 13.
         Very brief review.

*9 ANON. Review of The Ground We Stand On. Springfield
    Republican (31 August), p. 6.
         Cited in "John Dos Passos and His Reviewers," by William
    White, Bulletin of Bibliography, 20 (May-August 1950),
    45-47.

10 ANON. Review of The Ground We Stand On. Wisconsin Library
    Bulletin, 37 (November), 175.
         Brief review.

11 BARZUN, JACQUES. "Using the Past." Nation, 153 (13 September),
    227-228.
         Review of The Ground We Stand On which finds Dos Passos'
    intention excellent but the actual book a failure: "It is
    a failure of point of view, of technique, of proportion,
    of style." Finally, Barzun finds the book dull.

12 BEACH, JOSEPH WARREN. American Fiction: 1920-1940. New York:
    The Macmillan Co., pp. 25-44; 47-66.
         "John Dos Passos: The Artist in Uniform," pp. 25-46:
    Thinks Dos Passos to be a man of the "tenderest

1941

sensibilities" and an "inveterate lover of beauty" who,
nevertheless, portrays just the opposite in his novels.
Finds some faint indication in the characters of an inner
strength which is never outwardly manifested. Thinks the
narrative discontinuity of Dos Passos' work to be a mirror
of the social discontinuity which he portrays.
"John Dos Passos: Theory of the Leisure Class," pp. 47-
66: Considers the work from U.S.A. on an extension of the
earlier work with Dos Passos now exploring the roots of
social discontinuity and on a much larger scale. Thinks
Dos Passos' work to be credible and stimulating, possessing
a "bleak magnificence." While Beach does not think Dos
Passos appeals to the emotions, he does find his work
"morally educative."

13 BENET, STEPHEN VINCENT. "Americans Willing to Die for Their
    Faith." New York Herald Tribune Books (31 August), p. 3.
        Considers The Ground We Stand On "fascinating and ex-
    tremely readable." While the material is not as complete
    or balanced as it could be, Dos Passos does offer what
    "only an eloquent writer can give to history--a sense that
    the past is alive and the men of the past are alive."

14 BENET, STEPHEN VINCENT and ROSEMARY. "Dos Passos: Evolution
    of an American." New York Herald Tribune (21 September),
    p. 6.
        Summarizes Dos Passos' life and career, emphasizing that
    in many ways he is the most American writer of his genera-
    tion. Call him "the historian of America and Americans."

15 BROOKS, VAN WYCK. On Literature Today. New York: E. P. Dutton
    and Company, pp. 15, 26.
        Characterizes Dos Passos as among those writers--Brooks
    also includes Faulkner and Farrell--who "seem to delight in
    kicking their world to pieces, as if civilization were all
    a pretense and everything noble a humbug."

16 BROWN, FRANCIS. "A Testament of Faith in America by John Dos
    Passos." New York Times Book Review (31 August), p. 5.
        Calls The Ground We Stand On "a series of truly brilliant
    essays." Finds little cohesion, however, in the various
    portraits. Thinks Dos Passos missed his chance to develop
    a thesis which would unite the essays.

17 CARGILL, OSCAR. Intellectual America: Ideas on the March.
    New York: The Macmillan Co., pp. 160, 286, 349, 363, 674.
        Passing reference to Dos Passos in this general study.

18 CHAMBERLAIN, JOHN. "The Ground We Stand On." Harpers, 183
      (October).
      Calls The Ground We Stand On "excellent from the sensory
      point of view," noting that "Dos Passos is actually a better
      'novelist' when he is dealing with historical characters."
      Faults the book, however, for being too exclusive of certain
      types of men and views which, while perhaps not as compat-
      ible with Dos Passos' thesis, were nevertheless essential
      to the founding and development of the country.

19 COWLEY, MALCOLM. "Ancestors." New Republic, 105 (1 September),
      282.
      Considers The Ground We Stand On a new direction for Dos
      Passos in that it is history rather than fiction and more
      optimistic than earlier works. It is not seen as a com-
      pletely successful book, however, for, despite the evidence
      of the novelist's sharp eye for fresh and significant de-
      tail, Dos Passos is not able to provide the complete his-
      torical perspective: "His scholarship is intensive rather
      than extensive."

20 FADIMAN, CLIFTON, ed. Reading I've Liked. New York: Simon
      and Schuster, pp. 143-145.
      Calls Dos Passos a serious writer who grasps America at
      the center, who "works with cross sections, but the cross
      sections are of maximum density."

21 _____. Review of The Ground We Stand On. New Yorker, 17
      (30 August), 54-55.
      Feels the studies of The Ground We Stand On to be "too
      loosely grouped to exhibit any powerful unity." Neverthe-
      less, the cumulative effect is to show "how firmly rooted
      is the notion of democratic living," that it is "not a
      destroyable system but a manner of acting and feelings."

22 GARRISON, W. E. "Builders of Freedom." Christian Century,
      58 (24 December), 1610.
      Summary of The Ground We Stand On. Identifies Dos
      Passos' major concerns as "liberty, democracy, tolerance,
      and the development of a social and political order in
      which human rights have full scope."

23 HALE, WILLIAM HARLAN. Review of The Ground We Stand On.
      Common Sense (December), pp. 86-87.
      Calls The Ground We Stand On "a tract for the times."
      Feels that Dos Passos is too apt to digress, however, re-
      sulting in uneven pacing.

1941

24 HILLYER, R[OBERT] S. "Bookshelf." Atlantic Monthly
       (November).
          Finds The Ground We Stand On to be absorbing and "intel-
       ligent in each interpretation of event." Thinks Dos Passos'
       thesis to be "that the struggle between constantly forming
       and re-forming special groups and the self-governing masses
       is the very essence of our political vitality."

25 KAPUSTKA, STAN LEE. "A High Wind Blows In This Tree of Life."
       Chicago News (17 September).
          Calls Dos Passos a "delineator of history" and feels
       The Ground We Stand On "blows away the accumulated layers
       of historical dust and reveals the realistic foundation of
       freedom."

26 LOVEMAN, AMY. Review of The Ground We Stand On. Book-of-the-
       Month Club News (September).
          Feels that Dos Passos "has shed propaganda in favor of
       scholarly detachment and writes with dispassionateness and
       perspective."

27 LUCAS, DOROTHY F. Review of The Ground We Stand On. Library
       Journal, 66 (August), 667.
          Calls The Ground We Stand On "an excellent record of the
       self-governing tradition of America."

28 LYONS, EUGENE. The Red Decade: The Stalinist Penetration of
       America. Indianapolis: The Bobbs-Merrill Co., pp. 336-337,
       passim.
          Treats Dos Passos' changing attitudes towards communism
       and the Communists' changing attitudes toward him. Notes
       the political controversy stirred by Adventures of a Young
       Man.

29 M., D. Review of The Ground We Stand On. Partisan Review, 8
       (November-December), 516-517.
          Feels that "the pace is often so fast as to be merely
       cheap," and notes, with irritation, Dos Passos' tendency to
       form compound words, but admires the book for its read-
       ability and its detail.

30 NEVINS, ALLAN. "Roots of Democracy." Saturday Review of
       Literature, 24 (15 September), 6.
          Finds that Dos Passos' method in The Ground We Stand On--
       "to study the men in their own works and the record of
       their contemporaries, and to read his own conclusions"--
       gives the book originality and gleams of valuable insight,
       but causes a "deficiency in perspectives" which causes

Dos Passos to overvalue certain persons and events and
undervalue others.

31 R., W. K. "Democracy Called to Testify." Christian Science
Monitor (13 September), p. 11.
    Identifies the assumption behind The Ground We Stand On
to be that "we can find answers to the riddles of today in
the written record of the past." Finds the style lively
but quibbles occasionally with Dos Passos' emphases and
interpretations.

32 RUGOFF, MILTON. "Dos Passos, Novelist of Our Time." Sewanee
Review, 49 (October-December), 453-468.
    Traces Dos Passos' career from One Man's Initiation--1917
to Adventures of a Young Man. Calls him "the novelist of
the whole" for his panoramic style. Concludes that Dos
Passos is a writer "whose humanity renders him acutely
sensitive to the nature of his age while his intense idealism deeply colors his every reaction to it."

33 SEARS, WILLIAM R., JR. Review of The Ground We Stand On.
Churchman, 155 (15 September), 19.
    Calls The Ground We Stand On "an interesting and absorb-
ing venture into history . . . a very present comfort for
dismayed liberals in these troublous days."

34 T[HOMPSON], C. W. Review of The Ground We Stand On. Catholic
World, 154 (November), 244.
    Feels that "no praise can be too high" for The Ground We
Stand On, "the most interesting historical work I have read
in many a day." Finds the style graphic and pictorial, and
the book as a whole "a brilliant, fascinating panorama of
many of the most interesting historical persons in the
seventeenth and eighteenth centuries, English and American."

35 VAN GELDER, ROBERT. "An Interview with Mr. John Dos Passos."
New York Times Book Review (23 November), p. 2.
    Conversation in which Dos Passos discusses writer's
block; his fascination with Washington, D.C., which has
replaced his fascination with New York; his writing habits;
his one attempt to write a murder mystery; and his view of
himself as a writer.

36 WHIPPLE, LEON. "History for Our Times." Survey Graphic, 30
(October), 531-532.
    Finds The Ground We Stand On patriotic and
inspirational.

Writings about John Dos Passos

1942

1942 A   BOOKS - NONE

1942 B   SHORTER WRITINGS

1   ANON. The National Cyclopaedia of American Biography, Vol. F.
    New York: James T. White and Co., pp. 442-443.
    Biographical highlights.

2   ANON. Review of The Ground We Stand On. Common Ground
    (Winter).
    Feels the book contains "sound analysis, rich and color-
    ful detail, fine perspective, readability and even humor."

3   BRADFORD, CURTIS B. "John Dos Passos--A Defense." University
    Review, 8 (Summer), 267-272.
    Reaction to wartime criticism of Dos Passos and others
    of his generation that they are second rate artists because
    of the limits of their subject matter and their failures as
    artists. Bradford argues that Dos Passos' work directly
    confronts the essential themes of modern life and is written
    with a conscious and skillful artist's touch.

4   HEMINGWAY, ERNEST, ed. Men at War. New York: Crown Publishers,
    pp. xvi-xvii.
    Calls Three Soldiers "the first attempt at a realistic
    book about the war written by an American." Still,
    Hemingway thinks it has palled with time: "The dialogue
    rings false and the actual combat is completely unconvinc-
    ing." Thinks Dos Passos' use of slang dates the book and
    makes him a member of the "'twenty-three skiddoo' and 'isk
    ka bibble' school of American writing."

5   KAZIN, ALFRED. On Native Grounds: An Interpretation of Modern
    American Prose Literature. New York: Harcourt, Brace and
    Company, pp. 341-359, passim.
    Feels that Dos Passos, in his "unyielding oppositions"
    to all of society's degradations, in his "steady protest of
    a sensitive democratic conscience against the tyranny and
    the ugliness of society, against the failure of a complete
    human development under industrial capital"--in these
    things Dos Passos "rounds out the story of his generation
    and carries its values into the social novel of the thir-
    ties." Kazin thinks Dos Passos' novels are "the last
    essential testimony of his generation, and in many respects
    the most embittered." Finds the greatest strength of U.S.A.
    to be its narrative style: "the wonderfully concrete yet
    elliptical prose which bears along and winds around the

life stories in the book like a conveyor belt carrying
Americans through some vast Ford plant of the human spirit."

6 KUNITZ, STANLEY, and HOWARD HAYCRAFT, eds. Twentieth Century
   Authors: A Biographical Dictionary of Modern Literature.
   New York: H. W. Wilson, pp. 391-393.
      Calls Dos Passos a quiet, "dreamy, scholarly man" who
   has "not entirely fulfilled the high promise of his earlier
   work" but "is still growing."

1943 A BOOKS - NONE

1943 B SHORTER WRITINGS

1 ANON. "Demagogue at Work." Atlantic Monthly, 171 (April),
   146.
      Feels that Number One, "written under the spur of emer-
   gency, brings you powerfully to grips" with an American
   brand of dictatorship. Nevertheless, finds three flaws in
   the novel: Dos Passos does not arouse concern in the
   readers for the characters; he does not adequately convey
   the threat of such a demagogue; and his writing is still
   marred by his affectation in coupling words together."

2 ANON. "The People are You!" Time, 41 (15 March), 78.
      Calls Number One "a sad, harsh, funny companion piece"
   to Adventures of a Young Man, "that disenchanted odyssey of
   a left-wing idealist." Considers Chuck Crawford "the most
   noisome, best drawn demagogue in U.S. fiction." Feels the
   book would have been stronger if it had dealt more explicitly
   with the motivations, if it had more clearly shown the evil
   of the Chuck Crawford-Huey Long-"Pappy" O'Daniel kind of
   demagoguery.

3 ANON. Review of Number One. Booklist, 39 (1 April), 319.
      Feels there is little reason to feel sympathy for the
   characters of Number One which is realistic and convincing
   but "not one of the author's most impressive works."

*4 ANON. Review of Number One. Springfield Republican (7 March),
   p. 7e.
      Cited in "John Dos Passos and His Reviewers," by William
   White. Bulletin of Bibliography, 20 (May-August, 1950),
   45-47.

1943

5   ANON. "Wanted: A Dynamism." Commonweal, 37 (5 March), 497–
    498.
        Feels that, "in spite of vulgarity and sexual realism,"
    Number One is a good book, though not Dos Passos' best.
    Faults Dos Passos, however, for his mechanistic view of
    man's behavior. Calls for Christian novelists to create
    fiction reflecting the Christian outlook which, like Dos
    Passos' best work, "moves, jumps, crackles with the American
    tempo, American language, and . . . the American spirit."

6   BENET, STEPHEN VINCENT. "He Gets to the Senate With a Hillbilly
    Band." New York Herald Tribune Book Review (7 March), p. 3.
        Calls Number One "a brilliant portrait" of both a
    politician and the political arena. It lacks the depth,
    range, and solidity of the books of U.S.A., but it is an
    important book for its gritty portrayal of the "particular
    kind of fascism we could breed in these United States."

7   FADIMAN, CLIFTON. "Dos Passos--Burma & Dieppe." New Yorker,
    19 (6 March), 65–66.
        Finds Number One "a smoothly geared, expertly written,
    sharply observed book" which lacks the magnitude, the pano-
    ramic breadth of U.S.A. Feels the portrayal of Chuck
    Crawford is a mostly successful departure in characteriza-
    tion for Dos Passos, but considers Tyler Spotswood "simply
    another facet of that Lost Generation we've already for-
    gotten about."

8   FILLER, LOUIS. Randolph Bourne. Washington, D.C.: American
    Council on Public Affairs, pp. 112, 126.
        Mentions Bourne's acquaintance with Dos Passos through
    The Seven Arts magazine, and quotes from Dos Passos' bio-
    graphical sketch of Bourne in U.S.A.

9   GEISMAR, MAXWELL. "Young Sinclair Lewis and Old Dos Passos."
    American Mercury, 56 (March), 624–628.
        Compares Lewis' Gideon Planish and Dos Passos' Number
    One. Finds Lewis a youthful writer, his work dominated by
    an immense energy, while Dos Passos, though younger, "has
    always seemed a little sober for his years, and, at its
    weakest, his work has lacked the sheer vitality which
    usually marks Lewis' novels. Notes a "peculiar unreality"
    of the American world of Lewis and Dos Passos." The
    characters live in an "emotional miasma where they can
    never know real virtue or achieve real vice." Neverthe-
    less, thinks Dos Passos "our best informed and most con-
    sciously rational novelist."

10 GREGORY, HORACE. "Dos Passos and the Demagogue." <u>New York</u>
    <u>Times Book Review</u> (7 March), pp. 1, 18.
        Compares the irony and structure of <u>Number One</u> with
    Conrad's novels, particularly Under Western Eyes. Feels
    Dos Passos' novels offer a warning and should be read by
    all thinking Americans. Feels that "few characters in
    contemporary fiction are so brilliantly inspired and so
    faithfully exhibited to public view" as Homer Crawford.

11 JONES, HOWARD MUMFORD. "Sound-Truck Caesar." <u>Saturday Review</u>
    <u>of Literature</u>, 26 (6 March), 7-8.
        Sees <u>Number One</u> on two planes: as a document and as a
    novel. As a document it captures the essence of demagoguery
    and is vivid, adroit, and disturbing. As a novel, however,
    it sacrifices too much to the development of the main
    character and is, as a result, "naive in structure and
    without express conflict."

12 KAZIN, ALFRED. "Where Now Voyager?" <u>New Republic</u>, 108
    (15 March), 353-354.
        Points out that <u>Number One</u> and the books immediately
    preceding it are highly autobiographical and "it is their
    notebook character that explains why they have been so
    spasmodic in their brilliance, so nervous and uncertain
    and tame." Sees this and other works as a dismantling of
    the structure and coldly objective perspective of <u>U.S.A.</u>

13 McHUGH, VINCENT. "Dos Passos Trilogy Revalued." <u>New York</u>
    <u>Times Book Review</u> (5 September), p. 8.
        Retrospective view of <u>U.S.A.</u> in which McHugh concludes
    that "the author's verbal taste is, on the whole, very
    close to flawless," that while the biographies might seem
    dated, the "expert montage and sardonic humor" of the
    Newsreels is still effective, that the main characters
    "remain the skillfully chosen social representatives" they
    seemed on first reading. What has become clearer and more
    frightening is the aimlessness and purposelessness of Dos
    Passos' characters. McHugh regards <u>U.S.A.</u> as "the most
    formidable and accomplished novel of the American twenties
    and thirties."

14 MARSHALL, MARGARET. "Notes by the Way." <u>Nation</u>, 156
    (13 March), 384.
        Dos Passos has astutely recorded the demagogue mentality
    in <u>Number One</u>, but wonders whether the subject deserves a
    full-length study. Faults Dos Passos for his portrayal of
    Tyler Spotswood, "another of his dismal drinking young men,"

1943

who is "so obviously weak willed that one cannot help feeling he is an idealist because he is thwarted, not thwarted
because he is an idealist."

15 P., G. F. "Number One Is Story of Ruthless Demagog."
    Springfield Republican (7 March), p. 7e.
        While acknowledging that Dos Passos emphasizes only the
    seamier side of American politics, he nevertheless "master-
    fully" portrays "an authentic, important portion of the
    crazy quilt we call the United States."

16 SHORER, MARK. Review of Number One. Yale Review, N.S. 32
    (Summer), x-xii.
        Calls Dos Passos primarily a novelist of manners and
    feels the unintended effect of Number One is comic, for
    Dos Passos' narrative method--intensely realistic with lyric
    moments--"is inadequate to express the serious implications
    of the material."

17 STOVALL, FLOYD. American Idealism. Norman, Okla.: University
    of Oklahoma Press, pp. 147-150, 152.
        Finds the method of U.S.A. similar to the poetry of
    Whitman and Sandburg but sees little or none of their basic
    faith.

1944 A BOOKS - NONE

1944 B SHORTER WRITINGS

1 ADAMS, J. DONALD. The Shape of Books to Come. New York:
   Viking Press, Inc., pp. 73-78, passim.
       Feels that in his early (and best known) work, Dos
   Passos wrote under "the heavy hand of Dreiser," continuing
   the tradition of American naturalism. This tradition is,
   in part, responsible for Dos Passos' slanted portrayal of
   primarily the worst of American life. It is only in the
   later work, specifically Adventures of a Young Man and
   Number One, that Dos Passos is able to break through "the
   limitations of the naturalistic approach."

2 ANON. "America's Urgent Problems." Commonweal, 40
   (25 August), 449-450.
       Considers State of the Nation an outstanding socio-
   political study. Thinks it "difficult to imagine a reporter
   who approaches our national scene with greater seriousness."
   Admires the work for its "first-hand impression."

3   ANON.   "A Dos Passos Report on U.S."   Philadelphia Inquirer
    (23 July).
        Calls State of the Nation "a magnificent job of report-
    ing, and it makes for a book as warm and human as it is
    significant."

4   ANON.   "Novelist's Report on America."   Newark Evening News
    (20 July).
        Summary of State of the Nation.   Admires Dos Passos'
    lively and informative style.

5   ANON.   "Report of a Miracle."   Time, 44 (31 July), 91-92, 94-96.
        Calls State of the Nation "a report of a miracle," the
    miracle of a nation's ability to adapt and produce what is
    necessary, despite the fact that "the people who brought it
    about scarcely knew what they were doing."   Thinks the
    book's only real flaw is that it is overly objective, that
    it "does not give voice to emotions that his observations,
    and the people he observes, inspire."   Still, considers
    this Dos Passos' best book and the "best report on the war-
    time U.S. that any writer has given."

6   ANON.   Review of State of the Nation.   Booklist, 41
    (September), 18.
        Calls State of the Nation "an impressionistic but
    thought-provoking cross section of America at war."

7   ANON.   Review of State of the Nation.   The Chicago News
    (6 September).
        Very brief review.

8   ANON.   Review of State of the Nation.   Mademoiselle, 19
    (September).
        Faults Dos Passos for not developing a stronger narra-
    tive structure in State of the Nation: "The record might
    have been pared down to a terse, stenographic set of notes
    or it might have been enriched by the author's talents.
    As it stands, it is excellent but flaccid research."

9   ANON.   Review of State of the Nation.   Virginia Kirkus'
    Bookshop Service, 12 (15 May), 227.
        Calls State of the Nation "provocative and stimulating
    . . . a revealing and disturbing" book which engages the
    reader because it does not attempt to give all the answers.

10 ANON.   Review of State of the Nation.   Wisconsin Library
    Bulletin, 40 (October), 125.
        Thinks that "the material is of a kind to be soon dated,
    but, even so, still makes good reading."

1944

11 ANON. "SRC Poll on Novels and Novelists." <u>Saturday Review of
    Literature</u>, 27 (August), 61.
        In a survey of contributors to nominate the leading
    novelist and novel of the previous twenty years, Dos Passos
    was rated third behind Hemingway and Cather, and <u>U.S.A.</u> was
    also ranked third behind <u>Arrowsmith</u> and <u>A Farewell to Arms</u>.

12 BORLAND, HAL. "Dos Passos Reports on U.S.A." <u>Saturday Review
    of Literature</u>, 27 (2 September), 9.
        Calls <u>State of the Nation</u> "a kaleidoscope picture of
    America, working, squabbling, scheming . . . an America of
    endless opinions and countless little objectives." Wishes
    Dos Passos were less ironic in some reports, less impersonal
    in most. Finds irritating Dos Passos' idiosyncratic style.

13 COWLEY, MALCOLM. "The Generation That Wasn't Lost." <u>College
    English</u>, 5 (February), 233-239.
        Characterizes the novelists of Dos Passos' generation as
    international in their interests; technically expert;
    lyrical rather than naturalistic; rebellious but not revo-
    lutionary; progressively disillusioned; passive rather than
    active in their mood.

14 DE VOTO, BERNARD. <u>The Literary Fallacy</u>. Boston: Little,
    Brown and Co., pp. 111-113.
        Considers Dos Passos' fiction to be "conceived with
    great power" and "worked out with a technical mastery which
    no contemporary has excelled." Nevertheless, De Voto feels
    the characters are ant-like and fail to evoke our feelings.

15 DEWARD, ROBERT J. "Dos Passos Tells What People Over the
    Nation Think." <u>Sacramento Bee</u> (12 August).
        Calls <u>State of the Nation</u> "thought provoking."

16 DUFFUS, R. L. "Dos Passos Sketches Some Home-Front Americans."
    <u>New York Times Book Review</u> (23 July), p. 3.
        Objects to Dos Passos' method, in <u>State of the Nation</u>,
    of quick shifts of scene and character, often without
    identification, which "emphasizes the confusion [of con-
    temporary America] more than the possible coordination."
    The lack of specificity especially seems to indicate that
    "the reporter's method doesn't appear to interest him."
    Still, finds that, despite the flaws, there is much to be
    learned about homefront America in this book.

17 E., M. "Stop, Look, Listen!" <u>Boston Globe</u> (26 July), p. 15.
        Praises <u>State of the Nation</u> for, in it, "Dos Passos has
    not only written his most stimulating book, but has put the

arts back where they belong, out of the glass case and
ivory tower into the world we live in, the things we live
by."

18 ELWOOD, IRENE. "Man Who Had Look-See Reveals State of Nation."
    Los Angeles Times (30 July).
        Calls Dos Passos "impartial and unprejudiced" and State
    of the Nation "his best and most sincere book."

19 HART, JAMES D. The Oxford Companion to American Literature.
    Corrected edition. New York: Oxford University Press,
    pp. 202-203.
        Brief biographical sketch of Dos Passos.

20 JOHNSON, GERALD W. "Round the Perimeter of the Republic."
    Weekly Book Review (New York Herald Tribune) (23 July),
    p. 3.
        Calls State of the Nation an eyes open account of "a
    very great country accomplishing very great feats and per-
    petrating crimes and blunders on a scale commensurate with
    its triumphs." Feels the prose "ripples and sings," except
    when interrupted by Dos Passos' idiosyncratic combining of
    words. Appreciates the absence of a moral or a prophecy.
    Concludes that Dos Passos is a reporter, a poet, and philo-
    sopher and that this book is as important as any he has
    written.

21 JOHNSON, WENDELL. "Dos Passos Looks Over Americans." Chicago
    Sun Book Week (30 July), p. 3.
        Calls State of the Nation "a verbal panorama of the
    United States at war," a book which might not offer answers,
    but does pose provocative questions.

*22 JOUGHIN, G. L. Review of State of the Nation. Springfield
    Republican (20 August), p. 4d.
        Cited in "John Dos Passos and His Reviewers," by William
    White. Bulletin of Bibliography, 20 (May-August 1950),
    45-47.

23 MARSHALL, MARGARET. "Notes By the Way." Nation, 159
    (29 July), 131.
        Finds State of the Nation to be good reporting despite
    "the slight monotony of his sensory style after its first
    freshness wears off." Feels his conclusions are a state-
    ment of "a rather tired and negative faith" that we will
    probably hold onto our liberties despite poor national
    leadership.

1944

24 MAVITY, NANCY BARR. "American Mind Observed From All Angles
    for Pattern of Future." Oakland Tribune (6 August).
        Feels that Dos Passos, in State of the Nation, "is
    really clarifying America to Americans, demonstrating in
    the process that the frontier spirit is by no means a thing
    of the past."

25 MAYBERRY, GEORGE. "Alternatives to the Novel." New Republic,
    111 (24 July), 108.
        Calls State of the Nation "a book that is his best since
    The Big Money." Feels that Dos Passos is "always a better
    historian and reporter than a novelist," partly because of
    his inability to create full fictional characterization.
    Particularly admires the vivid portrayal of scene, especi-
    ally in the sections on Washington, D.C.

26 NICHOLS, ELIZABETH P. Review of State of the Nation. Library
    Journal, 69 (July), 601.
        Calls State of the Nation "an important book at the
    moment." Does not feel that Dos Passos is grinding any
    political axes.

27 NORTH, STERLING. "Realistic Report." New York Post
    (8 August).
        Calls State of the Nation "a refresher course in American
    realism . . . the most vital and most disinterested report
    on the state of the nation published during this war."

28 PEYRE, HENRI. Writers and Their Critics: A Study of
    Misunderstanding. Ithaca, N.Y.: Cornell University Press,
    352pp., passim.
        Passing references to Dos Passos. Reprinted, with
    slight changes in 1967 as The Failure of Criticism.

29 S., J. B. Review of State of the Nation. Infantry Journal
    (September).
        Calls the theme of State of the Nation "the questioning
    uncertainty about America's future."

*30 S., L. A. Review of State of the Nation. Christian Science
    Monitor (29 July), p. 14.
        Unlocatable. Cited in "John Dos Passos and His Re-
    viewers" by William White. Bulletin of Bibliography, 20
    (May-August, 1950), 45-47.

31 SEARLES, P. J. "What Americans Are Thinking." Boston Sunday
    Post (23 July).
        Calls State of the Nation a "clear eyed [and] sensitive"
    report on the strengths and weaknesses of America.

32 SMITH, THEODORE. Review of State of the Nation. San
     Francisco News (21 July).
          Calls State of the Nation a "hard-hitting" and "pungent"
     survey.

33 TROHAN, WALTER. "Dos Passos Tells What People Say." Chicago
     Tribune (13 August).
          Thinks State of the Nation has "the pace of a thriller,"
     and that Dos Passos "has an accurate ear which makes the
     character live in [the] briefest of glimpses."

34 WAGNER, CHARLES A. Review of State of the Nation. New York
     Sunday Mirror (23 July).
          Calls State of the Nation "reportage, but with the gift
     edge of eternals shining through."

35 WILSON, EDMUND. "Dos Passos' Reporting." New Yorker, 20
     (29 July), 57-58, 61.
          Finds State of the Nation to have "the remarkable quali-
     ties of all Dos Passos' writing as a reporter," especially
     his ability to capture "the sense of a community, a pro-
     ject, a meeting, or a slogan." Nevertheless, finds no
     moments when "the emotion of the writer fuses with and
     illuminates the thing it encounters till the reader is com-
     pletely convinced that what this emotion has written is the
     meaning of the thing itself."

1945 A BOOKS - NONE

1945 B SHORTER WRITINGS

 1 ANON. Review of First Encounter. New Yorker, 21 (6 October),
     98.
          Notes re-issue of One Man's Initiation--1917 under new
     title.

 2 EARNEST, ERNEST. A Forward to Literature. New York: D.
     Appleton-Century Co., Inc., pp. 142, 144.
          Sees Dos Passos as a good example of the type of writer
     who tries to represent the complexity of the modern world
     by showing the individual existing "not as a unit, but as
     part of an organism."

 3 GABRIEL, R. H. "Surveying the Nation." Yale Review, N.S. 34
     (Winter), 348-351.
          Feels that Dos Passos "excels in vivid, telling descrip-
     tion of swiftly moving, chaotic scenes," but that State of

1945

the Nation deals too much with such "surface phenomena" to be an accurate assessment of America in the mid 1940's.

4   HITCHCOCK, JAMES S.   Review of State of the Nation.   Grand Rapids Herald (18 February).
    Calls Dos Passos a "super-reporter" and feels that State of the Nation is "good medicine for all who are tempted to embrace every direful diagnosis of Uncle Sam's national ills as hopeless.

5   MOSS, HOWARD.   "A Dos Passos Novel Reissued."   New York Times Book Review (16 December), p. 11.
    Calls First Encounter "a bad novel, ill-formed and awkwardly written. . . . the characters, dialogue and structure . . . wooden and inept."

6   PEARSE, ANDREW.   "Dos Passos and the American Theme," in Focus One.   Edited by B. Rajan and Andrew Pearse.   London: Dennis Dobsen, pp. 115-125.
    Feels that, while Dos Passos has not proved himself a "great writer," he has demonstrated, particularly in U.S.A., that he has mastered the American theme: "the uprooted individual and his quest for social integration."

7   PLUMB, MILTON M., JR.   Review of First Encounter.   Library Journal, 70 (11 October), 890.
    Calls the re-issue of One Man's Initiation--1917 "timely," of interest for how it compares with descriptions of World War II.

8   SAUNDERS, LYLE.   Review of State of the Nation.   New Mexico Quarterly Review, 15 (Autumn).
    Calls State of the Nation "an informal, but nonetheless valid, report on the state of affairs in our country as soon by a keen and capable observer who has managed to hold his own biases to a minimum."

9   SLOCHOWER, HARRY.   No Voice is Wholly Lost: Writers and Thinkers in War and Peace.   New York: Creative Age Press, pp. 69-75, passim.
    Places Dos Passos firmly among the "lost generation." Feels he resolved the "duality of esthetic bohemianism and social radicalism" with his Camera Eye and Newsreels, respectively.

10 TATE, ALLEN.   "The New Provincialism."   The Virginia Quarterly Review (Spring), 262-272.

Arguing for the importance of regional consciousness in
literature, Tate maintains that without it there would be
nothing but travel literature, even if it might be on an
international level. Calls Dos Passos such a travel writer.
Reprinted: 1959.B22, 1968.B30.

1946 A BOOKS - NONE

1946 B SHORTER WRITINGS

1 ANON. "Dos Passos on War." Cleveland Press (24 September).
        Feels that Dos Passos, in Tour of Duty, "brings the
   atmosphere of the conflict very close to the reader," while
   posing some pertinent questions on international affairs.

2 ANON. Notice of Tour of Duty. San Francisco Chronicle
   (29 December).
        Notes Tour of Duty as one of a number of books written
   about World War II.

3 ANON. Review of Tour of Duty. American Mercury (December).
        Feels that Dos Passos' style is so far superior to the
   normal war correspondent's that it seems at first "a bit
   affected," but feels that his reporting is "much better"
   than anyone's else's.

4 ANON. Review of Tour of Duty. The Anniston Star (8 December).
        Calls Tour of Duty "a very human and understanding
   volume."

5 ANON. Review of Tour of Duty. Booklist, 43 (September), 13.
        Admires the "excellent reporting in a chatty, informal
   style" of Tour of Duty.

6 ANON. Review of Tour of Duty. Catholic World, 164 (November),
   188.
        Brief summary of contents of Tour of Duty.

7 ANON. Review of Tour of Duty. The Honolulu Advertiser
   (27 October).
        Brief review. Feels the book contains characters which
   might be autobiographical representations of both the
   younger and older Dos Passos.

8 ANON. Review of Tour of Duty. The Jewish Spectator
   (November).
        Brief note.

1946

9 ANON. Review of <u>Tour of Duty</u>. <u>Lewiston Journal</u> (19 October).
     Brief summary.

10 ANON. Review of <u>Tour of Duty</u>. <u>The Literary Guild Review</u>
     (October).
        Calls <u>Tour of Duty</u> "excellent and vivid . . . a powerful
     warning that we are repeating our mistakes of post-World
     War I."

11 ANON. Review of <u>Tour of Duty</u>. <u>Los Angeles Times</u> (25 August).
     Brief summary. Notes the book's objectivity.

12 ANON. Review of <u>Tour of Duty</u>. <u>Newark Evening News</u> (26 August).
        Calls <u>Tour of Duty</u> "a brooding attempt to tell us humbly
     what we need to know, so that we may do better with the
     peace today than his own generation did with that of 1919."

13 ANON. Review of <u>Tour of Duty</u>. <u>Oakland Post-Enquirer</u>
     (24 August).
        Admires Dos Passos' sharp eye and ear, noting that the
     soldiers' dialogue has "a stenographic quality."

14 ANON. Review of <u>Tour of Duty</u>. <u>Sacramento Bee</u> (23 November).
     Brief review.

15 ANON. Review of <u>Tour of Duty</u>. <u>St. Louis Star-Times</u>
     (30 October).
        Admires the "graphic precision" of Dos Passos' writing
     in a very brief review.

16 ANON. Review of <u>Tour of Duty</u>. <u>St. Louis Star-Times</u>
     (14 December).
        Calls Dos Passos' account one of the best pictures of
     the war yet written.

17 ANON. Review of <u>Tour of Duty</u>. <u>San Jose Evening News</u>
     (13 August).
     Brief summary.

18 ANON. Review of <u>Tour of Duty</u>. <u>Virginia Kirkus' Bookshop</u>
     <u>Service</u>, 14 (15 June), 289.
        Concedes that the material is already dated, but thinks
     that no writer has written so vividly about the war as Dos
     Passos.

19 ANON. Review of <u>Tour of Duty</u>. <u>The Weather League Messenger</u>
     (1 October).
     Brief review.

20 ANON. Review of Tour of Duty. Wisconsin Library Bulletin, 42
       (November), 148.
           Feels that "some of the unpleasant truths about the war
       are most effectively rammed home."

21 ANON. "The War." St. Louis Globe-Democrat (15 September).
           Admires Tour of Duty because "it never pontificates" and
       because Dos Passos' mind is "forever inquiring and alert."

22 ANON. "What They Said." St. Louis Post-Dispatch (27 August).
           Admires Dos Passos' vivid recreation of the sights and
       sounds of combat in Tour of Duty: "There is a feeling that
       the reader has looked and listened, has seen and heard, with
       only the slightest assistance of John Dos Passos."

23 BASSO, HAMILTON. "The Huey Long Legend." Life, 21
       (9 December), 106-108, 110, 112, 115-116, 118-119.
           Briefly outlines Long's career and argues that, despite
       two early and highly critical novels--one of which is
       Number One--the recent fiction, particularly Robert Penn
       Warren's All the King's Men and Adria Locke Langley's A
       Lion in the Streets, are "the stuff that legends are made
       of."

24 BLALOCK, JOHN V. "John Dos Passos' Report on War Tour."
       Durham Morning Herald (25 August).
           Summarizes Tour of Duty. Feels that Dos Passos' technique
       of offering merely "glimpses" of the war is, for the most
       part, "strangely effective."

25 BRIGHT, YVONNE YOUNGER. "War of the Conquerors." The San
       Francisco Argonaut (23 August).
           Calls Tour of Duty "an eloquent commentary on both the
       clean strength of a well-disciplined army force and the
       dangerously ineffectual American manner toward the European
       people."

26 BROOKHOUSER, FRANK. "Are We Losing the Peace? A Warning by
       Dos Passos." Philadelphia Inquirer (1 September).
           Calls Tour of Duty "top flight and highly perceptive re-
       porting," as a result of Dos Passos' "writing brilliance,
       his sensitivity, and his powers of observation."

27 BURNS, GEORGE R. "A Tour of Pacific Battlefield." Philadelphia
       Record (8 September).
           Regrets that Dos Passos can offer no solutions for the
       post-war world, but admires his vivid descriptions, parti-
       cularly of the Nuremberg trials.

1946

28 BUTCHER, FANNY. Review of U.S.A. Chicago Sunday Tribune
   (15 December).
   Calls U.S.A. "one of the greatest of modern American
   fictional classics."

29 BYRD, SIGMAN. "A Documentary View of the War Nobody Won."
   Houston Post (25 August).
   Calls Tour of Duty a "penetrating and fearless report."
   Summarizes a number of incidents from the book.

30 CHENEY, FRANCES. "Sensitive Report on War." The Nashville
   Tennessean (1 September).
   Admires Tour of Duty for Dos Passos' "ability to describe
   accurately" his observations and his "ability to convey
   impression without giving his own personal opinion."

31 CONROY, JACK. "Dos Passos Is Angry Man." Chicago Sun Book
   Week (25 August).
   Notes Dos Passos' new and suspicious attitude toward the
   Soviet Union. Feels that Dos Passos "has not lost his sharp
   ear for the salty speech of the common soldier."

32 CORT, JOHN C. Review of Tour of Duty. Commonweal, 44
   (20 September), 556.
   Finds that although "a good deal of the fire" has gone
   out of Dos Passos, in Tour of Duty he demonstrates that he
   is still a first-rate craftsman and a remarkably honest,
   humble, and revealing figure. Especially appreciates the
   last third of the book, about post-war Europe. Credits Dos
   Passos with the courage to point out America's blunders as
   well as its successes both during and after the war.

33 COYNE, CATHERINE. "Your Newsbook of the Week." Boston Herald
   (21 August).
   Calls Tour of Duty "a book for every thinking American
   . . . superb reporting by one of America's greatest
   writers."

34 DANIELS, JONATHAN. "The American War Procession." Saturday
   Review of Literature, 29 (3 August), 6-7.
   Considers Tour of Duty a "strong, beautiful, mature book
   about the war which can be both evil and magnificent and
   about peace which can be not only stupid and brutal, but
   blind."

35 DEMPSEY, DAVID. "Backwash of Victory." New York Times Book
   Review (25 August), p. 7.

Calls Tour of Duty a "leisurely, unexciting but highly
eventful book about the aftermath of victory." Identifies
Dos Passos' main interest as not the war itself, but
American's indecisive bungling of the events immediately
following the war. Concludes that "his focus is sharp and
the meaning plain: our two wars have not yet created one
world."

36 DE NOLASCO, TEDDY and SYLVIA CUMMINGS. Review of Tour of Duty.
    The Far East Advertiser (November).
        Feels that Dos Passos, "one of our most sensitive re-
    porters," is nevertheless guilty of simplifying his various
    subjects, of too readily portraying his characters in
    black and white.

37 DOUGLAS, M. STONEMAN. Review of Tour of Duty. Washington
    Times Herald (8 September).
        Admires the sketches of participants which provide a
    broader view "of the men who made military history."
    Reprinted: 1946.B38.

38 _____. "Vivid Account of War Depicted By Dos Passos." Miami
    Herald (11 September).
        Reprint of 1946.B37.

39 F., A. "Russia--Slave State." Books on Trial (December-
    January).
        Quotations from other reviews.

40 GLENN, TAYLOR. Review of Tour of Duty. Bridgeport Post
    (25 August).
        Calls the book "exciting and interesting and informing."

41 GOVAN, THOMAS P. "Will Fruit of Peace Be Fascism?"
    Chattanooga Times (September).
        Admits that the grim foreboding of Tour of Duty is not
    really pessimistic, but realistic and probably necessary.

42 GRAY, JAMES. Review of U.S.A. Chicago Daily News
    (4 December).
        Feels that the reissue of the novels in the trilogy em-
    phasizes "how serious and ambitious" Dos Passos' task was.

43 _____. "Tenderly Tolls the Bell for Three Soldiers," in his
    On Second Thought. Minneapolis: University of Minnesota
    Press, pp. 59-82.
        Thinks Fitzgerald, Hemingway, and Dos Passos to be "each
    in his different way . . . a glittering example of the

1946

psychology of the 'sad young men' of the 'lost generation.'"
Does not think Dos Passos as negative as many critics feel;
certainly Dos Passos has never portrayed as distressing a
"testimony against the human race" as in some of the scenes
in Tender is the Night. Dos Passos is simply more clinical
in his presentation, resulting in a sharper edge to his
portrayal. Reprinted: 1950.B53.

44 GREGORY, HORACE and MARYA ZATURENSKA. A History of American
    Poetry, 1900-1940. New York: Harcourt, Brace and Co.,
    pp. 250, 339, 415, 431.
        Draws parallels between the prose of Dos Passos and the
    poetry of Sandburg, Cummings, and Benet.

45 HAYES, SIBYL C. Review of Tour of Duty. San Jose Mercury
    Herald (8 September).
        Except for the reports from the Pacific islands, finds
    little that differs from the accounts of other
    correspondents.

46 HOFFMAN, FREDERICK J., CHARLES ALLEN, and CAROLYN F. ULRICH,
    eds. The Little Magazine: A History and a Bibliography.
    Princeton: Princeton University Press, 449pp., passim.
        Passing references to Dos Passos.

47 HOWES, ROYCE. "Dos Passos Depicts Men at War." Detroit Free
    Press (25 August).
        Calls Tour of Duty "a splendid piece of reporting."
    Admires Dos Passos' character portraits and finds his
    examination of post-war Europe most pertinent.

48 HUTCHENS, JOHN K. "People Who Read and Write." New York Times
    Book Review (22 September), p. 33.
        Report of conversation with Dos Passos in which he
    seemed "quite hopeful about American writers and not too
    pessimistic about the world."

49 JACKSON, JOSEPH HENRY. "Bookman's Notebook." This World
    magazine of the San Francisco Chronicle (22 August), p. 12.
        Thinks Tour of Duty is a thoughtful book, particularly
    in Dos Passos' analysis of post-war Europe.

50 JACKSON, MARGOT. Review of Tour of Duty. Akron Beacon-Journal
    (8 September).
        Admires Dos Passos' ability to create a "technicolor,
    three-dimensional slide picture," but finds the material
    "out-of-date and musty," without cohesion.

51 KALENICH, WAYNE A. Review of Tour of Duty. Library Journal, 71 (July), 976.
    Calls Tour of Duty "a series of short graphic cameos" which portray the life of the American soldier at the front.

52 KERN, JOHN DWIGHT. Review of U.S.A. Philadelphia Inquirer (15 December).
    Calls U.S.A. "Whitman-like and Herculean" in its attempt to portray "the entire America of his time." Calls Dos Passos a "neo-Preraphaelite" whose technique represents "an effort to recapture in fictional form a familiar device of medieval art. The 'Camera Eye' passages . . . suggest a religious work of the Middle Ages, with statues of saints on the borders and a small self-portrait of the artist in the corner." Compares Dos Passos with Dreiser but feels Dos Passos is stylistically more facile.

53 L[AYCOCK], E[DWARD] A. "Dos Passos Looks and Listens." Boston Daily Globe (22 August).
    Calls Tour of Duty "reporting of high caliber, reporting that will keep its value for a long time."

54 LEWIS, JASPER R. Review of Tour of Duty. Forum, 106 (October), 362.
    Brief review.

55 MacGREGOR, MARTHA. "Here's Your Country As Dos Passos Sees It." Washington Post (4 December).
    Calls U.S.A. a tour de force, entertaining while at the same time a work of serious social criticism. Reprinted: 1946.B56.

56 _____. Review of U.S.A. New York Post (9 December).
    Reprint of 1946.B55.

57 MEYER, CORD, JR. "Perceptive Reporting on Three Theaters of War." Weekly Book Review of the New York Herald Tribune (1 September), p. 2.
    Notes that the three part structure of Tour of Duty not only reflects the three different theaters of the war which Dos Passos visited but also the deepening concern about American policies which he and the soldiers he interviewed felt.

58 MURRAY, MARAIN. "Grand Reporting On War Fronts By Dos Passos." Hartford Times (17 August).

1946

> Compares Dos Passos' Tour of Duty with the war reports
> of Ernie Pyle: "where Pyle is personal, Dos Passos is photo-
> graphic. Where Pyle injects himself and his personality
> into everything he writes, Dos Passos lets the reader use
> his eyes and ears and nose. And yet the impressions made
> by the two are much alike." Calls the writing "as objective
> as a paid death notice."

59 NORTHROP, GUY. "Tour of Duty Mirrors War." Memphis Commercial
Appeal (1 September).
> Feels that Tour of Duty "finds Dos Passos at his height
> as a reporter. He writes with clarity and unity." Thinks
> the book is superior to anything Hemingway or Steinbeck
> wrote about the war.

60 O., W. H. "Dos Passos On The War." Birmingham (Alabama) News
(5 September).
> Does not feel that Tour of Duty is one of Dos Passos'
> best books, but admires the "understanding and moral force"
> with which Dos Passos presents his material.

61 OBERLIN, RICHARD. Review of Tour of Duty. Louisville Courier-
Journal (20 October).
> Feels that the account of the Pacific islands is over-
> burdened with scenic description, but that the account of
> post-war Germany is "the very stuff of an engrossing story."
> Speculates that this is because Dos Passos "was lost in the
> simple-minded Pacific, but entirely at home in the involved,
> devious, brutal and bitter diplomacy of Europe."

62 O'CONNOR, JOHN J. Review of Tour of Duty. America, 76
(2 November), 135-136.
> Feels that what distinguishes Tour of Duty from other
> wartime accounts is "Dos Passos' literary craftsmanship,
> his scrupulous objectivity, and the stenographic quality of
> his reporting. . . . The reader will have the curious im-
> pression of being led around by the hand by a highly intel-
> ligent and wonderfully observant but insensitive robot."

63 OLMSTEAD, HARRY C. II. "Cyclorama of Our Worldwide Ineptitude."
Hartford Courant Magazine (25 August).
> Quotes heavily from Tour of Duty, which is viewed as
> "simply the consistent diary of a keen, observant man
> [whose] accurate dialogue frequently carries the kick of
> a Missouri mule."

64 PHIPPS, ROBERT. "Dos Passos on the War." Omaha World-Herald
(25 August).

Admires Dos Passos' ability to capture "the combination of sights, sounds and meanings" of the war in Tour of Duty.

65 POLING, DANIEL A. Review of Tour of Duty. New York Christian Herald (5 August).
Admires the "vivid, conversational style" of Tour of Duty. Does not recommend for the Church library.

66 PRESCOTT, ORVILLE. Review of Tour of Duty. Cue (7 September).
Calls the book excellent: "casual, informal, perceptive, beautifully written and deceptively unpretentious."

67 ROBINSON, TED. Review of Tour of Duty. Cleveland Plain Dealer (8 September).
Feels that "nobody could have done a better job" at reporting the war. Only wishes that Dos Passos had written a novel about the war.

68 ROGERS, W. G. Review of Tour of Duty. San Jose News (22 October).
Feels that in this reworked compilation of previously published dispatches, "some pages have the musty flavor of an old history book."

69 S. "A Word Picture of War." Minneapolis Sunday Tribune (4 September).
Admires Dos Passos' ability in Tour of Duty, to create "word pictures where detail and characterization are so deftly chosen and presented that the reader feels himself present at the scene."

70 S., A. "Good Reporting." Infantry Journal, 59 (November), 66.
Feels that Tour of Duty "is an example of fine reporting, albeit some of it is of the travelogue variety."

71 S., R. "Americans in Germany." The Christian Science Monitor (1 September).
Admires the final, post-war section of Tour of Duty but feels the accounts of the war have lost their timeliness.

72 SARTRE, JEAN-PAUL. "American Novelists in French Eyes." Atlantic Monthly, 178 (August), 114-118.
Sees the discovery of Faulkner, Dos Passos, Hemingway, Caldwell, and Steinbeck, during the thirties, as the most important literary development in France. Sees the objective, non-analytical approach to fiction as their major contribution: "American authors have taught us that what we thought were immutable laws in the art of the novel were

1946

only a group of postulates which one might shift without
danger." Sartre feels that Dos Passos had the greatest
effect on his own fiction.

73 SNELL, GEORGE. "U.S.A.: Another Look At Another Printing of
the Great Dos Passos Trilogy." This World Magazine of the
San Francisco Chronicle (15 December).
    Calls U.S.A., "one of the great novels of our time . . .
the first and still the finest long fiction based on broad
social issues." Feels that Dos Passos may have overstated
his case in presenting "a terrible spectacle of life being
lived at breakneck pace, without aim, without much hope,
with few inherent values." Still, "the spectacle is
magnificent."

74 SONNEBORN, HARRY L. "Men in Conflict Etched Finely by Dos
Passos." Milwaukee Journal (25 August).
    Feels that Dos Passos, in Tour of Duty, succeeds in his
"limited objective: a clear, finely drawn picture of a man
who licked the jungle and the enemy, who tries to make
order out of rubble after the fighting, and who asks plain-
tively: What's it all about, what happens next, where do we
go from here?"

75 SPICEHANDLER, MIRIAM. Review of Tour of Duty. Justice
(15 August).
    Feels the book is written "with the brilliant clarity of
a camera eye."

76 TEWSON, W. ORTON. "Attic Salt-Shaker." Saint Paul Times
(30 September).
    Quotes, from Tour of Duty, passages about post-war
Vienna.

77 VAN GELDER, ROBERT. "An Interview with John Dos Passos."
Writers and Writing. New York: Charles Scribner's Sons,
pp. 327-340. Reprint of 1941.B35.

78 WATTS, RICHARD. "Reporter v. Editor." New Republic, 115
(2 September), 267-268.
    Feels that Dos Passos, in the first two parts of Tour
of Duty, "captures, through straightforward reporting . . .
a remarkable impression," but that in his sections which
deal with the Russians "Dos Passos seems an editorial writer
disguised as a reporter." This facade of objectivism,
which results from staged conversations, particularly
annoys Watts.

79 WICKHAM, BEN, JR. Review of U.S.A. Cleveland News
        (30 November).
            Feels that U.S.A. is still relevant and perhaps even of
        more interest in 1946 than when first published.

80 WILSON, EDMUND. "Dos Passos in the Pacific." New Yorker, 22
        (24 August), 66.
            Sees Tour of Duty as "probably the best thing he has
        written since he finished U.S.A." Praises his skill at
        continuous narrative as well as his genius for observation.
        Cites as an example his descriptions of sky and land while
        aboard a plane which Wilson thinks is "more brilliant than
        anything else yet attempted in this line."

81 WITMAN, SHEPHERD L. Review of Tour of Duty. Cleveland News
        (19 October).
            Feels that Dos Passos "lays open the body of war with
        clean incisions. He brings the spectator to view it with
        a style that stings like the flick of a whip."

82 ZINNER, HARRIET. "A Striking Indictment." Free World, 12
        (December).
            Feels that Tour of Duty displays the same "brilliant
        style" and "sympathy of characterization" that made U.S.A.
        "one of the most significant of American novels." Feels,
        however, that the section on the Pacific is too much a
        travelogue and that the portrait of post-war Germany is
        sometimes poorly handled.

1947 A BOOKS - NONE

1947 B SHORTER WRITINGS

 1 AARON, DANIEL. "'The Truly Monstrous': A Note on Nathanael
        West." Partisan Review, 14, no. 1, 98-106.
            Feels that while West's novels of the 1930s do not give
        as faithful a presentation of "a nation on the skids" as,
        for instance, "the colorful and violent documentaries of
        Dos Passos, "they do give us in an arresting and sometimes
        poetic way a glimpse of a mindless people . . . ripe for
        catastrophe."

 2 ANON. "Dos Passos Reviews Battle Experience." Springfield
        Daily News (7 March).
            Calls Tour of Duty "a series of vignettes, some tragic,
        some happy, and all of them interesting."

1947

3 ANON. Review of <u>Tour of Duty</u>. <u>Foreign Affairs</u>, 25
   (January), 340.
       Feels <u>Tour of Duty</u> reveals Dos Passos' "keen perception."

4 BEACH, JOSEPH WARREN. "Dos Passos 1947." <u>Sewanee Review</u>, 55
   (Summer), 406-418.
       Views Dos Passos as a social novelist whose ideology "is
   that of one trying to understand." Considers "the furthest
   triumph of art" in Dos Passos to be the submergence of his
   own personal style in that of his characters. Defends Dos
   Passos to those whose taste is more for psychological penetration of character. Beach argues that to read Dos Passos'
   novels in such a way is merely a sign of narrowness and is
   to deny his unique achievement.

5 BURGUM, EDWIN BERRY. <u>The Novel and the World's Dilemma</u>. New
   York: Oxford University Press, pp. 159, 224, 284, 304.
       Passing reference to Dos Passos.

6 CANBY, HENRY SEIDEL. <u>American Memoir</u>. Boston: Houghton
   Mifflin Company, pp. 342-343, passim.
       Feels Dos Passos created "a kind of literary television."
   Speculating that he wrote for his "exact contemporaries,"
   Canby finds "too much of the visual and auditory; too little
   depth and wisdom" in Dos Passos' novels.

7 COLEMAN, McALISTER. "Dos Passos and the War." <u>Nation</u>, 164
   (18 January), 80.
       Admires the vivid images and "the authentic speech"
   captured in <u>Tour of Duty</u>. Still, hopes that Dos Passos
   will resume his historical research.

8 COWLEY, MALCOLM. "Dos Passos and His Predecessors." <u>New York
   Times Book Review</u> (19 January), pp. 1, 29.
       Places <u>U.S.A.</u> in the naturalist tradition.

9 _____. "Not Men: A Natural History of American Naturalism."
   <u>Kenyon Review</u>, 9 (Summer), 414-435.
       Includes <u>Manhattan Transfer</u> and <u>U.S.A.</u> as examples of
   the naturalist novel. In defining the naturalist movement,
   Cowley maintains that the most important aspect of the
   movement is its denial of free will.

10 GAGEY, EDMOND M. <u>Revolution in American Drama</u>. New York:
    Columbia University Press, pp. 153-154.
        Feels that <u>The Moon is a Gong</u> was "deservedly a failure"
    but finds it interesting as an example of the concerns of
    the young intellectuals of the 1920s.

11 GEISMAR, MAXWELL. "John Dos Passos: Conversion of a Hero," in
    his <u>Writers in Crisis</u>. Boston: Houghton Mifflin Co., pp.
    87-139.
        Calls Dos Passos "the archetype of the rational writer
    within our tradition, the conscious, moral, progressive
    writer, the embodiment, not of the distructive rebel, but
    of all our communal and civilizational aspirations." Sees
    his education as a turning away from the "despairing and
    descriptive emotions of the isolated individual," and a
    turning "outward to deal with the structure of society, the
    patterns of our communal life, the technics and ideals of
    social progress." Having made this transition in the mid-
    twenties, while most of his contemporaries would ten years
    later, Geismar sees Dos Passos as "the true innovator and
    experimentalist."

12   . <u>The Last of the Privincials: The American Novel 1915-</u>
    <u>1925</u>. Boston: Houghton Mifflin Company, 416pp., passim.
        Various references to Dos Passos and the way he was in-
    fluenced by and extended certain themes and techniques of
    such writers as Cather and Anderson.

13 GURKO, LEO. <u>The Angry Decade</u>. New York: Dodd, Mead and Co.,
    pp. 50-52, passim.
        Feels the Rousseauism of Dos Passos is never more apparent
    than in <u>The 42nd Parallel</u> where "his personages are all good
    at birth and become corrupted by contact with an evil soci-
    ety." Thinks the novel to be an ideal literary expression
    of the bewilderment of the early depression.

14 K., A. "Dos Passos' Epic of Modern America." <u>New Orleans</u>
    <u>Times-Picayune</u> (18 May).
        Feels that while parts of <u>U.S.A.</u> seem dated, it remains
    "an artistic and moving story."

15 MORRIS, LLOYD. <u>Postscript to Yesterday: America: The Last</u>
    <u>Fifty Years</u>. New York: Random House, p. 68.
        Lists Dos Passos as one of the writers cynical about
    idealism in the age of the return to normalcy.

16 SHEPHERD, R. MARSHALL. "Correspondent's Odyssey." <u>Nashville</u>
    <u>Banner</u> (12 March).
        Brief review.

17 SNELL, GEORGE D. "John Dos Passos: Literary Collectivist," in
    his <u>Shapers of American Fiction, 1789-1947</u>. New York:
    E. P. Dutton Co., pp. 249-263, passim.

1948

Feels that Dos Passos "produced the first, and still the
most artistic, long fiction based on broad social issues."
Snell believes that Dos Passos has always considered technique to be "of primary importance," and notes Dos Passos'
fascination with modern experimentalism in the arts in
Europe. Considers Dos Passos the most artistic writer,
"perhaps because he has not always been happiest in his
role of realistic photographer." Thinks that U.S.A. "found
a new school in the American novel." After Adventures of a
Young Man, Snell sees a significant change in Dos Passos'
writing: he turns to the "storybook democracy" in his
American histories, and the more grimly pessimistic in his
novels.

1948 A BOOKS - NONE

1948 B SHORTER WRITINGS

1 BISHOP, JOHN PEALE. "Three Brilliant Young Novelists," in The
   Collected Essays of John Peale Bishop. Edited by Edmund
   Wilson. New York: Charles Scribner's Sons, pp. 229-233.
      Reprint of 1921.B6.

2 BLANKENSHIP, RUSSELL. American Literature as an Expression of
   the National Mind. New York: Holt, Rinehart & Winston,
   pp. 718, 759-761.
      Considers the politics of U.S.A. strident and to be the
   reason for omitting a central character. Admires the
   Biographies but considers the contributions of the other
   devices to be "dubious."

3 COWIE, ALEXANDER. The Rise of the American Novel. New York:
   American Book Co., pp. 721, 747, 749, 750, 752, 754.
      Occasional mention of Dos Passos, commenting briefly on
   his objectivity, his "hard-boiled manner" and his stylistic
   innovations.

4 FROHOCK, W. M. "John Dos Passos: Of Time and Frustration, I
   and II." Southwest Review, 33 (Winter, Spring) 71-80,
   170-179.
      Calls Dos Passos "a poet who has turned to the novel
   because its loose construction and lack of rules will let
   him do things which no other form will permit." Reprinted:
   1950.B52.

5 MAGNY, CLAUDE E. "Introduction to the Reading of Dos Passos."
   Art and Action: Twice A Year. Translated by Ralph Manheim.
   Nos. 16-17, pp. 230-244.
       Calls U.S.A. "the novel . . . that Zola and Upton Sinclair
   had vainly attempted to write . . . an important step in the
   development of the modern novel toward an impersonal art
   form." Magny closely examines the style of the various
   sections of U.S.A., and Dos Passos' use of time--"the objective, inexorable, almost spatialized time of society"--
   which she feels provides a thematic center for the trilogy.
   Thinks that, in U.S.A., Dos Passos "has achieved the point
   of perfection . . . where every quality becomes inseparable
   from a limitation," and wonders what that will bode for his
   later work.

6 SCHORER, MARK. "Technique as Discovery." Hudson Review, 1
   (Spring), 67-87.
       General article, highly critical of "the structural
   machinations" of Dos Passos which are seen as "desperate
   maneuvers" of a writer committed to a method whose limitations he despairs.

7 SPILLER, ROBERT E., et. al. Literary History of the United
   States. Vol. 2. New York: The Macmillan Company, pp.
   1302-1304, 1380, 1382, 1385-1387, passim.
       Calls Dos Passos "the embodiment of the rational artist
   in our tradition--the conscious, moral and progressive
   critic of our communal habits." Feels that, in the negative portrayal of his characters in U.S.A., Dos Passos
   defeats his own purpose "for if Dos Passos' people are
   really what he seems to think they are, there would be
   little value in the social revolution which is his central
   hope of redemption."

1949 A BOOKS - NONE

1949 B SHORTER WRITINGS

1 ALDRIDGE, JOHN W. "American's Young Novelists." The Saturday
   Review of Literature, 32 (12 February), 6-8, 36-37, 42.
       Discusses the burden on the new generation of American
   writers who would have to overcome the shadow of such
   writers as Dos Passos, Hemingway, Cummings, and Fitzgerald
   of whom Aldridge remarks: "Idiosyncrasy and defiance were
   part of their work because the things that had happened to
   them had happened to no generation before them."

1949

2 ANON. "Dos Passos' Design." <u>Newsweek</u>, 33 (3 January), 58.
 Finds <u>The Grand Design</u> vague and, at best, merely inventive rather than creative. Thinks Dos Passos' attitude
 toward Roosevelt and the New Deal are too ambivalent to be
 effective.

3 ANON. "Exiles and Others." <u>Saturday Review of Literature</u>, 32
 (6 August), 108-109.
 Notes Dos Passos as one of the famous American expatriate
 writers of the twenties.

4 ANON. "From Rebellion to Doubt." <u>Time</u>, 53 (3 January), 62.
 Finds <u>The Grand Design</u> successful as "top-of-the-mind
 journalism" but a failure as a novel because of weak
 characterization, a tendency to ridicule and preach, and
 the lack of unifying passion" which cemented the fragments
 of <u>U.S.A.</u>

5 ANON. "In New Writing Role." <u>Business Week</u>, no. 1032
 (11 June), p. 92.
 Notes that Dos Passos had been hired by General Mills,
 Inc., to write an "objective and human" story of the
 company.

6 ANON. "<u>Life</u> Congratulates." <u>Life</u>, 17 (22 August), 33.
 Notes Dos Passos' August 6 marriage to Elizabeth
 Holdridge.

7 ANON. Review of <u>The Grand Design</u>. <u>Booklist</u>, 45 (15 January),
 178.
 Brief summary of <u>The Grand Design</u>.

8 ANON. Review of <u>The Grand Design</u>. <u>Wisconsin Library Bulletin</u>,
 45 (March), 48.
 Brief review.

9 B., R. "From Babbitt to the Bomb." <u>Saturday Review of
 Literature</u>, 32 (6 August), 100-101.
 Notes that <u>The Naked and the Dead</u> has been compared with
 <u>Three Soldiers</u> but concludes that most critics felt that
 no novel of the post World War II period could compare with
 the best of Lewis, Anderson, Fitzgerald, Dreiser, or Dos
 Passos.

10 BLANKENSHIP, RUSSELL. <u>American Literature: As An Expression
 of the National Mind</u>. New York: Holt, Rinehart & Winston,
 pp. 759-760.
 Considers the technical innovations to be the most
 striking aspect of <u>U.S.A.</u>

11 BOURJAILY, VANCE. "John Dos Passos and A New Novel." This
    World Magazine of the San Francisco Chronicle (9 January),
    p. 11.
        Feels that Dos Passos' early novels, through U.S.A.,
    were at times clumsy but they touched a raw nerve, one had
    the feeling that "he was speaking for the people about whom
    he wrote." Finds the style of The Grand Design smoother
    but "we aren't there. The Grand Design doesn't crystalize
    what we feel about the New Deal." Concludes that Dos
    Passos' "point of view has grown narrower and narrower."

12 BRITT, GEORGE. Review of The Grand Design. Survey, 85
    (April), 232-233.
        Calls The Grand Design "negative and . . . sterile"
    social documentation.

13 COWLEY, MALCOLM. "Dos Passos and His Critics." New Republic,
    120 (28 February), 21-23.
        Observes that criticism of The Grand Design had fallen
    out primarily along political lines: conservative critics
    liked it; liberals hated it. Cowley questions the value
    of any novel which evokes primarily a political response.
    Then goes on to analyze in some depth a review of John
    Chamberlain in the New Leader in which Chamberlain claims
    that Dos Passos was never a great novelist but a great
    social reporter and feels the current novel is on a par
    with the others. Cowley argues that Dos Passos was not a
    great social reporter, that the extreme pessimism of his
    earlier novels was ill founded and then demonstrates the
    esthetic qualities of some of the earlier novels.

14 _____. "Washington Wasn't Like That." New Republic, 120
    (17 January), 23-24.
        While crediting Dos Passos with "an excellent memory for
    visual details, perhaps the best of any American novelist,"
    Cowley criticizes him for "losing his memory for the sound
    and sense of spoken English" in The Grand Design. Considers
    the contrived dialogue and equally contrived characteriza-
    tions "affronts to our sense of possibility" and goes on to
    point out a number of factual errors which pepper the novel.
    Concludes that it is not a novel at all: "It is a political
    or religious tract in which the characters, instead of
    being persons, are the bare bones of arguments."

15 DESMOND, EMMETT. "John Dos Passos Dissects Washington, New
    Deal Era." Chicago Sun (2 January), p. 8x.
        Thinks the writers of the twenties and thirties generally
    superior to the next generation, but feels they suffered
    from extreme political naivete. Thinks that to be the chief

1949

flaw of The Grand Design: while the characters are engaging
and convincing, Dos Passos seems to know or accept little
of political reality.

16 ELIAS, ROBERT H. Theodore Dreiser: Apostle of Nature. New
York: Alfred A. Knopf, pp. 254, 256.
Mentions the visit of Dreiser, Dos Passos and others to
the Hurlan Coal fields in 1931 and their subsequent indictment for criminal syndication. Reprinted: 1970.B12.

17 FAUSSET, HUGH I. A. "New Novels." Manchester Guardian
(24 June), p. 4.
Calls The Grand Design "art on the run," but thinks the
book has an "intimate realism and an exuberant narrative
power."

18 G., P. "The Author." Saturday Review of Literature, 32
(8 January), 8.
Brief sketch of the life and work of Dos Passos which
accompanies a review of The Grand Design.

19 GEISMAR, MAXWELL. "Dos Passos' New Novel of the New Deal
Years." New York Times Book Review (2 January), pp. 4, 13.
Calls The Grand Design an outstanding stylistic performance and thinks that Dos Passos has proven himself again
as "one of our best contemporary prose stylists." Unfortunately, the novel is also "entirely superficial" in
its presentation of the "modern collapse of values." Thinks
Dos Passos, as historian of American novelists, abuses
that role as his picture of the New Deal is "distorted to
the point of being obsessed."

20 GRENNAN, MARGARET R. Review of The Grand Design. Catholic
World, 168 (February), 409.
Calls The Grand Design "competent" but "in spite of its
technical excellence, we experience disappointment in reading the book" because of Dos Passos' "preoccupation with
setting and tone rather than with humanity." In general,
finds the treatment of the characters and situations of
the New Deal to be fair minded, "revealing its strength and
its weakness."

21 HART, H. W. Review of The Grand Design. Library Journal, 74
(1 January), 58-59.
Calls The Grand Design "a bitter satire against the
Kremlin's agents and dupes; a tribute and lament for New
Deal liberalism."

22 HICKS, GRANVILLE. "Dos Passos and His Critics." <u>American Mercury</u>, 68 (May), 623-630.
    Surveys criticism of <u>The Grand Design</u>, finding much of it overly partisan. Concludes, however, that this and recent novels are inferior to <u>U.S.A.</u> Feels that the bitter early novels were optimistic "for there was a promise of change," but after rejecting Marxism Dos Passos could find no social panacea to replace it. As a result, the passion which propels <u>U.S.A.</u> is missing: "He is against almost everything he writes about in <u>The Grand Design</u>, but his opposition is bewildered, ill tempered, often petulant, never passionate."

23 HOWE, IRVING. "John Dos Passos: The Loss of Passion." <u>Tomorrow</u>, 7 (March), 54-57.
    Feels that only in <u>U.S.A.</u> in which "the sense of history has become an absorbed passion," has Dos Passos been able to overcome serious technical flaws. Concludes that much of the later work, including <u>The Grand Design</u>, "fails because Dos Passos no longer sees himself passionately engaged in social rebellion." Reprinted: 1950.B57.

24 KALLICH, MARTIN. "A Bibliography of John Dos Passos." <u>Bulletin of Bibliography</u>, 19 (May-August), 231-235.
    Primary bibliography, listing Dos Passos' books and periodical publications.

25 _____. "A Textual Note on John Dos Passos' <u>Journeys Between Wars</u>." <u>Papers of the Bibliographical Society of America</u>, 43 (Spring), 346-348.
    Feels that the revisions of <u>Rosinante to the Road Again</u> for publication in <u>Journeys Between Wars</u> are an attempt to camouflage "his early romantic mysticism." As a result, Kallich feels that Dos Passos' thought at the time of the first World War is misrepresented.

26 MILES, GEORGE. Review of <u>The Grand Design</u>. <u>Commonweal</u>, 49 (28 January), 402.
    Finds <u>The Grand Design</u> unsuccessful "because the characters fail to impress as real people, because the writing is for the most part a journalistic listing and because the revelations are no longer revelations." Finds the work lacks "the skill and verve of earlier works."

27 MIZENER, ARTHUR. <u>The Far Side of Paradise: A Biography of F. Scott Fitzgerald</u>. Boston: Houghton Mifflin, pp. 111-112, passim.

1949

        Brief mention of Dos Passos in the context of how the
avant-garde of the 1920s mingled political rebelliousness
and hedonism.

28 MORRIS, LLOYD. "Dos Passos Offers Political Tract in Fiction."
     Weekly Book Review of the New York Herald Tribune
     (2 January), p. 3.
        Calls The Grand Design "a political tract, an angry,
embittered work . . . produced on the bench of desolation."
Concludes that Dos Passos, "an experienced and resourceful
novelist," must have consciously sacrificed art to argument
in this book.

*29 MUNN, L. S. Review of The Grand Design. Springfield
     Republican (30 January), p. 18a.
        Cited in "John Dos Passos and His Reviewers," by William
White. Bulletin of Bibliography, 20 (May-August 1950),
45-47.

30 PRESCOTT, ORVILLE. "Outstanding Novels." Yale Review, N.S.
     38 (Spring), 573.
        Calls The Grand Design "dull and mechanical as fiction,"
its only interest "is for the record, to show what the New
Deal seemed like to Mr. Dos Passos." Remarks that Dos
Passos is respectful of the idealism which initiated the
New Deal, contemptuous of the pragmatic politics which
made it function.

31 ROBINSON, HENRY MORTON. "Socio-Economic Surface." Saturday
     Review of Literature, 32 (8 January), 8-9.
        Offers Dos Passos "a few tough-hearted truths" about
The Grand Design. Feels that Dos Passos' greatest problem
is that he continues to work the exhausted mine of literary
naturalism. Also, Dos Passos ignores psychological man,
presenting him as entirely a socioeconomic creature. As a
result, the "characters are pygmies." Feels that unless Dos
Passos can change his portrayal of character to be more
inclusive "he cannot hope to be regarded as a continuing
force in American letters."

32 ROLLO, CHARLES J. "Reader's Choice." Atlantic Monthly, 183
     (February), 84-86.
        Thinks The Grand Design much more impressive than its
immediate predecessors because Dos Passos makes use of his
special talent, "his gift for sharp, pulsing documentation
of the social scene." Argues that Dos Passos' political
protest is not political at all, but "an expression of disgust with human beings, with Being itself" which will not
allow him to express affirmation.

33 SARTRE, JEAN-PAUL. What Is Literature? Translated by Bernard
      Frechtman. New York: Philosophical Library, p. 228.
        Feels that the success of Faulkner, Doss Passos, and
      Hemingway was the result of "the defense reflex of a litera-
      ture which, feeling itself threatened because its tech-
      niques and its myths were no longer going to allow it to
      cope with the historical situation, grafted foreign methods
      upon itself in order to be able to fulfill its function in
      new situations."

34 TRILLING, DIANA. "Fiction in Review." Nation, 168
      (22 January), 107-108.
        Is dismayed by the unfairness and bitter tone of The
      Grand Design. Asks "why could not the short acute vision
      of the world which Mr. Dos Passos had as a radical novelist
      have widened with the years to the compass of tragedy
      rather than narrowed as it has, to the compass of bitter-
      ness?" Feels the greatest fault is gross oversimplification
      of the democratic political system and adherence to the
      great-man notion of history which here attributes all to
      one man: FDR.

35 TRILLING, LIONEL. "Contemporary American Literature in Its
      Relation to Ideas." American Quarterly, 1 (Fall), 195-208.
        Concludes that it is a basic lack of intellectual power
      that makes Dos Passos--along with O'Neill and Wolfe--so
      inadequate aesthetically and emotionally despite our initial
      interest.

1950 A BOOKS

  1 POTTER, JACK. Bibliography of John Dos Passos. Chicago:
       Normandie House, 95 pp.
         Primary and selected secondary bibliography, with a very
       brief introduction by Dos Passos.

1950 B SHORTER WRITINGS

  1 A., E. S. "Dos Passos Studies the U.S." New Bedford Standard-
       Times (19 November).
         Calls The Prospect Before Us a "constructive message"
       that we need to come to know our country again.

  2 ANON. "Apathy of Our Citizens." St. Louis Post-Dispatch
       (27 December).
         Feels that The Prospect Before Us is interesting although
       it says nothing really new. Considers the lecture format to
       be particularly awkward and annoying.

1950

3 ANON. "Dos Passos Discusses U.S. Basic Ideals." Fort Worth
  Star-Telegram (31 December).
       Summarizes The Prospect Before Us.

4 ANON. "Double Dos Passos." New York Herald Tribune
  (28 September).
       Announces the forthcoming publication of District of
  Columbia and The Prospect Before Us.

5 ANON. "It's Not All Black." Columbia Missourian
  (21 October).
       Finds Dos Passos' prognosis for America, in The Prospect
  Before Us, sober but not discouraging.

6 ANON. "Master Reviews Modern Scene." Armarillo News
  (5 November).
       Summarizes the contents of The Prospect Before Us.
  Feels that "the ingenious form of the book doesn't make
  for as lively a give-and-take as might be expected."

7 ANON. "More Dos Passos." Daily Oklahoman (17 September).
       Notes the upcoming publication of The Prospect Before Us.

8 ANON. Note about District of Columbia. San Francisco
  Argonaut (29 September).
       Notes the forthcoming publication of District of
  Columbia.

9 ANON. Note about District of Columbia. Washington Post
  (17 September).
       Announces forthcoming publication.

10 ANON. "The Physician Forgets to Prescribe." San Francisco
  Argonaut (17 November).
       Regrets that, in The Prospect Before Us, "the author
  does not proceed beyond the diagnosis to suggest a remedy."

11 ANON. "Political Traveler." Newsweek, 36 (23 October), 102-
  103.
       Feels that Dos Passos' "word pictures" in The Prospect
  Before Us have "the bleached, unshadowed, unretouched,
  unromanticized authenticity of Mathew Brady's great Civil
  War photographs."

12 ANON. "Problem of Adjustment." Los Angeles Times
  (19 November).
       Dislikes the lecturer-audience structure of The Prospect
  Before Us, yet finds "the importance of the problems

1950

presented and the sincerity of the author" make it worthwhile reading.

13 ANON. Review of The Prospect Before Us. Booklist, 47
       (15 November), 110.
          Calls The Prospect Before Us a series of "occasionally
       lively lectures" with a "cautiously optimistic conclusion."

14 ANON. Review of The Prospect Before Us. Boston Globe
       (22 October).
          Calls the book "stimulating" and Dos Passos "the
       champion of the individual."

15 ANON. Review of The Prospect Before Us. Columbia (S.C.)
       Record (23 November).
          Calls the book "lively, humorous, often satirical, ini-
       mitably Dos Passos, which run[s] the gamut from exhortation
       to quip and paradox."

16 ANON. Review of The Prospect Before Us. Columbis (Ohio)
       Citizen (29 October).
          Calls the book "passionately in favor of the 'American
       Way of Life.'"

17 ANON. Review of The Prospect Before Us. Fort Wayne News-
       Sentinel (16 December).
          Feels the book offers an important warning about the
       dangers of socialism.

18 ANON. Review of The Prospect Before Us. Knoxville News
       Sentinel (29 October).
          Feels that "Dos Passos' thought is sharp and clear and
       his prose style very fine."

19 ANON. Review of The Prospect Before Us. The New Yorker, 26
       (11 November), 166-167.
          Calls the book "a rather tentative effort, sometimes
       provocative and sometimes provoking, to evaluate the mess
       that man has got himself into."

20 ANON. Review of The Prospect Before Us. San Antonio Express
       (12 November).
          Very brief review.

21 ANON. Review of The Prospect Before Us. San Francisco Call
       Bulletin (11 November).
          Calls the book "a thoughtful, 'whither-are-we-drifting'
       sort of dissertation."

1950

22 ANON. Review of <u>The Prospect Before Us</u>. <u>Virginia Kirkus</u>
    <u>Bulletin</u>, 18 (15 August), 505.
        Admires Dos Passos' reporting, but, "when he poses as a
    lecturer . . . he is stilted and dull." Feels the book has
    "a few high spots--a good many low spots."

23 ANON. "Think Piece." <u>Omaha World Herald</u> (5 November).
        Thinks that while <u>The Prospect Before Us</u> does not pro-
    vide answers, it does raise important questions about post-
    war American society.

24 ANON. "Time for Decision." <u>Buffalo Evening News</u> (28 October).
        Review of <u>The Prospect Before Us</u> which focuses on Dos
    Passos' warnings about the dangers of English socialism.

25 ANON. "The Traveller." <u>Time</u>, 56 (30 October), 106, 108-109.
        Sees <u>The Prospect Before Us</u> as a stage in Dos Passos'
    "long road back" from Marxism. Feels the lecturer-audience
    format of the book is a shrewd and persuasive means of show-
    ing the thinking of the average American. Identifies Dos
    Passos' primary concern as the danger of institutional
    bigness.

26 ANON. "Two Paeans for the American Way." <u>The Washington Post</u>
    (22 October).
        Calls <u>The Prospect Before Us</u> "a book which is passionately
    in favor of what remains of 'the American Way of Life.'"

27 ANON. "World-Wide Study of Men and Ideas." <u>Boston Sunday</u>
    <u>Post</u> (29 October).
        Calls <u>The Prospect Before Us</u> "a highly informative and
    stimulating book . . . a penetrating and understanding
    account of political and social attitudes."

28 B., E. T. "Dos Passos Studies Western World." <u>Lewiston-</u>
    <u>Auburn [Maine] Journal</u> (18 November).
        Calls <u>The Prospect Before Us</u> "a grassroots examination
    of postwar life in the western world." Notes "overtones of
    satiric humor."

29 B., J. "No Pleasant Prospect." <u>Youngstown [Ohio] Vindicator</u>
    (12 November).
        Calls <u>The Prospect Before Us</u> an "incisive, hard-hitting
    book."

30 B., V. A. "Dos Passos Tussles with Today's Ills." <u>Chicago</u>
    <u>Daily News</u> (25 October).
        Summarizes <u>The Prospect Before Us</u>, identifying Dos
    Passos' main concern as "centralization."

31 BAGDIKIAN, BEN H. "Political Travel." Providence Journal
      (22 October).
          Finds little new or of interest in The Prospect Before
      Us. Feels the book is stylistically jumbled and structurally
      pompous.

32 BAIRD, JOSEPH H. Review of The Prospect Before Us. Florida
      Sun (12 November).
          Calls The Prospect Before Us "a stimulating book" and
      admires the constructive attitude which has replaced Dos
      Pasos' earlier cynicism.

33 BARBER, LAWRENCE L., JR. "Buried Deep." Hartford Sunday
      Courant (26 November).
          Considers The Prospect Before Us generally well written,
      yet disappointing when compared to U.S.A.

34 BECK, WARREN. "Faulkner Versus Hemingway." Madison [Wis.]
      Journal (24 December).
          Summary of literary news of the year. Feels that
      Faulkner's star has risen while Hemingway's has fallen;
      Dos Passos and Steinbeck, "the two runners-up [have]
      lagged far behind."

35 BRADLEY, JOHN L. "World-Wide Study of Men and Ideas." Boston
      Post (29 October).
          Calls The Prospect Before Us "the work of a man who has
      obviously made sincere efforts to understand the civiliza-
      tions under his scrutiny."

36 BRANIGAN, ALAN. "The World Today." Newark News (3 December).
          Thinks The Prospect Before Us well structured and well
      written. Especially likes Dos Passos' analysis of political
      trends in Great Britain.

37 BREIT, HARVEY. "Talk With Mr. Dos Passos." New York Times
      Book Review (12 November), p. 53.
          Dos Passos says: that alternating between fiction and
      journalism is an old pattern for him, going back to the
      twenties; that he is attempting a "big term experiment":
      trying to create "a series of written photographs of in-
      stitutions as they develop"; that he finds American society
      more fluid and more encouraging than European society.

38 BRENNAN, JOSEPH PAYNE. "Dos Passos Fears Apathy." New Haven
      Sunday Register (19 November).
          Feels that although The Prospect Before Us "has its
      lapses of verbosity and tediousness, it remains stimulating
      and enormously informative."

1950

39 CLARK, JOHN ABBOT. "Saving Our Republic Is Individual Job."
    Chicago Sun Tribune (17 December), p. 8.
        Applauds Dos Passos' invocation of traditional values
    in The Prospect Before Us.

40 COHN, DAVID L. "Has Humanity Got Above Its Raisin?" New York
    Times Book Review (22 October), p. 16.
        Review of The Prospect Before Us--"no bookish book"--
    which focuses on Dos Passos' political questions.

41 COMMAGER, HENRY STEELE. "The Literature of Revolt," in his
    The American Mind. New Haven: Yale University Press, pp.
    267-271, passim.
        Calls Dos Passos "the most social minded of the social
    novelists" of his time and characterizes U.S.A. as "a kind
    of Domesday Book, a Calendar of Sin, and Index-Expurgatorius
    of economic malpractices."

42 CRIDEN, JOHN H. "Thoughts on Books." Boston Herald
    (23 October).
        Feels that The Prospect Before Us "comes to grips with
    the real world," and reveals Dos Passos' gifts as a "skill-
    ful reporter and political philosopher."

43 CROSSEN, KEN. "Novelist Dos Passos Objects to Government
    Interference." Los Angeles News (18 November).
        Feels that the execution of The Prospect Before Us does
    not live up to the material's promise: "I can't think of a
    better premise for a novel--nor have I ever seen a sorrier
    delivery of what is promised." Calls the book "some of the
    most boring reading I've done in ages." Concludes that the
    book is little more than a sentimental wish to return to
    the past.

44 D., E. V. "Dos Passos Surveys What People Expect." Hartford
    Times (19 December).
        Calls Dos Passos in The Prospect Before Us "an alert
    and observing reporter [who] depends upon people, not
    statistics. Finds the chapters on South America "especially
    sharp and colorful."

45 D[ANIEL], T[HOMAS] H. "Dos Passos Says Man Menaced by Con-
    centration of Powers." Columbia Record (8 December).
        Does not feel that Dos Passos' views, as expressed in
    The Prospect Before Us, are encouraging. Reprinted:
    1950.B46.

46 D., T. H. Review of The Prospect Before Us. Easley Progress
    (28 December).
       Reprint of 1950.B45.

47 DAVIS, CURTIS CARROLL. "A Novelist Looks At Our World."
    Baltimore Evening Sun (28 October).
       Summarizes the book and concludes that since there are
    many good journalists and but a few good novelists, Dos
    Passos would be wise to use his energies writing fiction.

48 DERBY, DONALD. "Corporate Bigness." Springfield Republican
    (12 November).
       Feels that, since The Prospect Before Us offers no
    solutions, "it would deserve little attention except for
    the fact that it was written by John Dos Passos." Identi-
    fies Dos Passos' major theme as the danger of "corporate
    bigness," whether it occurs in business, government, or
    labor.

49 DIAMOND, R. "Dos Passos Weighs Future Chances." Rochester
    Democrat and Chronicle (17 December).
       Feels that The Prospect Before Us, "with deft logic, and
    firm realism . . . succeeds in enlightening the populace as
    to the best way of coping with public problems."

50 F., P. "Not Entirely Hopeless." Charleston News-Courier
    (19 November).
       Feels that Dos Passos is an excellent reporter and ob-
    server in The Prospect Before Us, but that his imperson-
    ality is "repellant."

51 FREEHAFER, JOHN. Review of The Prospect Before Us.
    Philadelphia Forum (December).
       Feels that the "crackerbarrel philosophy" of the book
    is hardly enlightening, but admires Dos Passos' "vivid,
    panoramic reporting."

52 FROHOCK, W. M. "John Dos Passos: Of Time and Frustration," in
    his The Novel of Violence in America, 1920-1950. Dallas:
    Southern Methodist University Press, pp. 17-45, passim.
       Reprint of 1948.B4.

53 GRAY, JAMES. "Tenderly Tolls the Bells for Three Soldiers,"
    in Ernest Hemingway: The Man and His Work. Edited by
    John K. M. McCaffery. Cleveland: World, pp. 226-235.
       Reprint of 1946.B43.

1950

54 HACKFORD, R. R. "Apathy of Our Citizens." St. Louis Post-
     Dispatch (27 December).
         Calls The Prospect Before Us "a wandering collection of
     impressions strung together through the awkward device of
     pretending that the whole performance is a series of
     lectures."

55 HANSEN, HARRY. "John Dos Passos, Author and Farmer." Chicago
     Sunday Tribune (5 November).
         Hansen and Dos Passos talk about farming and also agree
     that Cummings' The Enormous Room is a "great American story."

56 HICKS, GRANVILLE. "The Politics of John Dos Passos." Antioch
     Review, 10 (Spring), 85-98.
         Noting Dos Passos' transition from the political left to
     the political right, Hicks maintains that "his political
     development is a significant phenomenon of our time."
     Finds it ironic that, when aligned with the left, Dos Passos
     shied away from dogmatism was flexible and open minded, but,
     in moving to the right, he "stumbled into a kind of abso-
     lutism." Sees Dos Passos' continuing dilemma to be an in-
     ability to find an alternative to the impersonality of
     both big business and big government. Concludes that Dos
     Passos has lost touch with his times and that is a particu-
     larly debilitating experience for a primarily impersonal
     social writer. Reprinted: 1971.A2; 1974.A3.

57 HOLLAND, E. L., JR. "Reporting A Nation." Birmingham News
     (24 October).
         Calls The Prospect Before Us an honest book, but feels
     that Dos Passos may have over-simplified the issues to the
     point of misrepresenting his subject.

58 HOWE, IRVING. "John Dos Passos: The Loss of Passion."
     Anvil and Student Partisan, 2 (Fall), 11-13.
         Reprint of 1949.B23.

59 IRVING, MARGARET. "Sober and Chilling Glimpses of the Brave
     New World." Worchester Sunday Telegram (29 October).
         Feels that the lecture portions of The Prospect Before
     Us are "needlessly patronizing," but that "the main body of
     the work is honest, sober, and a little chilling."

60 JACKSON, JOSEPH HENRY. "Dos Passos' Prognosis." San Francisco
     Chronicle (1 November).
         Summarizes the questions Dos Passos raises and answers
     in The Prospect Before Us. Feels that the lecture device
     "at first seems almost frivolous, but it turns out to be
     ideal for his purpose."

61 JACKSON, MARGOT. "Question He Asked Akron Persons Is Peg For
    Don [sic] Passos' New York." Akron Beacon Journal
    (19 November).
        Feels that, in The Prospect Before Us, "the meat, the
    rekindling of purpose, the feeling of uniting for the ex-
    citement of living, rather than warring, is ever uppermost."

62 JAUCHIUS, RONNIE. "Wry Analysis of Contemporary Scene."
    Columbus Dispatch (29 October).
        Calls The Prospect Before Us occasionally humorous, but
    basically a "dispassionate and penetrating observation" of
    the contemporary world.

63 KALLICH, MARTIN. "John Dos Passos: Liberty and the Father
    Image." Antioch Review, 10 (Spring), 99-106.
        Finds consistency in Dos Passos' career, in his "liber-
    tarian anarchism" which is "unmistakably accompanied, and
    in part conditioned, by an Oedipus Complex." Traces this
    anarchism through three stages: individualist; socialist
    (or syndicalist), and conservative. Reprinted: 1971.A2.

64 KEY, V. O., JR. "The Problem of Our Times." New Republic,
    123 (4 December), 19-20.
        Sees The Prospect Before Us as an "individual, episodic,
    personal" critique of contemporary society. Pinpoints Dos
    Passos' identification of the central problem of our times
    as "the contrivance of means to control, in the interest of
    individual men, by the corporations, or bureaucracies that
    boss us." Finds little original theory in the book but
    admires it as "a piece of perceptive reporting . . . on the
    anxieties, beliefs, and hopes of a real people."

65 KUHL, ARTHUR. Review of The Prospect Before Us. St. Louis
    Star-Times (22 November), p. 15.
        Feels the book is excellent when it is most descriptive,
    but that it degenerates as it progresses because it becomes
    too abstract, too dependent on vague generalizations.

66 L., E. A. "No Two Alike." Boston Globe (22 October).
        Calls The Prospect Before Us "stimulating" and calls Dos
    Passos "the champion of the individual."

67 L., G. "Dos Passos Discusses Prospect Before Us." Long Beach
    Press Telegram (12 November).
        Feels the structure of The Prospect Before Us seems
    awkward at first, but is, in fact, "perfect for the
    subject."

1950

68 LEVIN, HARRY. "Some European Views of Contemporary American
    Literature," in The American Writer and the European
    Tradition. Edited by Margaret Denny and William H. Gilman.
    Minneapolis: University of Minnesota Press, pp. 168-183.
         Notes Dos Passos' influence on French writers, particu-
    larly Sartre.

69 McHUGH, VINCENT. "Dos Passos and the Thirty Thousand Souls."
    in Writers of Our Years. Edited by A.M.I. Fiskin. Denver:
    The University of Denver Press, pp. 79-100.
         Emphasizes the breadth of Dos Passos' interests and in-
    fluences and the diversity of his writing, his individual-
    istic philosophy, and the rigorous objectivity of his style.
    Thinks that the technical innovations of U.S.A., which
    seemed so garish at first, have, with time, come to seem
    appropriate for his purpose.

70 MASON, ROBERT. "Dos Passos Lectures." Norfolk Pilot
    (21 October).
         Review of The Prospect Before Us which concentrates on
    Dos Passos' criticism of British socialism.

71 MEDLOCK, H. "Dos Passos Examines Future." Dayton News
    (3 December).
         Summary of The Prospect Before Us.

72 MIZENER, ARTHUR. "The Novel of Manners in America." Kenyon
    Review, 12 (Winter), 1-19.
         Discusses the problem of writing a modern American novel
    of manners by focusing on the work of Dos Passos and
    Fitzgerald. Thinks Dos Passos represents a strain of
    novelists whose primary interest is social, but he also
    possesses an ability to adequately create more personal
    characters who do more than merely represent social atti-
    tudes. Fitzgerald represents the other type of novelist
    whose focus is primarily on the individual. Feels that
    neither can quite wed the social and the personal, but
    feels that if there is to be a novel of manners in America,
    "it will probably come from Fitzgerald's kind of novel
    rather than Dos Passos.'"

73 MOWRER, EDGAR ANSEL. "Liberty and Democratic Participation."
    Saturday Review of Literature, 33 (4 November), 14-15.
         Summarizes the contents of The Prospect Before Us.

74 MURPHREE, ALEX. "A Pale-Pink Dos Passos Raps All Political
    Forms." Denver Post (19 November).

Notes Dos Passos' more recent conservatism. Considers
The Prospect Before Us to be incisive and well written,
"filled with apt observation."

75 NIXON, H. C. "Dos Passos Makes Report." Nashville Tennessean
      (31 December).
        Calls The Prospect Before Us "an attempt to mix the roles
      of reporter and editor within a fictionalized framework."
      Concludes that Dos Passos' "reporting is better than the
      editorializing or the fictionizing."

76 NORTH, STERLING. "Dos Passos." St. Petersburg Times
      (5 November).
        Summary of The Prospect Before Us which focuses on Dos
      Passos' criticism of British socialism. Reprinted: 1950.B77;
      1950.B78.

77 _____. "Dos Passos Study Finds Welfare State a Flop."
      Cleveland News (18 October).
        Reprint of 1950.B76.

78 _____. "2 Paeans For the American Way." Washington Post
      (22 October).
        Reprint of 1950.B76.

79 O'NEAL, COTHBURN M. "There's Yet Time For Freedom, Says Dos
      Passos." Dallas Times-Herald (29 October).
        Calls the thesis of The Prospect Before Us "valid and
      valuable" but finds the structure and style weak: "The
      mannerisms of the lectures, pitilessly painful as straight
      satire, become unbearably irritating as the means of es-
      tablishing a polemic."

80 P., R. L. "John Dos Passos Has Gone to Pot, His Latest Book
      Convinces Critic." Rocky Mountain News (22 October), p. 16a.
        Calls The Prospect Before Us "a tiresome and tiring bit
      of intellectual demagoguery which blunts itself by continual
      attack." Feels that Dos Passos has moved from an honest
      doubting liberalism "into a stage of omnipotent, self-
      confident conservation [sic]."

81 PORTER, EUGENE O. Review of The Prospect Before Us. El Paso
      Herald Post (9 December).
        Identifies Dos Passos' greatest concern as the survival
      of the individual and of society and his greatest foe as
      apathy.

1950

82 ROGERS, W. G. "Among New Books." Fitchburg [Mass.] Sentinel
(27 October).
     Does not find the form of The Prospect Before Us parti-
cularly effective or the views particularly new. Reprinted:
     _____. "Books In Review." Keene [N.H.] Sentinel
(20 November).
     _____. "Definite Ideas About World." Augusta [Ga.] Herald
(22 October).
     _____. "Literary Guidepost." Augusta [Maine] Kennebec
Journal (28 October).
     _____. "Literary Guidepost." Chambersburg [Pa.] Opinion
(30 October).
     _____. "Literary Guidepost." Grand Island [Nebr.] Independent
(27 October).
     _____. Review of The Prospect Before Us. Augusta [Ga.]
Chronicle (22 October).

83 ROLLO, CHARLES J. "Men Working." Atlantic Monthly, 186
(November), 96-98.
     Impressed with the preamble of The Prospect Before Us
which seems to promise an enlightened discussion of the
inevitable symbiotic relationship between modern technology
and collectivism, but finds the bulk of the book to be
mostly superficial despite brilliant reporting at times.
Identifies a basic paradox which informs the work: it
"reflects a curious blend of sentimental old fashioned
individualism and hard, forward looking devotion to technology, [which] looks to me like making the worst of both
worlds."

84 SHERMAN, JOHN K. "Dos Passos Fears Blight of Protective
Governments." Minneapolis Tribune (10 December).
     Considers The Prospect Before Us a balanced analysis of
the contemporary world.

85 STERN, MORT. "Our Fate in a Complex World." Arkansas Gazette
(5 November).
     Summarizes The Prospect Before Us. Feels that Dos
Passos' methods "are like those of the traveling medicine
men, but his medicine, if taken faithfully, might do a
world of good."

86 T., F. "Prospects for Freedom Analyzed by Dos Passos."
Amarillo News (10 November).
     Calls The Prospect Before Us "the latest in an increas-
ingly anxious and fevered parade of books aimed at per-
suading us, the apathetic public, to think again." Feels
that Dos Passos paints accurately "the mental confusion

under which the citizen today labors" but is "less satis-
factory in his solution" of grassroots political action.

87   THOMAS, NORMAN. "Casual Reflections of a Random Rover."
     New York Herald Tribune Book Review (5 November), p. 4.
        Thinks The Prospect Before Us is only "a minor event."
     Finds the lecture-discussion format banal and objects to
     Dos Passos' oversimplified analysis of the British Labor
     government.

88   URCH, ERWIN J. "Prospect Is Not All Black For These Battling
     Times." Toledo Blade (29 October).
        Calls The Prospect Before Us "accurate and realistic,"
     filled with "impressive observations and thoughtful
     interpretations."

89   W., L. A. "Downfall of Nations Is Bigness, Not 'Isms,' Dos
     Passos Warns." Columbia Missourian (20 November).
        Calls Dos Passos both "unreactionary" and "unliberal,"
     opposed to bigness in any form. Finds The Prospect Before
     Us a perceptive analysis of the problems of the present
     and challenges of the future, but feels that Dos Passos
     should go a step further and at least suggest methods of
     insuring a successful future.

90   WARD, LEO R. "Some Ideas About 'Isms.'" Books On Trial
     (December-January).
        Doesn't feel that The Prospect Before Us is "based on
     any profound knowledge of man and society or any exact
     knowledge of history, politics, or economics."

91   WHITE, WILLIAM. "John Dos Passos and His Reviewers."
     Bulletin of Bibliography, 20 (May-August), 45-47.
        Bibliography of reviews of Dos Passos' work, arranged
     by book, from Three Soldiers to The Grand Design.

92   WHITFORD, ROBERT C. Review of The Prospect Before Us.
     Brooklyn Eagle (10 December).
        Calls the book passionate and "closely reasoned," but
     finds the format somewhat distracting.

93   WILSON, EDMUND. "Archibald MacLeish and the Word," in his
     Classics and Commercials: A Literary Chronicle of the
     Forties. New York: Farrar, Straus, pp. 3-4.
        Reprint of 1940.B9.

1951

1951 A BOOKS - NONE

1951 B SHORTER WRITINGS

1 ALDRIDGE, JOHN W. "Dos Passos: The Energy of Despair," in his
   After the Lost Generation: A Critical Study of the Writers
   of Two Wars. New York: McGraw-Hill Book Company, pp. 59-
   81, passim.
       Surveys Dos Passos' career which is characterized as "a
   long process of running through and destroying the ideals
   which have seemed to him worthy of belief." Thinks that
   U.S.A. "achieved a perfect blend of protest and negation,"
   but he has finally "run through" all the ideals and is now
   "left with nothing." Reprinted: 1972.B1.

2 ANON. "Eighty Years With Dos Passos." Time, 58 (3 December),
   112.
       Feels the only ground covered in the eighty-year narra-
   tive time span of Chosen Country to be "from soapbox to
   soap opera and back." Thinks the hero, Jay Pignatelli, a
   bore and concludes that "Dos Passos was better when he was
   angry."

3 ANON. "Family Background." Newsweek, 38 (3 December), 98-99.
       Calls Chosen Country "a perfect period piece."

4 ANON. Review of Chosen Country. Virginia Kirkus Service, 19
   (15 October), 622.
       Finds the novel "abysmally boring," marred by "all of
   his weaknesses of loose construction, non-sequiturs, slip-
   shod writing, etc., and few of his strengths."

5 ANON. Review of The Prospect Before Us. Foreign Affairs, 30
   (October), 153.
       Brief review.

6 ANON. Review of The Prospect Before Us. Lewiston [Idaho]
   Tribune (28 January).
       Calls the book a "cautiously optimistic . . . object
   lesson in political and social trends in the western world
   today."

7 ANON. Review of The Prospect Before Us. Stars and Stripes
   (7 January).
       Feels that Dos Passos' findings are "disturbing, thought-
   provoking, but not without hope."

8   ANON.   Review of The Prospect Before Us. Tacoma News Tribune
     (19 February).
          Brief summary of the book.

9   ANON.   Short Notice.   Milwaukee Journal (6 December).
          Dos Passos recommends several recently read books.

*10 BROWN, DEMING B.   "American Authors in Soviet Russia: 1917–
     1951." Unpublished doctoral dissertation, Columbia
     University.
          Cited in "John Dos Passos Bibliography 1950–1966" by
     Virginia S. Reinhart. Twentieth Century Literature, 13
     (1967), 167–178.

11 BUTCHER, FANNY.   "Dos Passos Experiments With 'Feverish
     Honesty.'"   Chicago Sunday Tribune (9 December), p. 5.
          Considers Chosen Country an experimental novel which
     tests the premise that "philosphically, any man or woman
     is emotionally the sum of his forbears and, technically,
     that the story of any major character is the sum of the
     stories of his or her forbears."

12 BYAM, MILTON S.   Review of Chosen Country. Library Journal,
     76 (15 November), 1929.
          Calls Chosen Country "a hymn, written in the rich Dos
     Passos prose, that expresses a great love for our country,
     as it does for mankind, even though it details the evil
     too."

13 DERLETH, AUGUST.   "Books of Today." Madison Capital Times
     (3 March).
          Calls The Prospect Before Us "a grassroots examination
     of post-war life in the western world. . . . A book for
     our times."

14 DOWNER, ALAN S.   Fifty Years of American Drama, 1900–1950.
     Chicago: Henry Regnery Co., pp. 113–114.
          Notes Dos Passos' admiration for American popular forms
     of theatre: vaudeville, burlesque, and musical comedy.

15 DREISER, HELEN.   My Life with Dreiser. Cleveland and New
     York: The World Publishing Co., pp. 110, 225.
          Mentions Dos Passos.

*16 GELFANT, BLANCH H.   "The American City Novel, 1900–1940: A
     Study of the Literary Treatment of the City in Dreiser,
     Dos Passos and Farrell." Unpublished doctoral dissertation,
     University of Wisconsin.

1951

17 HOLLOWAY, MAURICE, S. J. Review of The Prospect Before Us. Indiana Catholic Record (25 January).
Feels that, while the style is often jumbled, "the book is a valuable effort in the fight for freedom."

18 LEAVIS, Q. D. "Hawthorne as Poet, Part II." Sewanee Review, 59 (Summer), 426-458.
Feels that Hawthorne, in The Blithedale Romance, had anticipated Dos Passos' "discovery of the Two Nations, symbolized at the end of U.S.A. in a neat parable but, compared with Hawthorne's, artistically barbarous."

19 LYNDENBERG, JOHN. "Dos Passos and the Ruined Words." Pacific Spectator, 5 (Summer, 1951), 316-327.
Detailed analysis of the novels of District of Columbia in which Lyndenberg suggests that this trilogy fails to measure up to U.S.A. for while "U.S.A. is rigidly amoral in form, but moral in its impress; District of Columbia is explicitly moral in many of its concerns, but amoral in its total effect." This because, while Dos Passos is essentially a moralist, his explicit pronouncements are peculiarly flat and lifeless, in part because his attitude toward his material changed from critical to cynical.

20 McLUHAN, HERBERT MARSHALL. "John Dos Passos: Technique vs. Sensibility," in Fifty Years of the American Novel: A Christian Appraisal. Edited by Harold C. Gardiner. New York: Charles Scribner's Sons, pp. 151-164.
Thinks that Dos Passos experiments in technique owe a great debt to Joyce, but while Joyce is concerned with both the outer and inner worlds of his characters, Dos Passos is only interested in the outer. "Joyce contemplates things for the being that is theirs. Dos Passos shows how they work or behave." Identifies "a pathos free from self-pity" as the "predominant and persistent note" in Dos Passos' writing. Reprinted: 1963.B69; 1971.A2; 1974.A3.

21 MATTHIESSEN, F. O. Theodore Dreiser, in the American Men of Letters Series. New York: William Sloane Associates, pp. 187, 229, 246.
Passing reference to Dos Passos.

22 MEHRING, WALTER. The Lost Library: The Autobiography of a Culture. Translated from the German by Richard and Clare Winston. Indianapolis: Bobbs-Merrill, p. 221.
In a listing of different categories of modernistic devices, mentions Dos Passos' work as the example of "American montage novels, presenting simultaneous big-city lives in slow motion."

23 MIZENER, ARTHUR. "Dos Passos' Story of the Yearning That Makes
    Americans." <u>New York Times Book Review</u> (2 December), p. 7.
        Believes <u>Chosen Country</u> "may well be John Dos Passos'
    best novel" because it possesses a sympathy for his charac-
    ters lacking in the earlier works. This sympathy is en-
    hanced by Dos Passos' normal fast-paced narrative and sharp
    eye for detail.

24 _____. "The Gullivers of Dos Passos." <u>Saturday Review</u>, 34
    (30 June), 6, 7, 34-36.
        Considers Dos Passos as a satirist in the Ben Jonson and
    Jonathan Swift tradition. Thinks that <u>U.S.A.</u> and the novels
    which follow are a brilliant extension of the picaresque
    tradition. Thinks Dos Passos' "flat, deadly accurate, and
    devastating prose" is a perfect vehicle for capturing the
    "essential horror" of the life he portrays. Reprinted:
    1971.A2; 1974.A3.

25 _____. <u>The Far Side of Paradise: A Biography of F. Scott
    Fitzgerald</u>. Boston: Houghton Mifflin Co., pp. xii, 111,
    112, 151.
        Several references to Dos Passos including a quotation
    from Fitzgerald's favorable review of <u>Three Soldiers</u>.

26 QUINN, ARTHUR HOBSON, ed. <u>The Literature of the American
    People</u>. New York: Appleton-Century-Crofts, Inc., pp. 651,
    880-882, 900, 957, 965.
        Finds the "stylistic oddities" of <u>U.S.A.</u> to be "ugly"
    and the pessimism almost unbearable: "Where everyone is
    rotten and everything is slimy, comparative values are
    impossible. Dos Passos presents us with such a monotony
    of disintegration that the reader's nerves become desensi-
    tized and refuse to function."

27 REYNOLDS, JOHN. "Long Range." <u>Cedar Rapids Gazette</u>
    (3 January).
        Calls <u>The Prospect Before Us</u> "a cleverly presented
    series of grassroots 'lectures.'"

28 RUGOFF, MILTON. "Rich Ore Mined From a Familiar Vein." <u>New
    York Herald Tribune Book Review</u> (2 December), p. 5.
        Thinks that <u>Chosen Country</u> "feels more like a major
    novel . . . than any Dos Passos has undertaken in a long
    time." Finds the characterization effective. Calls the
    mixing of the private and the public, similar to the tech-
    nique of <u>U.S.A.</u>, "the kind of writing in which Dos Passos
    is at his best."

1951

29 SCHERILL, JAMES. Sherwood Anderson: His Life and Work.
      Denver: University of Denver Press, pp. 135, 227, 286, 352.
      Briefly mentions Dos Passos in several contexts.

30 SMITH, HARRISON. "Welding the Past and the Present."
      Saturday Review of Literature, 34 (15 December), 19-20.
          Finds Chosen Country badly disjointed, little more than
      a collection of stories, many of which are in themselves
      excellent. Feels the novel is uneven and poorly balanced
      and finds the ending "as slick and as artificially em-
      broidered as a banal love story in a mass circulation
      magazine."

31 STRAUMANN, HEINRICH. American Literature in the Twentieth
      Century. London: Hutchinsen's University Library, pp. 33-
      40, passim.
          Views Dos Passos as one of the few successful moralists
      among contemporary novelists. Considers his ideas consis-
      tent throughout his career if he is viewed as an individual-
      ist whose primary sympathies lie with the underdog. Thinks
      the topicality of Dos Passos' fiction may make it unlikely
      to endure as long as the work of less gifted contemporaries.

32 WARFEL, HARRY REDCAY. American Novelists of Today. New York:
      American Book Company, pp. 122-124.
          Summary of the life and writings of John Dos Passos.

33 WHITE, WILLIAM. "More Dos Passos Bibliographic Addenda."
      Papers of the American Bibliographic Society, 45 (February),
      156-158.
          Primary and secondary items.

34 WINGFIELD, MARSHALL. "Individualism Is Lost In Prospect
      Before Us." Jackson Sun (4 February).
          Summary of the content of The Prospect Before Us: "The
      great question of the book is how can the ordinary individual
      avoid being crushed by corporate state, corporate capital,
      and corporate labor."

1952 A BOOKS - NONE

1952 B SHORTER WRITINGS

1 ANON. Review of Chosen Country. Booklist, 48 (1 January),
      159.
          Brief plot summary of Chosen Country.

1952

2 ANON. Review of <u>District of Columbia</u>. <u>Booklist</u>, 48 (15 April), 267.
   Notes the reprint in one volume of <u>Adventures of a Young Man</u>, <u>Number One</u>, and <u>The Grand Design</u>.

3 BAKER, CARLOS. <u>Hemingway: The Writer as Artist</u>. Princeton: Princeton University Press, pp. 18-46, passim.
   Occasional references to the personal and artistic relationship between Dos Passos and Hemingway.

4 BROOKS, VAN WYCK. <u>The Confident Years: 1885-1915</u>. New York: E. P. Dutton, pp. 325, 407, 542n.
   Notes the concern for the craft of writing in Hemingway and Dos Passos' generation.

5 BRUNN, ROBERT R. Review of <u>Chosen Country</u>. <u>Christian Science Monitor</u> (3 January), p. 7.
   Feels that <u>Chosen Country</u> has "a bouyant, almost joyous quality about it," in contrast both to Dos Passos' earlier work and the work of post-World War II novelists.

6 CHERNE, LEO. "The Writer and the Entrepreneur." <u>Saturday Review</u>, 35 (19 January), 10-11, 37-39.
   Traces the image of the American businessman in modern American literature, concluding that "the American writer has helped shape America's view of its businessmen." Briefly mentions Dos Passos.

7 COURNOS, JOHN and SYBIL NORTON. <u>Famous Modern American Novelists</u>. Famous Biographies for Young People Series. New York: Dodd, Mead and Co., pp. 116-117.
   Quotes Dos Passos' praise of Fitzgerald's writing.

8 COWLEY, MALCOLM. "A Natural History of American Naturalism," in <u>Critiques and Essays on Modern Fiction, 1920-1951</u>. Edited by John W. Aldridge. New York: Ronald Press, pp. 370-387.
   Reprint of 1947.B8.

9 GEIST, STANLEY. "Fictitious Americans." <u>Hudson Review</u>, 5 (Summer), 199-211.
   Examines the character, J. Ward Moorehouse, who is little more than "a creation of Publicity." Geist concludes that, perhaps "recent American literature has created no figure so extraordinary in its symbolic resonance and so terrifying in its symbolic truth."

10 GURKO, LEO. "Dos Passos: The Second Trilogy." <u>Nation</u>, 174 (29 March), 304-305.

1952

Finds District of Columbia a less exciting trilogy than
U.S.A., primarily because of the "querulous tone, a sharp
recession in the reality of their characters; and a con-
traction of outlook on Dos Passos' part." Nevertheless,
Gurko finds a number of scenes which rank among Dos Passos'
best, indicating that "he retains the power to arouse and
persuade."

11 HICKS, GRANVILLE. "Confusions of an Era." New York Times
Book Review (27 April), p. 5.
Feels that in District of Columbia the whole is less than
the sum of its parts for these are three novels different in
method: Adventures of a Young Man is a picaresque; Number
One is "a drama of intrigue and betrayal"; The Grand Design
is in the manner of U.S.A. Considers Dos Passos to be
uniquely qualified to be a political novelist but feels that
since U.S.A. he has had no coherent political position and
has thus never reattained the artistic heights of the first
trilogy.

12 HORTON, ROD W. and HERBERT W. EDWARDS. Backgrounds of American
Literary Thought. New York: Appleton-Century-Crofts, Inc.,
pp. 240n, 241, 317, 321, 399.
A number of references to Dos Passos who is characterized
as "a sensitive artistic temperament brought face to face
with the brutality and cold cynicism of the modern mater-
ialist world."

13 HUGHES, RILEY. Review of District of Columbia. Catholic
World, 175 (May), 152.
Brief summary of the trilogy which concludes that most
readers and reviewers "have found in these pages an un-
shaped mass of vulgarity, pornographic sex realism, and
pretty elementary political commentary."

14 JONES, HOWARD MUMFORD. The Bright Medusa. Urbana: University
of Illinois Press, p. 65.
Lists Three Soldiers as one of the novels of the revolt
of youth against age which were so popular among Dos Passos'
generation and which Jones feels were inspired, in part, by
Fitzgerald's This Side of Paradise.

15 K., A. Review of District of Columbia. This World Magazine
of the San Francisco Chronicle (27 July), p. 13.
Notes that the publication of District of Columbia
will probably generate more political than esthetic
discussion.

16 POSTER, WILLIAM. "The Progress of John Dos Passos." American
    Mercury, 74 (March), 115-118.
        Finds Dos Passos' naturalistic emphasis on "overwhelming
    mass of detail and elaborate reconstructions of history"
    irritating, especially in the early novels. Thinks that
    Chosen Country, while still primarily naturalistic, pos-
    sesses "a more genuine, measured, and moving emotional
    release" than the earlier works. Thinks that "Dos Passos
    has shown an unparalleled capacity for growth, maintaining
    a certain dignity and honesty even when most obviously in
    error."

17 ROLLO, CHARLES J. "U.S.A. Revisited." Atlantic Monthly, 189
    (January), 87-88.
        Finds Chosen Country reminiscent of U.S.A., but, while
    superior to District of Columbia, it still pales in com-
    parison to U.S.A.: "The affirmation of Dos Passos' maturity
    lacks the passion of his earlier revolt."

18 SAWYER, ROLAND. "A Grim View of Washington." Christian
    Science Monitor (2 April), p. 13.
        Admires, in District of Columbia, Dos Passos' "passion
    against wrongs and his knowledge of all the ways of wrong-
    doing," yet finds the trilogy difficult to read because
    "there is little but unrelenting gloom from cover to cover."

19 SCHWARTZ, DELMORE. "John Dos Passos and the Whole Truth," in
    Critiques and Essays on Modern Fiction, 1920-1951. Edited
    by John W. Aldridge. New York: Ronald Press, pp. 76-89.
    Reprint of 1938.B26.

20 WAGENKNECHT, EDWARD. "Novelists of the Twenties," in his
    Cavalcade of the American Novel: From the Birth of the
    Nation to the Middle of the Twentieth Century. New York:
    Henry Holt and Co., pp. 382-408, passim.
        Brief survey of Dos Passos' career which especially
    applauds the "vividness" of U.S.A. Still, even his best
    work is flawed from "using so deliberately flat a style
    and limiting his characterization so strictly to behavior-
    istic notation."

21 WHICHER, GEORGE F. "Reprints, New Editions." New York Herald
    Tribune Book Review (13 April), p. 13.
        Feels that District of Columbia and Arthur Meizer's
    introduction to it demonstrate conclusively that "the major
    thrust of Dos Passos' writing has been satirical."

1952

22 WILSON, EDMUND. "Dahlberg, Dos Passos and Wilder," in his
    The Shores of Light: A Literary Chronicle of the Twenties
    and Thirties. New York: Farrar, Straus and Young, pp.
    442-450.
        Reprint of 1930.B19.

23 ____. "Dos Passos and the Social Revolution," in his The
    Shores of Light: A Literary Chronicle of the Twenties and
    Thirties. New York: Farrar, Straus and Young, pp. 429-435.
        Reprint of 1929.B6.

1953 A BOOKS - NONE

1953 B SHORTER WRITINGS

1 BROOKS, VAN WYCK. The Writer in America. New York: E. P.
   Dutton and Co., pp. 117, 122, 160-161.
       Several references to Dos Passos. Discusses the diffi-
   culty with which members of his generation portrayed
   "goodness."

2 BROWN, DEMING. "Dos Passos in Soviet Criticism." Comparative
   Literature, 5 (Fall), 332-350.
       Chronicles the intense interest of Soviet critics in
   the writings of Dos Passos during the early 1930s. In
   attempting to understand Dos Passos' aesthetics and
   politics from a Marxist perspective, the Soviets realized
   earlier than many of their American counterparts that he
   was primarily an anarchistic and pessimistic novelist.
   Consequently, since 1936, Dos Passos' work has elicited
   only occasional, passing notice from Soviet critics.

3 GEISMAR, MAXWELL. Rebels and Ancestors: The American Novel,
   1890-1915. Boston: Houghton Mifflin Co., pp. 36, 378, 395,
   410n, 414.
       Several references. In a note, Geisman speculates that
   the direct descriptions of sexual passion in Dreiser's
   novels may indicate that the American revolution in sexual
   mores may have occurred in the years between 1900 and 1915
   and that postwar writers such as John Dos Passos were
   actually exploiting broken ground rather than breaking new
   ground themselves in their relatively graphic portrayal of
   sexuality.

4 McDONALD, GERALD D. Review of The Head and Heart of Thomas
   Jefferson. Library Journal, 18 (15 December), 2210.

114

Thinks that while the book may not be an "outstanding contribution, it is a careful study." Finds the first half a sober record and only later does Dos Passos touch the head and heart of his subject.

5   RUBIN, LOUIS D.   "Thomas Wolfe in Time and Place," in
     <u>Southern Renaissance: The Literature of the Modern South</u>.
     Edited by Louis D. Rubin and Robert D. Jacobs. Baltimore:
     Johns Hopkins Press, pp. 290-305.
        In contrasting the differences in style between souther-
     ners such as Wolfe, and non-southerners such as Hemingway
     and Dos Passos, Rubin concludes that "the prose of the
     Southern writer abounds in rich, variegated textual imagery,
     whereas the two Midwestern writers consciously strive for
     prose which is relatively poverty-stricken in sensuous
     material."

6   SPILLER, ROBERT E., et al.   <u>Literary History of the United</u>
     <u>States</u>.   New York: The Macmillan Co., pp. 1302-1304, 1385-
     1387.
        Brief discussion of Dos Passos as a social modernist,
     with bibliographical references.

<u>1954 A   BOOKS - NONE</u>

<u>1954 B   SHORTER WRITINGS</u>

1   ANDREWS, WAYNE.   "A Free Man."   <u>Commonweal</u>, 59 (29 January),
     432-434.
        Finds Dos Passos "perhaps the most sensitive" of
     Jefferson's biographers and applauds <u>The Head and Heart of</u>
     <u>Thomas Jefferson</u> for its novelistic technique, for not
     being shackled by the traditional biographical form.

2   ANON.   "Dos Passos Enters Field of History."   <u>Jackson Sun</u>
     (3 January).
        Notes that <u>The Head and Heart of Thomas Jefferson</u> is
     "more a history of the times in which Jefferson lived than
     a full-dress biography."

3   ANON.   "Influences on Young Jefferson Featured in Dos Passos'
     Study."   <u>Petersburg [Va.] Progress-Index</u> (31 January).
        Admires Dos Passos' attention to the influence of
     Jefferson's friends on his thought as revealed in <u>The Head</u>
     <u>and Heart of Thomas Jefferson</u>.

1954

4   ANON. "Jefferson By Dos Passos." Newsweek, 43 (1 February),
       78.
           A brief report of Dos Passos' current activity and a
       review of The Head and Heart of Thomas Jefferson. Feels
       that, while at times discursive and rambling, the novelistic
       techniques bring Jefferson alive.

5   ANON. "Jefferson Seen From the Inside." The Knoxville News-
       Sentinel (7 February).
           Congratulates Dos Passos on the warmth and vividness of
       his portrait of Jefferson in The Head and Heart of Thomas
       Jefferson.

6   ANON. "Novelist Dos Passos Enters Historical Writing Field."
       Salt Lake Tribune (24 January).
           Calls The Head and Heart of Thomas Jefferson "an excellent
       presentation of the world of the 18th century."

7   ANON. Review of The Head and Heart of Thomas Jefferson.
       Booklist, 50 (15 February), 237.
           Considers the book to be more a commentary on the life
       and times of Jefferson than a conventional biography.

8   ANON. Review of The Head and Heart of Thomas Jefferson.
       Frontiers (February).
           Finds Dos Passos inconsistent and overly simplistic in
       his treatment of Jefferson. The result is a blurred
       portrait.

9   ANON. Review of The Head and Heart of Thomas Jefferson.
       St. Louis Globe-Democrat (24 January).
           Calls the book "one of the most absorbing accounts of a
       founding father that ever has come to light." Especially
       admires the warmth and spontaneity of the Jefferson who
       comes to life in Dos Passos' pages.

10 ANON. Review of The Head and Heart of Thomas Jefferson. San
       Jose Mercury-News (24 January), p. 18.
           Admires the book for being both scholarly and of narra-
       tive interest.

11 ANON. Review of The Head and Heart of Thomas Jefferson.
       Vermont Sun News (8 February).
           Admires the way Dos Passos "recreates the mood and times
       which made Jefferson. . . . The result is to give body and
       spirit to the historical Jefferson."

12 ANON. Review of The Head and Heart of Thomas Jefferson. Virginia Kirkus Service, 21 (15 September), 654.
Considers this a "disappointing book . . . neither good Jefferson nor good Dos Passos."

13 ANON. Review of Most Likely to Succeed. Virginia Kirkus Service, 22 (1 June), 345.
Calls the novel "abysmally boring . . . a dreary tale."

14 ANON. "Turns To History." Spokane Daily Chronicle (14 January).
Notes the publication of The Head and Heart of Thomas Jefferson.

15 ANON. "Unmaking of an American." Time, 64 (27 September), 102.
Calls Most Likely to Succeed a "savage satire against the gulliberal," those who, like Dos Passos, toyed with Marxism in the twenties and thirties. Finds the satire merely shrill, however, and the characterization flat and concludes that Dos Passos, at 58, "starts to sound less like a social critic than a disappointed lover."

16 ASHFORD, GERALD. "John Dos Passos Gives Portrait of Jefferson." San Antonio Express and News (24 January), p. 4h.
Finds The Head and Heart of Thomas Jefferson strong on anecdote but disappointingly slim on analysis.

17 BARRON, LOUIS. Review of Most Likely To Succeed. Library Journal, 79 (August), 1399-1400.
Calls Most Likely To Succeed "an incredibly bad book" which indulges in "the worst kind of assassination" in its tired stereotypes. Calls Jud Morris, the novel's central character, "a particularly repulsive moral coward."

18 BERNARDIN, CHARLES W. "John Dos Passos' Harvard Years." New England Quarterly, 27 (March), 3-26.
Summary of Dos Passos' experiences at Harvard, including his friends, his writing, his work on the Advocate and the Monthly, and a partial list of his extensive reading during those years.

19 _____. "John Dos Passos' Textual Revisions." Papers of the Bibliographical Society of America, 48 (Winter), 95-97.
Feels, in contrast to Martin Kallich's assessment in the Spring 1949 number of Papers of the Bibliographical Society

1954

of America, that the textual revisions of <u>Rosinante to the Road Again</u> made when republished in <u>Journeys Between Wars</u> were justifiable as literary improvements and as a reflection of changes in Dos Passos' thinking during the intervening years.

20 BROWN, RALPH ADAMS. "Always Room For New Story on Jefferson." <u>Boston Sunday Herald</u> (24 January).
Considers <u>The Head and Heart of Thomas Jefferson</u> to be well researched and well written: "The book has balance as well as beauty--it deserves a wide audience and a Pulitzer Prize."

21 BULLOCK, FLORENCE HAPTON. "Case History of An American Communist." <u>New York Herald Tribune Book Review</u> (26 September), p. 3.
Calls <u>Most Likely To Succeed</u> "an illuminating novel" for it presents "a circumstantially authentic historical account of Communist methods." Calls the novel a blueprint of the communist program in the United States.

22 CLURMAN, HAROLD. "Communists by Dos Passos." <u>Nation</u>, 179 (9 October), 310.
Finds <u>Most Likely To Succeed</u> "a wretched piece of work" whose central character is "a phony, a mental incompetent, and a moral castrate." Feels that the book is libelous in its close parallels with Dos Passos' circle in the late twenties and early thirties.

23 COLLIER, BERT. "Dos Passos' Jefferson Is Deft Portrait." <u>Miami Herald</u> (14 February).
Admires the way Dos Passos places Jefferson in his political and intellectual milieu in <u>The Head and Heart of Thomas Jefferson</u>.

24 COMMAGER, HENRY STEELE. "Of Virginia and the World." <u>New York Times Book Review</u> (24 January), pp. 6, 18.
Finds <u>The Head and Heart of Thomas Jefferson</u> to offer little that is new in information or interpretation.

25 COWLEY, MALCOLM. <u>The Literary Situation</u>. New York: The Viking Press, pp. 36, 37, 41, 67, 78, 81, 244.
Reprints of a number of essays, several of which mention Dos Passos. In "War Novels: After Two Wars," Cowley concludes that Dos Passos was the primary model for the novelists of World War II. In "Naturalism, No Teacup Tragedies," calls <u>U.S.A.</u> "the most impressive and possibly the best of American works in the naturalistic tradition." In "The

Next Fifty Years in American Literature" mentions the influence of Dos Passos' devices for portraying collective
behavior.

26 DAVIS, ROBERT GORHAM. "The Twisting and Turning." New York
Times Book Review (26 September), pp. 4, 26.
    Calls the experiences of Most Likely To Succeed concrete
and vivid, yet "a little remote and unreal, like old snap-
shots looked at too often." Admires the characterization
but feels that the political satire fails to adequately
"engage Dos Passos' imagination and insight and sympathy
as a novelist."

27 DOHN, NORMAN. "Unique Book Interprets Jefferson." Columbus
Dispatch (7 February).
    Feels that The Head and Heart of Thomas Jefferson helps
maintain Dos Passos' "reputation as one of our outstanding
contemporary writers."

28 ENGLAND, J. MERTON. "Dos Passos on Thomas Jefferson."
Louisville Courier-Journal (24 January).
    Feels that while it is true that Jefferson often seems
to recede to the background, that allows Dos Passos to
develop the political and intellectual milieu in which he
moved. Concedes that while The Head and Heart of Thomas
Jefferson may not be a well-balanced biography, it does
magnificently reveal Jefferson's essence.

29 ENGLE, PAUL. "The Lucky Day for America." Chicago Sunday
Tribune Magazine of Books (24 January), p. 5.
    Finds The Head and Heart of Thomas Jefferson "brilliant
. . . with a fine care for interesting detail and with an
imagination broad enough to make those details glow with
the glittering daylight of history." Engle thinks the only
flaw is a lack of attention to Jefferson's "heart."

30 _____. "A Mixture of Idealist and Heel." Chicago Sunday
Tribune Magazine of Books (3 October), p. 9.
    Does not consider Most Likely To Succeed one of Dos
Passos' best novels for it is "lacking the overwhelming
sense of actual life which, for example, the great trilogy
U.S.A. always had." Furthermore, "the writing seems hasty
and trite." Nevertheless, Engle feels the novel serves an
important function of unmasking the deviousness of "the
disciplined disciples of the Marxist conspiracy."

31 FARRELL, JAMES T. "Some Observations on Naturalism, So Called,
in Fiction," in his Reflections at Fifty and Other Essays.
New York: The Vanguard Press, pp. 142-155.

1954

Cites Dos Passos and U.S.A., along with other "naturalist"
works, to demonstrate the diversity among its practitioners.

32 FRETZ, GENE. "When Unraveling Past, How Far Should One Go?"
Arkansas Gazette (24 January), p. 6f.
Critical of the excessive detail of The Head and Heart
of Thomas Jefferson as a result of which the writing, though
"sometimes beautiful" is more often confusing.

33 G[ARRISON], W. E. Review of The Head and Heart of Thomas
Jefferson. Christian Century, 71 (9 June), 706.
Calls the story of Jefferson "fascinating and informa-
tive," and a "superb portrait of his mind."

34 GELFANT, BLANCHE H. "John Dos Passos: The Synoptic Novel,"
in her American City Novel. Norman: University of Oklahoma
Press, pp. 133-174.
Thinks that Manhattan Transfer can be taken as "a kind
of text on the art of the city novel. . . . Perhaps no
other city novel reveals such sheer virtuosity in the handling of urban imagery and symbolism, such skill in creating
the city as an entity in itself, and such ingenuity in
making a complex form the vehicle of implicatory social
commentary."

35 GENZMER, GEORGE. "A Living Portrait." Nation, 178 (13 March),
222.
Finds The Head and Heart of Thomas Jefferson a triumph:
"A biography that is notably vivid, pictorial, sympathetic,
and original." Finds much of its freshness in the details
which have been added and equally in those often significant events which are quickly dismissed or eliminated altogether, for in this study, "achievement is subordinated to
character."

36 HART, ROBERT C. "Writers on Writing: The Opinions of Six
Modern American Novelists on the Craft of Fiction." Unpublished doctoral dissertation, Northwestern University,
489pp.
Study of six writers who may be considered realists yet
who differ considerably in their opinions on the function
of fiction. Describes Dos Passos as a specialist both in
language and the humanities.

37 HICKS, GRANVILLE. "Dos Passos: Fruits of Disillusionment."
New Republic, 131 (27 September), 17-18.
Considers Chosen Country and Most Likely To Succeed Dos
Passos' most autobiographical novels and his worst. Hicks

feels that without a cause to rally behind, Dos Passos
flounders. Feels that Dos Passos cannot "come to terms
with his own past." The result, in Most Likely To Succeed,
is a book which "has no emotion whatever, merely unhappy
boredom." Considers the decline of Dos Passos' career to
be "one of the saddest things that happened in recent
literary history."

38 HOWE, IRVING. "Perils of Americana." New Republic, 138
    (25 January), 16-17.
        Finds The Head and Heart of Thomas Jefferson a "rambling,
    formless chronicle" because Dos Passos seems "to consider
    accumulation a method, the absence of theory a sign of ob-
    jectivity, and 'concreteness' an almost magical virtue."
    Howe is disturbed that the book "is not colored but what
    is far worse bleached" by Dos Passos' conservative politics.

39 HUGHES, RILEY. Review of Most Likely To Succeed. Catholic
    World, 180 (December), 231.
        Credits Dos Passos with his usual success at portraying
    events, but the characters are flat, "the palest
    abstractions."

*40 JACKSON, J. H. Review of The Head and Heart of Thomas
    Jefferson. San Francisco Chronicle (28 January), p. 13.
        Cited in "John Dos Passos Bibliography 1950-1966," by
    Virginia S. Reinhart. Twentieth Century Literature, 13
    (1967), 167-178.

41 JOHNSON, GERALD W. "A New Jefferson Seen Through Men and
    Forces That Shaped Him." New York Herald Tribune Book
    Review (24 January), p. 5.
        Finds The Head and Heart of Thomas Jefferson to be a
    significant contribution for the Jefferson scholar for it
    emphasizes those people--rather than events--who had a
    direct influence on him. Feels that Dos Passos has cap-
    tured the "heart" of Jefferson better than any other
    scholar, but feels he misses on the "head," thinking
    Jefferson to be much more hard headed than Dos Passos
    admits.

42 KALLICH, MARTIN. "Mr. Kallich Replies." Papers of the
    Bibliographical Society of America, 48 (Winter), 97-98.
        Responds to Charles Bernardin's criticism in the Winter
    1954 issue of Papers, of Kallich's assessment of the textual
    changes made when parts of Rosinante to the Road Again were
    incorporated into Journeys Between Wars.

43 KENIERY, PAUL. Review of <u>The Head and Heart of Thomas</u>
    <u>Jefferson</u>. <u>Catholic World</u>, 178 (March), 476.
        Notes Dos Passos' emphasis on what seems to be side
    issues and obscure influences. Concludes that the book is
    not well enough balanced for the novice, but will be of
    interest to those familiar with Jefferson's life and career.

44 KOCH, ADRIENNE. "Hero of the Democracy." <u>Saturday Review of</u>
    <u>Literature</u>, 37 (13 March), 23, 40.
        Finds <u>The Head and Heart of Thomas Jefferson</u> "mechanical,
    only occasionally arresting, and often vitiated by its
    poverty of intellectual meaning."

45 KOPKE, RICHARD. "Jefferson Is Seen Student and Farmer."
    <u>Buffalo Courier-Express</u> (7 February), p. 42c.
        Finds the approach of <u>The Head and Heart of Thomas</u>
    <u>Jefferson</u> to break new ground by focusing on the private
    rather than the public Jefferson.

46 LEARY, LEWIS. <u>Articles on American Literature: 1900-1950</u>.
    Durham, N.C.: Duke University Press, pp. 72-73.
        Dos Passos checklist.

47 MURPHY, GEORGE D. "The Saga of a Fellow-Traveler."
    <u>Commonweal</u>, 61 (8 October), 19-20.
        Feels the surface glamor, gross motivation, and banal
    dialogue of <u>Most Likely To Succeed</u> seem to represent "the
    tragic exhaustion of a once formidable talent." Finds the
    greatest failing in characterization which turns "a sort
    of anti-communist morality play" into a farce.

48 ROGERS, W. G. "Dos Passos Writes Jefferson Era History."
    <u>Chicago Sun-Times</u> (24 January).
        Notes that while <u>The Head and Heart of Thomas Jefferson</u>
    seems circuitous, the result is a picture of "the formed,
    rounded and complete man." Reprinted: 1954.B49; 1954.B50.

49 _____. "Here's Third President As Novelist Sees Him."
    <u>Cleveland Plain Dealer</u> (31 January).
        Reprint of 1954.B48.

50 R[OGERS], W. G. "Jefferson Wanted Nation of Medium-Sized
    Farms." <u>Charlotte Observer</u> (24 January).
        Reprint of 1954.B48.

51 ROLO, CHARLES J. "Three Novels." <u>Atlantic Monthly</u>, 194
    (October), 98-99.

Finds <u>Most Likely To Succeed</u> "a rather dismal affair, whose sourness is unredeemed by any qualities of depth or brilliance." Concedes that the Communist abuses described in the book are entirely plausible but, by making the characters and the quality of their lives so disagreeable, Dos Passos resorts to the device of "giving the villain a devil's tail and surrounding him with fumes and sulpher."

52 RUBIN, LOUIS D. "All The King's Meanings." <u>Georgia Review</u>, 8 (Winter), 422-434.
Study of several novels based on the career of Huey Long, particularly Warren's <u>All The King's Men</u> and Dos Passos' <u>Number One</u>. Thinks that Dos Passos' novel limits its scope so that it is essentially a political novel, while Warren's is a political novel, but also "a social novel, a moral novel, a philosophical novel--a novel of the meaning of history and society and of man in time and place."

53 SHERMAN, THOMAS B. "Thomas Jefferson As A Human Being." <u>St. Louis Post-Dispatch</u> (24 January), p. 4b.
Considers <u>The Head and Heart of Thomas Jefferson</u> scrupulously researched and written, of interest to professional historian and general reader alike.

54 SIMMS, VIVIAN. Review of <u>The Head and Heart of Thomas Jefferson</u>. <u>Beaumont Journal</u> (22 January).
Calls the book "a work of integrity which is eminently readable." Considers Dos Passos especially strong in revealing Jefferson's intimate life.

55 SMITH, HARRISON. "A Red's Progress." <u>Saturday Review of Literature</u>, 37 (2 October), 31.
Considers <u>Most Likely To Succeed</u> a dreary, unbelievable novel which "suffers from too many long-winded speeches" and weak characterization.

56 SOLOMON, H. W. "Dos Passos Writes Book On Jefferson." <u>Delta Democrat-Times</u> (24 January).
Finds the writing in <u>The Head and Heart of Thomas Jefferson</u> flat and dull.

57 STRINGER, WILLIAM H. "Another Look at Thomas Jefferson." <u>Christian Science Monitor</u> (4 February), p. 11.
Calls <u>The Head and Heart of Thomas Jefferson</u> "refreshing and different," written in a "quick, succinct style."

58 STUMP, WILLIAM. "Communist Lure In The 1930's." <u>Baltimore Sun</u> (3 October), p. 15a.

1954

> Thinks that in <u>Most Likely To Succeed</u> Dos Passos "falls
> flat on his face. He can't seem to get interested in his
> task." The novel is, finally, "a surface treatment of a
> pertinent subject."

59 TILLYARD, E.M.W. <u>The English Epic and Its Background</u>. New
York: Oxford University Press, p. 62.
> Calls the "true American literary form" between 1890 and
> 1940 to be the documentary novel, "whether of Dreiser or
> Dos Passos."

60 W., E. W. Review of <u>The Head and Heart of Thomas Jefferson</u>.
<u>Wilmington Morning News</u> (25 January).
> Finds Dos Passos' approach "fresh." Considers it more a
> study of the times than the man.

61 WARE, OWEN. "Profile of a President." <u>The Columbia Record</u>
(21 January).
> Calls <u>The Head and Heart of Thomas Jefferson</u> "not so
> much biography as a fascinating account of the exciting and
> eventful times in which Jefferson lived."

62 WELLMAN, FREDERICK CREIGHTON. "The Human Jefferson." <u>Durham</u>
<u>Morning Herald</u> (31 January), p. 7.
> Calls <u>The Head and Heart of Thomas Jefferson</u> "a triumph.
> A gifted creative writer has presented to us a living
> biography."

63 WEST, ANTHONY. "Much Cry, Little Wool." <u>New Yorker</u>, 30
(27 February), 107-108, 110, 113.
> Criticizes <u>The Head and Heart of Thomas Jefferson</u> for he
> sees Dos Passos as emphasizing colorful irrelevancies,
> while "the true substance of their [the founding fathers]
> lives and their greatness goes into the discard on the
> ground that is too difficult or too dull for the general
> reader."

64 ZIEGNER, EDWARD. "Jefferson Is Shown From Different Angle."
<u>Indianapolis News</u> (6 February).
> By stressing Jefferson as "a farmer, a scholar, a man of
> letters," rather than Jefferson the statesman and politician,
> <u>The Head and Heart of Thomas Jefferson</u> "shows Jefferson in
> a somewhat new light, and it shows well."

<u>1955 A BOOKS - NONE</u>

1955 B SHORTER WRITINGS

1 ARDEN, EUGENE. "Manhattan Transfer: An Experiment in Tech-
    nique." University of Kansas City Review, 22 (December),
    153-158.
        An analysis of the relationship of form and content in
    Manhattan Transfer. Special interest in the fragmented
    portrayal of time.

2 BLOTNER, JOSEPH. The Political Novel. Garden City, N.Y.:
    Doubleday, pp. 15-16, 39-40.
        Examines the political implications of the District of
    Columbia trilogy.

3 CARPENTER, FREDERICK I. American Literature and the Dream.
    New York: Philosophical Library, p. 194.
        Notes that, in turning away from his earlier concern
    with realistically portraying a corrupt society, Dos Passos
    returned to the dream vision of American promise in his
    studies of the founding fathers.

4 FIEDLER, LESLIE A. "Adolescence and Maturity in the American
    Novel," in his An End To Innocence. Boston: Beacon Press,
    pp. 191-210.
        In exorcising the writers of the recent past, Fiedler
    concludes about Dos Passos: "We feel that all the famous
    technical devices are no more than mechanical substitutes
    for poetry, subterfuges to conceal from us the fact that he
    cannot create a convincing character."

5 KUNITZ, STANLEY, ed. Twentieth Century Authors: A Biographical
    Dictionary of Modern Literature, First Supplement. New
    York: H. W. Wilson, pp. 283-284.
        Revision of 1942 edition.

6 MacCRARY, TEX and JINX FALKENBURG. "New York Close-Up." New
    York Herald Tribune (8 November).
        Surveys Dos Passos' career. On his apparent political
    shift, Dos Passos remarks: "I have spent all my life trying
    to escape classification." When asked why he and other
    authors are not more forthcoming with stories from their
    lives, he responds: "'When a writer is involved in a story,
    he reworks it and uses it himself, and then scratches it
    off his pad and forgets it completely. That's why a good
    novelist so seldom writes a good autobiography.'"

7 MINER, WARD L. and THELMA M. SMITH. Transatlantic Migration:
    The Contemporary American Novel in France. Durham: Duke
    University Press, pp. 57-98, 217-221.

1955

Feels that, although Dos Passos has never been especially popular with the French reading public in general, "he shares with Faulkner the honor of influencing most strongly present-day French novelists." He is, therefore, Miner and Smith believe, primarily a writer's writer, "most important and influential in France as an innovator."

8 RUBIN, LEWIS D., JR. Thomas Wolfe: The Weather of His Youth. Baton Rouge: Louisiana State University Press, pp. 115-116, 167.
    Contrasts Wolfe's and Dos Passos' portrayal of urban life. Rubin thinks Wolfe's characters have more capability to experience--to feel--the life of the city. Considers Wolfe's city in You Can't Go Home Again to be reminiscent of European novels rather than those of Dos Passos or James T. Farrell.

9 SIEVERS, W. DAVID. Freud on Broadway: A History of Psycho-analysis and the American Drama. New York: Hermitage House, p. 242.
    Mentions Airways Inc. as a play which employed "the Strange Interludes technique of suspended motion and stream of consciousness soliloquies which the other characters on the stage do not hear--achieving at times an arresting and powerful effect."

10 UNTERMEYER, LOUIS. Makers of the Modern World: The Lives of Ninety-Two Writers, Artists, Scientists, Statesmen, Inventors, Philosophers, Composers, and Other Creators Who Formed the Pattern of Our Century. New York: Simon and Schuster, pp. 262, 328.
    Mentions Dos Passos' portrait of Thorstein Veblen and Henry Ford.

11 WILLIAMS, STANLEY T. The Spanish Background of American Literature. Vols. I and II. New Haven: Yale University Press, Vol. I, pp. 237-239; Vol. II, 271-283, passim.
    Calls Rosinante to the Road Again "Dos Passos' Walden": "at once a travel book, a poetic fantasy, a work of social criticism."

12 WYKES, ALAN. A Concise Survey of American Literature. London: Arthur Barker, Ltd., pp. 177-179, 193.
    Mentions the Whitmanesque quality of Dos Passos' plan and the Dickensian quality of his style in U.S.A., but finds his apparent ability to "conceive high drama only in terms of extremes" to be a serious flaw, "a failure of the imagination."

1956 A   BOOKS

1   ASTRE, GEORGES-ALBERT.   Themes et structures dans l'oeuvre de
    John Dos Passos.   Vol. 1.   Collection "Themes et structures."
    No. 1.   Paris: Lettres Modernes.
        First of a two-volume study (see 1958.A1) of the works
    of Dos Passos, with some emphasis on the biographical back-
    ground.   Traces the parallel development of ethical and
    esthetic concerns, stressing the interdependence of content
    and form.   This first volume covers the years 1896-1926.

1956 B   SHORTER WRITINGS

1   ALDRIDGE, JOHN W.   In Search of Heresy: American Literature in
    An Age of Conformity.   New York: McGraw-Hill Book Co.,
    210pp., passim.
        Numerous references to Dos Passos and his work.

2   ANON.   Review of The Men Who Made The Nation.   Virginia Kirkus
    Review, 24 (1 December), 882.
        Considers the book a "great contribution to a deepening
    appreciation and understanding of the American pattern of
    growth."   Feels that this and Carl Van Doren's Great
    Rehearsal (1945) are the two books which best bring the
    revolutionary period to life.

3   BREIT, HARVEY.   "John Dos Passos," in his The Writer Observed.
    Cleveland: World Book Company, pp. 143-145.
        Reprint of 1950.B37.

4   ENGLE, PAUL.   "A Dedicated Man's Views on Freedom."   Chicago
    Sunday Tribune (22 April), p. 2.
        Finds the great value of The Theme is Freedom is "as an
    honest document of the progress of an old fashioned
    liberal."

5   FARRELL, JAMES T.   "Some Observations on Naturalism, So Called,
    in Fiction," in his Reflections at Fifty and Other Essays.
    London: Neville Spearman, pp. 142-155.
        Reprinted from 1950.

6   GEISMAR, MAXWELL.   "The Theme is Fear."   Nation, 182 (14 April),
    305-306.
        Feels Dos Passos' disillusionment with the effects of
    the Russian Revolution apparently caused a psychic wound
    which is manifested in "a complete cessation of his creative
    energy and his human emotions."   Sees Dos Passos as obsessed

1956

by "demons in the shape of ideas." As a result, The Theme
is Freedom, which "should be an informal history of an
epoch . . . becomes a nightmare."

7 HECKSCHER, AUGUST. "One Lifetime." New York Herald Tribune
Book Review (15 July), p. 7.
    Considers The Theme is Freedom a testament to Dos
Passos' belief in the greatness of America, not necessarily
for what it is, but for what it has the potential to
become.

8 HORCHLER, R. T. "Significant Tract for the Time." Commonweal,
64 (11 May), 156-158.
    Finds the earlier essays collected in The Theme is
Freedom to be superior to the later ones and views the
commentaries about the essays--the confrontation of the
conservative and the radical--to be particularly impressive: as he "probes deeply into the mind and motives of
the younger Dos Passos . . . the result is true autobiography." Views Dos Passos as an impatient idealist who
reacts with "instant, violent opposition" to imperfections
in the status quo. As a result, finds a consistency in
Dos Passos' early radical opposition to big business and
later conservative opposition to big government.

9 KALLICH, MARTIN. "John Dos Passos Fellow Traveler: A Dossier
With Commentary." Twentieth Century Literature, 1
(January), 173-190.
    Chronicles the political and philosophical struggle
which Dos Passos underwent between 1925 and 1936.

10 KAZIN, ALFRED. On Native Grounds: An Interpretation of
Modern American Prose Literature. New York: Anchor
Press, pp. 265-282, passim.
    Reprint of 1942.B5.

11 PERLES, ALFRED. My Friend Henry Miller: An Intimate Biography.
New York: The John Day Company, p. 195.
    Mentions the 1940 meeting between Miller and Dos Passos.

12 RIDEOUT, WALTER B. "Class War," in his The Radical Novel in
the United States: 1900-1959. Cambridge: Harvard University
Press, pp. 310-317, passim.
    Rejects the opinion that there was ever in Dos Passos a
split between the esthetic and the radical. Instead,
Rideout feels that Dos Passos, even in his early work, was
able to fuse his three roles: historian, artist, and middle
class rebel. Attempts to explain why the far left embraced
Dos Passos in the early thirties.

13 ROGERS, LINDSAY. "A Novelist Answers the Threat." Saturday
   Review, 39 (31 March), 17.
       Briefly outlines the theme and structure of The Theme
   is Freedom.

14 SCHLESINGER, ARTHUR JR. "Notes and Comments From An Author's
   Notebook." New York Times Book Review (8 July), p. 3.
       Views Dos Passos as "essentially an anarchist." Finds,
   in The Theme is Freedom, a "curiously ill-natured, almost
   vengeful side to Dos Passos in his virulent and misleading
   hysteria about international communism and his implication
   that it is inexorably entangled in American affairs."

15 TAYLOR, WALTER FULLER. The Story of American Letters.
   Chicago: Henry Regnery Co., pp. 453-455.
       Feels that Dos Passos has made "the most ambitious effort
   to gather within a single fictional design the complexities,
   the dynamism, and the tensions of our twentieth-century
   society."

16 WALCUTT, CHARLES CHILD. "Later Trends in Form: Steinbeck,
   Hemingway, Dos Passos," in his American Literary Naturalism,
   A Divided Stream. Minneapolis: University of Minnesota
   Press, pp. 258-289.
       Feels that, in U.S.A., Dos Passos achieves "a perfect
   naturalistic form, in which the envelope of chaos contains,
   physically and metaphorically, the busy volitions of the
   individuals who move back and forth to weave its web."

1957 A BOOKS

 1 NELSON, F. WILLIAM. "An Analysis of John Dos Passos' U.S.A."
   Unpublished doctoral dissertation, University of Oklahoma,
   255pp.
       Analysis of the experimental techniques of U.S.A.,
   emphasizing the relationship between form and content.
   Stresses Dos Passos' minimal use of authorial intrusion.

1957 B SHORTER WRITINGS

 1 ANDERSON, CARL L. The Swedish Acceptance of American
   Literature. Stockholm: Almquist and Wiksell, pp. 82, 98,
   110.
       Brief mention of Dos Passos' Swedish reputation.

 2 ANGOFF, ALLAN, ed. American Writing Today: Its Independence and
   Vigor. New York: New York University Press, pp. 161-170,
   passim.

1957

Mentions Dos Passos as a critic of society and war novelist.

3 ANON. "The Novelist as Historian." Newsweek, 49 (11 February), 106.
Discusses Dos Passos' recent historical research and writing, noting that history has always been a primary concern in his work.

4 ANON. Review of The Men Who Made the Nation. Catholic World, 185 (June), vi.
Finds, in Dos Passos' treatment of Jefferson and Hamilton, a preference for the former and concludes: "Mr. Dos Passos is more keenly aware of the advantage of un-trammeled freedom than of the tremendous importance of authority."

5 ANON. Review of The Men Who Made the Nation. New Yorker, 33 (23 February), 130-131.
Brief review. Finds the book one among few which "convey a feeling of contemporaneousness," and "vividly bring to life" the men who founded the country.

6 ANON. Review of The Men Who Made the Nation. Wisconsin Library Bulletin, 53 (March), 366.
Feels these stories of the founding fathers are "told with eloquence."

7 ANON. "The Titans." Newsweek, 44 (11 February), 106-107.
Summarizes The Men Who Made the Nation and concludes that it is "basic American history, partisan but highly perceptive."

8 BEACH, JOSEPH WARREN. The Making of the Auden Canon. Minneapolis: The University of Minnesota Press, p. 139.
Speculates that Auden was reading Dos Passos while composing Letters from Iceland, evidenced by his own reference to letting "'the camera's eye record'" the details of his surroundings.

9 BRIDENBAUGH, CARL. "Great--and Lesser--Founding Fathers." New York Herald Tribune Book Review (10 February), p. 4.
Enjoys the impressionistic, humanizing portraits of The Men Who Made the Nation, but feels the book offers little new to the student of history. It is "the same old story, well told and ranking high is its genre but it is the same old story and its method is hackneyed."

10 BUTTERFIELD, L. H. "The American Revolution." Yale Review,
    46 (June), 624-627.
        Finds the cinematic technique of The Men Who Made the
    Nation to have a "graphic and transient" effect. As a
    result, "no pattern of meaning emerges from the welter of
    details."

11 COURNOS, JOHN. "Vivid Account of America's Early Leaders."
    Commonweal, 65 (20 March), 664-665.
        Finds The Men Who Made the Nation to be "scholarly with-
    out being pedantic, readable without having been subjected
    to the process popularly known as 'dramatization.'" Notes
    Dos Passos' preference for Jefferson over Hamilton.

12 CRAVEN, WESLEY FRANK. Review of The Men Who Made the Nation.
    William and Mary Quarterly, 15 (Fall), 120-121.
        Finds one of the chief virtues of the book to be that
    it "effectively places the history of the infant republic
    in the larger context of world affairs." Considers the
    total effect to be "extremely disappointing," however, for
    it offers nothing fresh in either detail or interpretation.

13 DAVIDSON, DONALD. Still Rebels, Still Yankees and Other
    Essays. Baton Rouge: Louisiana State University Press,
    p. 169.
        Lists Dos Passos with others characterized as novelists
    of social protest.

14 ELKINS, STANLEY. "A Novelist Looks at History." New Republic,
    135 (17 June), 20-21.
        Sees Dos Passos adapting the technique of the trilogies
    for The Men Who Made the Nation. Feels that Dos Passos is
    better at "recreating historical characters than he was at
    creating literary ones," but does not think the book has an
    adequate historical framework.

15 HENDERSON, ROBERT W. Review of The Men Who Made the Nation.
    Library Journal, 82 (15 January), 188.
        Highly recommends The Men Who Made the Nation, "a
    brilliant retelling of the post-revolutionary period."
    Feels the characters and events are "presented with
    dramatic clarity and compelling interest."

16 HOWE, IRVING, and LEWIS COSER. The American Communist Party:
    A Critical History (1919-1957). Boston: Beacon Press,
    pp. 274, 280, 281, 296, 299, 306.
        Passing reference to Dos Passos as a committed intel-
    lectual who always remained independent of the communists.

1957

17 KRUTCH, JOSEPH WOOD. The American Drama Since 1918: An Informal
    History. New York: George Braziller, pp. 36, 244.
        Revised edition of 1939.B21.

18 LANDSBERG, MELVIN. "Author Dos Passos." New York Times
    Magazine (7 July), p. 2.
        Letter refuting Harrison Salisbury's implication that
    Dos Passos was at one time a member of the Communist party.
    See Salisbury, 1957.B21.

19 McCORMICK, JOHN. Catastrophe and Imagination: An Interpretation
    of the Recent English and American Novel. London: Longmans,
    Green, pp. 77-78, 129-133, 154-155, passim.
        Discusses Dos Passos' fiction as typical of the best of
    American naturalism and considers him to be a leading ex-
    perimentalist in the novel.

20 MALONE, DUMAS. "While American History Was Marching On." New
    York Times Book Review (10 February), p. 4.
        Feels the effect of The Men Who Made the Nation is
    "kaleidoscopic, a shifting mosaic of men and measures with-
    out clearly discernable pattern." Admires Dos Passos'
    development of character, but misses "any deep consciousness
    of the meaning of historic events."

21 SALISBURY, HARRISON. "Writers in the Shadow of Communism."
    New York Times Magazine (9 June), pp. 10, 28, 30, 33-34.
        Refers to Dos Passos as one of a group of writers who
    was "first attracted by the communist dream, then repelled
    by the Soviet reality."

22 SARTRE, JEAN-PAUL. "John Dos Passos and 1919," in his Literary
    Essays. Translated by Annette Michelson. New York:
    Philosophical Library, pp. 88-96.
        Translation of 1947 article. Sartre admires the narra-
    tive method of 1919 which is characterized as "the jerky
    unreeling of a rough and uneven memory." Regards Dos Passos
    as "the greatest writer of our time." Reprinted: 1971.A2;
    1974.A3.

23 THODY, PHILIP. "A Note on Camus and the Contemporary American
    Novel." Comparative Literature, 9 (Summer), 243-249.
        Argues that the American influence was brief for most
    French writers. Sartre, for example, wrote only one book
    which owed its principal debt to Dos Passos.

24 WALTERS, RAYMOND, JR. "Pageant of the Founding Fathers."
    Saturday Review, 40 (17 August), 33.

Feels that Dos Passos, in The Men Who Made The Nation, sacrifices analysis of important events which shaped the founding of the U.S. for stories of the private lives of the founding fathers. Sees the book as "an entertaining, somewhat formless pageant that will beguile those whose historical knowledge is elementary and whose critical faculties are rudimentary."

25 WIGGINS, J. R. Review of The Men Who Made the Nation. American Historical Review, 63 (October), 226.
Feels the book "reflects the author's thorough understanding of the forces of history" despite questions about the appropriateness of Dos Passos' evaluation of some events. Admires the way Dos Passos avoids focusing his history on any one individual, but shows them in relation to each other.

26 YOUNG, LEO VERNON. "Values of the Young Characters in the Fiction of Dos Passos, Hemingway, and Steinbeck." Unpublished doctoral dissertation, Stanford University, 248pp.
Discusses the uses of Dos Passos, Hemingway, and Steinbeck for young students, noting the ways in which their values correspond to or diverge from traditional values as interpreted by the Educational Policies Commission of the National Education Association and The American Association of School Administrators.

1958 A BOOKS

1 ASTRE, GEORGES-ALBERT. Themes et structures dans l'oeuvre de John Dos Passos. Vol. 2. Collection "Themes et structures." No. 2. Paris: Lettres Modernes.
Second of a two-volume study (see 1956.A1) of the works of Dos Passos, with some emphasis on the biographical background. Traces the parallel development of ethical and esthetic concerns, stressing the interdependence of content and form. This second volume, subtitled Proces d'une Amerique ("An America on Trial"), covers the years 1926-1958.

*2 NEWMAN, PAUL. "The Critical Reputation of John Dos Passos, 1920-1950." Unpublished doctoral dissertation, University of Chicago.
Cited in "John Dos Passos Bibliography 1950-1966," by Virginia S. Reinhart. Twentieth Century Literature, 13 (1967), 167-178.

1958

3 WRENN, JOHN H. "John Dos Passos: Artist to Citizen." Un-
       published doctoral dissertation, University of Pennsylvania,
       260pp.
           Argues that artist and citizen are mutually exclusive
       terms and so, as Dos Passos begins to make peace with his
       country in the late thirties, he also begins to write less
       as an artist and more as a concerned citizen.

1958 B SHORTER WRITINGS

1 AARON, DANIEL. "Dos Passos Obsessed." New Leader, 41
       (2 June), 24.
           Calls The Great Days "a sad book, the weakest of Dos
       Passos' novels." Finds the characters flat and the con-
       victions unconvincing. Aaron thinks "the glow faded from
       his prose with the repudiation of his beliefs and the
       dislocation of his values."

2 ADAMS, PHOEBE. "Woes Unlimited." Atlantic Monthly, 201
       (May), 89-90.
           Feels The Great Days "is no more than a querulous wail
       that old men grow old and Utopia does not arrive." Further-
       more, finds the prose ragged, with "all the grace of
       Frankenstein's monster."

3 ANON. "Fallen Eagle." Time, 61 (31 March), 89-90.
           Calls The Great Days Dos Passos' "saddest, sorriest
       novel," weak on characterization despite great power in
       describing incidents and places.

4 ANON. Review of The Great Days. Booklist, 54 (15 May),
       534-535.
           Calls The Great Days "more conventional in style than
       the author's earlier work and more expressive of defeat
       than of social protest."

5 ANON. Review of The Great Days. New Yorker, 34 (21 June),
       102.
           Brief summary of the novel.

6 BITTNER, WILLIAM. The Novels of Waldo Frank. Philadelphia:
       University of Pennsylvania Press, pp. 122, 154, 159.
           Points out the similarities in the fragmented form of
       some of Frank's and Dos Passos' novels.

7 BLANKENSHIP, RUSSELL. American Literature as An Expression of
       the National Mind (Revised edition). New York: Holt,
       Rinehart and Winston, pp. 718, 759-761.
           Slight revision of 1949.B10.

8 BROOKS, VAN WYCK. <u>From a Writer's Notebook</u>. New York: E. P.
   Dutton & Co., pp. 36, 52, 107.
       Several references to Dos Passos' use of peculiarly
   modern conventions such as the use of the tavern or bar as
   a primary locale.

9 COWLEY, MALCOLM. "Success That Somehow Led to Failure." <u>New</u>
   <u>York Times Book Review</u> (13 April), pp. 4-5, 45.
       Thinks <u>The Great Days</u> "is not the novel we have the
   right to expect" after Dos Passos' previous triumphs. Feels
   the novel suffers from two basic stories which are never
   integrated, poor characterization, and missing crucial
   information. Thinks these flaws seriously mar the book.
   Cowley rejects the idea that Dos Passos' artistic decline
   is a result of his political views since other great
   writers have been able to change politically without
   apparent loss of ability. Finds Dos Passos' inability to
   feel for his characters to be the fatal flaw of this and
   other recent novels.

10 DICKENSON, A. T., JR. <u>American Historical Fiction</u>. New York:
   The Scarecrow Press, Inc., pp. 15, 79.
       Occasional references to Dos Passos' novels.

11 FARRELL, JAMES T. "How Should We Rate Dos Passos?" <u>New</u>
   <u>Republic</u>, 138 (28 April), 17-18.
       Praises the vivid description and technical inventiveness
   of <u>The Great Days</u>. Notes the disappointment of many critics
   with Dos Passos' political shift but argues that it should
   not have been unexpected, that he was always a novelist of
   disillusionment, whether with big business or big government. Warns that "a writer should not be judged in terms
   of immediate political considerations." Reprinted: 1976.B9.

12 GEISMAR, MAXWELL. "Dos Passos Yesterday and Today." <u>Saturday</u>
   <u>Review</u>, 41 (15 March), 21.
       Finds Dos Passos' work of the 1940s and 1950s to "have
   reflected a prevailing mood of despair, frustration, and
   black suspicion," and feels <u>The Great Days</u> is "the gloomiest
   and most desperate novel of all." Feels that perhaps his
   greatest failing, throughout his career but especially now,
   is that "the human core of his philosophical concepts is
   inadequate--is missing."

13 HEINEY, DONALD. <u>Recent American Literature</u>. Great Neck, N.Y.:
   Barron's Educational Series, Inc., pp. 132-139, passim.
       Brief summary of Dos Passos' life and major fiction.

*14 HOGAN, WILLIAM. Review of <u>The Great Days</u>. <u>San Francisco</u>
   <u>Chronicle</u> (18 March), p. 27.

1958

> Cited in "John Dos Passos' Bibliography 1950-1966," by
> Virginia S. Reinhart. <u>Twentieth Century Literature</u>, 13
> (1967), 167-178.

15 HYMAN, STANLEY EDGAR. "Some Trends in the Novel." <u>College
English</u>, 20 (October), 1-9.
Hyman feels that the caliber of the writing of the major
American writers of the twenties and thirties has signifi-
cantly declined and that Dos Passos' later novels "read like
some cruel satire on <u>U.S.A.</u>"

16 LEUCHTENBURG, WILLIAM E. <u>The Perils of Prosperity 1914-32</u>.
Chicago: University of Chicago Press, pp. 82-83, passim.
Passing reference to Dos Passos.

17 LISCA, PETER. <u>The Wide World of John Steinbeck</u>. New Brunswick,
N.J.: Rutgers University Press, pp. 4, 164, 176.
Briefly compares and contrasts several works by Dos
Passos with <u>The Grapes of Wrath</u>, the "chameleon" prose
style of which, Lisca feels, is partially indebted to Dos
Passos.

18 MAGILL, FRANK N., ed. <u>Cyclopedia of World Authors</u>. New York:
Harper and Row, pp. 302-304.
Brief biographical sketch.

19 RUGOFF, MILTON. "Story About A Man Who Was." <u>New York Herald
Tribune Book Review</u> (16 March), p. 8.
Feels that, in <u>The Great Days</u>, Dos Passos "puts together
scenes so loosely and impressionistically that the result
seems like improvisation--the ingredients of a novel still
to be written." Finds no vital present or promise of a
future to hold the book's many flashbacks together.

20 SMITH, JAMES STEEL. "The Novelist of Discomfort: A Reconsideration of John Dos Passos." <u>College English</u>, 19 (May),
332-338.
Sees Dos Passos as significantly different from other
social novelists in his attention to technique. Feels
that Dos Passos stressed technique and created his various
formal structures as an esthetic attempt to impose order on
an otherwise chaotic world.

21 STEVENSON, DAVID L. "The Lost Audience." <u>Nation</u>, 187
(2 August), 58-59.
Sees <u>The Great Days</u> as more a memoir than a novel.
Feels the book is an epitaph for the novel of social
awareness.

22 WEEKS, ROBERT P., ed. <u>Commonwealth vs. Sacco and Vanzetti</u>.
    Englewood Cliffs, N.J.: Prentice-Hall, pp. 261-263.
        Mentions Dos Passos' use of the Sacco and Vanzetti case
    in <u>U.S.A.</u> Weeks considers the use of the case "indirect yet
    fundamental" to the trilogy.

1959 A BOOKS

1 LANDSBERG, MELVIN D. "A Study of the Political Development of
    John Dos Passos From 1912 to 1936--With Emphasis Upon the
    Origins of <u>U.S.A.</u>" Unpublished doctoral dissertation,
    Columbia University, 420pp.
        Traces the influences on Dos Passos' political develop-
    ment: his father's attitudes; the threat of industrialism;
    the promise of the Bolshevik Revolution; his involvement in
    the twenties with the artists and writers of Greenwich
    Village; the Sacco & Vanzetti case; the Harlan miners'
    strike; and a whole series of similar events which seemed
    to point, to Dos Passos, to irreconcilable class differences
    in America. Landsberg also notes the influence of Veblen
    and Whitman.

1959 B SHORTER WRITINGS

1 ADAMS, J. DONALD. "Speaking of Books." <u>New York Times Book
    Review</u> (27 September), p. 2.
        Brief mention that Alfred Kazin, in an article about the
    difficulties of capturing the spirit of New York City in
    writing, fails to mention "the novelist that made the best
    try: Dos Passos in <u>Manhattan Transfer</u>."

2 ANON. Review of <u>Prospects of a Golden Age</u>. <u>Booklist</u>, 56
    (December), 213.
        Calls <u>Prospects of a Golden Age</u> "a lively, simply written
    narrative."

*3 ANON. Review of <u>Prospects of a Golden Age</u>. <u>Springfield
    Republican</u> (22 November), p. 12.
        Cited in "John Dos Passos Bibliography 1950-1966," by
    Virginia S. Reinhart. <u>Twentieth Century Literature</u>, 13
    (1967), 167-178.

4 ANON. Review of <u>Prospects of a Golden Age</u>. <u>Virginia Kirkus
    Service</u>, 27 (1 October), 774.
        Considers <u>Prospects of a Golden Age</u> a "balanced, tautly-
    written account of the men of the Revolution and their

1959

immediate successors." Finds the book "well documented, copiously illustrated, often witty."

5 BATES, WHITNEY. "Readable, Sound History." Baltimore Sun (17 February), p. 7a.
     Feels that The Men Who Made the Nation has "the perfect compatability of good writing and good history."

6 BRINNIN, JOHN MALCOLM. The Third Rose: Gertrude Stein and Her World. Boston: Little, Brown and Co., p. 257.
     Brinnin feels that, for the young Hemingway, Stein's approval was essential, "in spite of his association with such worthy literary friends" as Dos Passos.

7 CARGILL, OSCAR. Intellectual America: Ideas on the March. New York: The Macmillan Co., pp. 160, 286, 349, 363, 674.
     A number of references to Dos Passos.

8 CASEY, PHIL. "Dos Passos Speeds Up His Pen After 4 Decades of Writing." The Washington Post (16 July), p. 1b.
     Article about Dos Passos' interests and habits. Notes his admiration for Salinger, Faulkner, the early Hemingway, and E. E. Cummings.

9 COHEN, SYNDEY WOLFE, ed. International Celebrity Register. New York: Celebrity Register Ltd., p. 216.
     Biographical highlights.

10 COMMAGER, HENRY STEELE. "Their United Genius Built a Nation." New York Herald Tribune Book Review (27 December), p. 10.
     Finds Prospects of a Golden Age to be little concerned with ideas; rather, it presents "familiar men in familiar roles." Considers the book a gloss for The Men Who Made the Nation, "a companion piece which points a moral and adorns a tale."

11 CUNLIFFE, MARCUS. "In Praise of Yesterday." New York Times Book Review (20 December), p. 6.
     Calls Prospects of a Golden Age "a spic-and-span, gift album version, nearly all gloss and jollity, of the Revolutionary generation." Finds it a 180° shift from Dos Passos' position in U.S.A., and wishes that he could have found more veracity and dignity."

12 DODDS, JOHN W. "The Mediocre American." Huntington Library Quarterly, 22 (May), 163-177.
     Mentions Dos Passos in this discussion of the fragmented twenties in which the isolation of contemporary society, according to Dodds, was born.

13 GERSTENBERGER, DONNA and GEORGE HENDRICK. The American Novel,
1789-1959. Denver: Alan Swallow, pp. 57-60.
   Checklist of selected criticism, arranged by novel.

14 GOLDMAN, ERIC F. "Flashes of Some Founding Fathers."
Saturday Review, 42 (12 December), 21-22.
   Thinks Prospects of a Golden Age "proclaims the virtue
of liberty in the older, conservative meaning of the word,
and is written "with verve and a sure sense of portraiture."
Goldman finds it sad, however, that in order to find a model
for contemporary liberty, Dos Passos feels he must "ignore"
the heritage of the twentieth century--particularly the
thirties--and turn to examples nearly two centuries old.

15 LYDE, MARILYN JONES. Edith Wharton: Convention and Morality
in the Work of a Novelist. Norman: University of Oklahoma
Press, p. 168.
   Thinks that Wharton could not understand the disillusionment brought on by World War I for writers such as Dos
Passos because "in 1914 the world had suddenly become an
alien place" to her.

16 LYDENBERG, JOHN. "Cozzens' Man of Responsibility," in "Modern
Novelists and Contemporary American Society: A Symposium,"
edited by Louis D. Rubin. Shenandoah, 10 (Winter), 3-31.
   Describes how Cozzens finds heroes in the very characters
Dos Passos held up as most villainous: "'lawyers district-
attorneys collegepresidents judges.'"

17 MAY, HENRY F. The End of American Innocence. New York:
Alfred A. Knopf, pp. 243, 299, 325.
   Passing references.

18 OWENS, GWINN. "Unique Look at Early America." Baltimore Sun
(6 December), p. 27a.
   Calls Prospects of A Golden Age a "connoisseur's history,"
scholarly yet fascinating.

19 RUGGLES, ELEANOR. The West-Going Heart: A Life of Vachel
Lindsay. New York: W. W. Norton and Co., pp. 237, 299.
   Quotes Dos Passos' reaction to hearing Lindsay at
Harvard: "We went to kid, but were very much impressed in
spite of ourselves."

20 SOWERBY, HENRY. "'What Great Things Men Are Capable Of.'"
Christian Science Monitor (11 November), p. 13.
   Calls Prospects of a Golden Age "a gentle reminder of
a time . . . when the individual had come into his own."

1959

Considers it not as a history but as "a selection of telling
points in the careers of eminent Americans."

21 SPRINGER, ANNE M. "The American Novel in Germany: A Study of
the Critical Reception of Eight American Novelists Between
the Two World Wars." Unpublished doctoral dissertation,
University of Pennsylvania, 239pp.
    Survey of the reception of the authors. Concludes that
while Dos Passos was never a popular success, he was highly
regarded by the critics between 1922 and 1932.

22 TATE, ALLEN. "The New Provincialism," in his Collected Essays.
Denver: Alan Swallow, pp. 282-293.
    Reprint of 1945.B10.

23 VER STEEG, CLARENCE L. "Revolutionary Heroes As Seen by Dos
Passos." Chicago Sunday Tribune Magazine of Books
(6 December), p. 3.
    Feels there is an "abrupt, almost unfinished cast" to
Prospects of a Golden Age because of the impressionistic
and episodic "word portraits." As a result Ver Steeg does
not think the book measures up to its grand theme.

24 WASSERSTROM, WILLIAM. Heiress of All the Ages: Sex and
Sentiment in the Genteel Tradition. Minneapolis: University
of Minnesota Press, pp. 100, 101.
    Mentions Dos Passos as one of the writers who rejected
the genteel tradition, particularly its romantic vision of
love. Feels the War was the most important cause of this
rejection.

25 WOODWARD, ROBERT C. Review of Prospects of a Golden Age.
Library Journal, 84 (1 December), 3771.
    Finds Prospects of a Golden Age "reverent in tone,
spirited in style," full of fascinating detail on the
famous and obscure men who helped found our nation.

1960 A BOOKS

*1 DONNELL, RICHARD S. "John Dos Passos: Satirical Historican
of American Morality." Unpublished doctoral dissertation,
Harvard University.
    Cited in "John Dos Passos Bibliography 1950-1966," by
Virginia S. Rinehart. Twentieth Century Literature, 20
(May-August).

2 GORMAN, THOMAS R. "Words and Deeds: A Study of the Political
Attitudes of John Dos Passos." Unpublished doctoral dissertation, University of Pennsylvania, 285pp.
Feels Dos Passos is "basically a sensitive artist and an
aesthetic humanitarian concerned throughout with freedom,
liberty, and justice" whose shifting political attitudes
"have been more emotional responses to situations than
political positions."

3 LOWRY, EDWARD DANIEL. "The Writer as Technician: The Method
of John Dos Passos, 1925-1936." Unpublished doctoral
dissertation, New York University, 344pp.
Describes Dos Passos' use of techniques developed in
modern fiction, poetry, film, and painting in order to deal
with a new sort of reality: "the urban, industrial reality
of twentieth century America."

1960 B SHORTER WRITINGS

1 ANON. "Dos Passos Painting in U.N. Show." New York Times
(6 April).
Notes Dos Passos' donation of a water color to exhibi-
tion for benefit of UNICEF.

2 ANON. "Farmhouses Tell of Owners' Travels." Richmond News
Leader (13 April), p. 17.
Photos of Dos Passos' Spencer Point, Va. home.

3 BEACH, JOSEPH WARREN. American Fiction: 1920-1940. New York:
Russell and Russell, pp. 25-44, 47-66.
Paperback reprint of 1941.B12.

4 CHAMETZKY, JULES. "Reflections on U.S.A. as Novel and Play."
Massachusetts Review, 1 (February), 391-399.
Finds parallels in his college class's response to the
novel and the choice of material included in the play:
they share an emphasis on the technique but at the expense
of the biting social commentary.

5 CROSS, LESLIE. "The Shape of Books to Come." Milwaukee
Journal (25 December).
Notes the coming publication of Midcentury.

6 DURHAM, PHILIP and TAUNO F. MUSTANOJA. American Fiction in
Finland: An Essay and Bibliography. Helsinki: Societe
Neophilologique, pp. 48-49, passim.

1960

Say that Dos Passos is less popular in Finland than elsewhere in Europe. Find that while his material is intrinsically of interest, his style is often thought to be difficult and confusing.

7 FIEDLER, LESLIE. "Henry Roth's Neglected Masterpiece." Commentary (30 August), pp. 102–107.
   Mentions U.S.A. and Farrell's Studs Lonigan as the major works of the early thirties, works which, to the proletarian critics, would make Roth's Call It Sleep seem "woefully 'poetic' and uncommitted."

8 FIEDLER, LESLIE A. Love and Death in the American Novel. New York: Criterion Books, p. 441.
   Calls the novels of World War I such as Three Soldiers "more sentimental than social" in that they portray mass warfare as "essentially a conspiracy against the artistic sensibility."

9 FRIEDMAN, NORMAN. E. E. Cummings: The Art of His Poetry. Baltimore: Johns Hopkins Press, pp. 3, 34, 105.
   Mentions Cummings' political and stylistic differences with Dos Passos.

10 NYREN, DOROTHY, ed. A Library of Literary Criticism. Modern American Literature. New York: Frederick Ungar, pp. 140–145.
   Contains excerpts from a number of reviews of Dos Passos' work.

11 ROTHWEILER, ROBERT L. "Ideology and Four Radical Novelists: The Response of Dreiser, Anderson, Dos Passos, and Farrell." Unpublished doctoral dissertation, Washington University, St. Louis, 292pp.
   Feels the work of Dos Passos and the others has "provided discerning interpretations of certain aspects of recent American political history" and helps us to understand the appeal of communism during the time in which they wrote.

12 SPRINGER, ANNE M. "'Die Jungsten'--John Dos Passos, Ernest Hemingway, William Faulkner, Thomas Wolfe," in her The American Novel in Germany: A Study of the Critical Reception of Eight American Novelists Between the Two World Wars. Hamburg: Cram, de Gruyter & Co., pp. 75–95, passim.
   Notes that Three Soldiers was a huge commercial success upon its German publication in 1922. Succeeding books, while met with high critical acclaim, were never as popular,

142

perhaps because Dos Passos did not publish stories in the
magazines, but also because his subject and style may have
seemed "quite strange and obscure to the foreign reader."

13 THORP, WILLARD. American Writing in the Twentieth Century.
    Cambridge, Mass.: Harvard University Press, pp. 112, 130,
    136-142, 298.
        Feels that Dos Passos might have been a greater novelist
    if he had "followed the bent" of his earliest novels and
    continued writing in the Bildungsroman tradition. Spiller
    believes that Dos Passos was not temperamentally suited to
    dealing objectively with social issues and too much a per-
    fectionist to accept political realities. Furthermore,
    Dos Passos could never rise above being primarily a critic
    and argues that "the nausea of his later writing suggests
    a sense of guilt for having never found a social philosophy
    in which he could believe very long." Nevertheless, Spiller
    generally admires the technique of U.S.A. and feels that
    1919 and The Big Money are works of lasting value.

14 UNTERMEYER, LOUIS, ed. The Britannica Library of Great
    American Writing. Vol. II. Chicago: Britannica Press,
    pp. 1523-1524.
        Brief introduction to selections in anthology. Stresses
    Dos Passos' ear for the American idiom and his influence on
    later novelists.

15 WEAVER, BLANCHE HENRY CLARK. "Interesting Chronicle of
    Jeffersonian Era." Nashville Banner (30 December).
        Admires the technique of ignoring chronology and focus-
    ing on Jefferson's relationship to the other leading figures
    of his day in The Shackles of Power.

1961 A BOOKS

1 BRANTLEY, JOHN D. "The Fiction of John Dos Passos."
   Unpublished doctoral dissertation, University of Texas,
   196pp.
       Examines Dos Passos' use of "the machine" as symbol of
   the dehumanizing aspects of modern American life, as well
   as the structural devices and techniques he used to represent his theme.

2 HOLDITCH, WILLIAM K. "Literary Technique in the Novels of
   John Dos Passos." Unpublished doctoral dissertation,
   University of Mississippi, 458pp.

1961

     Study of Dos Passos' fiction as a committment to tech-
nique: "No other modern novelist has been more concerned
with technique as the basis for fiction, and no other has
produced more startling effects in form and structure."

3 WRENN, JOHN. John Dos Passos. United States Authors Series.
    New York: Twayne Publishers, 208pp.
     This first major study of Dos Passos is an attempt "to
break the stereotypes, to take a fresh look at Dos Passos'
work in the context of his life and times." Wrenn thinks
the three major misleading stereotypes are that he is a
member of a lost generation, that he was a fellow-traveller,
and that he became an arch-conservative apostate. Places
great emphasis on Dos Passos' psychological search for a
father figure, resulting from his love-hate relationship
with his own father. Wrenn gives attention to Dos Passos'
non-fiction interests and writings, including his plays,
his journalism, and his fiction. Thinks that Dos Passos'
method, in U.S.A., is tragic rather than satiric, and views
the trilogy as "a great agglomerate tragic history." Contains primary and selective secondary bibliography.

1961 B SHORTER WRITINGS

1 AARON, DANIEL. "The Adventures of John Dos Passos." Writers
    on the Left, Episodes in American Literary Communism. New
    York: Harcourt, Brace and Company, pp. 343-353, passim.
     Study of Dos Passos' relationship with the American
Communist Party. Concludes that, while Dos Passos' social
and political views grew more radical in the twenties and
early thirties, he "never found any form of collectivism
congenial." Thinks that "the death of Glenn Spotswood [in
Adventures of a Young Man] signified the end of Dos Passos'
turbulent affiliation with the radical movement."

2 ANON. "Dos Passos Brings Record Up To Date." Sunday Call
    Chronicle (16 April).
     Calls Midcentury "an exhaustive and deeply disturbing
study of contemporary America."

3 ANON. "John Dos Passos Honored By Drexel Library School."
    Philadelphia Evening Bulletin (21 April).
     Notes Dos Passos' comments on the public library system,
reading habits, and reading pedagogy.

4 ANON. "Out of the Past." Newsweek, 57 (27 February), 93.
     Calls Dos Passos "the perennial Lazarus of American
letters" and says that Midcentury "reopens the question of

his premature burial." Notes that this novel goes back to
the panoramic method of U.S.A., but that, thematically, it
merely amounts to "a rantingly disapproving history of the
rise of American labor." Finds Dos Passos obsessed with
his fears which make him sound "not like a great writer,
but like everybody's father-in-law."

5 ANON. Review of Midcentury. New Yorker, 37 (18 March),
   173-174.
      Feels Midcentury should be "read aloud by different
   voices rather than simply read" to capture its dissonance
   of style. Thinks the book never rises above "a morass of
   bitterness and old grief."

6 ANON. Review of Midcentury. Virginia Kirkus Service, 29
   (1 January), 43.
      Finds the form of Midcentury makes it difficult to
   classify the novel. Remarks on the "cynicism and bitterness . . . disillusionment and pathos, and occasional
   beauty and sentiment."

7 ANON. Review of Midcentury. Wisconsin Library Bulletin, 57
   (September), 306.
      Feels the novel "will interest readers who have lived
   through" the forties and fifties.

8 ANON. "The Sands of Power." Time, 77 (3 March), 91.
      Notes that Dos Passos, after decades of "diligent work
   and repeated failure," has turned back, almost in a gesture
   of despair, to the techniques of U.S.A. in Midcentury.
   Finds the characters manikins who "acquire a certain ani-
   mation and excitement by being placed on the revolving
   stage of twentieth century social and intellectual history.
   Concludes that though Dos Passos has lost much of the
   freshness, originality, and force of his earlier work,
   Midcentury still "compresses the events of recent decades
   into a remarkable kind of living newspaper."

9 ANON. "Well Disguised as a Novel." Newsday (25 February).
      Considers Midcentury a "planned attack on labor union
   corruption well disguised as a novel," but even more an
   indictment of the "manners and morals of the whole post-
   depression generation." Does not find the technique altogether successful: "it makes for jerky reading and a lack
   of focus; sometimes it is contrived and merely clever."

10 ANSON, CHERRILL. "Dos Passos: Changing with the Times."
   Baltimore Sunday Sun Magazine (22 January), p. 7.

1961

    Brief but wide ranging article which discusses Dos
Passos' recent reading, writing and research habits, political views, and family.

11 BAUER, MALCOLM. "Novelists Find Labor, Politics Betraying
    American Ideals." Sunday Oregonian (5 March).
        Feels that Midcentury "comes close to that high mark"
    established by U.S.A. Notes Dos Passos' shift in politics
    but asserts that "few can deny that there is a lot of truth"
    in Dos Passos' damnation of the labor movement and politi-
    cal liberals.

12 BUCHAN, BLISS S. "'The Death of the American Dream.'" New
    Orleans Times-Picayune (5 March).
        Finds the mood of Midcentury to be "that of utter
    hopelessness."

13 BUTCHER, FANNY. "Dos Passos Novel A Potent Exposé of Labor
    Abuses." Chicago Sunday Tribune Magazine of Books
    (26 February), p. 1.
        Calls Midcentury "a book with a message, a warning that
    all of the apples in the labor barrel are not sound, that
    today's youth is growing soft, that there are greed and
    corruption abroad in the land, and that there is fundamental
    good in man." Notes the similarities in method with U.S.A.

14 BUTLER, HENRY. "Labor History Is Dramatized." Indianapolis
    Times (26 February), p. 6.
        Compares Midcentury unfavorably with U.S.A.

15 CAPPON, R. J. "Dos Passos Changes To Angry Ex-Radical." Pine
    Bluff Commercial (26 February).
        Feels that Dos Passos had created, in Midcentury, an
    inferno which, unlike Dante's inferno, offers no redemption
    through "an overarching beatific vision." Finds the novel
    "curiously constructed, intermittently powerful and con-
    sistently angry." Reprinted: 1961.B16; 1961.B17.

16 _____. "New Dos Passos Novel Pillories Today's U.S."
    Cleveland Plain Dealer (26 February).
        Reprint of 1961.B15.

17 _____. "Midcentury Years: A Muddled Picture." Winston-Salem
    Journal and Sentinel (5 March).
        Reprint of 1961.B15.

18 CHASE, RICHARD. "The Chronicles of Dos Passos." Commentary,
    31 (May), 395-400.

Suggests several theories as to why the art of Fitzgerald and Hemingway seemed to grow and develop while the art of Dos Passos has seemed not to grow. First, believes Dos Passos' has the "impulse of the pamphleteer . . . inspired less by imagination than by anger and zeal." Second, Dos Passos, despite his obvious structural experiments, never developed a unique style, a personal language. Finally, Dos Passos, unlike Hemingway and Fitzgerald, "annihilated the sensitive, suffering, aspiring young hero" from whom he could have built more mature characters.

19 CLEARY, JOHN. "Dos Passos Offers Little That Is New." Hartford Times (4 March).
In reviewing Midcentury, concludes that "for all his skill, for all the fertility of his creative power, John Dos Passos has little new or challenging to offer. The inventiveness of style that so captured the taste of the reading public in the 1920s is dead. This style is there but its freshness has gone." Considers the biographical vignettes to be "jewels, polished to brilliance. But they have little depth." Feels that since Dos Passos is "neither reporter nor poet, neither chronicler nor creator of myth, he neither inspires nor informs."

20 CONROY, JACK. "Our Soul-Sick Century." Chicago Sun Times (5 March).
Stresses in this review of Midcentury the consistency of Dos Passos' "intense fear of and hatred for authoritarianism of any nature."

21 COPELAND, EDITH. "Dos Passos Novel Is Disturbing." Daily Oklahoman (26 February), p. 13b.
Feels that, in Midcentury, Dos Passos has "understated tragedy, relating it with such unexaggerated realism that the reader wishes he might have lived in almost any other time and place except the one which produced these stories. Feels that the novel's women are its weakest links: "They make very little differences to any one, in the world Dos Passos has pictured here."

22 CROSS, LESLIE. "Mr. Dos Passos Opens a Window." Milwaukee Journal (26 February), sec. 5, p. 4.
Notes the amount of research Dos Passos constantly does and quotes him: "'I'm for as much justice and individual freedom as can be squeezed out of life.'" Notes his interest in history and his journalistic technique.

23 DERLETH, AUGUST. Review of Midcentury. The Capital Times (30 March), p. 22.

1961

>   While he does not feel that Midcentury is as compelling
> as U.S.A., Derleth does consider it "highly effective" and
> "far and away better than most of the novels" of the year.

24 DWIGHT, OGDEN G. "Dos Passos Book Has a Raw Power." Des
    Moines Sunday Register (26 February).
        Does not feel that Midcentury can "be called a novel in
    the academic sense, but it has a raw power despite its
    irritating made-up words and intruding gaucheries. Explora-
    tion and subtlety are not in Dos Passos' paint-box, so one
    would not expect beauty, although there are a few gleams.
    Much has been sacrificed for technique."

25 FRANKLIN, JACOB. "Heartbeat of America." Worcester Telegram
    (26 February).
        Says of Midcentury: "No other work of fiction described
    so vividly the life of America's labor movement. . . .
    No other work is so suffused with the sprawl of America's
    economic and social stretchings in the first half of the
    twentieth century." Feels the novel represents a refine-
    ment of the technique of U.S.A.

26 FROHOCK, W. M. Strangers to this Ground: Cultural Diversity
    in Contemporary American Writing. Dallas: Southern
    Methodist University Press, pp. 145, 168.
        Feels that the best writers are "unimpressive when com-
    pared to two earlier nonconformists, John Dos Passos and
    Granville Hicks," who were both "men of rigorous aesthetic
    standards who treated their own alienation with respect
    shoring it up with serious ideas seriously handled, writing
    what they did from the vantage point of knowledge acquired
    by effort."

27 G., E. J. "Labor Picture at Midcentury." The Newark Advocate
    (2 March), p. 8.
        Sees Midcentury as "a strong protest against Communism
    and organized labor. Calls the novel "a concise view of
    the triumphs and tragedies of labor during the first half
    of the 20th century."

28 GELFANT, BLANCHE H. "The Search for Identity in the Novels of
    John Dos Passos." PMLA, 76 (March), 133-149.
        Survey of a number of novels spanning Dos Passos' entire
    career. Gelfant concludes that, despite the external and
    social emphasis of Dos Passos' work, he does create an
    archetypal character whose life is a quest for identity.
    Such a character is, typically, strongly influenced by an
    unhappy and insecure childhood marked by close attachment

to the mother and estrangement from the successful father.
As a result, he rejects conventional patterns of success
and often seeks refuge in hopeless causes, often political
and social ones. Views Chosen Country as one of Dos Passos'
first attempts to reconcile the hero with the father.
Reprinted: 1971.A2.

29 GEURINK, BOB. "Ruthian Swing For Dos Passos." Dayton Daily
    News (16 April).
        Feels that, in Midcentury, Dos Passos is attempting the
    great American novel but it falls short because he has
    boxed himself in, both stylistically and thematically.

30 GOLDEN, HARRY. Carl Sandburg. Cleveland & New York: The
    World Publishing Co., p. 168.
        Notes Sandburg's and Dos Passos' support, along with
    that of other writers, for Ezra Pound during his confine-
    ment at St. Elizabeth's Hospital.

31 GRIFFIN, DOROTHEA. "Shifts Exposé To Labor Union Corruption."
    Nashville Banner (10 March).
        Finds unchanged in Midcentury Dos Passos' "honesty in
    portraying men against forces that seem to deny their
    rights as human beings--and his rather pedestrian prose."
    Feels the book has considerable merit as "an exposé of the
    1960s," but lacks the fire of U.S.A.

32 GROSS, JOHN. "Past Masters." New Statesman, 62 (27 October),
    614-615.
        Finds Midcentury to be "little more than a crotchety
    attack on Labor rackets as the root of all un-American
    evil. . . ." Finds the various narrative devices hardly
    sufficient to transcend what sounds to all too much like
    the "growl of any bilious reactionary down at the country
    club."

33 HASSAN, IHAB H. "Love in the Modern American Novel: Expense
    of Spirit and Waste of Shame." Western Humanities Review,
    14 (Spring), 149-161.
        Study of the relationship between love and sex as a
    barometer of cultural values. Argues that in many modern
    American novels, including U.S.A., "sexual activity,
    brutalized and random, confessed to the failure of human
    relations in a society which offered no meaningful connec-
    tives between private and public actions."

34 HEATH, GARY EARL. "Dos Passos Describes Unions' Rise."
    Vermont Sunday News (5 March), p. 9.

1961

Finds U.S.A. and Midcentury similar in that both attack
"corruption and misuse of power." Especially likes the
portraits of historical characters.

35 HICKS, GRANVILLE. "Of Radicals and Racketeers." Saturday
Review, 44 (25 February), 25-26.
Identifies Dos Passos' major concerns in Midcentury as
the corruption of the labor movement, the sacrifice of
creativity for financial interests in the business world,
and the lack of conviction among contemporary youth. Considers this novel better than its immediate predecessors
and, though it lacks the passion of U.S.A., Midcentury
reveals Dos Passos' solid integrity and the sure hand of
the accomplished craftsman.

36 HORCHLER, RICHARD. "Prophet Without Hope." Commonweal, 75
(29 September), 13-16.
Thinks Midcentury a pale imitation of U.S.A., with
"tame and predictable" biographies, "mechanical and tire-
some" documentary sections, and hackneyed stories. Thinks
there is a basic philosophical consistency to Dos Passos'
work, but that his belief in the common man has always been
at odds with his rigorous determinism. This anomaly,
Horchler suggests, might provide a partial explanation
for Dos Passos' diminishing powers.

37 HUGHES, RILEY. Review of Midcentury. Catholic World, 193
(June), 197.
Feels that, in Midcentury, Dos Passos revives "with at
least partial success," the techniques of his earlier work.
Finds the "old magic" present in the biographical sketches
and occasional scenes, but feels the characters are shadows
and the dialogue banal.

38 INMAN, WALTER G. "New Dos Passos Hits Big Unions 'Tyranny.'"
Omaha World Herald (26 February), p. 26.
Feels that much of the reason for Dos Passos' critical
decline is "the rigidity of his more articulate critics
and, to some extent, of the intellectual temper of recent
years." Considers Midcentury "provocative" and "tremendously
interesting," and feels that Dos Passos "remains a genuine
master of English narrative--forceful and vivid, never dull."

39 JORDAN, JENICE. "Familiar Techniques of the New Dos Passos."
Columbus Dispatch (5 March), p. 12.
Lukewarm review of Midcentury. Favors the biographical
sketches, "written with the author's old mastery of narrative technique."

40 KENDIG, PERRY. "Dos Passos' New Novel." Roanoke Times
(9 February).
Evaluates Midcentury: "Not so good as Manhattan Transfer
and U.S.A., but better than District of Columbia--rather
heavy, a little tedious in spots--not a 'fun book'--but
a remarkable chronicle of our times, a serious novel well
worth the reading--this is Midcentury."

41 KIRKER, HAROLD and B. T. WILKIS. "Beard, Becker and the
Trotsky Inquiry." American Quarterly, 13 (Winter), 516-525.
Mentions Dos Passos as a member of the American Committee
for the Defense of Leon Trotsky in 1936.

42 LEWIN, JACQUELINE. "Dos Passos Frightens." Boston Globe
(26 February).
Calls Midcentury "an intense, frightening, powerful
book." Feels that the novel "seems to stand alone in the
literary milieu--something of an anachronism, a voice from
a past that is more distant in moral climate than in time."

43 LONG, THEODORE. "Labor Rackets In Contemporary U.S." Salt
Lake Tribune (12 March).
Thinks that while parts of Midcentury are successful,
others are much weaker, which causes the novel to "fall
short of being convincing."

44 LYDENBERG, JOHN. "American Novelists in Search for a Lost
World." Revue des Langues Vivantes, 27, 306-321.
Considers Dos Passos one of the most forward looking of
American novelists, perhaps the one most like the prescrip-
tion of the American as offered by Crevecoeur in his Letters
From an American Farmer: "The American is a new man; he must
therefore entertain new ideas and form new opinions," always
embracing the present.

45 McDOWELL, EDWIN. "Dos Passos Holds Up Mirror Before Nation."
The Arizona Republic (23 March), p. 24.
Feels that much of the negative criticism of Dos Passos
has been ideological but feels that Midcentury "should
silence all but the most extreme leftist critics," for it
is, McDowell believes, one of the best American novels of
recent years.

46 McLAUGHLIN, RICHARD. "Another Observation of American Scene."
Springfield Republican (16 April).
Feels that "while there is much of the old fire and
intensity" in Midcentury, "the book has considerably less
vigor or freshness."

1961

47 MacMANIS, JOHN. "Biography and Fiction Discerningly Blended."
   Detroit News (26 February).
   Feels that the prime purpose of Midcentury is "to record
   history and biography." Considers the novel a "well rounded
   account of events that have taken place within the lifetime
   of those who will read this book and will gain from it an
   understanding of undercurrent which many missed during the
   actual event."

48 MADDOCKS, MELVIN. "Dos Passos: Society as the Villain."
   Christian Science Monitor (2 March), p. 5.
   Explores the theme of flight in Midcentury and other Dos
   Passos novels. Finds that Dos Passos' use of this theme
   differs from other American novelists in that "they hint a
   dream of salvation behind the break-out; with Mr. Dos Passos,
   flight carries the sealed knowledge of damnation." Feels
   that, without the Marxist orientation of U.S.A., Midcentury
   seems overbearingly pessimistic. Also feels the novel is
   uneven stylistically. Concludes that the novel is "nothing
   much more than gallant nihilism."

49 MANOUSOS, JAMES W. Review of Midcentury. America, 105
   (15 April).
   Feels that Midcentury reads more like a writer's notebook
   than an epic. Thinks it fails as a novel of social protest
   because it is little more than "a petulant, recurrent whine."

50 MASLIN, MARSH. Review of Midcentury. San Francisco News-
   Call Bulletin (15 March).
   Finds Midcentury, like most of Dos Passos' fiction, to
   be overly pessimistic. Nevertheless, "much of Dos Passos'
   sympathy, inventiveness, and narrative skill is still there."

51 MATTHEW, CHRISTOPHER. "In A Big Novel, John Dos Passos Finds
   The People's Battle Unwon." Milwaukee Journal (26 February),
   pt. 5, p. 4.
   Calls Midcentury "one of the most impressive novels that
   John Dos Passos has written, and certainly his most remarkable since his famous U.S.A. trilogy." Feels that Dos
   Passos "rings the changes between man's despair and his
   glory." Calls Midcentury "a substantial achievement, both
   as fiction and as a record of the temper of the times."

52 MOORE, HARRY T. "The Return of John Dos Passos." New York
   Times Book Review (26 February), pp. 1, 51.
   Feels that, with Midcentury, Dos Passos "retrieve[s]
   a long-lost reputation with a single stroke." Finds it
   "written with a mastery of narrative styles, a grasp of
   character and a sense of the American scene."

53 MURRAY, JAMES F. Review of Midcentury. The Critic, 19
    (April-May), 27-28.
        Compares and contrasts Midcentury with U.S.A. Finds
    the technique similar but feels U.S.A. was surer and more
    exact. Discusses Dos Passos as a particularly American
    writer especially sensitive to the moods of his times.

54 NICHOLS, LEWIS. "Half-Century." New York Times Book Review
    (5 February), p. 8.
        Notes the upcoming publication of Midcentury. Reveals
    Dos Passos' habit of snipping out pieces of magazines,
    especially advertisements, to use in his books.

55 O'LEARY, THEODORE M. "Dos Passos Assails Our Ways." Kansas
    City Star (25 February).
        Thinks that while Midcentury is better than most of Dos
    Passos' recent novels, it falls considerably short of U.S.A.
    Feels that Dos Passos is attacking, in the novel, not just
    labor unions but the conspiracy between big labor and big
    business. Does not find the characters as convincing or
    the narrative as well integrated as in U.S.A.

56 PERKIN, ROBERT L. "Dos Passos Retains Hope for Humanity."
    Rocky Mountain News (19 April), p. 71.
        Dos Passos discusses his views on personal freedom,
    human progress, the roll of the novelist, and his evalua-
    tion of contemporary writers in interview.

57 ____. "One Man's Pegasus." Rocky Mountain News (5 March),
    p. 24a.
        Considers Midcentury to be structurally interesting in
    its "adaptation of the kaleidoscopic form of U.S.A. . . .
    but the fine old anger, shaped by sympathy, is gone."

58 POPKIN, GEORGE. "Corrupt Unions His Target." Providence
    Sun Journal (5 March).
        Thinks Dos Passos' obsession with theme in Midcentury
    results in flat characters who are little more than marion-
    ettes. Considers Dos Passos to be fundamentally "a writer
    of political and economic tracts dressed up in the clothes
    of his characters."

59 REDMAN, BEN RAY. "Dos Passos Regains Some of His Old Strength."
    St. Petersburg Times (26 February).
        Considers Midcentury "a skillfully constructed web in
    which the strands of fact and fiction intertwine and
    strengthen each other." Considers the novel more than mere
    reportage: "It is a successful, impressive achievement in
    one of the myriad of forms that the novel can assume."

1961

60 REID, MARGARET W. "Can This Be the Grand Old U.S.A.?"
Wichita Falls Times (12 March).
Feels that Midcentury is "powerfully written, intense,
interesting, and the interweaving of fact and fiction
heightens the sense of reality."

61 ROLO, CHARLES. "Reader's Choice." Atlantic Monthly, 207
(March), 112-113.
Thinks Midcentury "has a theme rich in possibilities for
a disillusioned radical" like Dos Passos, but that the book
is disappointing because he seems to have lost interest in
the creative process itself: "things are not represented,
not made vivid, they are merely stated." Feels that contemporary society arouses in Dos Passos "a diffuse aversion
quite lacking in the rebellious passion that energized his
early work." Nevertheless, feels the novel is valuable as
a social document which reveals in detail "the rottenness
within the house of labor."

62 ROWLAND, STANLEY JR. "As Our Heroes Go." Christian Century,
78 (24 May), 653-654.
Feels Midcentury lacks the "probing exploration of human
character which distinguishes a first-rate novel," but that
it has "the strength of good journalism: it documents our
times, it tells what people do to each other, and parts of
it make you mad enough to rush out and change things."

63 RUGOFF, MILTON. "U.S.A. Today: A Dos Passos Montage." New
York Herald Tribune (26 February).
Calls Midcentury "a jumbled book" with occasional
flashes of power, with all the "apparatus and techniques"
of U.S.A. "but little of the vision or insight." Feels
that the fiction is merely "thinly disguised propaganda"
which fails because "the message strangles the art."

64 SANDERS, DAVID. "The 'Anarchism' of John Dos Passos." South
Atlantic Quarterly, 60 (Winter), 44-45.
Tries to put Dos Passos' steady drift to conservatism
into context by asserting that Dos Passos has always been
essentially an individualist and an anarchist of the
Spanish mold, a position not entirely alien to midcentury
American conservatism. Traces the consistency of his
anarchism from the early "radical" novels to the later
"conservative" ones.

65 SANFORD, CHARLES L. The Quest for Paradise. Urbana:
University of Illinois Press, p. 265.

Considers the main theme of twentieth century American
literature to be "the dispossession from paradise, America's
abandonment of the security and innocence of an earlier day
through some essentially sinful act, an act most frequently
associated with industrialism and the commercial ethic."
Sanford locates the core of this disillusionment in the
Midwest and in such Midwestern writers as Masters, Anderson,
Lewis, Eliot, Dreiser, Farrell, Hemingway, Fitzgerald, and
Dos Passos.

66 SCHORER, MARK. Sinclair Lewis: An American Life. New York:
    McGraw-Hill Book Co., pp. 424, 455, 474, 759, 812.
        Several references to Lewis' admiration for Dos Passos'
    novels, particularly Manhattan Transfer.

67 SCHORETTER, HILDA N. "Dos Passos Attacks New Front."
    Richmond Times Dispatch (5 March).
        "John Dos Passos has made a long career of distinctive
    criticism of his time and his country, and his thunderous
    imprecations are tending to become feisty snarlings and
    yappings." Finds the effect of Midcentury "similar to
    that of the T.V. soap opera."

68 SHERMAN, JOHN K. "Midcentury is Pessimistic Panorama."
    Minneapolis Sunday Tribune (26 February).
        Calls Midcentury "a great spread of book, something like
    a huge mural in a city hall full of stories, incidents,
    symbols." Feels it is reminiscent in scope. Thinks that,
    despite its sour tone and the portions which "seem to be
    accumulation rather than crucially important," it is still
    powerful in its "vivid narration," "keenly observed detail,"
    and its "total impact."

69 STILWELL, ROBERT L. "A Massive Failure Difficult To Assay."
    Louisville Courier Journal (5 March).
        Admires the possibilities of Midcentury, but considers
    the novel to be "a dismal hodgepodge of specious thought
    and outrageously bad craftsmanship, one within which all
    potential for epic has been either choked by narrow vision
    or extinguished by wretched artistry." Concludes that
    Midcentury is "an almost complete fiasco both aesthetically
    and informationally."

70 TURNER, JIM. "Dos Passos Has 'Documentary' in New Novel."
    Cleveland Press (28 February).
        Feels that Midcentury has "a flavor of authenticity"
    that makes it read like a documentary.

1961

71 VEBECK, JAMES C. Review of Midcentury. The International
    Blue Printer (May), p. 68.
        Implies that Midcentury is a tired reworking of U.S.A.
    in which "unfortunately, Dos Passos gives no flesh and
    blood to his fictional characters."

72 VIDAL, GORE. "Comment." Esquire, 55 (May), 56–59.
        Although Vidal admires occasional sections of Midcentury,
    he finds Dos Passos' indictment of modern America "oddly
    disgusting": "his spirit strikes me as sour and mean and,
    finally, uncomprehending. To be harsh, he has mistaken the
    decline of his own flesh and talent for the world's decline.
    This is the old man's folly which a good artist or a gener-
    ous man tries to avoid." Feels that the decline of Dos
    Passos' reputation is understandable: "To paraphrase Holly-
    wood's harsh wisdom, the persistent writer is only as good
    as his last decade." Reprinted: 1962.B90; 1972.B30.

73 W., E. W. "Midcentury Dos Passos." Wilmington Morning News
    (6 March).
        Considers the biographies to be the best feature of
    Midcentury, "a highly uneven book." While the book is
    "often fascinating . . . it still leaves the reader with
    the feeling that the author has fallen far short of his
    intention of presenting a broad view of America at
    midcentury."

74 WHEILDON, LEONARD. "Dos Passos' Theme Still Is Freedom."
    The Boston Sunday Herald (26 February), p. 3a.
        Calls Midcentury a "big, brilliant, panoramic novel of
    the 40s and 50s."

75 WILLIAMS, HENRY L. "Good Guys Lose to Big Guys in Dos Passos'
    Midcentury." Peoria Journal Star (1 February).
        Admires most the fictional portrayals of Midcentury;
    feels the biographies lack the color of those from U.S.A.
    Thinks Dos Passos' goal to be to portray "a sick society
    dominated by the philosophy of 'grab n git.'"

76 WILSON, WILLIAM E. "A Big Novel By Dos Passos." Baltimore
    Evening Sun (10 March).
        Feels that Midcentury, like U.S.A. and District of
    Columbia, is "an impressive document and a depressing in-
    dictment of American society in the Twentieth Century."

77 YEISER, FREDERICK. Review of Midcentury. Cincinnati Inquirer
    (26 February).
        Summarizes Midcentury's plot and technique. Feels Dos
    Passos' bitterness is justifiable.

1962 A BOOKS

1 DAVIS, ROBERT GORHAM. John Dos Passos. University of
Minnesota Pamphlets on American Writers. Minneapolis:
University of Minnesota Press, 47pp.
Introduction to Dos Passos' career through Midcentury.
Thinks that Dos Passos' themes are the result of a mixture
of old fashioned patriotism and unrecognized psychological
needs. Calls his work, throughout his career, "a challenging commentary on the quality of American experience. . . .
In ways that Dos Passos does not recognize, his fiction as
a whole has drawn strength from its subject, his chosen
country."

*2 WINNER, ANTHONY. "The Needs of a Man: A Study of the Formation
of Themes, Characters, and Style in the Work of John Dos
Passos." Unpublished doctoral dissertation, Harvard
University.
Cited in "John Dos Passos Bibliography 1950-1966," by
Virginia S. Rinehart. Twentieth Century Literature, 13
(1967), 167-178.

1962 B SHORTER WRITINGS

1 AARON, DANIEL. "The Riddle of John Dos Passos." Harpers,
224 (March), 55-60.
Argues that there is a basic consistency throughout Dos
Passos' career in his belief in the individual. Feels that
he came to believe that big government and big labor came
to supplant big business as the major foe of the individual.
Gives considerable attention to Dos Passos' rocky relationship with the American Communist Party and discovery of his
affinity with the founding fathers. Concludes that Dos
Passos was consistent in his principles, that he was not "a
turncoat . . . who took the safe course. He remains the
oppositionist and seeker who refuses to make his peace."
Unfortunately, however, his art has diminished because "he
spent his talents lavishly and too emotionally on causes
he has since repudiated."

2 ANKENBRUCK, JOHN. "Wilson in Two Books." Ft. Wayne News
Sentinel (1 December).
Mentions Mr. Wilson's War.

3 ANON. "Dos Passos Delves Into World War I." Syracuse Post-
Standard (16 December).
Feels that Mr. Wilson's War is "a very valuable and distinguished one-volume review . . . and one that, incidentally, offers us many fresh and rewarding insights."

1962

4 ANON. "John Dos Passos on Woodrow Wilson." Cleveland Press
        (23 November).
            Calls Mr. Wilson's War "a brilliant piece of writing
        . . . a memorable picture of issues, events, people--a
        remarkable achievement."

5 ANON. "Mainstream of America." Fitchburg [Mass.] Sentinel
        (13 December).
            Admires Dos Passos' ability to breathe life into the
        historical figures of Mr. Wilson's War.

6 ANON. "Mr. Wilson's War Is Dos Passos High Point." Chicago
        Heights Star (13 December).
            Praises Dos Passos' "often unnerving ability to cloak a
        verdict or opinion with a sheath of living flesh."

7 ANON. Review of Brazil on the Move. New Orleans Times-
        Picayune (27 November).
            Calls the book "highly readable, very informative."

8 ANON. Review of Mr. Wilson's War. Beverly Hills Citizen
        (5 July).
            Announces the publication of Mr. Wilson's War.

9 ANON. Review of Mr. Wilson's War. Bristal Courier and
        Leavittown Times (13 December).
            Notes anecdotes from Mr. Wilson's War.

10 ANON. Review of Mr. Wilson's War. Burlington Free Press
        (12 December).
            Summarizes contents.

11 ANON. Review of Mr. Wilson's War. Christian Century, 79
        (28 November), 1453.
            Finds that, despite Dos Passos' move from "doctrinaire
        liberalism" to "chaotic conservatism," his survey of the
        Wilsonian years "is hardly marred by his bias."

12 ANON. Review of Mr. Wilson's War. Hudson Dispatch
        (20 December), pp. 12-13.
            Summary of Mr. Wilson's War.

13 ANON. Review of Mr. Wilson's War. Oregon Journal
        (8 December).
            Notes publication of Mr. Wilson's War.

14 ANON. Review of Mr. Wilson's War. St. Paul Pioneer Press
        (18 November).
            Brief summary.

15 ANON. Review of <u>Mr. Wilson's War</u>. <u>Rutland Herald</u>
(11 December).
Remarks on Dos Passos' ability to coordinate and synthe-
size the various themes of the book's large and complex
subject.

16 ANON. Review of <u>Mr. Wilson's War</u>. <u>St. Petersburg Times</u>
(26 November).
Calls <u>Mr. Wilson's War</u> "lucid and fascinating."

17 ANON. Review of <u>Mr. Wilson's War</u>. <u>Seattle Argus</u>
(14 December).
Briefly summarizes <u>Mr. Wilson's War</u>.

18 ANON. "World War I." <u>Hilo Tribune Herald</u> (16 December).
Applauds the narrative style of <u>Mr. Wilson's War</u>.

19 BARKHAM, JOHN. "Disappointments In Dos Passos' Book."
<u>Gary Post-Tribune</u> (25 November), p. 9d.
Admires the narrative style of <u>Mr. Wilson's War</u>, but
feels the scope is too large: "The book is curiously uneven,
with impressive passages offset by curt dismissals of
significant episodes." Reprinted:
_____. "Dos Passos Examines Role of Wilson in White House."
<u>Portland Maine Sunday Telegram</u> (2 December), p. 2c.
_____. "A Fresh Look at World War I." <u>Wichita Falls Times</u>
(16 December), p. 3.
_____. "History Made Human: Early Egghead Wilson." <u>Dallas
Morning News</u> (2 December), p. 5.
_____. "John Dos Passos Writes of Wilson and World War I."
<u>New York World Telegram and Sun</u> (23 November), p. 31.
_____. "The War to End All Wars." <u>Houston Post</u>
(30 December).
_____. "The Wilson Era and the War: Foresaken Ideals."
<u>St. Petersburg Times</u> (25 November), p. 11.

20 BAUER, MALCOLM. "Woodrow Wilson: 'Superior Kind.'" <u>Sunday
Oregonian</u> (25 November).
Summarizes <u>Mr. Wilson's War</u>.

21 BAUM, S. V., ed. <u>E. E. Cummings and the Critics</u>. E. Lansing:
Michigan State University Press, pp. 15, 99, 125, 126.
Several passing references to Dos Passos.

22 BENHAM, JOSEPH L. "Dos Passos' View of World War I Revolves
Around Wilson." <u>Columbia Missourian</u> (23 December).
Calls <u>Mr. Wilson's War</u> "a fascinating series of biog-
raphies of American leaders" of the first two decades of

1962

the twentieth century. Thinks the characterization of Wilson is particularly effective. Reprinted:

_____. Review of Mr. Wilson's War. Montgomery Advertiser (2 December).

_____. "Woodrow Wilson Well Portrayed." Sunday Call Chronicle (2 December), p. 6e.

_____. "World War I Era Sketched by Literary Craftsman." Bridgeport Sunday Post (13 December).

_____. "World War I Non-Fiction." Omaha World-Herald (30 December).

_____. "World War I Nonfiction Handled by Dos Passos." Durham Morning Herald (30 December), p. 5d.

23 BLOOM, EDWARD A. and LILLIAN D. BLOOM. Willa Cather's Gift of Sympathy. Carbondale: Southern Illinois University Press, pp. 191, 192, 247.

Mentions Cather's disdain for "the cult of fictional purpose," for those writers such as Dos Passos who aim "to reform society through literature." The authors conclude, however, that Cather may have had more in common with these writers than she cared to admit for they, like her, were motivated by a deep-seated idealism.

24 BOOTH, CHUCK ROBIE. "Dos Passos 'Objective and Perceptive in Major History.'" Utica Observer (9 December), p. 8b.

Calls Mr. Wilson's War "a major history . . . not top heavy or heel dragging, not loftily intellectual or a cut and dried listing of facts, figures, and dates. It is a thoughtfully weighted history."

25 BRADLEY, SCULLEY, et al., eds. The American Tradition in Literature. Vol. 2. Revised edition. New York: W. W. Norton and Co., pp. 1497-1499.

Brief general introduction to selections in this anthology.

26 BROUSSARD, LOUIS. American Drama: Contemporary Allegory From Eugene O'Neill to Tennessee Williams. Norman: University of Oklahoma Press, p. 51.

Quotes Dos Passos' favorable assessment of John Howard Lawson's Roger Bloomer.

27 BROWN, DEMING. "John Dos Passos," in his Soviet Attitudes Toward American Writing. Princeton, N.J.: Princeton University Press, pp. 83-108, passim.

Charts Soviet critics' reaction to Dos Passos and their numerous debates about whether his politics and esthetics made him a suitable model for Soviet writers. By the middle of the 1930s it was determined that he was not.

28 BRUNN, ROBERT R. "Dos Passos on World War I." Christian
    Science Monitor (3 December), p. 13.
         Finds Mr. Wilson's War written in a "pungent American
    idiom, well researched but always narratively interesting."
    Particularly admires the portraits of public persons.

29 BURNETT, BLANCHE. "Beleaguered President." San Francisco
    News Call Bulletin (15 December).
         Calls Mr. Wilson's War an important study. Notes the
    vivid historical portraits.

30 BUTLER, HENRY. Review of Mr. Wilson's War. Indianapolis
    Times (2 December), p. 10.
         Calls Mr. Wilson's War "clear and vivid." Notes that it
    is really a study of a whole nation preparing itself for
    war.

31 CLOUGH, F. GARDNER. Review of Mr. Wilson's War. New York
    Orange County Post (13 December), p. 7.
         Calls Mr. Wilson's War "graphic, lively, fascinating."
    Book is specially recommended for the general reader.

32 COLBY, ELBRIDGE. Review of Mr. Wilson's War. Best Sellers
    (1 December), pp. 355-356.
         While noting a number of flaws, Colby still calls Mr.
    Wilson's War "a readable and illuminating work."

33 COLLINS, AL. "Wilson: His Aftermath." Houston Chronicle
    (23 December).
         Feels that "what the narrative of Mr. Wilson's War may
    lack in continuity, Dos Passos makes up in entertainment,
    and certainly in information."

34 COWLEY, MALCOLM. "John Dos Passos: The Poet and the World,"
    in Literary Opinion in America. Vol. 2. Edited by M. D.
    Zabel. New York: Harper and Row, pp. 485-493.
         Reprint of 1932.B17.

35 DAVIS, E. DALE. "Dos Passos Lets The Facts Lie There."
    Detroit Free Press (2 December).
         Admires Dos Passos' ability as a "chronicler of his age"
    as evidenced in Mr. Wilson's War. Still, Davis feels the
    work might have had even greater impact had it used the
    experimental techniques Dos Passos had used elsewhere.

36 DAVIS, PAXTON. "John Dos Passos Looks at World War I."
    Roanoke Times (2 December).
         While Mr. Wilson's War spotlights Dos Passos' great
    talent for dealing with a large canvas, for Davis "this is

1962

a disappointing book and ultimately a distressing one" for
it lacks an "underlying, unifying concept of what the war
meant and still means." Instead, Dos Passos vents his
prejudices under the guise of objectivity.

37 DAVIS, R. A. Review of Mr. Wilson's War. Library Journal, 87
    (1 December), 4432.
        Considers the book well researched, well written, and
    interesting. Admires the objective portrait of Wilson.

38 EMERY, RICHARD. "Wilson's War or Peace." Springfield [Ill.]
    Star Journal-Register (25 November).
        Calls Mr. Wilson's War "a story made interesting by the
    delicate treatment of otherwise dull and monotonous
    happenings."

39 ETHRIDGE, JAMES M. and BARBARA KOPALA, eds. Contemporary
    Authors. Vols. 1-4. Revised. Detroit: Gale Research Co.,
    pp. 260-262.
        Brief sketch, bibliography, some comments on critical
    reputation.

40 FITZGERALD, F. SCOTT. The Letters of F. Scott Fitzgerald.
    Edited by Andrew Turnbull. New York: Charles Scribner's
    Sons, 633pp., passim.
        A number of references to Dos Passos.

41 GREBSTEIN, SHELDON NORMAN. Sinclair Lewis. United States
    Authors Series. New York: Twayne Publishers, pp. 121, 125,
    138.
        Mentions Lewis' praise of the younger generation of
    American writers, including Dos Passos, in his Nobel Prize
    acceptance speech.

42 GURKO, MIRIAM. Restless Spirit: The Life of Edna St. Vincent
    Millay. New York: Thomas Y. Crowell Co., p. 183.
        Mentions the arrest of Millay and Dos Passos for their
    leadership in demonstrations in support of Sacco and
    Vanzetti. Notes that Dos Passos was "one of the first
    writers to concern himself with the case."

43 H., B. M. "Dos Passos' Work Superb." Lafayette [Ind.]
    Journal Courier (24 November).
        Calls Mr. Wilson's War "a remarkably compact volume . . .
    a superb book, with its excellent writing and research . . .
    of award winning quality."

44 HALL, CODY. "Mr. Wilson's War. Great Story of Men and
     Issues." Anniston Star (25 November), p. 9b.
         Calls Mr. Wilson's War "a blockbuster of a book . . .
     lucid and fascinating . . . scholarly but lively." Admires
     the "surprises the book contains."

45 HAMILL, DOROTHY. "New Book About Woodrow Wilson." Johnson
     City [Tenn.] Press-Chronicle (25 December).
         Calls Mr. Wilson's War "excitingly written, with about
     it, frequently, a breathlessness of suspense." Especially
     likes the portraits.

46 HILL, BOB. Review of Mr. Wilson's War. Spokane Daily
     Chronicle (22 November), p. 36.
         Admires Dos Passos' ability to set down the revealing
     detail and the luminous anecdote.

47 HOFFMAN, FREDERICK J. Conrad Aiken. United States Authors
     Series. New York: Twayne Publishers, pp. 84, 103, 145.
         Finds echoes of Dos Passos in a number of Aiken's poems:
     "1915: The Trenches"; "House of Dust"; and "The Soldier."

48 HOLMESLY, STERLIN. "Dos Passos Gives Life to Wilson." San
     Antonio Express (2 December).
         Admires the honest, balanced portrayal of Wilson in
     Mr. Wilson's War: "this is history, not myth." Holmesly
     feels that "Dos Passos' prose no longer sings, but he moves
     clearly and rapidly, tying together the great political,
     economic, and military events."

49 J., F. P. "A Recreation of History." Worcester Telegram
     (25 November).
         Feels that Mr. Wilson's War demonstrates that "the deep
     well of compassion upon which he drew for his novels has
     not run dry."

50 JOHNSON, GERALD W. "When America Moved Into the World Arena."
     New York Herald Tribune Book Review (2 December), p. 10.
         Feels Mr. Wilson's War "unquestionably rates among Dos
     Passos' best" for sheer craftsmanship. Finds it "less
     didactic, more evenly balanced, broader in its philosophical
     aspects and sounder in its psychological judgements" than
     other recent books by Dos Passos. Calls the book "unemo-
     tionally dramatic."

51 JOHNSON, MICHAEL T. Review of Mr. Wilson's War. Montreal
     Star (1 December).

1962

Feels <u>Mr. Wilson's War</u> is important "both as a historical document and as pure entertainment." Thinks the length and density of detail might be excessive.

52 JONES, ARCHIE. "The Scholarly Vision of Woodrow Wilson." <u>Chicago Sun Times</u> (9 October).
Comments that, while <u>Mr. Wilson's War</u> is not the scholarship of the professional historian, "it is an equally valuable, exciting tale told by a perceptive and urbane man."

53 JOSEPH, ROBERT. "Dos Passos on World War I." <u>Beverly Hills Times</u> (28 December).
Calls <u>Mr. Wilson's War</u> "surely the best reading of the year," in which "there are no heros and no villains," just real, complex people.

54 KENNEDY, RICHARD S. <u>The Window of Memory: The Literary Career of Thomas Wolfe.</u> Chapel Hill: The University of North Carolina Press, pp. 4, 385.
Feels that Wolfe recorded twentieth-century civilization "in full scale more faithfully than Dos Passos, the only other American contemporary who attempted an imaginative compendium of his time."

55 **KENNY, HOWARD N. "Won the War But Lost the Peace—The Tragedy** of Woodrow Wilson." <u>Peoria Journal Star</u> (15 December).
Calls <u>Mr. Wilson's War</u> "a picture gallery . . . of history" and feels that Dos Passos "has performed a monumental task in marshalling up his facts, and useful service in allowing the reader a wide latitude in forming his own opinions about their import."

56 KNOLL, ROBERT E., ed. <u>McAlman and the Lost Generation: A Self-Portrait.</u> Lincoln: University of Nebraska Press, pp. 171, 228–229, 235, 241, 371.
Admires Dos Passos' ability to create believable American characters "without picking complete mental deficients, prize fighters, gangsters or hurt children of whatever age."

57 KNOX, GEORGE. "Voice in the <u>U.S.A.</u> Biographies." <u>Texas Studies in Literature and Language</u>, 4 (Fall), 109–116.
Calls the Biographies of <u>U.S.A.</u> "a hybrid of poetry and prose" and goes on to examine the special techniques which give them their power: "the collage of voices, incremental repetition of lines, varied endings, use of parentheses, Carlylean harangue." The aesthetic result of these techniques is that they "create unity while conveying a sense of disunity and disintegration."

58   LA BRECQUE, RICHARD T.   "War Won, Peace Lost."   Quincy [Mass.]
     Patriot Ledger (1 December), p. 8.
            Calls Mr. Wilson's War a "lightly written, neatly inter-
     woven account of America's role in World War I and in the
     search for world peace in its wake."

59   LEVI, ALBERT WILLIAM.   Literature, Philosophy and the
     Imagination.   Bloomington: Indiana University Press, p. 178.
            Feels that Sartre is attracted to Dos Passos primarily
     for his stylistic shifts "back and forth between objectivity
     and subjectivity . . . this vacillation and the curious
     atmosphere which it produces."

60   LEWIS, S. J., JR.   "Here's Real Woodrow Wilson."   Augusta
     Herald (9 December).
            Calls Mr. Wilson's War "a work which combines the
     scholarship and penetrating insight of the master historian
     with the vivid prose of the gifted novelist."

61   LIEBSON, PAULA.   "Just Browsing."   El Paso Times (25 November).
            Recounts anecdote concerning Mrs. Wilson and Henry Cabot
     Lodge as revealed in Mr. Wilson's War.

62   McINTIRE, LUCY B.   "Players Strut Stage."   Savannah Morning
     News Magazine (9 December).
            Feels that Dos Passos "has done a magnificent job of
     factual and documented reporting in Mr. Wilson's War without
     robbing this significant era of one bit of its drama and
     tense excitement."

63   MARSHALL, S.L.A.   "What Happened Over Here."   Saturday Review,
     45 (29 December), 42.
            Compares Mr. Wilson's War to F. L. Allen's Only Yesterday
     for its casual, chatty style.   Especially applauds Dos
     Passos' characterization of Wilson, and his ability to re-
     capture the mood of the American Expeditionary Force:
     "essentially a light hearted and gallant army."

64   MERGLER, WAYNE.   "World War Details Are In Series."   Columbus
     Enquirer (26 November).
            Calls Mr. Wilson's War "an interesting and detailed
     history."

65   MICHELS, SPENCER A.   "Dos Passos' Sensitive Study of Wilson."
     Peninsula Living (30 December).
            Calls Mr. Wilson's War "a very readable, sensitive and
     personal account of a fascinating era."

1962

66 MIZENER, ARTHUR. "The 'Lost Generation,'" in A Time of
    Harvest: American Literature 1910-1960. Edited by Robert E.
    Spiller. New York: Hill and Wang, pp. 73-82.
        Feels that the label "lost generation is a misnomer, for
    works such as Dos Passos' U.S.A. represent "the imagination
    afire with the possibilities for greatness in American
    life." Thinks that "the most difficult problem confronted
    by the novelists [of the generation] was that of bridging
    the gap between their heroes' heightened sense of the
    promises of life and the actualities of the society." The
    inevitable failure of the characters to achieve the promise
    makes the novels of Dos Passos, Hemingway, and Fitzgerald
    tragic according to Mizener.

67 NELSON, MARY JO. "Wilson Portrayed As Bitter, Little." The
    Daily Oklahoman (2 December).
        Stresses the negative personal traits of Wilson as por-
    trayed in Mr. Wilson's War.

68 NIXON, H. C. Review of Mr. Wilson's War. Nashville Tennessean
    (30 December).
        Feels that Mr. Wilson's War "reflects the combined
    qualities of John Dos Passos as novelist, biographer, and
    historian."

69 O'CONNOR, WILLIAM VAN. "A Note on the American Novel," in his
    The Grotesque: An American Genre and Other Essays. Cross-
    currents Modern Critiques. Carbondale: Southern Illinois
    University Press, pp. 32-36.
        Lists Dos Passos as an author and U.S.A. as a novel
    particularly concerned with American themes.

70 O'NEILL, JOHN P. "Dos Passos' Wilson's War: Coming-of-Age
    Portrait." The Atlanta Journal and Atlanta Constitution
    (2 December).
        Calls Mr. Wilson's War a "masterly demonstration" of
    historical writing." Particularly notes Dos Passos' choice
    of "the insightful scene or phrase."

71 PAGE, JAMES F., JR. "A New 'Feel' of Wilson Era, From the Pen
    of Dos Passos." Memphis Press (21 December).
        Believes that Dos Passos' method in Mr. Wilson's War
    allows the reader to get a "feel" for the times.

72 PAHLKE, ALFRED F. "Mr. Wilson's War Comes Back Very Much
    Alive." Milwaukee Journal (18 November).
        Admires the objectivity of Mr. Wilson's War which proves
    "highly dramatic" and "fascinating."

1962

73 PHILLIPS, HUBERT. "An Important New History Of the Wilsonian
    Years." Fresno Bee (9 December).
        Despite a few factual errors, Phillips considers Mr.
    Wilson's War to be an accurate account of the time and the
    man.

74 POSVAR, VLADIMIR L. "Dos Passos Dramatic In Mr. Wilson's War.
    Indianapolis Star (9 December).
        Feels that Dos Passos "waxes musical with the emotions"
    in the "dramatically pulsating text" of Mr. Wilson's War.

75 ROBERTSHAW, JIM. "World Destiny and Mr. Wilson." Greenville
    [Miss.] Delta Democrat Times (23 December).
        Admires Dos Passos' "sensitive selectivity" which makes
    the characters of Mr. Wilson's War "live and breathe."

76 RUBIN, MANNING. "Dramatic History of World War I." Charleston
    Evening Post (21 December), p. 9c.
        Calls Mr. Wilson's War "a tour de force . . . a notable
    achievement."

77 RUSSELL, FRANCIS. Tragedy in Dedham: The Story of the Sacco-
    Vanzetti Case. New York: McGraw-Hill Book Co., p. 421.
        Notes Dos Passos' arrest, along with other writers, for
    demonstating support of Sacco and Vanzetti.

78 SELLEN, ROBERT W. "Wilson in Love and War." Kansas City Star
    (2 December).
        Calls Mr. Wilson's War "a good narrative of events" but
    not much more. Bemoans the lack of analysis.

79 SHANDS, BILL. "How America Won War, Lost the Peace." San
    Mateo Times (1 December), p. 16a.
        Calls Mr. Wilson's War a "massive review of 23 tumultuous
    years of United States history." Shands admires Dos Passos'
    novelistic skill which results in an "engrossing, readable
    book."

80 SIMMS, LEROY. "Dos Passos Chronicles Worst Growing Pains."
    Huntsville Times (2 December), p. 5a.
        Calls Mr. Wilson's War "distinguished . . . interesting
    and readable history."

81 SINCLAIR, UPTON. The Autobiography of Upton Sinclair. New
    York: Harcourt, Brace and World, p. 232.
        Mentions Dos Passos' involvement in the production of
    Sinclair's play, Singing Jailbirds.

1962

82 SLOSSON, PRESTON. "Dos Passos In A Mellow Mood." Greensboro
    Daily News (23 December).
        Calls Mr. Wilson's War "history as it would be written
    by a good novelist rather than by a professional historian."
    Calls his portraits of historical figures "delightful."

83 SOMMERS, MARTIN. "A Sharp Penetrating Word Picture." Newsday
    (26 November).
        Considers Mr. Wilson's War the sharpest and most pene-
    trating picture of Wilson to date.

84 STALEY, THOMAS F. "Wilson--Man With a Dream." Tulsa World
    (23 December).
        Feels that Mr. Wilson's War is not a professional his-
    torian's study, but "a beautifully written factual but im-
    passionistic study of those important years in America's
    destiny." Thinks "Dos Passos' view of history is broader
    and more comprehensive in this work than it is in his recent
    novels and reportorial commentaries."

85 SWIGGART, PETER. The Art of Faulkner's Novels. Austin:
    University of Texas Press, p. 22.
        Mentions Dos Passos along with Faulkner and Wolfe as
    American novelists who attempted to fuse the European
    experimental techniques with an examination of contemporary
    American social issues. Swiggart feels that only Faulkner
    "was able to reconcile effectively psychological interests
    and experimental techniques with the social spirit of the
    time."

86 SYNON, JOHN J. "John Dos Passos Chronicles Wilson's War."
    Richmond News Leader (12 December).
        Calls Mr. Wilson's War a fine effort, despite a lack of
    documentation and, perhaps, too large a subject to treat in
    one book.

87 THOMPSON, W. Z. "The Struggle We Won and The Peace We Lost."
    Sunday Herald Leader (2 December).
        Calls Mr. Wilson's War a "masterful portrait of twenty
    turbulent years," which "reads like a first rate historical
    novel."

88 TRABING, WALLY. "Dos Passos Writes of Wilson's War." Santa
    Cruz Sentinel (5 December).
        Brief summary of Mr. Wilson's War.

89 TURNBULL, ANDREW. Scott Fitzgerald. New York: Charles
    Scribner's Sons, pp. 156, 228, 238, 276.

Several references to Dos Passos, including a comment on his praise for Fitzgerald's literary acuity, and his criticism of The Crack Up.

90 VIDAL, GORE. "The Demotic Novel: John Dos Passos," in his Rocking the Boat. London: Hernemann, pp. 151-150.
     Reprint of 1961.B47.

91 W., J. Review of Mr. Wilson's War. Auburn[N.Y.] Citizen-Advertiser (24 November).
     "Rich, immensely rewarding and highly readable, Mr. Wilson's War is one of the best books of the year--who knows, perhaps any year."

92 WATT, ROBERT G. "Mr. Wilson's War Not Joyful Account." Sarasota Herald-Tribune (23 December), p. 26.
     Feels that Dos Passos, in Mr. Wilson's War, "heaps contradictory comment upon historical fact." The result is a confusing yet fascinating picture of the man and the times.

93 WHEILDON, LEONARD. "President Wilson and War." The Boston Sunday Herald (9 December).
     Thinks that, in Mr. Wilson's War, "Dos Passos' main contribution is the color and realism he brings to a complicated and emotional period."

94 WILLEFORD, CHARLES. "Mr. Wilson's War Valuable Document for Historic Detail." Miami News (2 December).
     Calls Mr. Wilson's War "a sharply focused view of the times."

95 WILLIAMS, VERA. Review of Mr. Wilson's War. Long Beach Independent Press Telegram (16 December).
     Feels that Mr. Wilson's War establishes Dos Passos as "a first rate non-fiction as well as fiction writer."

96 WOODBURY, DR. GEORGE. Review of Mr. Wilson's War. Manchester [N.H.] Union Leader (12 December).
     Calls Mr. Wilson's War "a brilliant recapitulation of our recent history."

97 ZDINAK, PAUL. "Brilliant Study of Wilson." Pittsburgh Press (25 November).
     Calls Mr. Wilson's War "a highly spiced and colorfully detailed version of the Wilsonian era."

1963

1963 A BOOKS

1 CANARIO, JOHN W. "A Study of the Artistic Development of John
   Dos Passos In His Novels From One Man's Initiation--1917
   through U.S.A." Unpublished doctoral dissertation,
   University of Washington, 165pp.
   Study of Dos Passos' early novels argues that there is
   steady growth in the development of his social thought and
   toward complex aesthetic purposes. These two aspects are
   most convincingly merged in U.S.A., a complex "comic epic."

1963 B SHORTER WRITINGS

1 ALEXANDER, JAMES E. "Decision-Making and a Brazilian
   Travelogue." Pittsburgh Post Gazette (21 September).
   Disappointed that Brazil on the Move is primarily personal and "doesn't answer the need of any who want a bright
   illumination of this vast, important and spectacular land
   of Brazil."

2 ALLEN, ALBERT C. "Dos Passos Writes Love Note To Brazil . . .
   205 Pages Long." Louisville Times (30 November).
   Calls Brazil on the Move "a gentle hymn in praise of a
   people and a land."

3 ANDERSON, JACK R. Review of Mr. Wilson's War. Pasadena
   Independent Star-News (20 January).
   Admires Dos Passos' ability to portray Wilson clearly
   as a human being but faults him for numerous inaccuracies
   in details.

4 ANDERSON, LEE. "Dos Passos Evalues Wilson As 'Exceptionally
   Good Man.'" Chattanooga News Free Press-Times (4 January).
   Thinks Mr. Wilson's War is "beautifully written in simple
   and bright language . . . a significant account of Mr.
   Wilson's war, the President himself, his personality, his
   contemporaries, as well as a sketchbook of World War I."

5 ANON. "Do We Have A Social Conscience?" American Institute
   of Architects Journal, 40 (October), 6, 117.
   Prompted by Brazil on the Move, discusses the problems
   of Latin American slum conditions.

6 ANON. "Dos Passos Impressed By Brazil." Duluth Sunday News
   Tribune (1 December).
   Brief summary of Brazil on the Move.

7 ANON. Review of <u>Brazil On The Move</u>. <u>Booklist</u> (1 October),
p. 133.
Feels Dos Passos is best when "describing individual
people and places."

8 ANON. Review of <u>Brazil On The Move</u>. <u>Capitol Hill Spectator</u>
(1 October).
Considers <u>Brazil on the Move</u> a "pleasant, somewhat disjointed travelogue interspersed with a few personality
profiles reasonably well done."

9 ANON. Review of <u>Brazil on the Move</u>. <u>Chicago Heights Star</u>
(26 September).
Finds Dos Passos' knowledge of Brazil deep and the scope
of the book suitably broad.

10 ANON. Review of <u>Brazil on the Move</u>. <u>Chicago Sun Times</u>
(17 November).
Feels that Dos Passos writes with "affection, understanding, and hope."

11 ANON. Review of <u>Brazil on the Move</u>. <u>Hudson Dispatch</u>
(11 October).
Admires Dos Passos' ability to capture the flavor of
Brazil.

12 ANON. Review of <u>Brazil on the Move</u>. <u>Newsday</u> (28 November).
Calls <u>Brazil on the Move</u> "a disjointed and disappointing
book only because parts of it are so excellent."

13 ANON. Review of <u>Brazil On The Move</u>. <u>Roanoke Times</u>
(13 October).
Feels that Dos Passos' sympathetic descriptions of the
land, the people, and their problems in <u>Brazil on the Move</u>
add little really new about Brazil.

14 ANON. Review of <u>Mr. Wilson's War</u>. <u>Focus Midwest</u>, 2
(January), 25.
"Mr. Dos Passos' best book since <u>The Head and Heart of
Thomas Jefferson</u> and a wholly convincing account."

15 ANON. Review of <u>Mr. Wilson's War</u>. <u>Harpers</u>, 226 (January),
95.
Calls <u>Mr. Wilson's War</u> a "taut, selective, but readable
history."

16 ANON. Review of <u>Mr. Wilson's War</u>. <u>Honolulu Advertiser</u>
(3 February).
Calls the book "fascinating."

1963

17 ANON. Review of <u>Mr. Wilson's War</u>. <u>New Guard</u> (January).
        Brief summary.

18 ANON. Review of <u>Mr. Wilson's War</u>. <u>St. Albans [Vt.] News</u>
        (6 January).
        Calls <u>Mr. Wilson's War</u> "a book of importance and value,
        and one that is also highly readable."

19 ANON. Review of <u>Mr. Wilson's War</u>. <u>Tulsa World</u> (13 January).
        Brief summary.

20 ANON. "Unquestioning Narrative." <u>Economist</u>, 208 (10 August),
        517-518.
        Thinks the "technical tricks" of <u>Mr. Wilson's War</u> to be
        characteristic of Dos Passos, to "only emphasize the basic
        poverty of the writing, the generally tired prose, the
        stale repetition of familiar themes." Does, however, admire
        the impressionistic vitality of the middle section which
        deals directly with the war.

21 ANON. "Wilson Stopped Here But Stayed in Train." <u>Witchita
        Eagle and Beacon</u> (23 June).
        Calls <u>Mr. Wilson's War</u> "the work of an old pro, a fine
        craftsman, in places consummate, a performance with one
        hand tied behind him."

22 ANON. "Wilson's War." <u>Sacramento Union</u> (13 January).
        Notes the "remarkable job" Dos Passos has done, with
        his "very-nearly epochal" <u>Mr. Wilson's War</u>. Finds the style
        lucid and fascinating."

23 ANON. "Wilson's War Traced By John Dos Passos." <u>Catholic
        Standard</u> (18 January).
        Calls <u>Mr. Wilson's War</u> "readable and illuminating," but
        questions Dos Passos' use of selective anecdotes which
        might cause a distorted view of the characters and their
        world.

24 ANON. "Woodrow Wilson and the U.S. Role In First World War."
        <u>St. Catharines Standard</u> (2 February).
        Feels that while many of Dos Passos' judgments may
        arouse controversy, <u>Mr. Wilson's War</u> is a "brilliant
        account" and sure to be of particular interest to the
        general reader.

25 B., D. Review of <u>Mr. Wilson's War</u>. <u>World Affairs Council of
        Philadelphia</u>, 1 (Winter), 6, 7.
        Brief summary of the book.

26 B., J. "Mr. Wilson's War Is New Dos Passos Study." Lewiston
    Journal Magazine Section (29 April).
        Feels the emphasis is basically political but that the
    narrative sparkles with interesting anecdotes and illumina-
    ting character studies.

27 BAGG, DONALD B. Review of Brazil on the Move. Springfield
    Republican (6 October).
        Summary of the book which is considered "informal and
    informative."

28 BEDELL, W. D. "Growing Old, Tired Along With a Nation."
    Houston Post (22 November).
        Feels that Dos Passos might betray his own concerns
    about youth and age in Brazil on the Move, his study of
    this young country which Bedell feels is growing rapidly
    old.

29 BOGER, MARY SNEAD. "Dos Passos In Brazil." The Charlotte
    Observer (22 September).
        Notes Dos Passos' "spirit of adventurous hope" in Brazil
    on the Move which is called "a splendid book."

30 BONAFEDE, DOM. "A Labor of Love From Dos Passos." Miami
    Herald (15 September).
        Feels that the first half of Brazil on the Move resembles
    the style of National Geographic: "All the natives are
    friendly and smiling." Considers Dos Passos at his best
    when he "deal[s] with the complex, capricious and ironic
    political life of Brazil."

31 BOYNTON, PERCY H. "John Dos Passos," in his America in
    Contemporary Fiction. New York: Russell and Russell,
    pp. 185-203, passim.
        Reprint of 1940.B1.

32 BROCK, CHARLES. "Dos Passos Examines Brazil." Florida
    Times-Union (6 October).
        Admires Dos Passos' bright and inquisitive style in
    Brazil on the Move. Calls the book a "brilliant montage."

33 CARTER, MARGO. "A Large Nation Boldly Moves Ahead Despite
    Drawbacks." St. Petersburg Times (29 September), p. 12.
        Feels that Brazil on the Move displays Dos Passos' "art
    of the soft reproach and the loud hurrah and the little wry
    statement hidden in a paragraph of statistics."

1963

34 CHAMBERLAIN, JOHN. "Many Odd Tempests And a Seaworthy Cork."
    Wall Street Journal (8 January).
        Notes the nearly pure objectivity of Mr. Wilson's War.

35 CHAMBERS, LENOIR. "Mr. Wilson and World War I." The
    Virginian-Pilot (20 January), p. 6b.
        Feels that Mr. Wilson's War reveals Dos Passos more adept
    at portraiture than the presentation of large-scale military
    operations.

36 CLARK, GERALD. "Misses the Ferment In Modern Brazil."
    Montreal Star (21 September).
        Feels that Brazil on the Move is excellent in its
    novelistic portrayals of individuals, but weak in portrayal
    and analysis of the country's social and ideological
    ferment.

37 CONN, PETER J. "Dos Passos Treats Wilson's Role in World War
    One." The Cowl (6 March).
        Feels Mr. Wilson's War violates numerous standards for
    historical scholarship, yet still finds it "a volume that
    is eminently enjoyable and readable, and throughout which a
    high level of excitement and dramatic immediacy is
    sustained."

38 COSTELLO, CARL. "Dos Passos Reviews the Wilson Era." Duluth
    News Tribune (23 December).
        Despite disturbing flaws, Mr. Wilson's War is called "a
    work of power": "It is doubtful whether anyone has told the
    story of the American fighting in World War I so well in so
    small a space."

39 DUTHIE, O. B. "Brazil By Dos Passos." Pittsburgh Press
    (8 November).
        Notes the casual "off the cuff" style of Brazil on the
    Move.

40 EISINGER, CHESTER E. Fiction of the Forties. Chicago:
    University of Chicago Press, pp. 119-125, passim.
        Identifies the theme of all Dos Passos' writing during
    the forties as "the imperative need to guarantee the sur-
    vival of the individual in the modern state and to protect
    his liberties." Thinks Dos Passos' criticism of the New
    Deal is based upon his sense of the "frustration of the
    Jeffersonian and Whitmanian ideal." Thinks that Chosen
    Country reveals a "more buoyant confidence." Reprinted:
    1971.A2.

41 F., F. "He Left His Mark On U.S. History." Amarillo News-
    Globe (16 December).
        Thinks that Mr. Wilson's War "brings a novelist's
    talents to the writing of history. The history is factual,
    the writing glitters."

42 F., J. R. "Brazil Through a Traveler's Eyes." St. Paul
    Dispatch (12 October).
        Brief summary of Brazil on the Move.

43 _____. "Wilson, League Portrayed." St. Paul Dispatch
    (9 March).
        Calls Mr. Wilson's War a "well-knit, readable history."

44 FERREE, H. CLAY. "Brazil: Coming to the Fore." Winston-Salem
    Journal and Sentinel (29 September).
        Calls Brazil on the Move a "fascinating account."

45 _____. "Dos Passos: The Wilson Era." Winston-Salem Journal
    and Sentinel (13 January).
        Considers the chief value of Mr. Wilson's War to be "in
    the author's accomplishment in bringing together the many
    loose-end developments, events and personalities of the
    first two decades of the century."

46 FREEDMAN, RALPH. The Lyrical Novel. Princeton, N.J.:
    Princeton University Press, pp. 11, 14.
        Mentions Dos Passos' Camera Eye sections as an example
    of stream of consciousness technique.

47 FRESHWATER, PHILIP. "World War One Takes Book Front."
    Sacramento Bee (13 January).
        Notes that Mr. Wilson's War is part of a spate of
    recently published books concerning World War I.

48 G., A. A., JR. "A Big, But Brilliant Bite Of History."
    Northwest Arkansas Times (3 May).
        Feels that Mr. Wilson's War is "the best study of the
    war in recent months."

49 G., R. L. "Wilson Era in U.S. History." The Fayetteville
    Observer (21 April).
        Calls Mr. Wilson's War "good informative reading and a
    valuable reference work."

50 GERBIG, LEE. "Our Biggest Latin Neighbor." Columbus Dispatch
    (24 November), p. 15.

1963

Calls <u>Brazil on the Move</u> "an excellent up-to-date account" of the country.

51 GOLDHURST, WILLIAM. <u>F. Scott Fitzgerald and His Contemporaries</u>. Cleveland: The World Publishing Co., pp. 30-34, 40-41, passim.
Finds Dos Passos and Fitzgerald alike in their rejection of the popular aspirations and icons of their times, and in their unmasking of the sweetheart relationship of business and religion.

52 HALL, ELMER. "When War God Was Appeased." <u>Louisville Times</u> (3 January).
Summary of <u>Mr. Wilson's War</u>, a story told "in vigorous prose."

53 HARKNESS, DON. "1900-1920 Is Background For <u>Mr. Wilson's War</u>." <u>Tampa Times</u> (28 February).
Feels that Dos Passos' style--rich in detail--"is eminently successful" in bringing to life <u>Mr. Wilson's War</u>.

54 HAZO, SAMUEL. <u>Hart Crane: An Introduction and Interpretation</u>. New York: Barnes and Noble, Inc., p. 2.
Merely mentions Dos Passos as one of many of his and Crane's literary generation to be drawn to the bohemian atmosphere of New York and Paris.

55 HENDERSON, JAMES W. "<u>Mr. Wilson's War</u> Suggestively Described." <u>Saginaw News</u> (24 January).
Calls <u>Mr. Wilson's War</u> a "mature sensitive, discerning and wonderfully written account."

56 HICKS, GRANVILLE. "The Thirties: A Reappraisal." <u>Saturday Review</u>, 46 (4 May), 27-28.
Considers <u>U.S.A.</u>, <u>Studs Lonigan</u>, and <u>Grape of Wrath</u> the three most memorable novels of the thirties. Calls <u>U.S.A.</u> "the most ambitious attempt an American writer has ever made to show American life in all its complexity and to find some sort of pattern in it."

57 HILLMAN, SERRELL. "History Documents Dos Passos Trio." <u>Toronto Globe and Mail</u> (1 February).
Calls <u>Mr. Wilson's War</u> "a tired history of a fascinating era." Feels the style is windy and clumsy and that Dos Passos ignores the crucial cultural and social impact of the war.

58 HUMPHREYS, SEXON. "Life Added to History." Indianapolis News
       (4 February).
          Feels that Dos Passos' skill, as evidenced in Mr. Wilson's
       War, "is not in digging out the history but in making it
       real by his skillful writing."

59 JACKSON, KATHERINE GAUSS. Review of Mr. Wilson's War.
       Harpers, 226 (January), 95.
          Calls the book "taut, selective, but readable history."
       Applauds Dos Passos' ability to condense the vast material
       but feels it is sometimes too condensed.

60 JACOBSON, G. T. "He Got A War He Didn't Want." Dayton Daily
       News (13 January).
          Critical of the vast scope and lack of footnotes in
       Mr. Wilson's War. Does find this a good study for the
       amateur historian.

61 KIEMEN, MATHIAS C. "Dos Passos On Brazil." Baltimore Sun
       (29 September), p. 5d.
          Calls Brazil on the Move "eminently readable . . . the
       type of book deprecated by professional historians, but
       destined, perhaps, to have a wider influence than truly
       historical books."

62 KILLINGER, JOHN. The Failure of Theology in Modern Literature.
       New York: Abingdon Press, pp. 166-167, 203.
          Considers U.S.A. one of the novels which attempts to
       "salvage life from the flux of time, to give permanence
       through the ordering factor of the artistic mind."

63 KIRSCH, ROBERT R. "America and World War I: Idealism Meets
       Waterloo." Los Angeles Times (4 January).
          Says that Mr. Wilson's War evokes an emotional response
       and is thus "an excellent antidote to histories which,
       though more objective and scholarly, give the reader a
       sense of remoteness from the action."

64 KURZMAN, DANIEL. "Taking a Young Giant's Pulse." New York
       Herald Tribune Book Review (20 October), p. 10.
          Finds Brazil on the Move "dominated by a brooding nos-
       talgia." Admires the descriptions of persons and things,
       but thinks the political commentary shallow.

65 LEWIS, PAUL H. "Dos Passos Takes A Look At Brazil." Chapel
       Hill Weekly (22 December), p. 3b.

1963

Calls Brazil on the Move a "chatty narrative" which is
weakest in its discussion of politics.

66 LINK, ARTHUR. Review of Mr. Wilson's War. New York Times
Book Review (7 April), p. 41.
Finds Mr. Wilson's War to be "filled with errors in
nomenclature . . . and fact" which "reflect either care-
lessness or failure to assimilate the history of the
period, or both."

67 LONG, THEODORE. "World War I Study Brings Cast Vividly Alive."
Salt Lake Tribune (17 February), p. 19w.
Summary of Mr. Wilson's War which is considered "a
remarkably unprejudiced account."

68 LOWRY, E. D. "Manhattan Transfer: Dos Passos' Wasteland."
University of Kansas City Review, 30 (October), 47-52.
Traces the wasteland imagery through Manhattan Transfer.
Read in this light, Lowry concludes, the novel is not so
much naturalistic as an exploration of "the contours of
man's inner world."

69 McLUHAN, HERBERT MARSHALL. "Dos Passos: Technique vs.
Sensibility," in Modern American Fiction: Essays in
Criticism." Edited by A. Waton Litz. New York: Oxford
University Press, pp. 138-149.
Reprint of 1951.B20.

70 MacNEIL, NEIL. "A Lively Examination of Mr. Wilson's War."
Seattle Post-Intelligence (18 January).
Calls Mr. Wilson's War "brilliantly written," and feels
the account of the war is the book's highlight.

71 MAHONEY, JOHN J. Review of Mr. Wilson's War. Ave Maria
(26 January).
Admires the sheer volume of detail, even though it might
occasionally affect the fluidity of the narrative.

72 MASON, DONNA. "Dos Passos Pictures Brazil on the Move."
University of Toronto Varsity-Weekend Review (10 April).
Calls Brazil on the Move "a good introduction to a
little-known country and its people." Admires Dos Passos'
"journalistic sense" which allows him to present "a great
deal of information simply and fluently."

73 METZ, LEON C. Review of Brazil on the Move. El Paso Texas
Times (3 November).

Feels the book "is packed with some of the most trite, trivial subject matter ever to do an injustice to one of the most important countries in the western hemisphere." Thinks it a shame that Dos Passos avoids the complexities and controversies of Brazil.

74 MURPHY, JAMES B. Review of Mr. Wilson's War. Statesville Record and Landmark (22 March).
    Considers Dos Passos' major contribution in Mr. Wilson's War to be "his moving characterization of Woodrow Wilson."

75 MURPHY, RAYMOND. "'Mainstream Book On World War I.'" Newport News Daily Press (3 March).
    Calls Mr. Wilson's War "an informative book, written in a very readable style if one has no objections to odd word compounds and confusing tenses."

76 MURPHY, WILLARD. "Dos Passos Has Interesting Travelogue on Brazil Today." Arkansas Gazette (22 November).
    Feels that Brazil on the Move is "an interesting pot-pourri" which is at its best in its "untangling of the web of political intrigues and conflicts" of the country.

77 NOGGLE, BURL. "New Book Not Quite Up To Usual John Dos Passos." Baton Rouge Sunday Advocate (6 January).
    Feels Mr. Wilson's War is "a mediocre history" for, despite the often precise and vivid description, Dos Passos seems to ignore the fact that "history is also analysis." Concludes that "Dos Passos, historian, is no match for Dos Passos, novelist."

78 PETRIC, SIR CHARLES. "The United States in World Politics." Illustrated London News, 243 (13 July), 49.
    Credits Dos Passos with bringing vividly to life the characters and situations of Mr. Wilson's War. Applauds his realistic portrayal of the often brutal facts of the emergence of the American empire.

79 RASMUSSEN, ISABEL. "Dos Passos Really Loves and Knows Brazil, Its People." Waukegan News-Sun (12 October).
    Feels that the best parts of Brazil on the Move are Dos Passos' descriptions of the people.

80 REEDY, MARY ELIZABETH. Review of Mr. Wilson's War. The Sign, 42 (March), 64.
    Feels that Dos Passos "does a magnificent job of culling significant events and putting them together in a vivid narrative."

1963

81 ROBINSON, CECIL. With the Ears of Strangers: The Mexican In
   American Literature. Tucson: University of Arizona Press,
   pp. 166-167.
       Mentions the use of a Mexican setting in parts of The
   42nd Parallel.

82 ROVIT, EARL. Ernest Hemingway. United States Authors Series.
   New York: Twayne Publishers, p. 172.
       Feels that Hemingway "did not have the dogged serious-
   ness of vision and historical curiosity that . . . John Dos
   Passos possessed."

83 RUBIN, LOUIS D., JR. The Faraway Country: Writers of the
   Modern South. Seattle: University of Washington Press,
   pp. 109, 194, 235.
       Brief comparison of the writing of Dos Passos, Robert
   Penn Warren, and William Faulkner.

84 SAVAGE, FRANK B. "In Brazil--Westward Ho!" St. Louis Globe-
   Democrat (6 October).
       Feels that Dos Passos brings "not only good craftsman-
   ship" to Brazil on the Move, but also the perception of a
   novelist with the human touch.

85 SCRATCH, WALTER L. Review of Mr. Wilson's War. Hollywood
   Evening Outlook (21 January).
       Summary of the book.

86 SEVERSON, THOR. "Dos Passos Proves World War I is His Era."
   Sacramento Bee (23 December).
       Feels that Mr. Wilson's War shows Dos Passos as "crafts-
   man extraordinary." Admires Dos Passos' ability to present
   "both Wilsons: Wilson the Noble, Wilson the Terrible."

87 SHERMAN, GEORGE. "Brazil: A 'Sympathetic Interpreter's' View."
   Washington Sunday Star (22 September), p. 5B.
       Calls Brazil on the Move an "expertly written travelogue"
   which "makes Brazil come alive with all the grandeur and
   spirit of the old Wild West." Faults Dos Passos for his
   "failure to grasp the full power of Brazilian nationalism"
   when he seems to assert that Brazil's development is primarily a problem for the United States.

88 SMART, G. K. "An Ideal Topic For Dos Passos." Miami News
   (6 October).
       Feels that in Brazil on the Move Dos Passos has found
   "an ideal subject, one which brings back into his work the
   lyrical impressionism which so distinguished his earliest
   books."

89 SMITH, DIANA. "Wanderlogue of Love." <u>Worcester Telegram</u>
    (29 September).
        Considers <u>Brazil on the Move</u> a "fascinating, human and
    readable introduction to a vast and complicated country."

90 SMITH, RUTH. "About People Who Made History." <u>Orlando
    Sentinel</u> (3 February), p. 18e.
        Calls <u>Mr. Wilson's War</u> "engrossing reading. It is history
    in a series of well-told anecdotes."

91 STOLTZFUS, BEN. "John Dos Passos and the French." <u>Comparative
    Literature</u>, 15 (Spring), 146-163.
        Study of the influence of French thought on Dos Passos'
    fiction. Feels Dos Passos absorbed French poetry and
    painting--particularly impressionist and cubist--French
    sociology, and novelistic technique of unanimism. Concludes
    with a comparison of <u>U.S.A.</u> and Jules Romains' <u>Les Hommes
    de bonne volonté</u>. Reprinted: 1971.A1.

92 SWANSON, ROGER. "Brazil Struggles Toward Uncertain Future."
    <u>Kansas City Times</u> (13 November).
        Discusses Dos Passos' fear of communism as expressed in
    <u>Brazil on the Move</u>.

93 SZULC, TAD. "A Wish to Go It Alone." <u>New York Times Book
    Review</u> (10 November), p. 14.
        Admires Dos Passos' colorful description and love and
    enthusiasm for the people in <u>Brazil on the Move</u>, but wishes
    there was more analysis of "what makes the country what it
    is."

94 T., B. Review of <u>Mr. Wilson's War</u>. <u>Albuquerque Tribune</u>
    (23 March).
        Feels that <u>Mr. Wilson's War</u> can, at times, "smother with
    detail." Also feels that Dos Passos may be overly subjec-
    tive. Still, finds the book "engrossing."

95 TATUM, TERRELL. "Latin Giant." <u>Chattanooga Times</u>
    (27 October).
        Calls <u>Brazil on the Move</u> "magnificent" and "tremendously
    timely."

96 TAYLOR, A. J. P. "Flickering Figures." <u>New Statesman</u>, 66
    (12 July), 49.
        Finds the newsreel effect to dominate <u>Mr. Wilson's War</u>:
    "flickering figures move with an exaggerated briskness."
    While this method makes for compulsive reading, it also
    precludes any real depth of perception. Thinks Dos Passos

1963

would have been better to mine more recently unearthed material about Wilson.

97 TAYLOR, ROBERT W. Review of Mr. Wilson's War. The Diplomat (March).
Admires the fairness, rich detail, and fascinating presentation of Mr. Wilson's War.

98 THOMPSON, HUNTER S. "Failure to Deal With the Paradox of Brazil Ruins Dos Passos Book." National Observer (21 October).
Thinks that Brazil on the Move is "full of sharp, meaty, vivid little sketches that are as good as anything he did in Manhattan Transfer or The Big Money." Thompson faults Dos Passos, however, for not routing deeper to try to uncover and analyze the complexities of Brazilian culture.

99 WAKEFIELD, DAN. "Dos, Which Side Are You On?" Esquire, 59 (April), 112-114, 116-118.
Begins with an account of Dos Passos receiving an award from the conservative Young Americans for Freedom. Then Wakefield recounts his career in the manner of U.S.A., using bits of history, quotations from Dos Passos' writing, and from the criticism of others. Attempts to explain the enigma of his political views through Dos Passos' own words and evaluations of him by his colleagues and acquaintances.

100 WALDO, THAYER. "Dos Passos' Study of Brazil Spirited." Fort Worth Star-Telegram (29 September).
Feels that Brazil on the Move is "extraordinarily" effective at capturing the spirit of Brazil.

101 WASHBURN, BEATRICE. "Once a Red, Still Read." Miami Herald (19 April), p. 1d.
Talk with Dos Passos about his writing and politics.

102 WEST, PAUL. The Modern Novel. London: Hutchinson, pp. 264-283, passim.
Calls Dos Passos' detailed style "like a tragedy under a microscope." Calls U.S.A. "a capricious work, as irritating for its repetitions and lacunaeas exhilarating for its suggestion of urban, industrial bustle and economic tumult."

103 WILEY, BELL J. "First World War Viewed By John Dos Passos." Jackson Sun (3 February).
Calls Mr. Wilson's War "an absorbingly interesting book." Feels Dos Passos' "knowledge of men, events and moods is remarkably rich."

104 Z., R. "New Frontier." Cedar Rapids Gazette (24 November).
Brief summary of Brazil on the Move.

1964 A BOOKS

1 FITELSON, DAVID. "The Art of John Dos Passos: A Study of the
Novels Through U.S.A." Unpublished doctoral dissertation,
Emory University, 150pp.
Study of Dos Passos' early fiction. Fitelson is
interested in the work primarily as artistic experiments
rather than political or social commentary.

2 KNOX, GEORGE A. and HERBERT M. STAHL. Dos Passos and "The
Revolting Playwrights." Essays and Studies on American
Language and Literature, 15. Uppsala, Sweden: Uppsala
University Press, 241pp.
Study of Dos Passos' drama and his involvement with the
New Playwrights Theatre. Extensive discussion of Dos
Passos' views on the theatre, and details of production
background as well as criticism of Dos Passos' plays. The
authors think The Garbage Man "had been an exciting expressionistic experiment, not far off in manner and intent
from Manhattan Transfer," but think Airways, Inc., was "un-
coordinated, confused, overtalkative, and uneven." Conclude that "in fiction, he displayed artistic discipline,
in drama too little." Includes photographs of New
Playwrights Theatre sets and productions as well as repro-
ductions of various documents related to the group.

1964 B SHORTER WRITINGS

1 ALLEN, WALTER. The Modern Novel In Britain and the United
States. New York: E. P. Dutton, pp. 143-148, passim.
Thinks Dos Passos most closely resembles Whitman, but "a
Whitman who has fallen from the state of innocence."
Analysis of Dos Passos' technique in U.S.A.

2 ANON. Review of Occasions and Protests. Christian Century, 81
(4 November), 1372.
Finds the book stylistically provocative but thinks Dos
Passos "has become a rather weary and repetitive recaller
of an American past most of which never existed—and that
part which did now seems irretrievable."

3 BRESSLER, HARVEY J. "An All-or-Nothing Idealist." Commonweal,
81 (4 December), 366-367.

1964

Finds Occasions and Protests' subject matter dated and
editing uneven. Feels the essays are "totally without dis-
tinction." Blames a decline in Dos Passos' creative energy
on his inability to be moved by a "great cause" comparable
to those that have moved him in the past. Feels that,
while he "used to sound like an aroused social critic,
today he has come to sound more and more like a disappointed
lover."

4 BUSEY, JAMES L. Review of Brazil on the Move. American
   Political Science Review, 58 (June), 456–457.
      Calls Brazil on the Move "an entertaining and pleasing
   introduction to some aspects of the country." Unfortunately
   "no definable thread of meaning runs through the book."

5 BUTTERFIELD, ROGER. "For Young Readers: Presidents and Their
   Place In History." New York Times Book Review (18 October),
   p. 30.
      Calls Thomas Jefferson: The Making of a President "a
   vivid and robust portrayal of Jefferson."

6 COOPERMAN, STANLEY. "Christ in Khaki: Religion and the Post
   W. W. I Literary Protest." Western Humanities Review, 18
   (Autumn), 360–372.
      Shows the ways in which allied propagandists used reli-
   gious appeals to exhort their soldiers. Feels they
   attempted with some success, to make it into a religious
   war, a holy crusade. Shows how the hypocrisy of such propaganda was rejected by many modern writers, including Dos
   Passos, who participated in the war. The result was a
   "religious cynicism" which permeated into war novels.

7 DE OLIVEIRA CAMPOS, ROBERTO. "Diplomat Comments On Book About
   Homeland." The Diplomat (February).
      In commenting on Brazil on the Move, Campos notes a
   number of flaws but feels that, on the whole the book is
   "readable and compassionate."

8 EASTMAN, MAX. Love and Revolution: My Journey Through an
   Epoch. New York: Random House, pp. 464–465, passim.
      Occasional reference to Dos Passos who is described as
   "so shy that he seems cold as an empty cellar with the door
   locked when you meet him. Those flames of passion and sky-
   licking imageries that illumine his novels are damped down
   so they don't even smoke in social intercourse."

9 FARRELL, JAMES T. "Some Observations on Naturalims, So Called,
   in Fiction," in Selected Essays. Edited by Luna Wolf. New

York: McGraw-Hill, pp. 21-34.
Reprint of 1954.B31.

10 FEIED, FREDERICK. No Pie in the Sky: The Hobo as American
    Cultural Hero in the Works of Jack London, John Dos Passos,
    and Jack Kerouac. New York: Citadel Press, pp. 41-56,
    passim.
        Calls U.S.A. "the most complete portrait of the hoboes"
    of the first part of the century. Focusing his discussion
    on Mac and Ben Compton, Feied feels that Dos Passos creates
    hoboes who are uniquely political in their views and signi-
    ficance. Dos Passos' hoboes share none of the optimism or
    romance of those of either London or Kerouac.

11 FIEDLER, LESLIE. "The Beginning of the Thirties: Depression,
    Return and Rebirth," in his Waiting for the End. New York:
    Stein and Day, pp. 32-64.
        Feels that U.S.A., which had "seemed for a while the
    great book of the age," is, in fact, a "dull, pseudo-
    experimental" work.

12 GORMAN, THOMAS RICHARD. "Dos Passos and the Drama." Speech
    Monographs, 32 (Spring), 420-426.
        Overview of Dos Passos' work with the New Playwrights
    and his own three plays. Finds the plays themselves flawed
    but credits Dos Passos with paving the way for later play-
    wrights to blend new ideas in form and content.

13 HOFFMAN, FREDERICK J. The Mortal No: Death and the Modern
    Imagination. Princeton, N.J.: Princeton University Press,
    pp. 476-478, passim.
        Notes the influence of Dos Passos on Mailer's The Naked
    and the Dead, especially in the matter of fact, unemotional
    treatment of death.

14 HOHENBERG, JOHN. Foreign Correspondence: The Great Reporters
    and Their Times. New York: Columbia University Press,
    p. 312.
        Mentions Dos Passos as a correspondent of the Spanish
    Civil War.

15 HUFFORD, KENNETH. Review of Thomas Jefferson: The Making of a
    President. Christian Science Monitor (5 November), sec. B,
    p. 6.
        Feels that "few books about Thomas Jefferson have been
    written with more care "than Thomas Jefferson: The Making
    of a President. Finds it a "balanced and readable biography
    for young people (or adults)."

1964

16 HULET, CLAUDE L. "The Goal: Economic Freedom." Saturday
Review, 47 (15 February), 43-44.
While noting Dos Passos' lack of scholarly background,
Hulet considers Brazil on the Move a vivid introduction to
the country for Americans. He finds especially interesting
Dos Passos' synthesis of political history.

17 KEYFITZ, NATHAN. Review of Brazil on the Move. American
Journal of Sociology, 70 (July), 115-116.
Calls Brazil on the Move highly competent journalism, a
travelogue. Notes Dos Passos' success at capturing the
flavor of the Vargas dictatorship and of the governments
which followed it.

18 KEYSER, SHERIDAN T. "An Account of Brazil." Newsport News
[Va.] Daily Press (9 February).
Calls Brazil on the Move "informative and entertaining."

19 KING, MARY LYNN CARLSON. "Mr. Dos Passos Takes An Intimate
Look At Brazil." Greensboro Daily News (12 January).
Says that Brazil on the Move is "well written, hap-
hazardly organized, hastily edited, and all the more fascinating for those very reasons."

20 KNOX, GEORGE. "Dos Passos and Painting." Texas Studies in
Literature and Language, 6 (Spring), 22-38.
Notes Dos Passos' accomplishments as a painter and argues
that his experience as a painter affected and paralleled
his writing style.. Discusses his career up to U.S.A. as a
move from fin de siècle romanticism to impressionism to
cubism. Reprinted: 1971.B2.

21 LANDSBERG, MELVIN. "John R. Dos Passos: His Influence on the
Novelist's Early Political Development." American Quarterly,
16 (Fall), 473-485.
Briefly summarizes the life, career, and writing of Dos
Passos' father and tries to suggest ways in which his ideas
may have influenced the novelist.

22 LEHAN, RICHARD. "The Trilogies of Jean-Paul Sartre and John
Dos Passos." Iowa English Yearbook, 9 (Fall), 60-64.
Argues that Sartre's trilogy, Les Chemins de la Liberté,
owes "a huge debt" to U.S.A., both for its technique and for
Dos Passos' "ability to immerse a reader in a historical
situation and to create a kind of existential reality,"
which Sartre tried to emulate. Reprinted: 1971.A2.

23   LYDENBERG, JOHN. "Dos Passos' U.S.A.: The Words of the Hollow
     Men," in Essays on Determinism in American Literature.
     Edited by Sydney J. Krause. Kent, Ohio: Kent State
     University Press, pp. 97-107.
          Argues that Dos Passos' main concern in U.S.A. is with
     the debasement of our language, its perversion by the
     "forces of modern society and ancient prejudices which
     renders it unable to express the truth." Reprinted:
     1971.A2; 1974.A3.

*24 McCREADY, JAMES R. "Dos Passos on the Issues of Time."
     Baltimore Sun (16 December), p. 36a.
          Cited in "John Dos Passos Bibliography 1950-1966," by
     Virginia S. Reinhart. Twentieth Century Literature, 13
     (1967), 167-178.

25   MILLER, MABEL. "Short History of Burgeoning Brazil." Sioux
     City Sunday Journal (12 January).
          Calls Brazil on the Move an interesting account of a
     fascinating country.

26   MILLGATE, MICHAEL. "John Dos Passos," in his American Social
     Fiction: James to Cozzens. New York: Barnes and Noble,
     pp. 128-141, passim.
          Feels that the entire presentation of American society
     in U.S.A. is based on moral indignation: "His rationale may
     have been economic and political, but his impetus, however,
     closely identified with the rational, was moral and
     emotional." Traces the origins of Dos Passos' view of
     society, emphasizing the influence of Thorstein Veblen.
     Also impressed with the "ease, swiftness, and flexibility
     of his narrative."

27   MIZENER, ARTHUR. "The Dilemma of the American Novelist," in
     his The Sense of Life in the Modern Novel. Boston: Houghton
     Mifflin, pp. 148-154, passim.
          Discusses Dos Passos' dilemma: "It is difficult not to
     feel that Dos Passos is a man who found himself confronted
     by two irreconcilable senses of life, the personal and the
     public, and resolved his difficulty by an act of will,
     forcing his main attention onto a rigidly public sense of
     life and allowing his personal sense of it expression only
     on carefully limited occasions." Mizener thinks this
     results in two-dimensional characterization, and absence
     of a sense of inner life.

28   O'CONNOR, WILLIAM VAN, ed. Seven Modern American Novelists:
     An Introduction. Minneapolis: University of Minnesota
     Press, pp. 9, 98, 101, 116, 151.

1964

> Several references. Feels Fitzgerald's "May Day," with
> its "three plots with intertwining action," is similar to a
> Dos Passos chronicle novel.

29 OLINER, STANLEY. Review of Occasions and Protests. Library
    Journal, 89 (1 November), 4365.
    > Considers "notable" the word portraits of prominent
    Americans in Occasions and Protests.

30 RABKIN, GERALD. Drama and Commitment: Politics In The American
    Theatre of the Thirties. Bloomington: Indiana University
    Press, pp. 30, 81, 128, 129, 142, 143.
    > A number of references to Dos Passos, particularly to
    his artistic relationship to John Howard Lawson.

31 RITALIN, THANE. Review of Occasions and Protests. Best Seller,
    24 (15 November), 323-324.
    > Finds Occasions and Protests animated with vitality and
    dedication. Feels there are few creative writers "as
    meaningfully concerned as he is with whatever it is that is
    gnawing at our national vitals." Considers the verbal por-
    traits to be an "inimitable synthesis of the journalist's
    and the fictionist's visions and techniques."

32 RUOFF, GENE W. "Social Mobility and the Artist in Manhattan
    Transfer and The Music of Time." Wisconsin Studies in
    Contemporary Literature, 5 (Spring), 64-76.
    > Notes the dissimilarities between Dos Passos and Anthony
    Powell but goes on to point up a basic and crucial similar-
    ity; that in their works knowledge is to be gained not from
    a study of the hidden inner man as in Joyce or Proust, but
    from "empirical analyses of the relation between the indi-
    vidual and social forces."

33 STEWART, D. J. Elbow Room for the Eye. National Review, 16
    (1 December), 1072-1073.
    > Focuses on the "emphatic 'visualism'" of Dos Passos in
    this review of Occasions and Protests. Finds Dos Passos'
    greatest passion to be the clear perception of things and
    his greatest foe in that or those who would impose blinders,
    who would blur the vision.

34 SWIFT, ESTHER M. Review of Thomas Jefferson: The Making of a
    President. Library Journal, 89 (15 September), 117.
    > Calls this book an outstanding biography for children.

35 WITHAM, W. TASKER. The Adolescent in the American Novel 1920-
    1960. New York: Frederick Ungar Publishers, pp. 15, 94,
    160, 262, 284.

Several references to Dos Passos' use of adolescent
characters.

1965 A   BOOKS - NONE

1965 B   SHORTER WRITINGS

1 ALSTON, E. B. "A Collection of Essays By An Astute Observer."
   Newport News Daily Press (7 March).
       Calls Dos Passos "lucid and forthright" and Occasions
   and Protests "serious and worthwhile."

2 ANON. "Between the Bookends." Clovis [N. Mex.] News Journal
   (13 May).
       Calls Occasions and Protests a "relaxed, but informative,
   view of the history of the past three decades" which empha-
   sizes Dos Passos' concern with individual freedom.
   Reprinted:
   Crossett [Ark.] News Observer (13 May).
   Crown Point [Ind.] Lake County Star (4 June).
   Cuero [Tex.] Record (13 May).
   Eunice [La.] News (13 May).
   Fulton [Miss.] Times (13 May).
   Houston [Miss.] Times-Post (20 May).
   Lake Wales [fla.] Highlander (14 May).
   Lima [Ohio] News (12 May).
   Pampa [Tex.] News (17 May).
   Santa Ana [Calif.] Register (25 May).

3 ANON. Review of Occasions and Protests. Choice, 1 (January),
   478.
       Feels Occasions and Protests "completes the linear move-
   ment of Dos Passos from the left to the right." Finds many
   of the earlier essays to seem more conservative when taken
   out of context and juxtaposed with later work.

4 ANON. Review of Occasions and Protests. Miami Courier
   (30 January).
       Calls the book "a collection of essays and articles of
   diverse quality." Reprinted: 1965.B6; 1965.B7.

5 ANON. Review of Occasions and Protests. New England Farmer
   (June).
       Calls the book "one of the better collections of the
   writing and opinions of a good author and a conservative."

1965

6 ANON. Review of <u>Occasions and Protests</u>. <u>Philadelphia Courier</u>
   (30 January).
      Reprint of 1965.B4.

7 ANON. Review of <u>Occasions and Protests</u>. <u>Pittsburgh Courier</u>
   (30 January).
      Reprint of 1965.B4.

8 ANON. Review of <u>Occasions and Protests</u>. <u>Social Education</u>, 29
   (April), 263.
      Calls <u>Occasions and Protests</u> "a book of competently
   written essays that . . . beat the drum for more individual
   liberty while, at the same time, suggesting we place our
   wagons in a circle so that we might beat off an attack by
   Communists (who are inside the circle)."

9 BERTHOFF, WARNER. <u>The Ferment of Realism: American Literature</u>,
   <u>1884-1919</u>. New York: The Free Press, pp. 37, 47, 283.
      Several references to Dos Passos. Notes Dos Passos'
   contribution to the modern development of the realist novel.

10 BORENSTEIN, WALTER. "The Failure of Nerve: The Impact of Pio
   Baroja's Spain on John Dos Passos," in <u>Nine Essays in Modern</u>
   <u>Literature</u>. Edited by Don Stanford. Baton Rouge:
   Louisiana State University Press, pp. 63-87.
      Examines the thematic similarities in the work of Dos
   Passos and Baroja. Concludes that Dos Passos found, in
   novels such as <u>La lucha por la vida</u>, "both inspiration and
   corroboration of ideas that had long been stirring within
   his troubled mind."

11 BRAINE, JOHN. "A Novelist Should Stick to His Last." <u>New</u>
   <u>York Times Book Review</u> (10 January), pp. 1, 24.
      Calls <u>U.S.A.</u> "the great American novel." It was "a
   mansion built at a time when every other author was building
   Cape Cod Cottages." Still, <u>Occasions and Protests</u> is a
   "sad, drab book" because Dos Passos loses his objectivity,
   because he lowers himself to mouthing common sentiments.
   Dos Passos, and any novelist, it is held, lose their power
   when they try to speak their views directly.

12 BROOKS, VAN WYCK. <u>Van Wyck Brooks: An Autobiography</u>. New
   York: E. P. Dutton and Co., 103pp., passim.
      A number of references to Dos Passos including brief
   personal sketches, and some evaluation of his writing.
   Brooks feels that "few things were more interesting than
   the development of this remarkable writer."

1965

13 CARGILL, OSCAR. "Anatomist of Monsters," in his Toward a
    Pluralistic Criticism. Carbondale: Southern Illinois
    University Press, pp. 150-188.

        Briefly compares Robert Penn Warren's Willie Stark with
    Dos Passos' Chuck Crawford and concludes that Warren's
    creation is more realistic, more plausible. Also notes the
    influence of expressionist film on Dos Passos.

14 DE POTO, ALFRED. "With Old Magic." The Newark News
    (7 March).
        Feels that, in Occasions and Protests, Dos Passos "demon-
    strates that he has not lost his ability to stir readers."
    While the reader would not question the power of the writing,
    DePoto feels there is much in the subject matter with which
    to quarrel.

15 DUTHIE, O. B. "Nostalgic Collage." Pittsburgh Press
    (21 February).
        Considers Occasions and Protests effective because Dos
    Passos has "no social theory to promote, no conviction to
    sell."

16 EBY, CECIL D. "We Agree, But We Did That Anyway." Roanoke
    Times (18 April).
        Wonders at the need for Occasions and Protests for it
    "describes the symptoms of the cancer [upon society], a
    disease we recognize all too well, but evades the important
    matter of prescribing a cure."

17 FAULKNER, WILLIAM. "Address to the American Academy of Arts
    and Letters in Presenting the Gold Medal for Fiction to
    John Dos Passos," in Essays, Speeches and Public Letters.
    Edited by James B. Meriwether. New York: Random House,
    pp. 153-154.
        Speech delivered in New York, May 22, 1957. Reprinted
    from Proceedings of the American Academy of Arts and Letters
    and the National Institute of Arts and Letters. Second
    series. New York, 1958.

18 FELIX, DAVID. Protest: Sacco-Vanzetti and the Intellectuals.
    Bloomington: Indiana University Press, pp. 12-13, 171, 204,
    232, 241, 242-243, 247.
        Mentions Dos Passos' involvement in, and the effect on,
    his subsequent views of the Sacco and Vanzetti affair.
    Considers the Sacco and Vanzetti sections of U.S.A. to be
    the weakest part of the trilogy.

19 FETLER, JOHN. "Current Books." Colorado Springs Gazette-
    Telegraph (6 May).
        Mentions Occasions and Protests.

1965

20 GIFFORD, DON. "The Individual vs. Society." New Leader, 48
   (15 March), 18-19.
      Despite dust jacket claims that Occasions and Protests
   intends to raise questions, not to present "settled theory,"
   finds a very settled and very hollow theory of individualism. Considers this theory based on a naive, anti-
   intellectual notion of a natural man "who shares 'certain
   simple realities which are universal to all men.'"

21 GORDON, ROSALIE. "Collection From A Master." America's
   Future (23 April), pp. 5, 6.
      Calls Occasions and Protests "a rich and rewarding volume
   by a master craftsman." Lambasts those liberal critics
   "who forsook concern for individual liberty" and who have
   branded Dos Passos a "turncoat."

22 GORMAN, THOMAS RICHARD. "Dos Passos and the Drama." Speech
   Monographs, 32 (November), 420-426.
      Surveys Dos Passos' activity as a critic of theatre, a
   playwright, and a founder of the New Playwrights Theatre.

23 HARRIS, PHIL. "Challenges From Dos Passos." Tampa Tribune
   (14 February).
      Calls Occasions and Protests "a sort of potpourri of the
   life and times of John Dos Passos . . . a lucid and facile
   writer."

24 MEYER, ROY W. The Middle Western Farm Novel in the Twentieth
   Century. Lincoln: University of Nebraska Press, p. 222.
      Includes a summary of Leroy Mac Leod's 1934 novel, The
   Crowded Hill which attempts "to catch the flavor of the
   times by the use of a device comparable to Dos Passos'
   'Newsreels'" but is not, Meyer feels, as successful.

25 SPILLER, ROBERT E. "The Alchemy of Literature," in his The
   Third Dimension, Studies in Literary History. New York:
   Macmillan, pp. 153-171.
      Finds Dos Passos working with a direct, specific, real-
   istic approach to his subject in Three Soldiers and moving
   toward symbolic structure in U.S.A. Finds, however, that
   Dos Passos cannot, in this work, offer his reader any
   clarifying generalization about the ultimate meaning of
   the symbolic presentation.

26 STEGNER, WALLACE, ed. The American Novel: From James Fenimore
   Cooper to William Faulkner. New York: Basic Books, pp.
   207, 220.
      Passing references.

27 STUHLMANN, GUNTHER, ed. <u>Henry Miller Letters to Anais Nin</u>.
New York: G. P. Putnam's Sons, pp. 17, 143, 370, 376.
Several passing references to Dos Passos and a personal
evaluation from Miller: "You say Dos Passos is not very
human. Did you meet him? I had quite the opposite impres-
sion--found him very warm and likable. Don't judge from
his books."

28 SWANBERG, W. A. <u>Dreiser</u>. New York: Charles Scribner's Sons,
pp. 384-386, 391, 403, 406, 413, 424, 447, 495.
A number of references to contacts between Dos Passos
and Dreiser, from their visit to the Harlan County coal
fields and on.

29 WARD, JOHN W. "Lindbergh, Dos Passos, and History." <u>Carleton
Miscellany</u>, 6 (Summer), 20-41.
Feels that the two popular views of Lindbergh's flight--
that it was either a triumph of the individual or a triumph
of the machine--provide the poles of conflict of <u>U.S.A.</u>,
which is characterized as "the coldest, most mercilessly
despairing book in our literature."

1966 A BOOKS

1 BELKIND, ALLEN J. "Satirical Social Criticism in the Novels
of John Dos Passos." Unpublished doctoral dissertation,
University of Southern California, 337pp.
Feels that there has been much confusion in Dos Passos
criticism because critics have tried to label him simply
a realist or naturalist and overlook his true genius as a
satirist. Belkind attempts to remedy the situation by
analyzing the satirical elements in a number of Dos Passos'
novels.

2 EVANS, WILLIAM ALFRED. "Influences On and Development of John
Dos Passos' Collectivist Technique." Unpublished doctoral
dissertation, University of New Mexico.
Studies Dos Passos' journey towards developing an appropriate form to express his collectivist views, culminating
in <u>U.S.A.</u>

1966 B SHORTER WRITINGS

1 ALDRIDGE, JOHN W. <u>Time to Murder and Create: The Contemporary
Novel in Crises</u>. New York: David McKay Publishers, pp.
11, 16, 69, 146.

1966

Mentions the indebtedness, in their first novels, of
Norman Mailer, James Jones, and Irwin Shaw to "the pano-
ramic-naturalist view of society that Dos Passos made
fashionable in U.S.A. and Manhattan Transfer."

2 ALEXANDER, HOLMES. Review of The Shackles of Power. Tampa
Tribune (7 August).
Feels that, in one sense, The Shackles of Power is
flawed by Dos Passos' focus on personality; in another
sense, this focus—particularly when on Jefferson—makes
the book "a deeply moving work."

3 ANON. "Dos Passos Looks At Jefferson Era." Galveston News
(21 May).
Calls The Shackles of Power "a memorable portrait of
Thomas Jefferson . . . rich in detail . . . an impressive
full-length portrait."

4 ANON. "Dos Passos Studies Jefferson." Sioux City Journal
(12 June).
Calls The Shackles of Power a "bright, refreshing look"
at the Jeffersonian era, an "enlightening overview of the
time."

5 ANON. "Dos Passos Tells of 'Best Times.'" Fort Lauderdale
News-Sun-Sentinel (27 November).
Thinks that The Best Times shows that, though Dos Passos
was often accused of "running away from himself he was
actually running at top speed, despite recurrent illness
and an often empty wallet, toward the whole wide world."

6 ANON. "Dos Passos Writes His Memoirs." The Grand Rapids
Press (20 November).
Notes that The Best Times is basically reportorial
rather than analytic. Reprinted: 1966.B

7 ANON. "The Hidden Artist." Time, 88 (18 November), 127.
Review of The World in a Glass and The Best Times which
attempts to pinpoint the reasons for the eclipse of Dos
Passos' literary reputation. Concludes that there were
basically three: a change in literary fashion which "left
him beached with the wreckage of the realistic novel," his
changing political views, his reluctance to exploit his
own personality.

8 ANON. "High Drama." Omaha World-Herald (19 June).
Calls The Shackles of Power "fine historical drama."

9 ANON. "John Dos Passos." Tulsa World (4 December).
Very brief summary of The Best Times.

10 ANON. "New Edition." Boston Sunday Globe (4 December).
        Notes the publication of District of Columbia.

11 ANON. Review of The Best Times. McClurgs Book News (October).
        Short review. Feels The Best Times presents Dos Passos'
        basic thought: "his deep belief in the Puritan ethic, the
        value of hard work as moral nourishment, the traditions of
        the yeoman."

12 ANON. Review of The Best Times. Monroe [Mich.] News
        (12 December).
        Calls The Best Times "an interesting book about a man
        who has had an interesting life and recalls his best times
        with verve."

13 ANON. Review of The Best Times. Virginia Kirkus Review, 34
        (1 October), 1087.
        Calls The Best Times "Dos Passos' best book in years,"
        a surprisingly warm book, primarily free from gossip, the
        stories which are told, "pretty wonderful."

14 ANON. Review of District of Columbia. Los Angeles Herald-
        Examiner (9 October).
        Calls Dos Passos "a literary titan" and feels that
        District of Columbia is a worthy heir to U.S.A.

15 ANON. Review of District of Columbia and Most Likely to
        Succeed. Roanoke Times (20 November).
        Notes the reissue of District of Columbia and Most Likely
        to Succeed. Feels that in the latter work "the solidity
        of the author's fictional world comes through beautifully."

16 ANON. Review of The Shackles of Power. Chicago American
        (8 May).
        Feels that the book is flawed by "labyrinthine" sentences
        and "frequent unsupported proclamations."

17 ANON. Review of The Shackles of Power. Chicago Heights Star
        (8 May).
        Finds the book "far too long . . . and spotted with awk-
        ward writing."

18 ANON. Review of The Shackles of Power. Choice, 3 (October),
        710.
        Brief review. Finds the "scholarship respectable, the
        insights those of a skilled journalist and analyst, the
        writing that of an experienced novelist."

1966

19 ANON. Review of The Shackles of Power. Christian Century, 83
    (11 May), 624.
        Feels book will help restore some of the lost esteem for
    Dos Passos, for he "eschews some of the ideology which has
    marred much of his recent work."

20 ANON. Review of The Shackles of Power. New Yorker, 42
    (28 May), 143.
        Finds the book "unsystematic and chatty, paying . . .
    much attention to individuals." Does not consider it a
    definitive study but finds it "in its affectionate familiar-
    ity with the illustrious dead, more than entertaining."

21 ANON. Review of The Shackles of Power. Newsday (7 May).
        Admires Dos Passos' ability to make the past come alive.

22 ANON. Review of The Shackles of Power. Virginia Kirkus Review,
    34 (15 January), 94.
        Admires the biographical portraits of the principal
    characters, particularly Burr and Jefferson, but finds
    the book as a whole "diffuse" and "awkwardly arranged."

23 ANON. Review of World In A Glass. Atlantic Monthly, 218
    (September).
        Feels that the coherence of World In A Glass "derives
    from the fact that the country here described was always
    a central character in Dos Passos' fiction." Feels that,
    despite Dos Passos' political shift, "a remarkably consis-
    tent picture emerges . . . [because] the personal and
    national values remain resilient."

24 ANON. Review of World In A Glass. Los Angeles Herald-
    Examiner (18 December).
        Considers The World In A Glass a "bountiful selection"
    of Dos Passos' work.

25 ANON. Review of World In A Glass. Virginia Kirkus Review, 34
    (1 July), 644.
        Notes the excellent introduction by Kenneth Lynn of this
    collection of fifty years of Dos Passos' writing--"a
    mammoth lifetime's work." Concludes that "although Dos
    Passos has been faulted for the obtrusiveness of his opin-
    ions, for the slackness of his documentary style, his work
    has been both representative and significant and no one has
    questioned its essential sincerity, indignation and 'formi-
    dable independence.'"

26 ANON. "Skullduggery In Early Day Washington." Springfield
    State Journal-Register (22 May).
        Brief review of The Shackles of Power.

27 ANON. "The Three Jefferson Decades." The Gary Sunday Post-
      Tribune Panorama (8 May).
           Reprint of 1966.B

28 B., C. K. "Dos Passos and Left Bank Companions." St. Louis
      Globe Democrat (5 November).
           Calls The Best Times "good humored and modest [with]
      touches of the old magic."

29 [BARKHAM, JOHN]. "Absorbing Detail Fills Narrative." The
      Grand Rapids Press (8 May), p. 29.
           Finds The Shackles of Power "absorbing in its detail."
      As a result, "the book offers a crowded and often dramatic
      panorama" of emerging America. Reprinted: 1966.B32;
      1966.B33.

30 BARKHAM, JOHN. "Dos Passos: Age And The Writers." Hackensack
      Record (17 December).
           Account of conversation with Dos Passos in which the
      author says he has no plans to write a sequel to The Best
      Times. Dos Passos says the more deliberate pace of his
      recent books is "the natural result of aging."

31 [BARKHAM, JOHN]. "Dos Passos the Man." Lincoln Sunday Journal
      and Star (20 November).
           Thinks it disappointing that Dos Passos excludes any
      discussion of the process of writing from The Best Times,
      but still thinks the memoir is "a highly entertaining chap-
      ter of personal history." Reprinted:
      B[arkham], J[ohn]. "Dos Passos the Man Appears." Albany
           Times Union (20 November).
      Barkham, John. "Dos Passos Writes of Friends, Travels."
           Norfolk Virginian Pilot (20 November).
      B[arkham], J[ohn]. "Informal Memoir by Dos Passos."
           Philadelphia Sunday Bulletin (1 December).
      Barkham, John. Review of The Best Times. Dallas Morning
           News (20 November).

32 BARKHAM, JOHN. "John Dos Passos' History of the Jefferson
      Period." Toledo Blade (15 May).
           Reprint of 1966.B29.

33 _____. "Three Decades of Jefferson." San Francisco Chronicle
      (10 June).
           Reprint of 1966.B29.

34 BELLMAN, SAMUEL I. "Dos Passos Balance Redressed." Los
      Angeles Times Calendar (23 October).

1966

>   Feels that the reissue of <u>District of Columbia</u> and <u>Most
> Likely to Succeed</u> may help Dos Passos "take his rightful
> place among the major American writers of the 20th century."

35 BILLINGS, CLAUDE. Review of <u>The Best Times</u>. <u>Indianapolis Star</u>
    (10 December).
>   Feels Dos Passos' memoir will give the reader "a much
> better appreciation of the great writer he is."

36 BLOTNER, JOSEPH. <u>The Modern American Political Novel, 1900–
    1960</u>. Austin: University of Texas Press, pp. 215-217, 312–
    315, 360-361, passim.
>   Many references to Dos Passos and his works. Blotner
> does not feel that Dos Passos was caught in the trap of
> sacrificing art to politics as many other politically
> oriented writers were.

37 BROWN, FRANK C. Review of <u>The Shackles of Power</u>. <u>Best Sellers</u>,
    26 (1 June), 96.
>   Feels that there is much that Dos Passos leaves out but
> that the character portrayals are matchless.

38 BROWN, TERRY. "John Dos Passos Looks Back At Writing Career."
    <u>Pasadena Independent Star-News</u> (18 December).
>   Calls <u>The Best Times</u> "restless and dynamic . . . less
> informal than it is viable and eventful."

39 BUSSEY, EVAN. Review of <u>The Shackles of Power</u>. <u>Charleston
    News and Courier</u> (20 November).
>   Feels the book is well written and offers "good insight"
> into Jefferson and his times.

40 BUTTERS, TOM. "Social Truths Brought Out By Dos Passos."
    <u>Indianapolis Star</u> (18 December).
>   Feels that the reissues of <u>Most Likely to Succeed</u> and
> <u>District of Columbia</u> only show how quickly Dos Passos'
> work becomes dated. Harshly critical of the "sophomoric
> dialogue" and the "political naivete" of the novels.

41 BYCZYNSKI, STUART. "Dos Passos Novel Exciting and Perceptive."
    <u>Baltimore News American</u> (16 October).
>   Feels that the significance of <u>Most Likely to Succeed</u>
> "rests on a chronicling--not of generations, which are
> temporary--but of human nature and human personality and
> human reactions, which are largely universal and do not die
> easily." Calls it "an interesting, exciting and greatly
> rewarding novel."

42 BYRD, SCOTT. "Dos Passos, New and Old, Makes Engaging Reading."
    Charlotte Observer (6 November).
    Congratulates Kenneth Lynn for his intelligent and taste-
    ful editing of World In A Glass, a collection which "reminds
    us of what a shrewd and skillful writer Dos Passos is--and
    what an entertaining one." Also, admires the "rambling
    informality of genial conversation" which characterizes the
    style of The Best Times which "may seem almost cheerfully
    old-fashioned."

43 CALDWELL, STEPHEN F. "Occasional Sparks." Hackensack Record
    (3 December).
    Feels that The Best Times alternates between passages
    which are "mere outlines, devoid of content and without
    impact" and passages "filled with humanity and beauty."
    Unfortunately, he feels, these latter passages are all too
    infrequent.

44 CALTON, WILLIAM B. "The Age of Jefferson." Washington Post
    Book Week (29 May), p. 13.
    Finds The Shackles of Power to lack "balance, focus,
    structure, cohesiveness, theme, and continuity." The re-
    sult is "little more than a study in personalities inter-
    spersed with episodic narrative."

45 CAPPON, R. J. "Jefferson Force Remains Evident." Allentown
    [Pa.] Call-Chronicle (29 May).
    Calls The Shackles of Power "old-fashioned" history in
    the sense that it focuses on men more than institutions and
    social forces. Nevertheless, feels that it "succeeds
    admirably." Reprinted:
    _____. "Novelist Dos Passos Turns Historian In Study of
    Jefferson." Fort Smith [Ark.] Southwest-Times Record
    (29 May).
    _____. Review of The Shackles of Power. Portland [Me.]
    Sunday Telegram (29 May).
    _____. "Study of Jeffersonian Era Made by John Dos Passos."
    Jackson Sun (31 July).

46 CARBERRY, EDWARD. "Turning New Leaves: A Past Recaptured."
    The Cincinnati Post and Times Star (19 November), p. 2.
    Calls Dos Passos "the U.S.'s most distinguished living
    novelist," and considers The Best Times enchanting.

47 CHAMBERLAIN, JOHN. "Shedding Friendships." The Freeman, 16
    (November), 60-64.
    Review of The Best Times which stresses the importance
    of Dos Passos' unusual childhood which "made him a curious

1966

but somewhat aloof spectator of life." Discusses the
Hemingway-Dos Passos relationship and their falling out
during the Spanish Civil War. Feels that their friendship
ended at least partially because Dos Passos "kept on growing intellectually where Hemingway did not."

48 CHAMBERLIN, WILLIAM HENRY. "A Novelist's Approach To
   Jeffersonian Years." Wall Street Journal (2 August), p. 14.
      Calls Dos Passos, himself, "Jeffersonian in his distrust
   of excessive state power," and finds The Shackles of Power
   to be "agreeable reading."

49 COOKE, JACOB E. Review of The Shackles of Power. Pennsylvania
   Magazine of History and Biography (October), pp. 542-543.
      Faults Dos Passos for over-reliance on secondary sources
   and for not even using the most important secondary sources.

50 CORBETT, EDWARD D. J. Review of The Best Times. America, 115
   (17 December), 808-809.
      Admires many of the portraits of Dos Passos' contempo-
   raries, but feels that "there's a world-weariness about the
   tone of this memoir--the ennui of the man who has experienced
   everything and has been more often disillusioned than in-
   spirited by what he has seen and heard and felt."

51 COWLEY, MALCOLM. The Faulkner-Cowley File: Letters and
   Memories, 1944-1962. New York: The Viking Press, pp. 142-
   143, 145-147, passim.
      A number of references to Dos Passos, including a letter
   from Cowley about the Gold Medal of the Institute for Fiction
   which Dos Passos received in 1957. In writing to Faulkner
   to ask him to make the presentation, Cowley says of Dos
   Passos: "of course his recent work hasn't been up to the
   level of what he did in the twenties and thirties, but he
   did a lot then; he took chances; he put other novelists in
   his lasting debt."

52 CULLER, JOHN. "Author Documents Jefferson's Tenure In The
   White House." Columbus Enquirer (15 August).
      Calls Shackles of Power not only educational and enlight-
   ening, but enjoyable reading as well. Especially likes Dos
   Passos' account of the military aspects of the revolution.

53 DAUGHTREY, ANITA. "Informal Memoirs By John Dos Passos."
   The Fresno Bee (25 December), p. 13f.
      Feels that, in The Best Times, Dos Passos writes with
   "humor, good taste, and zest," of those select times which
   nurtured his personal growth. Thinks that the account of
   his father "outshines, emotionally, the rest of the book."

54 DAVIS, ROBERT GORHAM. "The Good Old Days." New York Times
    Book Review (25 December), pp. 4, 17.
        Thinks The Best Times valuable because it "tells how his
    sensibility was formed, where his feeling of history came
    from, and why he so much enjoyed life" in his early career.
    Feels that, like Hemingway's A Moveable Feast, this is a
    "remining of a romantic past" instead of an analysis of the
    effects of the past.

55 DERLETH, AUGUST. "Of John Dos Passos." Madison Capital Times
    (22 December), p. 5.
        Feels that District of Columbia is powerful because of
    "the passionate sincerity of Dos Passos' hatred of our
    failure." Calls World In A Glass "a very good sampling."

56 FRENCH, WARREN. The Social Novel at the End of an Era.
    Carbondale: Southern Illinois University Press, pp. 11-12,
    165.
        Thinks Dos Passos is locked into attitudes which pre-
    clude his artistic development, a problem which some of his
    contemporaries--including Hemingway, Faulkner, and Steinbeck
    --have avoided.

57 FRESHWATER, PHILIP C. "Dos Passos Gets Second Look--and
    Deservedly So." The Sacramento Bee (27 November).
        Calls Dos Passos the most underrated American writer,
    partly because of "political fashion" and partly because
    "Dos Passos has turned out in recent years some potboilers
    and some work which amounts to a parody of himself." Sur-
    veys the reissues of a number of recent novels, but feels
    the best introduction to Dos Passos' work is World In A
    Glass which indicates "what Dos Passos is ultimately aiming
    at: a history of our century shorn of the falsity that for-
    mal history imposes."

58 GRAY, RICHARD A. Review of The Shackles of Power. Library
    Journal, 91 (15 April), 2056, 2058.
        Calls The Shackles of Power "an excellent example of the
    method of historical montage," and "entertaining popular
    history."

59 GREBSTEIN, SHELDON NORMAN. John O'Hara. United States
    Authors Series. New York: Twayne Publishers, pp. 18, 19,
    150.
        Feels O'Hara's achievement comparable to Dos Passos' and
    Sherwood Anderson, and bemoans the fact that he has received
    considerably less critical recognition.

1966

60 GREENE, DANIEL. "Dos Passos Recalls the Old Literary Lions."
   National Observer (19 December), p. 19.
   Feels that, after a slow beginning, which focuses on Dos
   Passos' father, the narrative of The Best Times "perks up"
   and becomes a fascinating tale of the Lost Generation.

61 GREENWOOD, WALTER B. "John Dos Passos In Autobiography Is
   Chatty, Revealing." Buffalo Evening News (26 November).
   Feels that Dos Passos, "at age 70, is still a remarkably
   lively writer and thinker." Calls The Best Times a "chatty
   and revealing autobiography."

62 GRESHAM, WILLIAM D. "Three Books by Dos Passos." Wilmington
   Morning News (20 December).
   Feels that no author "has drawn on so large a canvas with
   so many variegated colors" as Dos Passos. Feels that World
   In A Glass is a fair sampling of that work. Finds little
   of interest in the re-issue of Most Likely to Succeed. Considers the style of The Best Times to be "as good as his
   best novels," but thinks it sad that the book spans only the
   early years of Dos Passos' career.

63 GRIMES, ROY. Review of The Shackles of Power. The Victorian
   Advocate (29 May), p. 10.
   Feels that Dos Passos can reveal history with "life-size
   clarity."

64 H., B. H. "Shackles of Power by Dos Passos." Springfield
   Sunday Republican (14 August), p. 12c.
   Calls The Shackles of Power "a book of artistic narrative
   qualities as well as of firm informative values."

65 HANDLIN, O. "Reader's Choice." Atlantic Monthly, 218
   (September), 140.
   Thinks that World In A Glass displays, in its selections
   from Dos Passos' novels, a "remarkably consistent picture
   . . . despite the shift of political position of the author.
   . . . From beginning to end, Dos Passos conveys a sense of
   the strivings for dignity of the people in all their
   variety."

66 HANSEN, HARRY. "Monticello and After." Saturday Review, 49
   (7 May), 99.
   Considers The Shackles of Power a fluid, well researched
   survey of Jefferson the statesman and private citizen and
   applauds the wide ranging attention to the social and political framework within which Jefferson moved.

67 HARRIS, STANLEY E., JR. "Refreshing, Impartial Account Of
      Significant Historic Era." Savannah Morning News (15 May).
         Finds The Shackles of Power "interesting but lacking in
      intensity."

68 HASWELL, RICHARD E. Review of The Shackles of Power. St. Louis
      Post-Dispatch (1 August).
         Feels that, for Dos Passos in The Shackles of Power,
      "history is biography, or rather, a web of interwoven
      biographies."

69 HAVIGHURST, WALTER. "Life's Best Years." Chicago Tribune
      (20 November), p. 7.
         Finds Dos Passos, in The Best Times, "generous in
      appreciation of his friends, laconic about his own work
      [providing] just an occasional glimpse of the developing
      novelist." Reprinted: 1966.B70.

70 _____. Review of The Best Times. The Shreveport Times
      (27 November).
         Reprint of 1966.B69.

71 HICKOK, RALPH. Review of The Shackles of Power. New Bedford
      Standard and Times (24 May).
         Admires Dos Passos' ability to bring a scene alive.

72 HICKS, GRANVILLE. "John Dos Passos Reminisces." Saturday
      Review, 49 (26 November), 33-34.
         Finds the most rewarding portions of The Best Times to
      be those in which Dos Passos writes about his contemporaries.
      Wonders about the considerable attention given to foreign
      travels, events covered in more detail in the travel books.
      Concludes that reading the memoir left him with renewed
      interest for the man.

73 HINDUS, MILTON. "Memoir of Youth." Boston Sunday Globe
      (27 November), p. 20a.
         Calls The Best Times "a very attractive piece of auto-
      biography . . . a memoir of youth written with great
      verve by a man who has remained extraordinarily young in
      spirit even while growing mature in his outlook upon the
      world."

74 HOFMANN, FRANK. "Writer's Memoir More Travelogue." Dayton
      Daily News (11 December).
         Compares The Best Times with A Moveable Feast. Feels
      that, unlike Hemingway, Dos Passos "stresses too often the

1966

> wrong things," making his book more a travelogue than a
> living account of the creative period in which he lived.

75 HOGAN, WILLIAM. "A Dusting Off of Dos Passos 'Failures.'"
    San Francisco Chronicle (27 September).
    > Notes the reissue of two Dos Passos novels which are
    > often considered failures: District of Columbia and Most
    > Likely to Succeed.

76 HOLDITCH, KENNETH. "One Man's Initiation: The Origin of
    Technique in the Novels of John Dos Passos," in Explorations
    of Literature. Edited by Rima D. Reck. Baton Rouge:
    Louisiana State University Press, pp. 115-123.
    > Feels the innovations in structure and use of symbols
    > and archetypal characters--all hallmarks of his later work
    > --in One Man's Initiation demonstrates the importance of
    > this first novel as a kind of apprenticeship.

77 HOWELL, I. L. "Masterful Historical Analysis." Columbus
    Dispatch (19 June).
    > Calls The Shackles of Power a "definitive" study.

78 HUBLER, RICHARD G. "Jefferson Versus Burr, Marshall." Los
    Angeles Times (5 June).
    > Calls the experience of reading The Shackles of Power
    > comparable to that of reading a fine novel: "all the
    > modulations and amplifications of fiction are here, almost
    > infinitely varied."

79 _____. "With Dos Passos." Los Angeles Times (4 December).
    > Calls The Best Times "a quietly charming, deliberately
    > disorganized exercise in remembrance."

80 IRVING, MAGGIE. "With Candor And Dignity." Worcester Telegram
    (11 December).
    > Calls The Best Times "gentle, unaffected . . . untouched
    > by spite."

81 JOHNSON, GERALD W. "America in the Early Nineteenth Century."
    Baltimore Evening Sun (16 May).
    > Compares Dos Passos' approach to history in The Shackles
    > of Power with Henry Adams in his work about the same period.
    > Calls Adams a classicist and Dos Passos an impressionist.

82 JORDAN, FOREST. Review of The Best Times. Long Beach Press
    Telegram (24 November).
    > Calls The Best Times "a walking tour through the fond
    > memories of [Dos Passos'] past." Feels that the account of

the early years is "a bit too precious," but calls the book lively for the most part.

83 K., J. J. "Dos Passos Reminisces on His Best Times." Richmond News Leader (9 November).
    Feels that the essential aim of a memoir is to entertain and that The Best Times scores "a superlative bull's-eye. . . . Through every paragraph, every sentence, every line, the essential goodness and kindness of the man shows through."

84 KAPLAN, HAROLD. "The Solipsism of Modern Fiction," in his The Passive Voice: An Approach to Modern Fiction. Athens: Ohio University Press, pp. 3-21.
    Critical of Dos Passos' "simplistic" psychological and sociological portrayal of human behavior. Concludes that Dos Passos' "field of vision is at the extreme of externality, so preoccupied by the superpersonal design of social and biological process that the agents within it seem mindless."

85 KITCHING, JESSIE. Review of The Best Times. Publishers Weekly, 190 (10 October), 72.
    Thinks Dos Passos' anecdotal approach is careless and casual and finds the book to be old literary gossip, neither "vivid [n]or interesting."

86 LIPTZIN, SOL. The Jew in American Literature. New York: Bloch Publishing Company, p. 153.
    Cites Dos Passos as a non-Jew who, nevertheless, characterized Jews in a generally sympathetic manner.

87 LOBDELL, JARED. "A Good Story Well Told." National Review, 18 (26 July), 738-739.
    Admires The Shackles of Power for its compelling narrative interest, but feels it sacrifices historical accuracy in its interpretations—particularly the heavy-handed treatment of Aaron Burr—and in its organization.

88 LYNN, KENNETH S. "Dos Passos' Chosen Country." New Republic, 155 (15 October), 15-18, 20.
    A general survey of Dos Passos' ideas and career which praises the vast scope of Dos Passos' art and especially applauds "the veritable anthology of the American idiom," that is U.S.A. Implies that Dos Passos has been—at least through most of his career—not out of step with the times, but ahead of them. Reprinted: 1966.B89.

1966

89 _____ . Introduction to <u>World in a Glass: A View of our Century</u>
<u>Selected from the Novels of John Dos Passos</u>. Boston:
Houghton-Mifflin Co., pp. v-xv.
Reprint of 1966.B88.

90 McDOWELL, EDWIN. "John Dos Passos Writes Tribute To The Age
of Thomas Jefferson." <u>The Arizona Republic</u> (25 September).
Calls <u>The Shackles of Power</u> "objective" and "eminently
fair."

91 McDOWELL, JOHN. "Dos Passos Book on Jefferson 'Lively.'"
<u>Fort Wayne News-Sentinel</u> (14 May).
Calls <u>The Shackles of Power</u> "an excellent historical
work"--a "lively account of a lively era."

92 MacGREGOR, MARTHA. "The Week in Books." <u>New York Post</u>
<u>Magazine</u> (29 October), p. 15.
Dos Passos chats about <u>The Best Times</u>: "'I wanted to get
down . . . a little picture of my father'"; painting: "'very
amusing occupation'"; and the literati: "'never been much
for these literary gatherings.'"

93 McHUGH, VINCENT. Review of <u>The Best Times</u>. <u>San Francisco</u>
<u>Examiner-Chronicle</u> (18 December), p. 45.
Feels that, of his generation, Dos Passos "had the
largest sense of those connections between events and
periods and generations that maintain the continuity of a
people." Hopes that <u>The Best Times</u> "is the first panel of
a longer autobiography."

94 MADDOCKS, MELVIN. "'Lost Generation' Drop-Out." <u>Christian</u>
<u>Science Monitor</u> (23 November), p. 15.
Feels that <u>The Best Times</u> contains some of Dos Passos'
best writing in years. In addition, the memoir offers a
unique and convincing view of his generation: "He has quite
deliberately grafted his autobiography onto the memory of
his father. The startling effect is to contradict the
whole assumption of the catch-phrase--Lost Generation.
Rather than dramatizing himself in the conventional posture
of the self-disinherited, Dos Passos has, through the
powerful and attractive presence of John Dos Passos Sr.,
thrust his own roots deep into America and its past. . . .
Dos Passos, by implication, has built a good case for the
Lost Generation being a continuing chapter in the tradition
of the American artist rather than a violent break with it."

96 MAILER, NORMAN. <u>Cannibals and Christians</u>. New York: Dial
Press, p. 98.

On Dos Passos' inability to revitalize American fiction: "Manners may be sufficient to delineate the rich but one needs a vision of society to comprehend the poor, and Dos Passos had only revulsion at injustice, which is ultimately a manner."

96 MILLGATE, MICHAEL. The Achievement of William Faulkner. London: Constable and Company, pp. 55, 81, 145, 291, 321.
    Feels the influences behind The Sound and the Fury were primarily European, but concedes "the possibility of certain minor influences from Sherwood Anderson and John Dos Passos."

97 MILNE, GORDON. The American Political Novel. Norman: University of Oklahoma Press, pp. 105-106, 136-138, passim.
    Mentions the District of Columbia trilogy which Milne thinks "adds up to a distinct accomplishment, by a man more touched than most by political concern, and more skilled than most in dramatizing that concern."

98 MOTTLEY, ROBERT. "Dos Passos Scans Life." Roanoke World News (15 December).
    Feels that Dos Passos keeps The Best Times "personal and tightly focused."

99 MOYNAHAN, JULIAN. "Quiet American." Observer Review (4 February).
    Feels that The Best Times lacks the "heart-stopping clarity" of Hemingway's A Moveable Feast.

100 MURRAY, JOHN J. Review of The Best Times. Bestsellers, 26 (15 December), 348-349.
    Feels the memoir is lively and informative, written with "the painter's peculiar perspective of looking at things in all their dimensions," but finds it only "second best" when compared to A Moveable Feast."

101 N., K. Review of Most Likely to Succeed. Oregon Journal (3 December).
    Brief summary of the book.

102 NICHOLS, LEWIS. "A Thought." New York Times (13 November).
    Brief profile on Dos Passos on the occasion of the publication of The Best Times.

103 NOLTE, WILLIAM H. H. L. Mencken: Literary Critic. Middletown, Conn.: Wesleyan University Press, pp. 167, 168, 170-171, 240-241, passim.

1966

Numerous references to Dos Passos and his early work
(Three Soldiers; Manhattan Transfer). Nolte often uses the
critical reaction to these books to demonstrate the differences between Mencken's criticism and those of other
critical schools, particularly the Humanists.

104 O., E. B. "We Repeat the Past." St. Paul Pioneer Press
     (12 June).
         Brief review of The Shackles of Power. Comments on how
     the present often repeats the past.

105 O'LEARY, THEODORE M. "Time Now for Another Look at the Words
     of Dos Passos." Kansas City Star (25 December).
         Calls The Best Times "a deliberately random sort of
     work." Thinks it unfortunate that most readers will come
     to the book to read about Hemingway and Fitzgerald rather
     than Dos Passos, then proceeds to relate Dos Passos' im-
     pressions of his two contemporaries. Admires The World In
     A Glass, but calls Kenneth Lynn's introduction inadequate
     because it fails to "note the decline of Dos Passos' powers
     as a novelist after political disillusionment set in."

106 O'NEILL, JOHN. Review of The Best Times. The Atlanta Journal
     and the Atlanta Constitution (27 November).
         Calls The Best Times an account of "full, full years
     excellently reported: precisely phrased, vivid, and objec-
     tive," but feels that this period between the wars was long
     ago dated.

107 OVERBECK, S. K. "Moveable Feast." Newsweek, 68 (21 November),
     134 B.
         Recounts anecdotes from The Best Times. Concludes that
     the memoir vibrantly captures the playfulness and later
     loss of the "golden boys" of modern American writing.

108 PAGE, JOSEPH A. "Dos Passos Puts 1930s in Focus." The Sunday
     Denver Post (27 November).
         Admires the wide-angle sweep of District of Columbia.

109 PASLEY, VIRGINIA. "Critic's Corner." Newsday (19 November).
         Calls The Best Times a lively memoir. Summarizes Dos
     Passos' political changes.

110 PFEIFFER, TED. "Reading History Is Fun, If It's Written in
     Dos Passos' Delightfully Chatty Style." Louisville Times
     (17 June).
         Calls The Shackles of Power a fine book "despite a cer-
     tain lightness of tone in dealing with events of great
     importance."

111 POORE, CHARLES. "Books of the Times." New York Times
(29 December).
Feels that in The Best Times the point of view is often
crusty and the humor only occasionally hits the mark.
Still, Poore finds "this idiosyncratic book" enjoyable.

112 POTTER, JACK. "Dos Passos: A Grasp of American Life."
Chicago Daily News (5 November).
Notes that, at one time, Dos Passos was, like Mencken,
"a kind of hero of the intellectuals," and feels that "no
writer has ever had anything like his grasp of American
life, from the councils of government to the novels of the
destitute." Thinks Dos Passos has been consistent in his
attacks on the powerful, but that "the touch of malice that
gave a cutting edge when he apostraphized Henry Ford was
resented when applied to Eleanor Roosevelt." Feels that
each reader must decide whether Dos Passos "is a prophet
largely without honor or the wreckage of a noble talent."

113 RAVITZ, ABE C. "Dos Passos and His Literary Friends." The
Plain Dealer (20 November).
Calls The Best Times "easy, pleasant reading, abounding
in anecdote and low-pressure talk about the American
literary community during its committed days."

114 REA, ROBERT R. "Thomas Jefferson's World." Washington D.C.
Evening Star (10 June).
Feels that the view of Jefferson which Dos Passos offers
in The Shackles of Power "possesses a vigor and reality that
can only come from a remarkable intimacy with the sources
of history and a rare ability to make them speak for
themselves."

115 REDDING, SAUNDERS. "The Negro Writer and American Literature,"
in Anger and Beyond: The Negro Writer In The United States.
Edited by Herbert Hill. New York: Harper and Row, pp. 1-19.
Considers Dos Passos to be a model for the experimental
tendencies in black writing which emerged in the early
thirties.

116 RIDEOUT, WALTER B. The Radical Novel in the United States:
1900-1954. Cambridge, Mass.: Harvard University Press,
pp. 247, passim.
Numerous brief references to Dos Passos and his work.

117 RINGER, AGNES C. Review of World in a Glass. Library Journal,
90 (15 December), 5394.
Calls World in a Glass an "admirable selection" of Dos
'Passos' writing. Considers his genius to lie "in his

1966

ability to integrate biography and autobiography, poetry, history, and criticism in panoramic novels."

118 ROSENFELD, ARNOLD. "Dos Passos Revisited." The Houston Post (27 November).
Notes the fact that U.S.A. was once banned from the University of Texas library. Feels that The Best Times, which shows how much Dos Passos has mellowed, "is distinguished by a series of comfortable sketches."

119 ROUSH, STANLEY. "Jefferson's Hand on Young Nation." Springfield [Mo.] Sunday News and Leader (8 May).
Thinks that The Shackles of Power is written "with scholarly research and compelling literary skill."

120 SANDERS, DAVID. "'Lies' and the System: Enduring Themes from Dos Passos' Early Novels." South Atlantic Quarterly, 65 (Spring), 215-228.
Study of the novels through Streets of Night which isolates a crucial thematic interest of Dos Passos' which develops then: "that institutions can grow beyond the point of being controlled by the human beings who create them."

121 SCOTT, GLENN. "J.D.P." Norfolk The Virginia-Pilot (18 December).
Remembers, on the occasion of the publication of The Best Times, a meeting with Dos Passos in the early 1950s at Washington and Lee University.

122 SHERMAN, JOHN K. Reviews of The Best Times and World In A Glass. Minnesota Tribune (20 January).
Calls Dos Passos one of the greatest writers of his generation and "one of the 'coolest,' the least prima donna" as well. Considers The Best Times the result of a "marvelously precise 'eye' goaded by a tireless curiosity . . . transferred to prose so lacking in conscious style or effect as to constitute a style in itself." Feels World In A Glass provides an excellent introduction to Dos Passos' world.

123 SHOWERS, PAUL. "The Jumble Shelf." New York Times Book Review (4 December), p. 38.
Calls World in a Glass an "impressive picture, a record of events and attitudes made vivid through fictional recreations and biographical summaries."

124 SMITH, MILES A. "Author Dos Passos As A Young Adventurer." Fayettesville Observer (20 November).

Calls The Best Times "a sprightly, exuberant, conversa-
tional memoir . . . and a not altogether modest account."
Reprinted:
[SMITH, MILES A.]. "Author Looks Back." Bloomington
Pantagraph (20 November).
_____. "Author's Memoir Sprightly, Exuberant."
Jackson City Patriot (13 November).
_____. "Dos Passos Looks Back With Gusto."
Philadelphia Enquirer (20 November).
S[MITH], M[ILES]. "Dos Passos Memoir Recalls a Zesty
Life." Columbis Dispatch (20 November).
[SMITH, MILES A.]. "Dos Passos Reviews Events With Gusto."
Winona, Minnesota News (20 November), p. 11.
SMITH, MILES A. "Dos Passos Tells About His Life."
Augusta Chronicle-Herald (20 November).
[SMITH, MILES A.]. "Dos Passos Tells About His Life."
Fredericksburg [Va.] Free Lance-Star (19 November).
SMITH, MILES A. "Dos Passos Tells of Early Years."
Salina Journal (2 December), p. 8.
[SMITH, MILES A.]. "'I'm Sinbad' By Dos Passos." Reno
Gazette (14 December).
SMITH, MILES A. "John Dos Passos Tells of His Life and
Those He Knew Along the Way." Poughkeepsie Journal
(20 November).
[SMITH, MILES A.]. "A Not-Too-Modest Dos Passos Memoir."
Middletown Journal (27 November).
_____. Review of The Best Times. Battle Creek Enquirer
and News (20 November).
SMITH, MILES A. Review of The Best Times. Rock Island
Argus (26 November).
[SMITH, MILES A.]. Review of The Best Times. Vallejo
Times-Herald (11 December).
SMITH, MILES A. "Sprinkling of Spice." Baltimore News
American (20 November).

125 SPARKS, DAVID S. "Eddies in The Mainstream." Baltimore
Sunday Sun (19 June), p. 22a.
    Admires Dos Passos' narrative expertise, but feels that
he misses, in The Shackles of Power, many of the most important issues and concerns of the times.

126 STELLA, CHARLES. "Other Writers Viewed Gently by Dos Passos."
Cleveland Press (9 December).
    Feels that The Best Times "is an unqualified delight,"
and reveals Dos Passos to be "gentle, modest, reserved and
always at pains to make excuses for churlish actions of his
fellow writers."

1966

127 STEVENS, HOLLY, ed. <u>Letters of Wallace Stevens</u>. New York:
     Alfred A. Knopf, pp. 286-287.
        Stevens criticizes, in a 1935 letter, the left as repre-
     sented in the <u>New Masses</u> in general, and Dos Passos in
     particular: "The other day I saw an article by Dospassos
     [sic] on Ford, which was an atrocious piece of writing and
     an incredible piece of thinking; and yet Dospassos is re-
     garded as an international figure. The literary world is a
     very small world and it takes almost nobody at all to look
     like a giant killer. <u>Masses</u> is just one more wailing place
     and the whole left now-a-days is a mob of wailers."

128 STOREY, ED. "Moral Tone of Government Shown Not So Saintly In
     Jefferson Era." <u>Newport News Daily Press</u> (29 May), p. 11.
        Feels that <u>The Shackles of Power</u> is valuable for it shows
     that, just as in the present, the early days of the nation
     had both its scoundrels and its saints.

129 STUCKEY, W. J. <u>The Pulitzer Novels: A Critical Backward Look</u>.
     Norman: University of Oklahoma Press, pp. 10, 32, 106, 149,
     162, 211.
        Many references to Dos Passos and his work. Includes
     <u>Three Soldiers</u> as one of the novels to appear shortly after
     World War I which questioned the standards of conventional
     morality.

130 THOMPSON, JEAN. "30 Years' Jeffersonia Jammed In." <u>Miami
     Herald</u> (12 June).
        Feels that the first third of <u>The Shackles of Power</u>, up
     to the end of Jefferson's presidency, is too "loosely-
     joined," but that the rest of the book is exciting and in-
     formative reading.

131 TOWLE, LAWRENCE W. "Our Great Experiment." <u>Hartford Courier</u>
     (14 August).
        Calls <u>The Shackles of Power</u> "perhaps more Jefferson
     biography than it is straight American history. Calls the
     book "a highly readable history, packed with facts, but
     never making the reader feel that he is being overwhelmed."

132 VAN MATRE, LYNN. "<u>World In A Glass</u> Captures Dos Passos'
     Genius, Insight." <u>Columbia Missourian</u> (4 Deember).
        Feels that <u>World In A Glass</u> demonstrates Dos Passos'
     genius and shows that his "literary world is, indeed, the
     image of an era."

133 VARBLE, RACHEL McBRAYER. Review of <u>The Shackles of Power</u>.
     <u>Register of the Kentucky Historical Society</u> (October), pp.
     340-342.

Calls the book's narrative "often pell-mell, sometimes slangy, but unfailingly vivid."

134 VERSTEEG, CLARENCE L. "An Era Rich with Personalities."
     Chicago Tribune Books Today (29 May), p. 8.
     Feels that Dos Passos' narrative gifts make this a fine impressionistic history, despite "the slighting of a number of issues which would normally loom large in such a volume."

135 WATTS, RICHARD, JR. Review of The Best Times. New York Post
     (13 December), p. 68.
     Feels The Best Times reveals Dos Passos as "a man of the rarest tolerance and mellowness."

136 WELLEJUS, ED. "Informal Memoir." Erie Daily Times
     (31 December).
     Calls The Best Times "a consistently interesting walking-tour through the fond memories of Dos Passos' life."

137 WILLS, GARRY. Review of The Best Times. Ave Maria
     (26 November).
     Notes The Best Times as one of a number of good, recent books by conservative authors.

138 WILSON, W. EMERSON. "The 19th Century's First Three Decades."
     Wilmington Morning News (9 May).
     Admires the character sketches in The Shackles of Power. Feels the book will enhance Dos Passos' reputation as an historian.

139 WOODRESS, JAMES, ed. American Literary Scholarship, 1964.
     Durham, N.C.: Duke University Press, pp. 141, 142, 147, 153, 155, 218-219.
     Reviews Dos Passos criticism of the year.

140 YOUNG, MARGUERITE. "A Journey Back to the Beginning." New
     York Post (17 November).
     Calls The Best Times "enthralling not only because Dos Passos' life has been crowded with unusual adventures and fabulous people and colorful places, but because he brings to this autobiographical study an exquisite accuracy and an imaginative interpretation . . . [he] is not only the incurably romantic Don Quixote. He is also the realistic Sancho."

141 YOUNG, PHILIP. Ernest Hemingway: A Reconsideration. University
     Park: The Pennsylvania State University Press, pp. 66, 99, 141, 148, 163.

1966

References to the relationship between Hemingway and Dos
Passos. Speculates that U.S.A. may have, in some way, influenced the social themes of To Have and Have Not.

142 ZINSER, BEN. Review of The Shackles of Power. Long Beach
Press-Telegram (25 May), p. 3c.
     Feels that Dos Passos "sketches masterfully his many
characters."

1967 A BOOKS

1 LYNDE, LOWELL F. "John Dos Passos: The Theme Is Freedom."
Unpublished doctoral dissertation, Louisiana State
University.
     Emphasizes Dos Passos' main concern as individual freedom
and his main socio-political influence the bitter and pessimistic Veblen rather than the optimistic Marx. Believes
that only when critics accept Dos Passos' intellectual heritage will they appreciate the consistency of his views and
elevate him to his proper critical stature.

1967 B SHORTER WRITINGS

1 BIGSBY, C. W. E. Confrontation and Commitment: A Study of
Contemporary American Drama, 1959-66. London: Macgebbon
and Kee, pp. 113, 118, 136-137.
     Believes that Dos Passos, and other politically committed
playwrights such as Sinclair and Lawson, were "prepared to
sacrifice artistic integrity to social expediency."

2 BRANDT, GEORGE. "Cinematic Structure in the Work of Tennessee
Williams," in American Theatre. Edited by John Russell
Brown and Bernard Harris. Stratford-Upon-Avon Studies 10.
London: Edward Arnold Publishers, pp. 163-188.
     Thinks Manhattan Transfer is a good example of the fact
that American novelists were quick to adapt film techniques.

3 BRITTIN, NORMAN A. Edna St. Vincent Millay. United States
Authors Series. New York: Twayne Publishers, p. 61.
     Mentions Dos Passos' involvement with Millay in the
defense of Sacco and Vanzetti.

4 BRYER, JACKSON R. "Broad Look At Dos Passos." Baltimore
Sunday Sun (15 January), p. 5.
     Feels that District of Columbia and Most Likely to Succeed
share the theme of the individual's struggle against a

dehumanizing society. Feels Dos Passos' concern with the
theme also causes its weakness for "the author is often
more concerned with what he has to say than how he says it."
Feels that Dos Passos' talent is unconventionality and he
is weakest when, as in Most Likely To Succeed, he ties himself to conventional narrative.

5 CHAMBERLAIN, JOHN. "'Dos' and the Underdog." Harpers, 234
   (January), 97.
      Feels that The Best Times reveals that Dos Passos was
   never an ideological radical or conservative; his interests
   were simply always with the underdog, whether he be a victim of big business or big government. It was always the
   institutions he opposed.

6 COOPERMAN, STANLEY. World War I and the American Novel.
   Baltimore: Johns Hopkins University Press, pp. 141-145,
   175-181, passim.
      Thematic study of the significance of World War I for a
   generation of American novelists. Extensive discussion of
   Dos Passos' contribution to the development of the modern
   American war novel.

7 COWLEY, MALCOLM. "Afterthoughts on Dos Passos," in his Think
   Back on Us. Edited by Henry Dan Piper. Carbondale:
   Southern Illinois University Press, pp. 298-301.
      Reprint of 1936.B13.

8 _____. "John Dos Passos: The Poet and the World," in his
   Think Back on Us. Edited by Henry Dan Piper. Carbondale:
   Southern Illinois University Press, pp. 212-219.
      Reprint of 1932.B17.

9 _____. "The Twenties in Montparnasse." Saturday Review, 50
   (11 March), 51, 55, 98-101.
      Quotes from The Best Times a passage about the buoyancy
   of youth which, although written about New York, could well
   be a summary of the life of the expatriates in Paris in the
   twenties.

10 DAHLBERG, EDWARD. Epitaphs of Our Times: The Letters of Edward
    Dahlberg. New York: George Braziller, pp. 12, 239, 258.
       Considers Dos Passos a "lowly clerk" of literature and
    calls him, Faulkner, and Hemingway "bestial provincial
    scribblers."

11 GORDON, WILLIAM A. The Mind and Art of Henry Miller. Baton
    Rouge: Louisiana State University Press, pp. 4, 34.

1967

Considers Dos Passos to be one of those writers who
"became for the most part politically oriented . . . [whose]
art did not keep pace with their enthusiasm for justice."

12 HART, JEFFREY. "John Dos Passos." National Review, 19
    (24 January), 93, 95-97.
        Notes Dos Passos' dedication to modernist technique: "as
    far as technique is concerned he is our most inventive
    novelist." Feels that, taken together, Dos Passos' novels
    are "clearly non-political," offering only the argument
    that modern life is not humane, regardless of politics.

13 HOLDITCH, KENNETH. "One Man's Initiation: The Origin of
    Technique in the Novels of John Dos Passos," in Explorations
    of Literature. Edited by Rima Dell Peck. Baton Rouge:
    Louisiana State University Press, pp. 115-123.
        Finds in Dos Passos' first novel many of the techniques
    "in embryonic form" which Dos Passos was to employ in later
    fiction. Notes particularly the use of juxtaposition,
    irony, and symbolism which dramatizes Dos Passos' lifelong
    conviction that "the modern world enslaves man and defeats
    individualism of any kind."

14 JOSEPHSON, MATTHEW. Infidel in the Temple: A Memoir of the
    Nineteen-Thirties. New York: Alfred A. Knopf, passim.
        Many references to Dos Passos and particularly to his
    political development. Considers Dos Passos to be, among
    New Republic contributors of the twenties, "one of the few
    who wrote as a convinced Marxist." By the thirties, when
    the communists had become "quite an army and thoroughly
    organized," Dos Passos saw them no longer as a vehicle for
    individual revolt, but as a threat to the individual.
    Josephson feels the "living newspaper" technique employed
    by the Federal Theatre Project was directly influenced by
    Dos Passos' "Camera eye" technique of using "vignettes of
    public personages figuring in the news of the day." From
    his description, it seems that Josephson meant either the
    biographies or newsreels rather than the camera eye.

15 LEDBETTER, KENNETH. "The Journey of John Dos Passos."
    Humanities Association Bulletin, 18 (Fall), 36-48.
        Surveys Dos Passos' career through Midcentury. Emphasizes
    the basic consistency of Dos Passos' philosophical anarchism.

16 LEWIS, R. W. B. The Poetry of Hart Crane: A Critical Study.
    Princeton, N.J.: Princeton University Press, p. 298n.
        After quoting from "The River," Lewis remarks, in a note,
    that "this device--of juxtaposing glamorous transcontinental

movement, along with financial and technological power,
with the figure of the hungry vagrant--was exploited by
John Dos Passos in the final pages of U.S.A. . . . for a
rather different artistic purpose. Devoted as Dos Passos
was to Whitman, it was the democratic and egalitarian rather
than the visionary Whitman that he sought to recover."

17 MIZENER, ARTHUR. "The Big Money," in his Twelve Great American
     Novels. New York: New American Library, pp. 87-103.
          Considers the technical innovations of U.S.A. to be
     "devices for emphasizing in a dramatic way the general
     social significance of individual men's experiences."
     Feels Dos Passos is "the only major American novelist of
     the twentieth century who has had the desire and power" to
     envelope his characters in their environment in this way.

18 MOSSIEN, ROSEMARY H. "Dos Passos Not Up to Par." Rochester
     Times-Union (3 January).
          Sees little in Most Likely to Succeed to compare with
     Manhattan Transfer or U.S.A. Does not care "a tinker's
     damn" about the novel's characters and subject matter.

19 PEYRE, HENRI. The Failures of Criticism. Ithaca, N.Y.:
     Cornell University Press, passim.
          Emended edition of Writers and Their Critics, 1944.

20 REINHART, VIRGINIA S. "John Dos Passos, 1950-1966: Bibliog-
     raphy." Twentieth Century Literature, 13 (October), 167-178.
          Primary and secondary bibliography which includes books,
     critical articles, book reviews, dissertations, and foreign
     publications.

21 RUBIN, LOUIS D. The Teller in the Tale. Seattle: University
     of Washington Press, p. 103.
          Mentions Dos Passos as a kind of novelist other than the
     type, typified by James and Proust, who chronicle the
     society of the drawing room.

22 RULAND, RICHARD. The Rediscovery of American Literature:
     Premises of Critical Taste, 1900-1940. Cambridge, Mass.:
     Harvard University Press, pp. 24, 54, 192, 293.
          Survey of American criticism with occasional mention
     of Dos Passos.

23 SANDERS, DAVID. John Hersey. United States Authors Series.
     New York: Twayne Publishers, pp. 24, 56, 98, 137, 139.
          Mentions the influence of Dos Passos' war novels--
     particularly Three Soldiers--on Hersey's chronicles of

1967

World War II. Also notes that Hersey is, like Dos Passos,
an "unclassifiable" writer, "both blessed and cursed by the
compulsion to deal with a wide variety of subjects and to
attempt a great diversity of fictional forms." As a result,
Sanders feels, neither writer has received the critical
attention he deserves.

24 SKLAR, ROBERT. "Dos Passos' Restless Times." Nation, 204
(16 January), 87-88.
Feels that Dos Passos' "fiction and reputation through
a generation have leapfrogged over each other downhill."
Thinks both World In A Glass and The Best Times will help
the reader understand how Jean-Paul Sartre could have called
Dos Passos the greatest writer of his time.

25 _____. F. Scott Fitzgerald: The Last Laocoon. New York:
Oxford University Press, passim.
Notes Fitzgerald's admiration for Dos Passos' early works
but Sklar speculates that he always viewed Dos Passos as a
serious competitor and, when it appeared that Dos Passos was
in some way overtaking him, artistically or commercially,
he suffered severe emotional distress.

26 [SMITH, MILES A.]. "Dos Passos' Memories of a Special Era."
Corpus Christi Caller-Times (1 January).
Reprint of 1966.B124.

27 STEINER, GEORGE. Language and Silence. New York: Atheneum
Press, pp. 116, 359, 387.
Places Dos Passos in a tradition, beginning with Defoe,
in which the novel is a vehicle through which "history is
made private." Also thinks that "the case of [Gunter] Grass
is one of many to suggest that it is not Hemingway, but Dos
Passos who has been the principal American literary influence
of the twentieth century."

28 TURNBULL, ANDREW. Thomas Wolfe. New York: Charles Scribner's
Sons, p. 277.
Quotes from Fitzgerald's review in which Wolfe is ranked
with Hemingway, Dos Passos, Wilder, and Faulkner as "one
of a group of talents for fiction such as rarely appears in
a single hatching."

29 VALENTI, LEONARD G. "Giant Slice Of This One Man's Life."
Newark News (2 January).
Calls The Best Times "a labor of love" written with a
"crisp and flavorful style."

30 WAKEFIELD, DAN. "Return to Paradise." <u>Atlantic Monthly</u>, 219
   (Fall), 102-104, 106, 108-110.
      Calls <u>The Best Times</u> a "fragmentary but fascinating
   memoir . . . the best 'album' I know of the literary
   figures of the twenties." Particularly attracted by "the
   warm and generous glimpses of his talented contemporaries."

31 WARREN, LUCIAN C. "Dos Passos Lacks Fire In Memoirs."
   <u>Buffalo Courier Express</u> (8 January).
      Finds <u>The Best Times</u> flavorless because Dos Passos gives
   no clues to the reasons for his own personal changes and
   because of his pedestrian namedropping.

32 WEST, THOMAS REED. "John Dos Passos: The Libertarian Cause,"
   in his <u>Flesh of Steel: Literature and the Machine in
   American Culture</u>. Nashville: Vanderbilt University Press,
   pp. 54-70.
      Feels Dos Passos has been "a dissenter of singularly
   broad temperment" and identifies his major theme as liberty.
   Nevertheless, Dos Passos continually revised his view of
   liberty and its threats and so, West believes, his career
   falls into three relatively distinct periods: 1) covering
   the first few post-war years in which liberty is seen as
   "self-expression in the domain of the aesthetic, the
   imaginative, the humanely sensuous"; 2) from the mid-twenties
   through the thirties in which "the massiveness, the energy
   of machine civilization" is seen as in opposition to the
   individual spirit; 3) from the late thirties on, freedom is
   seen as "a cool adherence to constitutional methods, a
   capacity for compromise and self-restraint."

33 WIDMER, ELEANOR. "The Lost Girls of <u>U.S.A.</u>: Dos Passos'
   Movie," in <u>The Thirties: Fiction, Poetry, Drama</u>. Edited by
   Warren French. Deland, Fla.: Everett Edwards, pp. 11-19.
      Credits Dos Passos with an outstanding ability to convey
   the sense of place and of travel, but feels his writing
   "breaks down" in characterization. Finds this flaw most
   acute in his treatment of women characters: "Dos Passos . . .
   handles women with a gentility closely akin to Edwardianism
   and defeats them by stock situations, lugubrious determinism,
   and his particular brand of social consciousness <u>cum</u>
   caricature."

34 WOODRESS, JAMES, ed. <u>American Literary Scholarship, 1965</u>.
   Durham, N.C.: Duke University Press, pp. 162, 163, 169, 236.
      Reviews Dos Passos criticism of the year.

1968

1968 A BOOKS

1 BRANTLEY, JOHN D. The Fiction of John Dos Passos. Studies in
    American Literature. Vol. 16. The Hague: Mouton & Co.
        Broad survey of Dos Passos' career. Brantley concludes
    that "John Dos Passos is a better biographer than a poet,
    a better poet than historian, a better historian than a
    novelist. He chose to write novels; therefore his best
    novels are those which make most use of his other talents,
    which are considerable. It is this set of circumstances
    which makes Manhattan Transfer, U.S.A., and Midcentury his
    best works."

2 JOYNER, CHARLES WINSTON. "John Dos Passos and World War I:
    The Literary Use of Historical Experience." Unpublished
    doctoral dissertation, University of South Carolina, 312pp.
        A comparative analysis of Dos Passos' war experiences
    and his three novels about the war: One Man's Initiation--
    1917, Three Soldiers, and 1919. Considers Dos Passos'
    experience to be essential to his later view of the relation-
    ship of man to society.

1968 B SHORTER WRITINGS

1 ALLSOP, KENNETH. "The Importance of Being Ernest (Hemingway)."
    The Evening News (18 January).
        Feels that Dos Passos' The Best Times is, with a few
    exceptions, flat, the material "not so much tapped from the
    life blood of a creative writer as drawn out of a filing
    cabinet of notes."

2 ANDREWS, LYMAN. "A Wink From the Corpse." London Times
    (20 January).
        Feels that The Best Times "is full of sharply observed,
    unexpected detail. In the sparest of prose, he hands us
    continued surprises."

3 BILLINGTON, MICHAEL. "Dos Passos: An Informal Memoir." The
    Birmingham [Eng.] Post (10 February).
        Calls The Best Times "a causal, pleasantly unhurried
    journey through the first thirty years or so of the author's
    life." Thinks the book gives one "a good, racily written
    impression of what it is like to be one of the talented
    young, eager to travel and hungry for experience."

4 CONNOLLY, CYRIL. "To Be Young Was Very Heaven." The London
    Sunday Times (21 January).

Calls The Best Times a "charming, happy-making, skill-
fully written" memoir. Comments on Dos Passos' circle of
writer and artist friends: "Dos Passos was much the nicest
of them. . . . He was modest, kind and unmalicious--and
has always remained so . . . his modesty helps him to give
a sensitive and sympathetic picture of his group."

5 CRAIG, DAVID. "The Defeatism of 'The Waste Land,'" in T.S.
Eliot: The Waste Land. Edited by C. B. Cox and Arnold P.
Hinchliffe. New York: Macmillan and Co., pp. 200-215.
Calls the Belinda character of The Waste Land "a neurotic
who cannot stand being alone with her own thoughts--a type
psychologically and socially akin to Eveline Hutchins of
U.S.A."

6 DAVIS, EARLE. Vision Fugitive: Ezra Pound and Economics.
Lawrence: The University Press of Kansas, pp. 43-44, 65-67.
Notes that many young writers of Pound's time, including
Dos Passos, shared his disgust for modern civilization.
Finds similarities between Pound's Cantos and the biographies
of U.S.A.

7 EARNEST, ERNEST. Expatriates and Patriots: American Artists,
Scholars, and Writers in Europe. Durham, N.C.: Duke
University Press, pp. 265, 271.
Mentions the hostility of many Americans toward their
leading artists and writers, including Dos Passos, as one
of the reasons for their expatriation.

8 FAULKNER, WILLIAM. Lion in the Garden: Interviews with William
Faulkner, 1926-1962. Edited by James B. Merriwether and
Michael Millgate. New York: Random House, 121-122, passim.
A number of references to Faulkner's ranking of the five
most important writers of his time, ranking them in terms of
the "magnificence of their failure." Dos Passos rates
second or third, behind Wolfe or Wolfe and Faulkner, de-
pending on the interview.

9 FIEDLER, LESLIE. "The Two Memories: Reflections on Writers
and Writing in the Thirties," in Proletarian Writers of the
Thirties. Edited by David Madden. Carbondale: Southern
Illinois University Press, pp. 157, 167, 187, 190.
Several references to Dos Passos in the context of the
proletarian writers' movement.

10 FEYER, GRATTAN. "An American Panorama." The Irish Times
(13 January).

1968

> Feels that throughout Dos Passos' career his greatest
> strength has been "an insatiable curiosity about men's lives
> and an undogmatic puritanism, which believes there is a
> moral order underneath, but not one to be readily defined."
> Feels that The Best Times reveals these traits, though in a
> "minor key."

11   GURKO, LEO. "John Dos Passos' U.S.A.: A Thirties Spectacular,"
in Proletarian Writers of the Thirties. Edited by David
Madden. Carbondale: Southern Illinois University Press,
pp. 46-63.
> Argues that, although Dos Passos' writing had certain
> things in common with the proletarian writers, there were
> three major differences: first, his novels began at a high
> emotional pitch and gradually declined while most prole-
> tarian novels ended on a rising note; second, Dos Passos
> rigorously avoided propagandizing; third, Dos Passos looked
> on power as an evil while the proletarians saw it as a
> necessary means to an end. Gurko considers the triumph of
> U.S.A. to be "primarily a triumph of organization, but an
> organization so complex and ordered as in itself to consti-
> tute an original vision of its subject."

12   HARDCASTLE, BARBARA. "Lived to the Full." The Yorkshire Post
(1 January).
> Finds The Best Times sharp and affectionate and Dos
> Passos equally adept at evoking pathos and humor.

13   HUDSON, JOHN. "Nice Guy Among Pens and Bulls." The Boston
Evening News (17 February), p. 8.
> Thinks The Best Times "sizzles with people." Compares
> the memoir with Hemingway's A Moveable Feast and admires
> how "Dos Passos paints without malice" his literary
> associates.

14   JAMES, CLIVE. "He Didn't Stifle." New Statesman, 75
(1 March), 272-273.
> Argues that The Best Times reveals that, despite the
> political controversies surrounding him, Dos Passos "was
> never a political writer at all." His was the artist's
> individualistic response rather than the politician's
> dogmatic one. Thinks the memoir contains some of his best
> writing in years and never lacks interest: "Dos Passos is
> deeply cultivated, has been everywhere, done everything."

15   JANSSENS, G. A. M. The American Literary Review: A Critical
History 1920-1950. The Hague: Mouton & Co., pp. 24, 139,
172-173, 243-244.

Notes Dos Passos as a contributor to and subject of reviews in a number of literary reviews beginning with the
Harvard Monthly.

16 McALEER, JOHN J. Theodore Dreiser: An Introduction and
    Interpretation. New York: Barnes and Noble, pp. 2, 54, 60.
    Quotes from a 1937 letter to Dos Passos from Dreiser in
    which he expresses his disillusionment with the Soviet
    Union and from a 1938 letter in which he tells of his goal
    to establish a community founded on the Quaker concept of
    "spiritual relationship."

17 MADDEN, CHARLES F., ed. "John Dos Passos," in his Talks With
    Authors. Carbondale: Southern Illinois University Press,
    pp. 3-11.
    Interview with Dos Passos with considerable discussion
    of Midcentury.

18 MAYNARD, REID. "John Dos Passos' One-Sided Panorama."
    Discourse, 11 (Autumn), 468-474.
    Assessment of U.S.A.: "Running through all four frames
    of the trilogy is the cynical theme of despair, defeat,
    corruption, frustration, and loss of values once cherished.
    Dos Passos' panoramic view is indeed one-sided for it is
    an incredibly negative society that he has presented in
    U.S.A.

19 MUNSON, GORHAM. "A Comedy of Exiles." Literary Review, 12
    (Fall), 41-75.
    General reminiscence, mentioning Dos Passos.

20 NORMAN, CHARLES. The Case of Ezra Pound. New York: Funk and
    Wagnall, p. 196.
    Mentions Dos Passos' statement advising Pound's release
    from confinement in St. Elizabeth's.

21 POWELL, ANTHONY. "Contrast in Life Styles." The Daily
    Telegraph (29 February).
    Calls The Best Times "an interesting and accomplished
    book." Admires Dos Passos' vivid character sketches of his
    famous contemporaries.

22 REEVES, PASCHAL. Thomas Wolfe's Albatross: Race and Nationality
    in America. Athens: University of Georgia Press, p. 1.
    Feels that Wolfe attempted "to portray the vast complex-
    ity of his native land on a scale which surpassed all of his
    contemporaries and was approached only by Dos Passos."

1968

23   REYNOLDS, STANLEY. "Not-So-Hard Times." The Guardian
        (19 January).
             Notes how the comfortable, middle class American
        novelists--particularly Dos Passos and Hemingway--attempted
        in their language and subject matter to spiritually descend
        "to the level of the lower classes." Thinks The Best Times
        is essentially a statement of moneyed-class bitchiness.

24   ROSS, ALAN. "Special Notices." London Magazine (March),
        p. 97.
             Calls The Best Times "a literary feat." Compares it
        favorably with Hemingway's A Moveable Feast: "Where
        Hemingway was boastful and malicious, . . . Dos Passos,
        with little loss of focus, is modest and tolerant." Calls
        Dos Passos' account of Hemingway a "brilliant, relaxed
        characterization."

25   ROSS, FRANK. "The Assailant-Victim in Three War-Protest
        Novels." Paunch, No. 32 (August), pp. 46-57.
             Examination of Three Soldiers, A Farewell to Arms, and
        The Naked and the Dead. Notes Dos Passos' use of juxta-
        position of selective details for ironic and satiric effect;
        also notes, in Chisfield and other characters, an example
        of the function of war in creating dehumanized "killing
        machines."

26   SANDELIN, CLARENCE K. Robert Nation. United States Authors
        Series. New York: Twayne Publishers, p. 20.
             Characterizes Nathan's Peter Kindred (1920), as well as
        Dos Passos' One Man's Initiation--1917, as "novels that
        appeared just after World War I in which the sad young men
        of a lost generation identified themselves and their dolor."

27   SEIB, KENNETH. James Agee: Promise and Fulfillment. Pitt
        Pittsburgh: University of Pittsburgh Press, p. 53.
             Considers Agee's criticism of American education and
        society "as caustic as Upton Sinclair's exposure of the
        Chicago stockyards, Sinclair Lewis' denunciation of Main
        Street, and John Dos Passos' arraignment of capitalism."

28   ST. JOHN, DONALD. "Interview with Hemingway's 'Bill Gorton.'"
        Connecticut Review, 1 (April), 5-12.
             Interview with Bill Smith, the model for Bill Gorton in
        The Sun Also Rises and also the brother of Dos Passos' first
        wife Kate. Smith and wife Marion discuss Kate's hatred for
        Hemingway for his treatment of his second wife Pauline and
        speculate that the unfavorable treatment of the fictionalized
        Hemingway character in Chosen Country is a reflection of

that hatred. Smith feels that Chosen Country wasn't "effective" because it was second hand, because so much of the information for it came from Kate.

29 STEWART, RANDALL. "The Social School of American Criticism," in Regionalism and Beyond: Essays of Randall Stewart. Edited by George Core. Nashville, Tenn.: Vanderbilt University Press, pp. 172-177.
Calls U.S.A. an example of the "approved social fiction" which Granville Hicks and other social critics regarded as a model.

30 TATE, ALLEN. "The New Provincialism," in his Essays of Four Decades. Chicago: The Swallow Press, p. 536.
Reprint of 1945.B10.

31 VAN NOSTRAND, A. D. Everyman His Own Poet. New York: McGraw-Hill, p. 250.
Sees U.S.A. and Midcentury as examples of the American novelists' obsession with the notion of a "consummate national fiction," of "the great American novel."

32 WAGER, WILLIS. American Literature: A World View. New York: New York University Press, pp. 229-233, passim.
Considers the technique of Dos Passos' early work to be "musico-dramatic" and that of U.S.A. to be "presentational and architectonic." Mentions Dos Passos' "great influence among writers in the Latin countries." Also notes the influence of Dos Passos' war novels on those of Mailer, Jones, and Heller.

33 WEINTRAUB, STANLEY. The Last Great Cause: The Intellectuals and the Spanish Civil War. New York: Weybright and Talley, pp. 267-277, passim.
Fairly detailed account of Dos Passos' participation in the Spanish Civil War, focusing on his increasing disillusionment with the cause, partially a result of the execution of his friend, Jose Robles. Briefly discusses Adventures of a Young Man and Dos Passos' magazine articles on the war.

34 WIDMER, KINGSLY. "The Way Out: Some Life-Style Sources of the Literary Tough Guy and the Proletarian Hero," in Tough Guy Writers of the Thirties. Edited by David Madden. Carbondale: Southern Illinois University Press.
Considers Dos Passos' "Vag" an example of the "wandering consciousness" of the social protest literature of the thirties.

1968

35 WOODRESS, JAMES, ed. <u>American Literary Scholarship: An Annual,</u>
    <u>1966</u>. Durham, N.C.: Duke University Press, pp. 160, 169,
    265.
       Reviews Dos Passos criticism of the year.

<u>1969 A BOOKS - NONE</u>

<u>1969 B SHORTER WRITINGS</u>

1 ALLEN, WALTER. <u>The Urgent West: The American Dream and Modern</u>
   <u>Man</u>. New York: E. P. Dutton, pp. 156, 206, 208-210, 214.
      Calls Dos Passos "a latter day Whitman . . . a Whitman
   who has fallen from the state of innocence." Finds the
   technical devices of <u>U.S.A.</u> to be exhilarating; considers
   the novel weakest in the more conventional sections.

2 ANON. "Dos Passos Still Pertinent." <u>Seattle Times</u> (25 May).
      Feels that <u>Occasions and Protests</u> and <u>One Man's</u>
   <u>Initiation--1917</u> "offer an interesting insight into the
   life and writings of John Dos Passos."

3 ANON. "How Traders Won an Empire." <u>Kansas City Star</u> (4 May).
      Brief review of <u>The Portugal Story</u>.

4 ANON. "John Dos Passos On Portugal." <u>Petersburg [Va.]</u>
   <u>Progress-Index</u> (22 May), p. 6.
      Calls <u>The Portugal Story</u> "a scholarly rather than popular
   history," yet a particularly lively one written in a "lean,
   economical style."

5 ANON. "A Miscellany of the Newest Books." <u>Long Beach</u>
   <u>Independent</u> (5 June), p. 17A.
      Calls the unexpurgated reissue of <u>One Man's Initiation--</u>
   <u>1917</u> a "powerful indictment of war." Reprinted: 1969.B6.

6 ANON. "A Miscellany of the Newest Books." <u>Long Beach Press-</u>
   <u>Telegram</u> (4 June).
      Reprint of 1969.B5.

7 ANON. Notice of <u>The Portugal Story</u>. <u>The Columbia Record</u>
   (13 April).
      Notes forthcoming publication.

8 ANON. "Portugal's Brief Glory Told By John Dos Passos." <u>San</u>
   <u>Diego Union</u> (18 May).
      Brief summary of <u>The Portugal Story</u>.

9 ANON. Review of The Portugal Story. Arizona Republic
(2 September).
Notes the amount of original research in The Portugal
Story, which is "no mere retelling of familiar tales."

10 ANON. Review of The Portugal Story. Columbus Dispatch
(1 June).
Calls the book a "labor of love."

11 ANON. Review of The Portugal Story. Indianapolis Star
(27 April).
Brief description of the book.

12 ANON. Review of The Portugal Story. Jackson [Mich.] Citizen-
Patriot (13 April).
Calls The Portugal Story "engrossing." Reprinted:
1969.B21.

13 ANON. Review of The Portugal Story. National Observer
(11 April).
Brief review.

14 ANON. Review of The Portugal Story. New Yorker, 45 (24 May),
139.
Feels The Portugal Story is told with "care and narrative
vigor." Notes Dos Passos' admiration for the courage of
Portuguese seamen and explorers.

15 ANON. Review of The Portugal Story. The Newark News
(22 June).
Finds the book dry and disappointing.

16 ANON. Review of The Portugal Story. Orlando [Fla.] Sentinel
(1 June).
Thinks The Portugal Story adds the flesh and blood to
what most Americans learn of Portuguese history.

17 ANON. Review of The Portugal Story. The Pittsburgh Press
(20 April).
Calls the book "well documented and interestingly written
for the layman."

18 ANON. Review of The Portugal Story. Portland Oregonian
(27 April).
Brief review.

19 ANON. Review of The Portugal Story. Publishers Weekly, 195
(10 February), 70.

1969

> Calls the book "a labor of love," but, while admiring
> some of the individual tales, feels "the sum suggests a
> mausoleum hung with time, cobwebs and forgotten trophies."

20 ANON. Review of The Portugal Story. South Bend Tribune
     (8 June).
     Brief review.

21 ANON. Review of The Portugal Story. Witchita Falls Times
     (20 April), p. 4.
     Reprint of 1969.B12.

22 ANON. "Strangely Happy." Times Literary Supplement
     (7 August), p. 873.
     Finds that "happiness, oddly, is the keynote" of One
     Man's Initiation--1917. Feels that the war, for Dos Passos,
     was "the eternal undergraduate trip to Paris."

23 BAKER, CARLOS. Ernest Hemingway: A Life Story. New York:
     Charles Scribner's Sons, pp. 127-128, 158-161, passim.
     Many references to the relationship of Dos Passos and
     Hemingway.

24 BARKHAM, JOHN. "The Author Speaks." San Juan [P.R.] Star
     (11 May), pp. 20-21.
     Conversation with Dos Passos upon the publication of The
     Portugal Story. Dos Passos reports that the research for
     the book, which took two years to write, was fascinating.
     Expresses his dismay with the American educational system
     and obscenity in fiction. Reveals plans for a book on
     Easter Island and a novel.

25 [BARKHAM, JOHN]. "Dos Passos Does Well by Portugal." Grand
     Rapids Press (11 May).
     Admires the scholarship and style of The Portugal Story:
     "Told in his crispest, liveliest, unsentimental manner, the
     story is rich in colorful personalities and events of
     historic significance." Reprinted:
     _____. "Dos Passos Writes of the Glory That Was Portugal."
     Victoria Advocate (27 April).
     _____. "How the Portuguese Helped Shape History of the
     West." Toledo Blade (27 April).
     _____. "Portugal's Heroic Past Recounted." Newport News
     Daily Press (25 May).

26 BELANGER, HERB. "A World Power in Decline." Seattle Times
     (10 August).

228

Summarizes <u>The Portugal Story</u>. Feels that, in his account of Portugal's golden age, Dos Passos' "pride at being descended from the adventurers of that era shines through."

27 BENSON, JACKSON J. <u>Hemingway: The Writer's Art of Self Defense</u>. Minneapolis: University of Minnesota Press, p. 3.
    Considers the basic object of Dos Passos' and Hemingway's writing to be similar, but finds Dos Passos' style rational and systematic and Hemingway's emotional.

28 BLAKE, N. M. "The Rebels," in his <u>Novelists' America: Fiction as History, 1910-1940</u>. Syracuse, N.Y.: Syracuse University Press, pp. 163-168, 193-194, passim.
    Studies Dos Passos' growing disenchantment with the political left through an examination of Dos Passos' fiction of the thirties.

29 BONOMO, JOSEPHINE. "Dos Passos Tells Of Portuguese Lore." <u>Newark News</u> (22 June).
    Calls <u>The Portugal Story</u> "a short, readable" history.

30 BRADDY, MAMIE. "Imperial Portugal Recalled." <u>Winston Salem Journal and Sentinel</u> (8 June).
    Calls <u>The Portugal Story</u> both "colorful" and "complete."

31 BRITT, A. S. Review of <u>The Portugal Story</u>. <u>Savannah Evening Press Sunday Magazine</u> (8 June).
    Calls <u>The Portugal Story</u> "a thrilling and gripping account," of a country virtually unknown to Americans.

32 BRYER, JACKSON R., ed. <u>Fifteen Modern American Authors: A Survey of Research and Criticism</u>. Durham, N.C.: Duke University Press, passim.
    A number of references to Dos Passos in the various bibliographies.

33 CARLISLE, RICHARD. "Power In Front of the Throne." <u>Quincy [Mass.] Patriot Ledger</u> (20 June).
    Summary of <u>The Portugal Story</u>, "a book worth recommending to history buffs and travelers to Lisbon."

34 CASTO, JAMES. "On History and Politics." <u>Huntington [W. Va.] Press Advertiser</u> (27 July).
    Mentions <u>The Portugal Story</u>.

35 CHAPLIN, GEORGE. Review of <u>The Portugal Story</u>. <u>The Honolulu Sunday Star-Bulletin and Advertiser</u> (18 May).
    Brief review.

1969

36 COOPER, H. H. "Dos Passos Writes of Portugal." <u>Washington</u>
<u>Star</u> (4 May).
Summarizes many episodes of <u>The Portugal Story</u>, a book
written with "mildness and modesty."

37 COOPER, SHELBY. "Writer John Dos Passos--Literary Giant."
<u>The Pensacola News-Journal</u>
Conversation in which Dos Passos discusses contemporary
Portugal, differences among the Portuguese, contemporary
American writing, and student unrest.

38 DRUMMOND, ANNE. "So Many Facts They Overwhelm." <u>Springfield</u>
<u>[Mo.] News and Leader</u> (1 June).
Feels that <u>The Portugal Story</u> is burdened with too much
factual information: "perhaps a little more imagination and
a bit of dramatic guessing would have added a little
sparkle."

39 DUMBELL, JAMES M. "The Prismatic Odyssey Of A Miniscule
Nation." <u>Charlotte Observer</u> (27 April).
Feels that <u>The Portugal Story</u> "might have been the life
work of a lesser author." Admires Dos Passos' ability to
"humanize the times . . . and make a story that reads like
a contemporary fiction."

40 DUPEE, F. W. and GEORGE STADE, ed. <u>Selected Letters of E. E.</u>
<u>Cummings</u>. New York: Harcourt, Brace and World, passim.
Many references and three letter-poems to Dos Passos.
Dupee and Stade include, in the forward, a brief discussion
of Dos Passos' appreciation for Cummings.

41 FENTON, JAMES. "Seeing the Show." <u>New Statesman</u>, 78 (July),
121.
Finds the style of <u>One Man's Initiation--1917</u> to be
still fresh and the book, in general, to be a good reflection of the spirit of the time.

42 FLAHERTY, JOE. "Portrait of A Man Reading." <u>Book World</u>
(13 July), pp. 1, 2.
Dos Passos discusses his reading interests in this interview. Mentions Faulkner, Joyce, Proust, Dreiser, and
possibly Solzhenitsyn as "the great novelists of the
twentieth century." Also speaks favorably of Fitzgerald,
Barth, Updike, and James Baldwin. Dos Passos says, however,
that he has always preferred reading history to fiction.

43 FRENCH, WARREN, ed. <u>The Forties: Fiction, Poetry, Drama</u>.
Deland, Fla.: Everett Edwards, pp. 8, 21, 198, 262.

Includes several references, including Dos Passos' high
praise for parts of The Naked and The Dead.

44 GALLAWAY, B. P. "U.S.A. Novelist Dos Passos Pens History of
    Portugal." Abilene Reporter News (4 May).
        Admires the "novelist's fascination with the human element
    within the essential currents of history" which have charac-
    terized all of Dos Passos' histories, but feels that The
    Portugal Story is also notable for its rigorous scholarship.

45 GIBBS, WAYNE E. Review of The Portugal Story. Camden Courier
    Post (23 April).
        Calls the book "a moving account . . . a powerfully
    written story by a powerful storyteller." Thinks "the
    theme of adventure and exploration is the thread of con-
    tinuity in this tapestry of modern Portugal."

46 GILLIAM, STANLEY. "Portugal's Story Gobs Down in Blobbish
    Prose." Sacramento Bee (29 June).
        Feels that The Portugal Story is "overly anecdotal . . .
    and overdetailed," and is written in a "stilted and pedantic
    style."

47 GOULD, JEAN. The Poet and Her Book: A Biography of Edna St.
    Vincent Millay. New York: Dodd, Mead & Co., pp. 183-184.
        Mentions the involvement of Millay, Dos Passos, and
    other writers in the defense of Sacco and Vanzetti.

48 GREENWOOD, WALTER B. "Enthusiastic Report On Explorers of
    Old." Buffalo News (3 May).
        Calls The Portugal Story "a solid and scholarly study,"
    but one lacking in historical or artistic vision.

49 H., C. H. "Dos Passos' Book On Portugal Called A Richly
    Detailed History." Charleston News and Courier (18 May),
    p. 3d.
        Calls The Portugal Story "an excellent history . . .
    vivid . . . rich in detail."

50 HERRON, IMA HONAKER. The Small Town in American Drama.
    Dallas: Southern Methodist University Press, p. viii.
        Mentions the 1960 dramatization of U.S.A. by Dos Passos
    and Paul Shyre.

51 KAZIN, ALFRED. "John Dos Passos: Inventor in Isolation."
    Saturday Review, 52 (15 March), 16-19.
        Overview of Dos Passos' career with a special focus on
    U.S.A. which he considers, in its technical inventiveness

and freshness of style, more a novel of the twenties than
the thirties. Feels the use of history to supply the structure of the novel is "what distinguishes the extraordinary
invention that is Dos Passos' U.S.A." Finds it a multi-
faceted structure: "a way of objectifying one vulnerable
individual's experience to the uttermost--of turning even
the individual life into a facet of history. Particularly
admires the biographies, but thinks that "Dos Passos' con-
traption, his new kind of novel, is in fact . . . the
greatest character in the book itself."

52 KNOX, GEORGE. "A Novelist's Portugal." Riverside [Calif.]
 Sunday Press-Enterprise (3 August).
        Feels that The Portugal Story lacks "dramatic quality
    and vitality."

53 LAWRENCE, FLOYD B. "Two Novelists of the Great War: Dos Passos
    and Cummings." University Review, 36 (October), 35-41.
        Compares The Enormous Room and Three Soldiers. Feels
    that "Dos Passos' paralyzing horror in remembering decidedly
    interfered with his story and its scope." Cummings, on the
    other hand, "through his skillful handling of the humor of
    detachment and compassion, wrote a novel containing the
    immediacy of the most enduring fiction."

54 LEEDS, BARRY H. The Structured Vision of Norman Mailer. New
    York: New York University Press, pp. 15-16, passim.
        Calls Dos Passos "the most obvious influence on The
    Naked and the Dead, particularly in its structure."

55 LEHAN, RICHARD. Theodore Dreiser: His World and His Novels.
    Carbondale: Southern Illinois University Press, pp. xiii,
    177, 182.
        Mentions Dos Passos' acknowledged indebtedness to
    Dreiser and their connection in radical activities, in-
    cluding their tour and reporting of the Harlan coal fields.

56 LORZ, MIKE. "Dos Passos Tells Vivid Story of Portugal's Rise,
    Downfall." Columbus Citizen-Journal (3 May).
        Admires Dos Passos' portrait of Portugal's empire years
    in The Portugal Story, but feels he is too sketchy in
    chronicling its decline.

57 LOWE, ARNOLD H. "Dos Passos Gets Inside Old Portugal."
    Minneapolis Tribune (18 May).
        Calls The Portugal Story "a scholarly book . . . written
    by a man who knows how to write." Feels that Dos Passos
    reveals his resourcefulness and his perceptiveness of men
    and events."

58 LOWRY, E. D. "The Lively Art of Manhattan Transfer." PMLA,
     84 (October), 1628-1638.
         Feels that Manhattan Transfer is an early and excellent
     example of Dos Passos' attempt to use traits of other
     modernistic forms--including photography, films, and even
     vaudeville--to create a holistic picture of modern life.

59 MANIJAK, WILLIAM. "Portugal History Proves Scholarly,
     Stimulating." Fort Wayne News Sentinel (24 May).
         Feels that The Portugal Story "is scholarly in its
     deeper penetration through the translation of sources, yet
     . . . reads like a novel."

60 MOSSMAN, JOSEF. "Portugal's Glory Told By a Master." Peoria
     Journal Star (13 May).
         Calls Dos Passos "one of the supreme masters of litera-
     ture," and thinks The Portugal Story reads like "a medieval
     minstrel's fascinating narration."

61 PETERSON, RICHARD K. Hemingway: Direct and Oblique. The
     Hague: Mouton & Co., pp. 59-60, 88, 97.
         Notes the distrust of words shared by both Dos Passos
     and Hemingway. Speculates that the irony of both might
     have been used to conceal romantic temperaments.

62 PONTE, MANUEL L. "A 'Prodigal Grandson' Returns to Portugal."
     St. Louis Post-Dispatch (11 May), p. 4c.
         Feels that The Portugal Story is written with "a novel-
     ist's affection for history." Thinks the book will provide
     a useful introduction to Portugal for Americans, who tend
     to be ignorant of the country's important history.

63 PRESCOTT, ORVILLE. Review of The Portugal Story. New York
     Times Book Review (17 August), p. 10.
         Feels The Portugal Story "should interest any lover of
     popular history" for it is both scholarly and lively. If
     there is a fault it may be that Dos Passos does not do
     enough to convey the emotional atmosphere of the place.

64 PRYCE-JONES, ALAN. "Lively Portugal Story Related by Dos
     Passos." Newsday (8 July).
         Feels that Dos Passos, in The Portugal Story, "has told
     his brilliant story in rather too jaunty a fashion," empha-
     sizing "the glory days of the empire and its flamboyant
     heroes, but saying too little about its decline and less
     striking but equally important leaders." Nevertheless,
     considers the book, on the whole, excellent. Reprinted:
     1969.B65.

1969

65 ____. "Portugal, A History Told in Jaunty Fashion."
   Detroit News (27 July).
   Reprint of 1969.B64.

66 RAHV, PHILIP. Literature and the Sixth Sense. Boston:
   Houghton Mifflin, pp. 358-368.
   Review of Arnold Houser's Social History of Art which
   mentions the similarity of the narrative techniques employed by Proust, Joyce, Woolf, and Dos Passos and the
   technique of the film.

67 RUHLE, JURGEN. Literature and Revolution: A Critical Study of
   the Writer and Communism in the 20th Century. Translated
   by Jean Steinberg. New York: Frederick A. Praeger, pp.
   467-478, passim.
   Passing reference to Dos Passos.

68 S., F. S. "Its Role In History Was Major." Roanoke Times
   (15 June), p. 10c.
   Does not think The Portugal Story is an exceptional
   book, but "found it interesting and worthwhile reading,"
   for the lay reader rather than the historian.

69 SANDERS, DAVID. "John Dos Passos: The Art of Fiction, 44."
   Paris Review, 12 (Spring), 146-172.
   Wide ranging interview in which Dos Passos discusses in
   some detail his theory of the novel. Reprinted: 1976.B20.

70 ____. "Manhattan Transfer and 'The Service of Things,'" in
   Themes and Directions in American Literature: Essays in
   Honor of Leon Howard. Edited by Ray B. Browne and Donald
   Pizer. Lafayette, Ind.: Purdue University Press, pp.
   171-185.
   Stresses the importance of Dos Passos' postwar travels
   in shaping the themes of Manhattan Transfer, and in his discovery of the montage technique which he applied to the
   novels.

71 SCHIFF, PEARL. "First Dos Passos Novel (63 Copies Sold)
   Offered." The Boston Globe (22 May), p. 28.
   Feels that the reissue of One Man's Initiation--1917
   will be of interest only to the student of American litera-
   ture, the "college English major writing a thesis on Dos
   Passos."

72 SELLEN, ROBERT W. "History as Vaudeville Act on Paper."
   The Kansas City Times (11 May).
   Feels that "if popular history is designed to amuse the
   reader," The Shackles of Power is a huge success. But, "if

diversion is not enough, if popular history is also intended
to inform, [it] is barely at the high school level."

73 [SMITH, MILES A.]. "Dos Passos Pens History of Portugal."
    Indianapolis Star (20 July).
        Calls The Portugal Story "dry, plodding, and undramatic."
    Reprinted: 1969.B74; 1969.B75.

74 SMITH, MILES A. "Portugal History Too Detailed." St. Paul
    Pioneer Press (18 May).
        Reprint of 1969.B73.

75 _____. Review of The Portugal Story. San Francisco Examiner
    (1 May).
        Reprint of 1969.B73.

76 ST. JOHN, DONALD. "Interview with Hemingway's 'Bill Gorton'
    (Part II)." Connecticut Review, 3 (October), 5-23.
        Continues discussion of Dos Passos' fictionalized por-
    trayal of Hemingway in Chosen Country.

77 STARK, JOHN. "Dos Passos' Portugal Story Is Exciting and
    Thrilling." The Jackson [Ind.] Sun (6 July), p. 3c.
        Calls The Portugal Story "a history that will delight
    all adventure-loving readers."

78 STUHLMANN, GUNTHER, ed. The Journals of Anais Nin, 1939-1944.
    London: Peter Owen, p. 123.
        Quotes a letter from Henry Miller which mentions Dos
    Passos.

79 SULLIVAN, WALTER. "The New Faustus: The Southern Renascence
    and the Joycean Aesthetic," in Southern Fiction Today:
    Renascence and Beyond. Edited by George Core. Athens:
    University of Georgia Press, pp. 1-15.
        Calls U.S.A. one of a number of books of its time
    "dealing with the decline of accustomed belief."

80 TEMPLE, BRUCE G. "Scholars Will Like The Portugal Story."
    Louisville Times (15 May).
        Calls The Portugal Story a textbook which will send
    scholars "running to revise their lectures," but will have
    little interest for the average reader. Faults Dos Passos
    for revealing little of the personality of the place and
    time.

81 TENCH, SHARON. "Story of Portugal Historical Narrative."
    Pensacola News-Journal (25 May), p. 8b.

1969

> Feels that, while parts of The Portugal Story "are
> laborious with dry details, the overall appearance sparkles."

82   UNTERECKER, JOHN. Voyager: A Life of Hart Crane. New York:
     Farrar, Straus and Geroux, pp. 294, 334, 393, 641.
     Several references to Dos Passos.

83   VITELLI, JAMES R. Van Wyck Brocks. United States Authors
     Series. New York: Twayne Publishers, pp. 21, 77, 98, 145,
     152.
     Passing reference to Dos Passos.

84   WALDMEIR, JOSEPH H. "Novelists of Two Wars," in his American
     Novels of the Second World War. The Hague: Mouton & Co.,
     pp. 39-55.
     Finds the novels of World War I, including Dos Passos',
     to be characterized by a fiercely pessimistic iconoclasm
     directed at all of society.

85   WARD, JOHN WILLIAM. "Dos Passos, Fitzgerald, and History,"
     in his Red, White, and Blue: Men, Books, and Ideas in
     American Culture. New York: Oxford University Press, pp.
     38-61.
     Thinks the theme of both U.S.A. and The Great Gatsby to
     be that "the meaning of America, after its initial promise,
     has been lost as Americans go whoring after false Gods."
     Thinks both link this sense of loss symbolically to the
     Edenic fall: "both books at climactic moments project the
     sense of loss, of failure, of betrayal, through the viola-
     tion of greenness, of meadows, of open, inviting, unravaged
     nature." Reprinted: 1974.B3.

86   WICKES, GEORGE. "The Education of John Dos Passos," in his
     Americans in Paris, 1909-1939. Garden City, N.Y.: Doubleday
     and Co., pp. 83-102.
     Discusses the significance of French art and culture to
     Dos Passos' development as a writer.

87   WOODRESS, JAMES, ed. American Literary Scholarship, 1967.
     Durham, N.C.: Duke University Press, pp. 169, 180-181, 307.
     Reviews Dos Passos criticism of the year.

1970 A BOOKS

1   ENGLAND, DONALD GENE. "The Newsreels of John Dos Passos' The
    42nd Parallel: Sources and Techniques." Unpublished
    doctoral dissertation, University of Texas at Austin, 331pp.

Study of the sources, use, and implications of the Newsreels. Thinks that "Dos Passos' craftsmanship is almost a
reversal of the usual artistic process. We expect a writer
to use his imagination to inform us about our factual world.
Dos Passos has sparked our imagination by using facts,
carefully selected and artfully arranged."

1970 B   SHORTER WRITINGS

1   ANON. "A Darling Whitman." Time, 96 (12 October), 12.
     Obituary calls Dos Passos "the last major survivor of
the literary generation that included Hemingway, Fitzgerald,
Steinbeck and Faulkner." Feels that many of Dos Passos'
earlier work "often seem as archaic as the rhetoric of the
Wobblies. But there are also passages that seem eerily
prescient," as when he reveals the anger which sounds so
much like the anger of the New Left.

2   ANON. "Dos Passos, U.S.A. Trilogy Author Dies." Chicago
     Tribune (29 September), p. 12.
     Notes, upon his death, Dos Passos' major accomplishments
and his increasingly conservative politics.

3   ANON. "John Dos Passos Dies At 74." Baltimore Sun
     (29 September), pp. 1a, 13a.
     Summary of Dos Passos' life and career.

4   ANON. "John Dos Passos Dead at 74; Acclaimed for U.S.A.
     Trilogy." New York Times (29 September), p. 1.
     Notes Dos Passos' death.

5   ANON. "Novelist John Dos Passos, 74, Author of U.S.A., Dies
     in Md." Washington Post (29 September), p. 1a.
     Calls Dos Passos "one of the most influential of 20th
Century American novelists." Notes that some critics
consider U.S.A. "the nearest thing we have had to the great
American novel."

6   BERRY, THOMAS ELLIOTT. The Newspaper in the American Novel:
     1900-1969. Metuchen, N.J.: The Scarecrow Press, Inc.,
     pp. 75-77, 101, 156.
     Feels Dos Passos is basically critical of the power and
practices of the newspaper industry as it is portrayed in
U.S.A. and The Great Days. Berry considers Dos Passos'
portrayal of newspapermen as characters--Jimmy Herf in
Manhattan Transfer, for instance--to be stereotypic.

1970

7 CHAMBERLAIN, JOHN. "Dos Passos: Last of the Big Four."
    National Review, 22 (20 October), 1100-1101.
        Attempts to counter the prevailing opinion expressed in
    Dos Passos' obituaries that his political shift from left
    to right was accompanied by and even caused a decline in his
    art. Chamberlain argues that Dos Passos' performance,
    throughout his career, was more even than that of Lewis,
    Fitzgerald, Hemingway, or Wolfe. Calls Dos Passos a
    "seeker . . . forever young, forever growing."

8 CONANROE, JOEL. William Carlos Williams' "Paterson": Language
    and Landscape. Philadelphia: University of Pennsylvania
    Press, p. 38.
        Mentions that the only place in which Williams uses the
    "pyrotechnics" of "typewriter art" in Paterson is on page
    164, and is "possibly influenced by Manhattan Transfer, in
    which the phrases appear crisscross to suggest the breaking
    apart of language."

9 COWLEY, MALCOLM. "A Natural History of American Naturalism,"
    in A Many-Windowed House: Collected Essays on American
    Writers and American Writing. Edited by Henry Dan Piper.
    Carbondale: Southern Illinois University Press, pp. 116-152.
        Expanded version of 1947.B9.

10 DURANT, WILL and ARIEL DURANT. Interpretations of Life: A
    Survey of Contemporary Literature. New York: Simon and
    Schuster, pp. 39, 186.
        Mentions an act of kindness by Hemingway toward Dos
    Passos and the latter's influence on Sartre.

11 EARNEST, ERNEST. The Single Vision: The Alienation of American
    Intellectuals. New York: New York University Press, pp.
    92-97, passim.
        Feels that Dos Passos' early work reveals "a paranoid
    hatred of the human race."

12 ELIAS, ROBERT H. Theodore Dreiser: Apostle of Nature. Ithaca,
    N.Y.: Cornell University Press, pp. 254, 256.
        Reprint of 1945.B16, slightly emended.

13 GEISMAR, MAXWELL. "The Shifting Illusion, Dream, and Fact,"
    in American Dreams, American Nightmares. Edited by David
    Madden. Carbondale: Southern Illinois University Press,
    pp. 45-57.
        Considers the "lost generation" twice lost, alienated
    expatriates from not only World War I but from their own
    culture as well. This second loss, Geismer feels, was the
    most important one.

14 GILMER, WALKER. <u>Horace Liveright, Publisher of the Twenties</u>.
    New York: David Lewis, pp. 121-124.
        Occasional references to Dos Passos including comments
    about his help in the publication of <u>In Our Time</u>.

15 GOLDMAN, ARNOLD. "Dos Passos and His <u>U.S.A.</u>" <u>New Literary
    History</u>, 1 (Spring), 471-483.
        Examines the epic elements of <u>U.S.A.</u> Concludes that it
    is not a mock epic but an epic turned inside out, a chron-
    icle of a nation's demise: "John Dos Passos appears to have
    been a Twentieth Century man by instinct and to have found
    the burden intolerable. <u>U.S.A.</u> is the epic of his
    discovery."

16 HOFFA, WILLIAM. "Norman Mailer: <u>Advertisements for Myself</u>, or
    A Portrait of the Artist as a <u>Disgruntled Counter-Puncher</u>,"
    in <u>The Fifties: Fiction, Poetry, Drama</u>. Edited by Warren
    French. Deland, Fla.: Everett Edwards, pp. 73-82.
        Considers Dos Passos, Farrell, Malraux, and Hemingway to
    be Mailer's dominant literary progenitors.

17 HUBBELL, JAY B. "1922: A Turning Point in American Literary
    History." <u>Texas Studies in Literature and Language</u>, 12
    (Fall), 481-492.
        Survey of the American literature of the early twenties
    which concludes that it was a time of dramatic change from
    the Victorian era to the modern. Mentions Dos Passos as
    one who helped bring about the change.

18 KEATS, JOHN. <u>You Might As Well Live: The Life and Times of
    Dorothy Parker</u>. New York: Simon and Schuster, pp. 108, 114.
        Mentions Dos Passos as one of the circle of writers and
    artists associated with Gerald and Sarah Murphy.

19 KENNEDY, RICHARD S. and PASCHAL REEVES, eds. <u>The Notebooks of
    Thomas Wolfe</u>. 2 Vols. Chapel Hill: The University of North
    Carolina Press, pp. 331, 332, 786, 886, 887.
        Several references to Dos Passos.

20 LASK, THOMAS. "America As a Character." <u>New York Times</u>
    (29 September), p. 47.
        Appraisal of Dos Passos' work. Considers him primarily
    a naturalist, one particularly concerned with "fiction as
    technique." Feels that Dos Passos may be remembered by only
    one book, <u>U.S.A.</u>, "but in its range and reach, in its will-
    ingness to meet head on the possibilities of American life,
    it is large enough to be considered a life's work."

1970

21 LIPPMAN, THOMAS W. "John Dos Passos: America Was His Main
   Character." Washington Post (29 September), p. 4c.
   Feels that Dos Passos' novels "presented a kind of
   fictionalized history of this century as Mr. Dos Passos
   observed it--history in which America was the central
   character and the outlook for her future was gloom."
   Summarizes his life and career.

22 LUDINGTON, CHARLES T., JR. "The Neglected Satires of John Dos
   Passos." Satire Newsletter, 7 (Spring), 127-136.
   Argues that if Dos Passos' novels, throughout his career,
   are treated as satiric chronicles, "as one man's highly
   critical, often scornful, but never totally despairing
   vision of American society--then they have a value few
   critics have been willing to accord them."

23 MADDEN, DAVID. James M. Cain. United States Authors Series.
   New York: Twayne Publishers, Inc., pp. 113, 165, 168, 169.
   Lists Dos Passos as one of the many serious writers who
   used the "tough guy" type popularized by Cain.

24 MARTIN, JAY. Nathanael West: The Art of His Life. New York:
   Farrar, Straus and Giroux, pp. 101-102, 145-146, passim.
   Many references to Dos Passos, particularly to his
   acquaintanceship with West through the literary journals
   and the Greenwich Village social circuit of the late
   twenties and thirties.

25 MILFORD, NANCY. Zelda: A Biography. New York: Harper and
   Row, pp. 93, 94, 96, 106, 133, 137, 370.
   Several references to social relations between Dos
   Passos and the Fitzgeralds. Includes quotes about Scott
   and Zelda by Dos Passos.

26 MILLER, WAYNE CHARLES. An Armed America: Its Face in Fiction.
   New York: New York University Pres, pp. 108-116, 132-134,
   passim.
   Feels that Three Soldiers and One Man's Initiation--1917
   establish "the form that most of the novels occasioned by
   World War II and the Korean War would take." Miller draws
   parallels between Three Soldiers and A Farewell to Arms,
   and One Man's Initiation--1917 and In Our Time. Considers
   Dos Passos to be the "first [American] novelist since
   Melville to use the military novel as a vehicle for social
   analysis."

27 PAVESE, CESARE. "John Dos Passos and the American Novel," in
   American Literature, Essays and Opinions. Translated by

Edwin Fussel. Berkeley: University of California Press, pp. 91-106.

Notes that, in U.S.A., "Dos Passos has chosen no longer to tell his story by means of episodes but through passages of biography." Finds Dos Passos' greatest strength in his objective, rapid, journalistic air of the man who is in a hurry and can't waste his time searching for effects."

28 ROSMOND, BABETTE. Robert Benchley: His Life and Good Times. Garden City, N.Y.: Doubleday and Co., pp. 139, 160.

Mentions Dos Passos as one of the well known people who participated, with Benchley, in attempts to prevent the execution of Sacco and Vanzetti.

29 ROSS, ISHBELL. The Expatriates. New York: Thomas Y. Crowell Co., pp. 235, 262, 264.

Mentions Dos Passos' experiences as an expatriate.

30 SCHWARTZ, DELMORE. "John Dos Passos and the Whole Truth," in Selected Essays of Delmore Schwartz. Edited by Donald H. Dike and David H. Zucker. Chicago: The University of Chicago Press, pp. 229-245.

Reprint of 1938.B26.

31 SOKOLOV, RAYMOND A. "Dos Passos, 1896-1970." Newsweek, 76 (12 October), 117-118.

Says Dos Passos was "a giant of a sensibility, with appetites for experience that were never appeased . . . a restless and insatiable lover of the American people." Summarizes Dos Passos' career, concluding that his "vision and humanity" were every bit as powerful as Hemingway's."

32 VICKERY, OLGA W. "The Inferno of the Moderns," in The Shaken Realist: Essays in Modern Literature in Honor of Frederick J. Hoffman. Edited by Melvin J. Friedman and John B. Vickery. Baton Rouge: Louisiana State University Press, pp. 147-164.

Examines the influence of Dante, particularly in his imagery and symbolism in The Inferno, on modern writers. Analysis of how the "city of Dis has been fully recognized and powerfully re-created in . . . Manhattan Transfer."

33 WEINBERG, HELEN. The New Novel In America: The Kafkan Mode in Contemporary Fiction. Ithaca, N.Y.: Cornell University Press, pp. 109, 167.

Concludes that the "activist mode" in contemporary literature--typified by Mailer and Bellow--owes more to Dreiser and Dos Passos than to Hemingway.

1970

34 WHITE, WILLIAM. American Literary Scholarship, An Annual,
    1968. Edited by J. Albert Robbins, Durham, N.C.: Duke
    University Press.
       Reviews Dos Passos criticism of the year.

35 WHITMAN, ALDEN. "Fame From Early Books." New York Times
    (29 September), pp. 1, 47.
       Summarizes Dos Passos' life and career with special
    attention to his political changes.

36 WOODRESS, JAMES. Willa Cather: Her Life and Art. New York:
    Pegasus, p. 195.
       Quotes from a review of H. L. Mencken (see 1922.B17) in
    which he maintains that Cather's war novel, One of Ours,
    is "spoiled" by Three Soldiers, for "no war story can be
    written in the United States without challenging comparison
    with it."

1971 A BOOKS

1 BAKER, JOHN DAVID. "John Dos Passos, Chronicler of the
   American Left." Unpublished doctoral dissertation, Case
   Western Reserve University, 256pp.
      Considers Dos Passos' work "a remarkably comprehensive
   chronicle of the radical left by a sensitive participant."
   Examines a number of actual and fictional characters as
   "representative radical types." Thinks Dos Passos' political
   thought was consistent.

2 BELKIND, ALLEN, ed. Dos Passos, the Critics and the Writers'
   Intention. Crosscurrents/Modern Critiques. Carbondale:
   Southern Illinois University Press, 349pp.
      Contents: pp. vii-xii: Preface by Harry T. More. Very
   brief overview of Dos Passos' career with a personal remi-
   niscence of the author.
      pp. xiii-xvii: Notes on the contributors.
      pp. xix-lxi: Introduction by the editor. Overview of
   Dos Passos' career based on the critical interpretations
   by the book's contributors.
      pp. 1-21: "Dos Passos and the 'Lost Generation,'" by
   Alfred Kazin. Reprinted from On Native Grounds. New York:
   Harcourt, Brace & Co., 1942, pp. 341-359.
      pp. 22-34: "John Dos Passos: The Poet and the World," by
   Malcolm Cowley. Reprinted from The New Republic, 70
   (27 April 1932), 303-305.
      pp. 35-43: "The America of John Dos Passos," by Lionel
   Trilling. Reprinted from Partisan Review, 4 (April 1938),
   26-32.

1971

pp. 44-53: "The Gullivers of John Dos Passos," by Arthur Mizener. Reprinted from The Saturday Review of Literature, 34 (30 June 1951), 6-7, 34-35.

pp. 54-69: "Manhattan Transfer: Collectivism and Abstract Composition," by Joseph Warren Beach. Condensed from American Fiction: 1920-1940. New York: Macmillan, 1941.

pp. 70-80: "John Dos Passos and 1919," by Jean-Paul Sartre. Reprinted from Literary Essays. Translated by Annette Michelson. New York: Philosophical Library, 1957, pp. 88-96.

pp. 81-92: "Dos Passos and Naturalism," by Charles C. Walcutt. Reprinted from American Literary Naturalism: A Divided Stream. Minneapolis: University of Minnesota Press, 1956, pp. 280-289.

pp. 93-105: "Dos Passos' U.S.A.: The Words of the Hollow Men," by John Lydenberg. Reprinted from Essays on Determinism in American Literature. Edited by Sidney J. Krause. Kent, Ohio: Kent State University Press, 1964, pp. 97-107.

pp. 106-121: "The Politics of John Dos Passos," by Granville Hicks. Reprinted from Antioch Review, 10 (March 1950), 85-97.

pp. 122-135: "The 'Anarchism' of John Dos Passos," by David Sanders. Reprinted from South Atlantic Quarterly, 60 (Winter 1961), 44-55.

pp. 136-145: "Dos Passos and the New Liberalism," by Chester E. Eisinger. Reprinted from Fiction of the Forties. Chicago: University of Chicago Press, 1963, pp. 118-125.

pp. 146-155: "John Dos Passos: Liberty and the Father Image," by Martin Kallich. Reprinted from Antioch Review, 10 (March 1950), 100-105.

pp. 156-196: "The Search for Identity in the Novels of John Dos Passos," by Blanche H. Gelfant. Reprinted from PMLA, 74 (March 1961), 133-149.

pp. 197-218: "John Dos Passos and the French," by Ben Stoltzfus. Reprinted from Comparative Literature, 15 (Spring 1963), 146-163.

pp. 219-226: "The Trilogies of Jean-Paul Sartre and John Dos Passos," by Richard Lehan. Reprinted from Iowa English Yearbook, 9 (1964), 60-64.

pp. 227-241: "John Dos Passos: Technique vs. Sensibility," by Marshall McLuhan. Reprinted from Fifty Years of the American Novel. Edited by Harold C. Gardiner. New York: Charles Scribner's Sons, 1951, pp. 151-164.

pp. 242-264: "Dos Passos and Painting," by George Knox. Reprinted from Texas Studies in Literature and Language, 6 (1964), 22-38.

1971

<u>1971 B   SHORTER WRITINGS</u>

    1 ALLEN, WALTER. <u>The Urgent West: The American Dream and Modern</u>
       <u>Man</u>. New York: E. P. Dutton Co., pp. 156, 206, 208–210,
       214.
          Calls Dos Passos "a latter-day Whitman who has fallen
       from [Whitman's] state of innocence; for him, in <u>U.S.A.</u>,
       the brotherhood of man is frustrated by the fact of twen-
       tieth century American life. What Dos Passos shows us is a
       United States that is the negation of the brotherhood of
       man Whitman conceived it to be."

    2 BERTHOFF, WARNER. "Edmund Wilson and His Civil War," in his
       <u>Fictions and Events: Essays in Criticism and Literary</u>
       <u>History</u>. New York: E. P. Dutton Co., pp. 264–287.
          Considers Dos Passos--along with Wilson--of a breed of
       "professional, moderately freethinking and highly self-
       regarding, middle class intellectuals," and feels Dos
       Passos' career was "an odd and eventually debilitating
       lover's quarrel" with such an outlook.

    3 BLAKE, NELSON M. <u>Novelist's America: Fiction as History, 1910–</u>
       <u>1940</u>. Syracuse, N.Y.: Syracuse University Press, pp. 163–
       194, passim.
          Examines Dos Passos' major novels. Concludes that he
       was, throughout his career, the stubborn rebel, opposing,
       on principle, the powers that be.

    4 BORGES, JORGE LUIS, with ESTHER ZEMBORAIN DE TORRES. <u>An</u>
       <u>Introduction to American Literature</u>. Lexington: The
       University Press of Kentucky, p. 48.
          While admitting that Dos Passos' importance is undeniable,
       Borges finds <u>U.S.A.</u> to leave "a final impression of sadness
       and futility since it suffers from a lack of passion and
       faith."

    5 CADY, EDWIN H. <u>The Light of Common Day: Realism in American</u>
       <u>Fiction</u>. Bloomington: Indiana University Press, p. 68.
          Compares Dos Passos to Norris, concluding that neither
       is a truly epic novelist.

    6 CHURCHILL, ALLEN. <u>The Literary Decade</u>. Englewood Cliffs, N.J.:
       Prentice-Hall, pp. 57–58, 119–120, 193–194, passim.
          Summarizes the critical reaction to <u>Three Soldiers</u> and
       <u>Manhattan Transfer</u>.

    7 COHN, RUBY. "Less Than Novel," in her <u>Dialogue In American</u>
       <u>Drama</u>. Bloomington: Indiana University Press, pp. 170–225.

Considers the language of Dos Passos "dull because he is primarily a journalist rather than a poet and because he cannot make us care about his characters." Contains a short plot summary and critique of each of Dos Passos' plays.

8   COINDREAU, MAURICE EDGAR. The Time of William Faulkner: A French View of Modern American Fiction. Edited and translated by George McMillan Reeves. Columbia: University of South Carolina Press, 247pp., passim.
    A number of references to Dos Passos in this collection of essays.

9   COOK, BRUCE. The Beat Generation. New York: Charles Scribner's Sons, pp. 48, 133.
    Mentions the influence of the "lost generation" of the twenties on the beats. Thinks "Vag" of U.S.A. served as a model for the beats.

10 CRANE, JOAN ST. C. "Rare of Seldom Seen Dust Jackets of American First Editions: V." Serif, 8 (June), 27-28.
    Describes dust jacket of Three Soldiers.

11 DAHLBERG, EDWARD. The Confessions of Edward Dahlberg. New York: George Braziller, passim.
    Waspish assessment of Dos Passos. Characterizes him as "a pleasant, unoriginal man, quite myopic, with a levantic bald-looking face." Feels Dos Passos is one of the novelists of his generation who "considered ignorance a kind of genius . . . [whose] dimensions were pygmean."

12 FEENEY, JOSEPH JOHN. "American Anti-war Writers of World War I: A Literary Study of Randolph Bourne, Harriet Monroe, Carl Sandburg, John Dos Passos, E. E. Cummings, and Ernest Hemingway." Unpublished doctoral dissertation, University of Pennsylvania, 275pp.
    Study of the diversity of approaches for dealing with the war. Notes Dos Passos' use of concrete diction and generalizations for ironic effect.

13 GLICKSBERG, CHARLES F. The Sexual Revolution In Modern American Literature. The Hague: Martinus Nijhoff, p. 31.
    Cites Manhattan Transfer as a forerunner of later sexual explicitness in American literature.

14 GUTTMAN, ALLEN. The Jewish Writer in America: Assimilation and the Crisis of Identity. New York: Oxford University Press, pp. 38-39, 145, 154-155, 172.
    Notes Dos Passos' influence on two Jewish writers--Meyer Levin and Norman Mailer.

1971

15 KRIEGEL, LEONARD. Edmund Wilson. Carbondale: Southern
    Illinois University Press, pp. 14, 34, 35, 42, 69.
        Several references to Dos Passos. Notes that the novelist
    Hugo Bamman in I Thought of Daisy was "drawn, for the most
    part, from John Dos Passos."

16 KRONENBERGER, LOUIS, ed. Atlantic Brief Lives: A Biographical
    Companion to the Arts. Boston: Little, Brown and Company,
    pp. 234-235.
        Brief biographical sketch.

17 KUEHL, JOHN and JACKSON R. BRYER, eds. Dear Scott/Dear Max,
    The Fitzgerald-Perkins Correspondence. New York: Charles
    Scribner's Sons.
        Numerous references to Dos Passos. Perkins remarks, in
    1933, on Dos Passos' weak sales: "I do not think that his
    way of writing and his theory makes books that people care
    to read unless they are interested objectively in society
    or in literature purely for its own sake. His whole theory
    is that books should be sociological documents, or something
    approaching that. I know that I never took one up without
    feeling that I was in for three or four hours of agony only
    relieved by admiration of his ability."

18 LEE, BRIAN. "History and John Dos Passos," in The American
    Novel and the Nineteen Twenties. Edited by M. Bradbury and
    D. Palmer. London: Edwin Arnold, pp. 197-213.
        Thinks Dos Passos' best fiction "has a pessimism different
    in kind and more profound than that found in the works of
    any of his American contemporaries." Thinks that to view
    Dos Passos as merely a novelist of social protest is to view
    him too narrowly: "What his image of America in the twenties
    compels us to see and believe is a truth so evident that
    even Life magazine propounds it now. Twentieth-Century man
    has created physical and spiritual environments for himself
    which will not allow him to go on living as a human being.
    . . . This is the social tragedy of our times."

19 McCORMICK, JOHN. The Middle Distance, A Comparative History of
    American Imaginative Literature: 1919-1932. New York: The
    Free Press, pp. 93-97, passim.
        Thinks Three Soldiers fails because of its rhetoric,
    because it "clearly derives from the Walter Pater-Algernon
    Charles Swinburne manner of registering of human emotion."
    Considers Manhattan Transfer to be "the first [American]
    novel to attain complete objectivity outside the tradition
    of naturalism." Notes the influence of Joyce, but calls
    Dos Passos unique for accepting the influence without sacri-
    ficing his own voice.

246

20 MAGEE, JOHN D. "An Analytical Study of John Dos Passos'
    Manhattan Transfer." Unpublished doctoral dissertation,
    Ball State University, 194pp.
        Calls Manhattan Transfer a masterpiece of experimental
    art and considers it to be an adventurous extension of the
    Whitman tradition. Also, the novel is viewed as an impor-
    tant source of knowledge about New York in the early
    twentieth century.

21 MICHAELSON, L. W. "My 85¢ Supper with Mr. U.S.A." English
    Record, 22 (Winter), 36-39.
        Humorous account of hosting "the famous author" at a
    campus speaking engagement.

22 MOTTRAM, ERIC. "The Hostile Environment and the Survival
    Artist: A Note on the Twenties," in The American Novel in
    the Nineteen Twenties. Edited by Malcolm Bradbury and
    David Palmer. Stratford-Upon-Avon Studies 13. London:
    Edwin Arnold, pp. 233-262.
        Discusses how Dos Passos, in Manhattan Transfer, makes
    use of "the multiple narrative of Griffith, the montage of
    Eisenstein and spatial discontinuities associated with
    Joyce" to portray the city "as a machine for living death."
    Also mentions Dos Passos' satirization of the cult of
    hero-worship in U.S.A.

23 MUSTE, JOHN M. "Norman Mailer and John Dos Passos: The
    Question of Influence." Modern Fiction Studies, 17
    (Autumn), 361-374.
        Agrees with other critics that Dos Passos strongly in-
    fluenced Mailer, but thinks that The Naked and the Dead
    owes more to Three Soldiers than U.S.A. Muste feels that
    Dos Passos was one of few novelists of World War I to por-
    tray the war as a natural outgrowth of modern civilization.

24 PEARCE, RICHARD. "Pylon, Awake and Sing, and the Apocalyptic
    Imagination of the 30's." Criticism, 13 (Spring), 131-142.
        Notes similarities between the imagery of Yeats' "Second
    Coming" ("Turning and turning in the widening gyre/The
    falcon cannot hear the falconer;/Things fall apart, the
    centre cannot hold") and the imagery and symbolism of
    American writers of the thirties. Feels that Dos Passos,
    in U.S.A., is "focused entirely on the 'widening gyre' [of]
    America's destructive energy."

25 PIPER, HENRY DAN. "Social Criticism in The American Novel in
    the Nineteen Twenties," in The American Novels in the Nine-
    teen Twenties. Edited by Malcolm Bradbury and David Palmer.

1971

Stratford-Upon-Avon Studies 13.   London: Edwin Arnold,
pp. 59-83.
  Briefly discusses Dos Passos.   Feels that he attempted,
in U.S.A., "to relieve the monotonous journalistic narrative
of naturalism," but only revealed "the shortcomings of his
imagination."

26 REEVES, PASCHAL.   Thomas Wolfe and the Glass of Time.   Athens:
University of Georgia Press, pp. 86-89, passim.
  Compares Dos Passos' and Wolfe's stylistic method and
thematic concerns.

27 REILLY, JOHN M.   "Dos Passos Et. Al.: An Experiment in Radical
Fiction."   Midwest Quarterly, 12 (Summer), 413-424.
  Examines the sources and influence of Dos Passos' "collective" novels which, Reilly feels, were an attempt to
find a revolutionary style to complement the revolutionary
social views which they would express.

28 ROBBINS, J. ALBERT, ed.   American Literary Scholarship, 1969.
Durham, N.C.: Duke University Press, pp. 125, 201, 210, 226,
272, 355.
  Reviews Dos Passos criticism of the year.

29 SCHORER, MARK.   "John Dos Passos: A Stranded American."
Atlantic Monthly, 227 (March), 93-96.
  Notes that Dos Passos' death marked the end of an era in
American literature.   Summarizes Dos Passos' career with
high praise for U.S.A., for its scope which makes it
"probably as close as we will ever come . . . to that
chimera, the Great American Novel," and for its stylistic
brilliance.   Feels that Dos Passos finally outlived his
generation and so lost the vital pulse of the times.   The
result was a series of flawed and minor books interrupted
only by his fine memoir, The Best Times.

30 SQUIRES, RADCLIFFE.   Allen Tate: A Literary Biography.   Pegasus
American Authors Series.   New York: Pegasus, p. 187.
  Mentions Dos Passos' lack of involvement in the controversy which swirled around Pound's 1949 selection as winner
of the Bollingen Prize: Dos Passos "pleaded ignorance of
the situation."

31 STENERSON, DOUGLAS C.   H. L. Mencken: Iconoclast From Baltimore.
Chicago: The University of Chicago Press, p. 220.
  Considers Dos Passos to be one of the writers to justify
Mencken's prophesy, in The American Language, that "the idiom
of everyday speech would form an increasingly important
part of the American literary tradition."

32 TITCHE, LEON L., JR. "Doblin and Dos Passos: Aspects of the
      City Novel." <u>Modern Fiction Studies</u>, 17 (Spring), 125-135.
      Comparison of Alfred Doblin's expressionistic novel,
      <u>Berlin Alexanderplatz</u> (1929), and <u>Manhattan Transfer</u>: "In
      Manhattan and Berlin, the best monuments to man's energies,
      intellect, and capabilities are preserved. Here also is
      found the worst in man." Shows how both portray the aliena-
      tion and loss of identity of modern urban life. Finds a
      crucial thematic difference in the desires of their charac-
      ters: "With Doblin, the character is outside the social
      periphery, battering it to get in"; in <u>Manhattan Transfer</u>,
      "the characters are within, fighting to get out."

33 TOMKINS, CALVIN. <u>Living Well Is the Best Revenge</u>. New York:
      Viking Press, 148pp., passim.
      Dos Passos is mentioned several times in this examination
      of the expatriates Gerald and Sara Murphy and their circle.

34 WATKINS, FLOYD G. <u>The Flesh and the Word: Eliot, Hemingway,</u>
      <u>Faulkner</u>. Nashville: Vanderbilt University Press, pp. 5-6.
      Mentions Dos Passos' character, J. Ward Morehouse, as an
      example of "a user of empty words . . . one of the most com-
      mon kinds of characters in literature written after [Woodrow]
      Wilson and the sentimental patriots had deadened the
      language."

<u>1972 A BOOKS</u>

1 LANDSBERG, MELVIN. <u>Dos Passos' Path to U.S.A.: A Political</u>
     <u>Biography, 1912-1936</u>. Boulder: The Colorado Associated
     University Press, 292pp.
     Biography of Dos Passos through the publication of <u>The</u>
     <u>Big Money</u>. Landsberg's primary purpose is "to describe the
     genesis of Dos Passos' political and social views." Focuses
     on the importance of Dos Passos' relationship with his
     father, of his Harvard years, of his war experiences, of
     his relationship with the political left, and of his per-
     ception of post-war society as decadent.

2 SANDERS, DAVID, ed. <u>The Merrill Studies in "U.S.A."</u> Charles E.
     Merrill Studies. Columbus, Ohio: Charles E. Merrill Publish-
     ing Company, 102pp.
     Contents: pp. iii-v: Preface by the editor.
     pp. 1-3: "A Sad 'Big Parade,'" by Matthew Josephson.
     Reprinted from <u>The Saturday Review of Literature</u>, 9
     (19 March 1932), 600.
     pp. 4-7: "The End of a Trilogy," by Malcolm Cowley.
     Reprinted from <u>The New Republic</u>, 88 (12 August 1936), 23-24.

1972

pp. 7-11: "Private Historian," Anonymous. Reprinted from Time, 28 (10 August 1936), 51-52.

pp. 11-16: "The Moods and Tenses of John Dos Passos," by Granville Hicks. Reprinted from New Masses, 27 (26 April 1938), 22-23.

pp. 17-21: "Dos Passos and the U.S.A.," by T. K. Whipple. Reprinted from The Nation, 146 (19 February 1938), 210-212.

pp. 21-28: "The America of John Dos Passos," by Lionel Trilling. Reprinted from Partisan Review, 4 (April 1938), 26-32.

pp. 30-37: "John Dos Passos and 1919," by Jean-Paul Sartre. Reprinted from Literary Essays. New York: Philosophical Library, 1957, pp. 88-96.

pp. 38-43: "From On Native Grounds," by Alfred Kazin. Reprinted from On Native Grounds. New York: Harcourt, Brace & Co., 1942, pp. 353-359.

pp. 44-48: "From After the Lost Generation," by John W. Aldridge. Reprinted from After the Lost Generation. New York: McGraw-Hill, 1951, pp. 71-76.

pp. 48-54: "The Fulfillment of Form in U.S.A.," by Blanche H. Gelfant. Norman: University of Oklahoma Press, 1954, pp. 166-174.

pp. 54-59: "From American Literary Naturalism: A Divided Stream," by Charles C. Walcutt. Reprinted from American Literary Naturalism: A Divided Stream. Minneapolis: University of Minnesota Press, 1956, pp. 283-289.

pp. 60-67: "Reflections on U.S.A. as Novel and Play," by Jules Chametzky. Reprinted from The Massachusetts Review, 1 (Winter 1960), 392-399.

pp. 67-78: "U.S.A.," by John H. Wrenn. Reprinted from John Dos Passos. New York: Twayne Publishers, 1961, pp. 154-166.

pp. 78-86: "Voice in the U.S.A. Biographies," by George Knox. Reprinted from Texas Studies in Language and Literature, 4 (Spring 1962), 109-116.

pp. 86-95: "Dos Passos' U.S.A.: The Words of the Hollow Men," by John Lydenberg. Reprinted from Essays on Determinism in American Literature. Edited by Sidney J. Krause. Kent, Ohio: Kent State University Press, 1964, pp. 97-107.

3 SMITH, JUAN EDWARD, JR. "John Dos Passos: Historian of Twentieth Century American Culture." Unpublished doctoral dissertation, University of Minnesota, 305pp.

Surveys critically the failings of previous Dos Passos criticism, which he feels has focused on only a handful of works while ignoring the many others. Argues that by examining the entire corpus of Dos Passos' writing it becomes

1972

clear that he was, throughout his career, consistent in his political views which were essentially those of a traditional American individualism and the role of the writer as "a historian of the culture in which he lived."

1972 B SHORTER WRITINGS

1 ALDRIDGE, JOHN W. "Dos Passos: The Energy of Despair." The Devil in the Fire: Retrospective Essays on American Literature and Culture, 1951-71. New York: Harper's Magazine Press, pp. 106-123.
   Reprint of 1951.B1.

2 BAKER, CARLOS. Hemingway, The Writer as Artist. 4th edition, revised. Princeton: Princeton University Press, 458pp., passim.
   Many references to Dos Passos.

3 BLAKE, FAY M. The Strike in the American Novel. Metuchen, N.J.: The Scarecrow Press, Inc., pp. 264-265, passim.
   Briefly discusses Dos Passos' anti-communist position in Adventures of a Young Man.

4 BLUEFARB, SAM. "John Andrews: Flight From the Machine State," in his The Escape Motif in the American Novel: Mark Twain to Richard Wright. Columbus: Ohio State University Press, pp. 61-72.
   Considers John Andrews to be "a man who possesses all of the essential characteristics of the Dos Passos hero--the romantic rebel against regimentation, the sensitive young artist--opponent of all repression." Thinks Three Soldiers to be "only incidentally a novel about World War I." Instead, Bluefarb considers it one more example of the escape motif which runs through American literature.

5 BUTCHER, FANNY. Many Lives--One Love. New York: Harper and Row, pp. 35, 141.
   Mentions Three Soldiers and U.S.A.

6 CRUNDEN, ROBERT M. From Self to Society, 1919-1941. Englewood Cliffs, N.J.: Prentice-Hall Company, pp. 54, 80, 101, 133, 181.
   A number of passing references to Dos Passos.

7 DITSKY, JOHN. "Carried Away by Numbers: The Rhapsodic Mode in Modern Fiction." Queen's Quarterly, 79 (Winter), 482-494.

1972

> Considers cataloguing "a major organizing principle of a
> [contemporary] fiction which has thrown away traditional
> concepts of 'purposes' and 'meanings.'" Thinks Dos Passos'
> use of cataloguing, particularly in the Newsreels of U.S.A.
> "strike the reader like dots that make up newspaper photo-
> graphs, though in actual fact they are just . . . manipula-
> table forms of 'objectivity.'"

8 DOWDY, ANDREW. "Hemingway & Surrealism: A Note on the Twenties
   Twenties." Hemingway Notes, 2 (Spring), 3-6.
     Mentions Dos Passos' praise for a passage from The
   Torrents of Spring.

9 FEENEY, JOSEPH J., S.J. "American Anti-War Writers of World
   War I: A Literary Study of Randolph Bourne, Harriet Monroe,
   Carl Sandburg, John Dos Passos, E. E. Cummings, and Ernest
   Hemingway." Unpublished doctoral dissertation, University
   of Pennsylvania, 275pp.
     Discusses the imagery and use of irony in Dos Passos'
   war novels.

10 FLANNER, JANET. Paris Was Yesterday, 1925-1939. Edited by
    Irving Drutman. New York: The Viking Press, p. xviii.
      Notes that Dos Passos was "popular and esteemed by all
    the other male writers in Paris," and that "the French
    regarded him as the most normal, typical American."

11 GEISMAR, MAXWELL. Ring Lardner and the Portrait of Folly.
    New York: Thomas Y. Crowell Co., pp. 1, 46, 117.
      Several references to Dos Passos. Geismar argues that
    Lardner's writing is reflective of the twenties, a period
    which seemed gay and carefree on the surface but was, in
    fact, "a period full of shame and scandal and moral debase-
    ment." Cites U.S.A. as evidence.

12 HOLMAN, HUGH C. The Roots of Southern Writing: Essays on the
    Literature of the American South. Athens: University of
    Georgia Press, pp. 89, 189.
      Draws parallels between the southern fugitives and the
    writers of the "lost generation": Dos Passos, Hemingway,
    et al.

13 HUBBELL, JAY B. Who Are the Major American Writers? Durham,
    N.C.: Duke University Press, passim.
      Frequent references to Dos Passos and his critical
    reputation.

14 KLIMO, VERNON (JAKE) and WILL OURSLER. <u>Hemingway and Jake: An</u>
    <u>Extraordinary Friendship</u>. Garden City, N.Y.: Doubleday,
    passim.
        Many references to Dos Passos and his relationship with
    Hemingway.

15 LANE, JAMES B. "<u>Manhattan Transfer</u> as a Gateway to the 1920s."
    <u>Centennial Review</u>, 16 (9 August), 293-311.
        Considers <u>Manhattan Transfer</u> a representative although
    superior novel of the twenties, both in its subject matter
    and stylistic innovations. Sees Dos Passos as "in many ways
    a traditionalist, an individualist, and a moralist."

16 LONGSTREET, STEPHEN. "John Dos Passos Goes to War," in his
    <u>We All Went to Paris: 1776-1971</u>. New York: Macmillan, pp.
    350-353, passim.
        Considers Dos Passos typical of the "frightfully decent
    fellows" who joined the Norton-Harjes Volunteer Ambulance
    Service.

17 McILVAINE, ROBERT M. "Dos Passos' Reading of Thorstein Veblen."
    <u>American Literature</u>, 44 (November), 471-474.
        Discusses Veblen's influence on the social and economic
    thought of Dos Passos and how such thought was diametrically
    opposed to the thinking of Dos Passos' father, John Randolph
    Dos Passos.

18 McLENDON, JAMES. <u>Papa: Hemingway in Key West</u>. Miami: E. A.
    Seeman Publishing, passim.
        Describes Dos Passos' importance in introducing Hemingway
    to Key West and his participating in Hemingway's Key West
    "mob."

19 MAGNY, CLAUDE-EDMONDE. <u>The Age of the American Novel: The</u>
    <u>Film Aesthetic of Fiction Between the Two Wars</u>. Translated
    by Eleanor Hochman. New York: Frederick Ungar Publishing
    Co., pp. 105-143, passim.
        Extensive discussion of Dos Passos' fiction, particularly
    in two chapters "Dos Passos' <u>U.S.A.</u>, or the Impersonal
    Novel," and "Time in Dos Passos," but also throughout the
    book. Stresses how the technique of the film was adapted
    by Dos Passos and others as a means of portraying the speed,
    energy and chaos of modern American society.

20 MEI, FRANCESCO. "Culture and Technique in Tate," in <u>Allen Tate</u>
    <u>and his Work: Critical Evaluations</u>. Edited by Radcliffe
    Squires. Minneapolis: University of Minnesota Press, pp.
    273-277.

1972

Cites Dos Passos and others to disprove the myth that
"American writers lack university education and know little
of European thought, history, and literature."

21 MORAN, RONALD. <u>Louis Simpson</u>. United States Authors Series.
New York: Twayne Publishers, p. 26.
Mentions Simpson's Columbia M.A. thesis: "One Man in His
Time," about Dos Passos.

22 MOTTRAM, ERIC. "Living Mythically: The Thirties." <u>Journal of
American Studies</u>, 61, 267-287.
Calls Dos Passos "the major novelist of alienation in
the 1930's, portraying the "dissolution of the family and
the community in the 1930's."

23 MURRAY, EDWARD. "John Dos Passos and the Camera-Eye:
<u>Manhattan Transfer</u> and <u>U.S.A.</u>," in his <u>The Cinematic
Imagination: Writers and Motion Pictures</u>. New York:
Frederick Ungar Publishing Co., pp. 168-178, passim.
Details Dos Passos' borrowing of film technique. Concludes that "by imitating the structure and style of motion
picture too closely, and by failing to subordinate his
borrowings to material that remains essentially literary--
as did the stream of consciousness novelists--Dos Passos
contributed to that genre which Virginia Woolf contemptuously
dismissed as the 'movie novel.'"

24 PROFFER, CARL R., ed. and trans. <u>Soviet Criticism of American
Literature in the Sixties: An Anthology</u>. Ann Arbor: Ardis
Publishers, pp. 29, 31, 74, 96, 165.
Several references to Dos Passos.

25 ROBBINS, J. ALBERT, ed. <u>American Literary Scholarship, 1970</u>.
Durham, N.C.: Duke University Press, p. 236.
Reviews Dos Passos criticism of the year.

26 SARASON, BERTRAM D. <u>Hemingway and the Sun Set</u>. Washington,
D.C.: NCR Microcard Editions, passim.
Frequent mention of John Dos Passos.

27 SMILEY, SAM. <u>The Drama of Attack: Didactic Plays of the
American Depression</u>. Columbia: University of Missouri
Press, p. 77.
Feels that the best American playwrights of the depression
agreed with Dos Passos' assertion that "if a writer works
genuinely with insight and intelligence . . . he will be
on the side . . . of liberty, fraternity, and humanity."

28 TAYLOR, KAREN MALPEDE. People's Theatre in Amerika. New
   York: Drama Book Specialists.
       Contains a number of documents from the Radical theatre
   including portions of plays, essays, reviews, etc. Included
   is a reprint of Dos Passos' "Did the New Playwrights Theatre
   Fail?" from The New Masses.

29 VALGEMAE, MARDI. Accelerated Grimace: Expressionism in the
   American Drama of the 1920s. Carbondale: Southern Illinois
   University Press, pp. 73-74, 118-121, passim.
       Many references to Dos Passos and the New Playwrights'
   Theatre as well as a brief analysis of The Garbage Man,
   which Valgemae characterizes as "thoroughly expressionistic
   . . . a grotesquely distorted vision of modern America."

30 VIDAL, GORE. "John Dos Passos At Midcentury," in Homage to
   Daniel Shays: Collected Essays 1952-1972. New York: Random
   House, pp. 96-102.
       Reprint of 1961.B72.

31 YOUNG, PHILIP. "American Fiction, American Life: An Address
   to the Peace Corps," in his Three Bags Full, Essays in
   American Fiction. New York: Harcourt, Brace, pp. 154-171.
       Cautions against viewing the generally dark vision of
   the modern American novel to be intended to or in fact be a
   representative portrait of American society. Calls U.S.A.
   "an epic of monumental, national failure" in which "success
   is empty and failure is pregnant."

1973 A BOOKS

1 LUDINGTON, TOWNSEND, ed. The Fourteenth Chronicle: Letters and
   Diaries of John Dos Passos. Boston: Gambit, 676pp.
       Rich selection of letters and journal entries from 1910
   to 1970. Ludington provides brief but useful biographical
   introductions to the letters which are grouped
   chronologically.

2 SMITH, IVAN E., JR. "John Dos Passos: Historian of Twentieth-
   Century American Culture." Unpublished doctoral dissertation, University of Minnesota.
       Attempts to correct two basic flaws in evaluations of
   Dos Passos' work: a tendency to focus almost exclusive
   attention on the two trilogies, and an uncalled-for politi-
   calization of Dos Passos criticism. Smith views Dos Passos
   as a pragmatic experimenter whose vision for America was
   always essentially traditional.

1973

1973 B SHORTER WRITINGS

1 ALDRIDGE, JOHN W. "Afterthoughts on the 20's." Commentary,
   56 (November), 37-41.
      Feels that "too many of the 20's writers remained locked
   into their first youthful responses to an experience that
   was too overwhelmingly intense to serve as very much more
   than the material of an often brilliant, but very personal
   and limited literature." Aldridge feels that all Dos Passos
   "essentially had to support his intricately panoramic
   vision of American society were the values of adversary
   politics, and . . . as he grew older, his vision did not
   deepen: only his politics aged."

2 BAKISH, DAVID. Richard Wright. New York: Frederick Ungar
   Publishing Co., p. 82.
      Mentions that Dos Passos and Wright, along with many
   other writers, were active supporters of the Republicans in
   the Spanish Civil War.

3 BOGAN, LOUISE. What the Woman Lived, Selected Letters of
   Louise Bogan, 1920-1970. Edited by Ruth Limmer. New York:
   Harcourt, Brace, Jovanovich, pp. 121, 137, 167.
      Mentions a Wallace Stevens-Dos Passos run-in in Key West.
   Also includes Bogan's assessment of Dos Passos as a writer
   ("If Dos Passos is a novelist, I'm a gazelle!") and as a
   man ("if ever there was a fake human being and a punk
   writer, J. Dos P. is that one").

4 BROER, LAWRENCE R. Hemingway's Spanish Tragedy. University,
   Ala.: The University of Alabama Press, p. 4.
      Mentions the pleasure Hemingway took in introducing Dos
   Passos to bullfighting.

5 BURNS, EDWARD, ed. Staying on Alone: Letters of Alice B.
   Toklas. New York: Liveright, pp. 151, 193.
      Toklas offers her own and Stein's view of Dos Passos:
   Stein "liked him--he had the Spanish charm--she tried to
   read his novel written after the other war but it didn't
   interest her. She told an American lady . . . that his
   brains were addled--and she never tried to read any more of
   his books." Toklas mentions that she tried but couldn't
   read Manhattan Transfer: "it didn't hold my attention."

6 COWLEY, MALCOLM. "Dos Passos: The Learned Poggius." Southern
   Review, N.S. 9 (Winter), 7-17.
      Survey of Dos Passos' career. Considers Dos Passos'
   greatest achievement to be in his widely influential experiments in the form of the novel. Thinks Dos Passos' decline

was not so much the result of his change in political
thinking as in his coming to value his opinions more than
his characters. As a result, he came to feel a "tired
aversion" for his characters. Reprinted 1973.B7.

7 _____. "Dos Passos: The Learned Poggius," in his A Second
Flowering: Works and Days of the Lost Generation. New
York: The Viking Press, pp. 74-89.
Reprint of 1973.B6.

8 _____. "What Books Survive from the 1930's?" Journal of
American Studies, 7, 293-300.
Calls U.S.A.--along with For Whom the Bell Tolls and The
Grapes of Wrath--the "three big novels" of the 1930s.
Cowley feels the novel may seem "absurdly pessimistic"
forty years later but feels "the book holds together like
a great ship freighted with the dead and dying, and it ex-
presses what many people besides the author felt in those
years when the nation seemed to be careening into the
depths."

9 DIGGINS, JOHN P. The American Left in the Twentieth Century.
The Harbrace History of the United States. New York:
Harcourt, Brace, Jovanovich, passim.
A number of references to Dos Passos and quotations from
his writing, particularly from the biographies of radical
leaders which appear in U.S.A.

10 ELIAS, ROBERT H. "Entangling Alliances with None": An Essay
on the Individual in the American Twenties. New York:
W. W. Norton & Co., pp. 164, 171-178.
Finds in Dos Passos' work of the twenties only limited
answers to modern man's alienation: to merely walk vaguely
away from society as Jimmy Herf does at the end of
Manhattan Transfer or to totally externalize society as
does Conga Jake in the same novel.

11 FABRE, MICHEL. The Unfinished Quest of Richard Wright.
Translated from the French by Isabel Barzun. New York:
William Morrow and Co., pp. v, xvi, 84, 136, 170, 417, 427.
Many references to Dos Passos. Fabre points out several
instances of Wright's indebtedness to Dos Passos.

12 GADO, FRANK, ed. "John Dos Passos," in First Person,
Conversations on Writers and Writing. Schenectady, N.Y.:
Union College Press, pp. 31-62.
Interview conducted in 1968 which ranges over many
topics: the SDS and student rebellion in general; the harm-
ful effects of television; historians as literary artists;

his interest in painting; and its effect on his fiction; the influence of the film montage of Griffith and Eisenstein; evaluations of Cowley, Hemingway, Fitzgerald, Barth, Updike, and Mailer; and various influences on his writing.

13 FOSTER, RICHARD. "Norman Mailer," in Seven American Stylists from Poe to Mailer: An Introduction. Edited by George T. Wright. Minneapolis: University of Minnesota Press, pp. 238–273.

Quotes Mailer as admitting the influence of the naturalists Farrell and Dos Passos, but Mailer feels he went beyond them, to a kind of mysticism.

14 FRANK, WALDO. Memoirs of Waldo Frank. Edited by Alan Trachtenberg. Amherst: University of Massachusetts Press, pp. x, 88, 132, 193.

Briefly evaluates Dos Passos' analysis of Spain and the Spanish writer Pio Baroja and mentions his attendance at a meeting to form New Masses.

15 GOLD, HERBERT. "The Literary Lives of John Dos Passos." Saturday Review World, 1 (11 September), 32–35.

Feels that "Dos Passos' letters and diaries [in The Fourteenth Chronicle] offer a new experience, an autobiographical treasure more intimate and touching than his novels."

16 HASSAN, IHAB. Contemporary American Literature 1945–1972: An Introduction. New York: Frederick Ungar Publishing Co., pp. 1, 65.

Feels that the "surrealistic form" of Mailer's The Naked and the Dead, as well as the war novels of John Hawkes, Thomas Berger, Joseph Heller, and Kurt Vonnegut, are reminiscent of Dos Passos.

17 HUGHSON, LOIS. "In Search of the True America: Dos Passos' debt to Whitman in U.S.A." Modern Fiction Studies, 19 (Summer), 179–192.

Notes the similarities and differences between Whitman and Dos Passos, particularly in their shared sympathy for the powerless, the outcast, and the downtrodden and also in their vision of America's Edenic potential for which both writers looked to the past.

18 KAZIN, ALFRED. Bright Book of Life: American Novelists and Storytellers from Hemingway to Mailer. Boston: Little, Brown and Company, pp. 10–16, passim.

Discusses the high value placed on art and artists by
Hemingway, Dos Passos, and others of their generation.

19 KVAM, WAYNE E. Hemingway in Germany: The Fiction, the Legend,
    and the Critics. Athens: Ohio University Press, pp. 3, 44,
    100, 119, 120.
    Several references to Dos Passos.

20 LEHAN, RICHARD. "French and American Literary Existentialism:
    Dos Passos, Hemingway, Faulkner," in his A Dangerous
    Crossing: French Literary Existentialism and the Modern
    American Novel. Carbondale: Southern Illinois University
    Press, pp. 35-79.
    Explores the philosophical and literary influence of
    these American writers on the French existentialists,
    particularly Sartre and Camus. Notes especially the simi-
    larities between Sartre and Dos Passos in style and thematic
    concerns.

21 McILVAINE, ROBERT. "Dos Passos' Three Soldiers." Explicator,
    31 (March), item 50.
    Examines two scenes from the novel to show that Andrews'
    wound is a result of an act of sympathy for all life and
    that the wound leads to a rise in his integrity which will
    guarantee that he will never "'fall into line again.'"

22 MEINKE, PETER. "Swallowing America Whole." New Republic, 169
    (22 September), 28-31.
    Compares Dos Passos' early writing with Allen Ginsberg's.
    Feels that the two reasons for Dos Passos' lack of popular
    success are "the negative thrust of his work . . . and his
    failure to create characters with whom readers could iden-
    tify." Feels that The Fourteenth Chronicle reveals "a decent
    and generous man of boundless enthusiasm and energy."

23 NICOL, CHARLES. "The Camera Eye." National Review, 25
    (7 December), 1365-1366.
    Feels that The Fourteenth Chronicle bears out the idea
    that the major movement of Dos Passos' career was his "slow
    rapprochement with America." Thinks the letters reveal Dos
    Passos to be a "kind, honest, intelligent man, and a good
    writer."

24 PEARSALL, ROBERT BRAINARD. The Life and Writings of Ernest
    Hemingway. Amsterdam: Rodopi NV, pp. 94-95, passim.
    A number of references to Dos Passos, including his view
    of Hemingway's The Torrents of Spring as a "double cross"

1973

and his advice that Hemingway should cut many of the intro-
spective passages of Death in the Afternoon.

25 RALEIGH, JOHN HENRY. "History and the Burdens: The Example of
    Norman Mailer," in Uses of Literature. Edited by Monroe
    Engel. Cambridge, Mass.: Harvard University Press, pp.
    163-186.
        Notes Dos Passos' influence on Mailer, particularly
    evident in The Naked and the Dead. Feels that Mailer has
    always tried and failed to emulate and surpass the great
    writers of the American twenties, including Dos Passos.

26 ROBBINS, J. ALBERT, ed. American Literary Scholarship, 1971.
    Durham, N.C.: Duke University Press, pp. 209, 210, 224-225,
    247, 249, 379.
        Reviews Dos Passos' criticism of the year.

27 RUBIN, LOUIS D., JR., ed. The Comic Imagination in American
    Literature. New Brunswick, N.J.: Rutgers University Press,
    p. 75.
        Identifies Ichabod Crane as an American literary type
    used by many writers, including Dos Passos.

28 SCOTT, NATHAN A., JR. Three American Moralists: Mailer, Bellow,
    Trilling. South Bend, Ind.: University of Notre Dame Press,
    pp. 23, 24, 31, 109.
        Mentions Dos Passos' influence on Mailer.

29 SHAW, SAMUEL. Ernest Hemingway. Modern Literature Monographs.
    New York: Frederick Ungar Publishing Co., p. 38.
        Mentions Dos Passos' objections to Hemingway's decision
    to publish The Torrents of Spring.

30 STEWART, DONALD OGDEN. "An Interview." Fitzgerald/Hemingway
    Annual, pp. 83-89.
        Stewart recalls Dos Passos briefing him on Paris and
    helping to arrange a meeting with Hemingway.

31 WEEKS, EDWARD. Review of The Fourteenth Chronicle. Atlantic
    Monthly, 232 (October), 128.
        Calls The Fourteenth Chronicle an "exciting and forth-
    right collection."

32 WELLS, WALTER. Tycoons and Locusts: A Regional Look at
    Hollywood Fiction of the 1930's. Carbondale: Southern
    Illinois University Press, p. 120.
        Feels that Dos Passos' opinion that The Last Tycoon is
    "'one of those literary fragments that from time to time

260

appear . . . and profoundly influence the course of human
events'" to be overly enthusiastic.

1974 A BOOKS

1 BECKER, GEORGE J. John Dos Passos. Modern Literature Monographs. New York: Frederick Ungar Publishing Co., 142pp.
Surveys the career and writings of an "artist-observer."
The first chapter is a biographical sketch. Fairly in-depth
discussion of Manhattan Transfer and U.S.A.; briefer treatment of other works. Primary and secondary bibliography of
selected major works.

2 FERGUSSON, DIANE SMITH. "John Dos Passos: The Novelist as
Satirical Chronicler." Unpublished doctoral dissertation,
University of South Carolina, 291pp.
Feels that Dos Passos is rightly noted primarily for his
stylistic and technical innovations, but that the unique
"combinations of history, satire, and poetry" of his contemporary chronicles, from Manhattan Transfer to Midcentury,
are "an important addition to American literature."

3 HOOK, ANDREW, ed. Dos Passos: A Collection of Critical Essays.
Twentieth Century Views. Englewood Cliffs, N.J.: Prentice-
Hall, Inc., 192pp.
Contents: pp. 1-12: Introduction by the editor.
pp. 13-14: "Dos Passos' Own Views," from "The Situation
in American Writing." Partisan Review (Summer 1939), pp.
25-27.
pp. 15-30: "The Politics of John Dos Passos," by Granville
Hicks. Reprinted from The Antioch Review, 10 (March 1950)
85-98.
pp. 31-35: "Dos Passos and the Social Revolution," by
Edmund Wilson. Reprinted from his Shores of Light. New
York: Farrar, Straus & Giroux, Inc., 1952, pp. 429-435.
pp. 36-52: "John Dos Passos: The Synoptic Novel," by
Blanche H. Gelfant. Reprinted from her The American City
Novel. Norman: University of Oklahoma Press, 1954, pp.
133-151.
pp. 53-60: "Manhattan Transfer: Dos Passos' Wasteland,"
by E. D. Lowry. Reprinted from The University Review, 30
(October 1963), 47-52.
pp. 61-69: "John Dos Passos and 1919," by Jean-Paul
Sartre. Reprinted from Literary and Philosophical Essays
of Jean-Paul Sartre. Translated by Annete Michelson.
London: Rider & Company, 1955, pp. 88-96.

1974

    pp. 70-75: "A Serious Artist," by F. R. Leavis. Re-
printed from <u>Scrutiny</u>, 1 (September 1932), 173-179.
    pp. 76-86: "John Dos Passos: The Poet and the World,"
by Malcolm Cowley. Reprinted from <u>The New Republic</u>, 70
(27 April 1932), 303-305.
    pp. 87-92: "Dos Passos and the U.S.A.," by T. K. Whipple.
Reprinted from <u>The Nation</u>, 146 (19 February 1938), 210-212.
    pp. 93-100: "The America of John Dos Passos," by Lionel
Trilling. Reprinted from <u>The Partisan Review</u>, 4 (April
1938), 26-32.
    pp. 101-119: "Dos Passos, Society, and the Individual,"
by Alfred Kazin. Reprinted from "All the Lost Generations,"
in <u>On Native Grounds</u>. New York: Harcourt, Brace & Co.,
1942, pp. 341-359.
    pp. 120-127: "Dos Passos, Fitzgerald, and History," by
John William Ward. Reprinted from his <u>Red, White, and Blue:
Men, Books and Ideas in American Culture</u>. New York: Oxford
University Press, Inc., 1969, pp. 38-47.
    pp. 128-144: "Time in Dos Passos," by Claude-Edmonde
Magny. Reprinted from her <u>The Age of the American Novel:
The Film Aesthetic of Fiction Between the Two Wars</u>. Trans-
lated by Eleanor Hochman. New York: Frederick Ungar
Publishing Co., 1972.
    pp. 145-147: "The Radicalism of <u>U.S.A.</u>," by Walter B.
Rideout. Reprinted from his <u>The Radical Novel in the United
States: 1950-1954</u>. Cambridge, Mass.: Harvard University
Press, 1956, pp. 162-164.
    pp. 148-161: "John Dos Passos: Technique vs. Sensibility,"
by Herbert Marshall McLuhan. Reprinted from <u>Fifty Years of
the American Novel</u>. Edited by Harold C. Gardiner. New
York: Charles Scribner's Sons, 1951, pp. 151-164.
    pp. 162-170: "The Gullivers of Dos Passos," by Arthur
Mizener. Reprinted from <u>The Saturday Review of Literature</u>,
34 (30 June 1951), 6-7, 34-36.
    pp. 171-180: "The Chronicles of Dos Passos," by Richard
Chase. Reprinted from <u>Commentary</u>, 31 (May 1961), 395-400.

1974 B   SHORTER WRITINGS

1 BAKER, JOHN D. "Whitman and Dos Passos: A Sense of Communion."
<u>Walt Whitman Review</u>, 20 (March), 30-33.
    Feels that Dos Passos was his generations' heir to the
"Whitman revolution": "Though they differed over industrialism because of their disparate perspectives, worked from
separate aesthetic models (Whitman, the opera; Dos Passos,
muralist painting), and created within different literary
forms, the two men shared a basic philosophy. Both believed

in the centrality of the dignity of the individual, the
need to return to the ideals of the Founding Fathers, and
the writer as the spokesman for a nation."

2 BLOTNER, JOSEPH. Faulkner: A Biography. 2 Volumes. New York:
Random House, pp. 1221-1222, 1665-1667, passim.
Many references to Dos Passos.

3 BROUGHTON, PANTHEA REID. William Faulkner: The Abstract and
the Actual. Baton Rouge: Louisiana State University Press,
p. 13.
Mentions Dos Passos' "camera eye" as "an experiment
setting forth objectivity as the highest aesthetic end.
As a level of meaning, style established that the concrete
is true, the abstract false."

4 BUTTERFIELD, STEPHEN. Black Autobiography In America. Amherst:
University of Massachusetts Press, p. 142.
Argues that while the method of Claude McKay's A Long
Way From Home owes much to those of Steinbeck and Dos
Passos, the point of view is "distinctively black."

5 DIGGINS, JOHN P. "Visions of Chaos and Visions of Order: Dos
Passos as Historian." American Literature, 46 (November),
329-346.
After establishing that in U.S.A. "the historical dimension first emerges in Dos Passos' work, both as a structural
device and as a mode of comprehension," Diggins goes on to
analyze Dos Passos' approach to the histories of his later
career. Identifies Dos Passos as a historicist in the
Daniel Boorstein mold, rather than an idealist such as
Perry Miller.

6 DUMAS, BETHANY K. E. E. Cummings: A Remembrance of Miracles.
London: Vision Press, passim.
Many references to Dos Passos. Dumas frequently quotes
from The Best Times.

7 FURNAS, JOSEPH CHAMBERLAIN. Great Times: An Informal Social
History of the U.S. 1914-1929. New York: G. P. Putnam's
Sons, pp. 66-68, 70-71, passim.
Numerous references to and quotations from Dos Passos who
is treated as a representative figure of the time.

8 GELFANT, BLANCHE. Review of Dos Passos' Path to U.S.A.: A
Political Biography, 1912-1936. American Literature, 45
(January), 621-622.
Faults Landsberg's biography for not presenting signifi-
cant new material and for avoiding the most interesting

1974

aspect of Dos Passos' writing: his use of language, his
attempt to capture "the speech of the people."

9   GOLDSTEIN, MALCOLM. The Political Stage: American Drama and
    Theater of the Great Depression. New York: Oxford University
    Press, pp. 11-14, 20-24, passim.
        Discusses Dos Passos' involvement with the New
    Playwrights' Theatre.

10 GRAHAM, DON and BARBARA SHAW. "Faulkner's Small Debt to Dos
    Passos: A Source for the Percy Grimm Episode." Mississippi
    Quarterly, 27 (Summer), 327-331.
        Identifies the "Paul Bunyan" sketch of 1919, which had
    appeared in the New Masses under the title "Wesley Everest,"
    as the source of the Percy Grimm episode in Light in August.

11 GUNN, DREWEY WAYNE. American and British Writers in Mexico,
    1556-1973. Austin: University of Texas Press, pp. 55, 63,
    77, 80, 90-93.
        Discusses Dos Passos' great interest in Mexican culture
    and politics and speculates that his Mexican experiences
    had an influence on the U.S.A. trilogy. Considers the
    trilogy to be a fictional attempt at a mural, the very art
    form that Dos Passos was most fascinated by in Mexico.
    Identifies some possible models for Dos Passos' characters.

12 HAYASHI, TETSUMARO, ed. A Study Guide To Steinbeck: A Hand-
    book to his Major Works. Metuchen, N.J.: The Scarecrow
    Press, p. 284.
        Notes Dos Passos' capsule biography of James Dean in
    Midcentury as evidence of the emblematic "adulation of Dean"
    whose first major film, East of Eden, was based on the
    Steinbeck novel.

13 HENDERSON, HARRY B., III. Versions of the Past: The Historical
    Imagination In American Fiction. New York: Oxford University
    Press, pp. 241-246, passim.
        Draws parallels between Dos Passos and Henry Adams, both
    characterized as "hopeless" progressives who adhered to a
    progressive ethic but could see little hope for its realiza-
    tion to the modern world. Henderson further compares Dos
    Passos to Edith Wharton both of whom, he believes, used the
    economic theories of Thorstein Veblen as a touchstone.

14 HICKS, GRANVILLE. Granville Hicks in the New Masses. Edited
    by Jack Alan Robbins. Port Washington, N.Y.: Kennikat
    Press, pp. 29-33, 51, 53-55, 64-65, 133-138, 272.

1974

Dos Passos is discussed in some depth in various essays: "The Complex Novel"; "The Problem of Documentation"; "Notes of a Novelist"; "The Moods and Tenses of John Dos Passos."

15 KAPLAN, JUSTIN. Lincoln Steffens: A Biography. New York: Simon and Schuster, pp. 211, 227, 229, 276, 310.
    Passing reference to Dos Passos.

16 LEWIS, THOMAS S. W., ed. Letters of Hart Crane and His Family. New York: Columbia University Press, pp. 229, 233.
    Mentions Crane's anticipation of spending Thanksgiving, 1923, with Dos Passos.

17 MERSMANN, JAMES F. Out of the Vietnam Vortex: A Study of Poets and Poetry Against the War. Wichita: The University Press of Kansas, pp. 58, 208.
    Feels the spirit of much of the literature of World War I, including 1919, to be essentially comic. Thinks that "anger at the misuse of language to manipulate and obscure" is the primary force behind the "Newsreels" as well as behind much of the poetry of the Vietnam War.

18 ROBBINS, J. ALBERT, ed. American Literary Scholarship, 1972. Durham, N.C.: Duke University Press, pp. 151, 249, 346, 362.
    Reviews Dos Passos criticism of the year.

19 ROBINSON, CHARLES E. "James T. Farrell's Critical Estimate of Hemingway." Fitzgerald-Hemingway Annual [1973] pp. 209-214.
    Quotes from unpublished letter of 1936 in which Farrell gives an account of Hemingway's judgment of his contemporaries. Farrell notes that he likes Dos Passos very much: "He says that he thinks the best part of Dos Passos are his portraits and that he also liked some of the early camera eye sketches, particularly those dealing with experiences he had known of."

20 SAMPSON, EDWARD C. E. B. White. United States Authors Series. New York: Twayne Publishers, pp. 60, 162.
    Feels that White was "perhaps closer to the truth politically" during the thirties than Dos Passos and other American writers sympathetic to the left.

1974

21 SCHULTZ, MAX F. <u>Bruce Jay Friedman</u>. United States Authors
Series. New York: Twayne Publishers, pp. 57-58.
Feels that while mid-century America has grown too disparate for the "effort at comprehensiveness of detail"
of a Dos Passos, Friedman "perseveres in this social realist
tradition, with the difference that he is not afraid to use
the terse style of the caricaturist."

22 SLOANE, DAVID E. E. "The Black Experience in Dos Passos'
<u>U.S.A.</u>" <u>CEA Critic</u>, 36 (March), 22-23.
Argues that Dos Passos' relatively scanty treatment of
the black experience in <u>U.S.A.</u> is "objective social realism
with a significant point" for it represents "a racism which
forces black people to the periphery of American life."

23 SMOLLER, SANFORD J. <u>Adrift Among Geniuses: Robert McAlman,
Writer and Publisher of the Twenties</u>. University Park:
Pennsylvania State University Press, pp. 144-147, passim.
Mentions Dos Passos' initial disdain for the expatriates
and McAlmon's enthusiastic evaluation of Dos Passos' work.

24 SOLOTAROFF, ROBERT. <u>Down Mailer's Way</u>. Urbana: University of
Illinois Press, pp. 3, 5, 14.
Considers <u>The Naked and the Dead</u> to be derivative in
both style and theme of the great novels of World War I
and particularly of Dos Passos.

25 STADE, GEORGE. "The Two Faces of Dos Passos." <u>Partisan
Review</u>, 41, no. 3, 476-483.
Review of <u>The Fourteenth Chronicle</u>. Compares Dos Passos
with George Orwell and feels he would have been the American
Orwell had he died in 1950 and not lived to produce the
later and lesser work of the fifties and sixties.

26 STENGER, WALLACE. <u>The Uneasy Chair, A Biography of Bernard
De Voto</u>. New York: Doubleday and Co., pp. 17, 232.
Mentions Dos Passos.

27 SULLIVAN, JEREMIAH. "Conflict in the Modern American Novel."
<u>Ball State University Forum</u>, 15 (Spring), 28-36.
Feels that Robert Penn Warren and Norman Mailer share
with the realists Dreiser, Anderson, Twain, James, and Dos
Passos a sense of radical commitment, "but their commit-
ments are based on wishes rather than realities."

28 VANDERWERKEN, DAVID L. "Dos Passos' Streets of Night: A
     Reconsideration." Markham Review, 4 (October), 61-65.
          Feels that critics have overlooked "the tight structural
     pattern of the novel." Feels the formal structure is es-
     tablished by "an elaborate series of triangular relation-
     ships" and that each character possesses, within his
     consciousness, another triangle "which seems to owe much
     to Freud's theory of the tripartite division of the psyche."
     Vanderwerken also identifies the wheel as another "con-
     trolling image." He concludes that, although the scope is
     smaller, in this novel, as in his other fiction, Dos Passos
     establishes a pattern of the characters' lives which
     "become metaphoric alternatives for the nation."

1975 A BOOKS

1 ORTH, WILLIAM J. "The Later Novels of John Dos Passos."
     Unpublished doctoral dissertation, Temple University.
          Considers the later fiction of Dos Passos which Orth
     believes is of very high quality when properly read as
     satire.

1975 B SHORTER WRITINGS

1 AICHINGER, PETER. The American Soldier in Fiction, 1880-1963:
     A History of Attitudes Toward Warfare and the Military
     Establishment. Ames: Iowa State University Press, pp. 17-
     19, 22-23, 39, 42, passim.
          Many references to Dos Passos and his war writing.

2 CARVER, CRAIG. "The Newspaper and Other Sources of Manhattan
     Transfer." Studies in American Fiction, 3 (Autumn),
     167-180.
          Feels that fragments of the newspaper and other popular
     media not only enhance the theme of Manhattan Transfer, but
     mirror the very shaping of the novel: "the discontinuous
     structure, the pervasive sensationalism, the self-imposed
     limitation of recording only external phenomena and behavior,
     and, to an extent, the characterization which tends to be
     simplistic and stereotyped is much the way human behavior
     is simplified and categorized by the less sophisticated
     journalism of seventy years ago."

3 CHUPACK, HENRY. James Purdy. United States Authors Series.
     New York: Twayne Publishers, p. 129.

1975

Notes Purdy's affinity with such naturalists as Dreiser,
Farrell, and Dos Passos, but feels his characters evoke
more compassion than theirs since his characters' own
"emotional deficiencies" rather than an "indifferent uni-
verse" are the source of their sufferings.

4 CLEMENS, WALTER. "Houdini, Meet Ferdinand." Newsweek, 86
(14 July), 73, 76.
Review of E. L. Doctow's Ragtime. Notes Dos Passos
among others who have experimented with the mix of history
and fiction.

5 COWLEY, MALCOLM. "Century's Ebb." New York Times Book Review
(9 November), p. 6.
Feels that Century's Ebb, the last of Dos Passos "contemporary chronicles," leaves one "with more admiration for
the series as a whole, including the later books that have
been too easily rejected." Especially likes the character
of Jay Pignatelli who so resembles Dos Passos, himself:
"shy, persistent, often disappointed by persons he trusted,
and determined to maintain a stubborn integrity."

6 COX, MARTHA HEASLEY and WAYNE CHATTERTON. Nelson Algren.
Boston: Twayne Publishers, p. 61.
Briefly compares Algren's Somebody in Boots with The 42nd
Parallel, both "American road stories . . . vigorous American
versions of the older picaresque tale."

7 DAY, MARTIN S. A Handbook of American Literature: A
Comprehensive Study from Colonial Times to the Present Day.
St. Lucia, Queensland: University of Queensland Press, pp.
474-476, passim.
Characterizes Dos Passos as "a disillusioned Whitman."
Considers U.S.A.'s framework to be the "epic and exciting
quality of the trilogy."

8 DIGGINS, JOHN P. Up from Communism, Conservative Odysseys in
American Intellectual History. New York: Harper and Row,
pp. 74-117, 233-268, 350-360, passim.
Critical study of Dos Passos' writing and career which
focuses on Dos Passos' own odyssey from left to right.

9 EISENBERG, DIANE U. Malcolm Cowley: A Checklist of His
Writings, 1916-1973. Carbondale: Southern Illinois
University Press, passim.
Numerous bibliographical references to articles by
Cowley on Dos Passos.

10 FORD, HUGH. <u>Published in Paris: American and British Writers,</u>
     <u>Painters, and Publishers in Paris, 1920-1939</u>. New York:
     Macmillan Publishing Co., passim.
        A number of references to Dos Passos including mention
     of his encouragement of and support for young Hemingway.

11 HARRIS, LEON. <u>Upton Sinclair: American Rebel</u>. New York:
     Thomas Y. Crowell Company, pp. 276, 298, 326, 346, 385.
        Passing reference.

12 HAYMAN, DAVID. "An Interview with Alain Robbe-Grillet."
     <u>Contemporary Literature</u>, 16 (Summer), 273-285.
        Robbe-Grillet remarks that it is odd that "in literature
     I feel closer to the novelists of the last generation, to
     Faulkner, or even to Dos Passos, you know, even to
     Hemingway."

13 HOBHOUSE, JANET. <u>Everybody Who Was Anybody: A Biography of</u>
     <u>Gertrude Stein</u>. London: Weidenful and Nicolson, p. 125.
        Mentions Dos Passos' visit to Stein's Paris flat. Stein
     thought him "charmingly Spanish though his 'brains were
     addled.'"

14 HOLMAN, C. HUGH. <u>The Loneliness at the Core: Studies in</u>
     <u>Thomas Wolfe</u>. Baton Rouge: Louisiana State University
     Press, pp. 98-102, 160, 161.
        Contrasts Wolfe and Dos Passos, writers who are often
     linked for their novels of the thirties. Notes the differ-
     ences in their socioeconomic background, their age, their
     experiences and, perhaps most importantly, their methods:
     while Dos Passos tried to portray his world in rigorously
     objective terms, Wolfe filtered the world through the sub-
     jective impressions of his protagonist.

15 KENNER, HUGH. <u>A Homemade World: The American Modernist Writers</u>.
     New York: Alfred A. Knopf, pp. 14, 128.
        Brief mention of Dos Passos.

16 KRIEGEL, LEONARD. "The Stuff of Fictional History."
     <u>Commonweal</u>, 102 (19 December), 631-632.
        Notes the similarities and differences between <u>U.S.A.</u>
     and E. L. Doctorow's <u>Ragtime</u>: "In Dos Passos' great trilogy,
     the biographical is used as a counterweight to the fic-
     tional. In Doctorow, the stuff of J. P. Morgan is, indeed,
     the stuff of fictional life."

17 LIGHT, MARTIN. <u>The Quixotic Vision of Sinclair Lewis</u>. West
     Lafayette, Ind.: Purdue University Press, p. 26.
        Mentions Lewis' acknowledgement of Dos Passos and others
     in his Nobel Prize Address.

1975

18 MARIANI, PAUL L. <u>William Carlos Williams: The Poet and His
Critics</u>. Chicago: American Library Association, p. 54.
Quotes from Frank W. Dupee's 1940 <u>New Republic</u> review of
<u>White Mule</u> that Williams was "'merely rewriting Dos Passos
according to Imagist principles.'"

19 MORSE, JONATHAN IRVING. "Forms of Disillusion in Fitzgerald
and Dos Passos." Unpublished doctoral dissertation, Indiana
University, 187pp.
Argues that in Dos Passos' fiction, particularly <u>U.S.A.</u>,
"all social norms have disintegrated and the only organizing
principle is that of disillusion," and that "the continuing
popularity of <u>U.S.A.</u> is due to its brutally thorough demon-
stration that the 1920's view of individuality expressed
within a viable social context was an illusion."

20 RADFORD, JEAN. <u>Norman Mailer: A Critical Study</u>. London: The
Macmillan Press, Ltd., pp. 76, 77.
Notes Dos Passos' influence on <u>The Naked and the Dead</u>.

21 SALE, ROGER. Review of <u>Ragtime</u>. <u>New York Review of Books</u>, 22
(7 August), 21-22.
Feels that, in <u>Ragtime</u>, E. L. Doctorow's "story makes
his history predictable and easy just as politics makes Dos
Passos' history predictable and easy in <u>U.S.A.</u>"

22 SMITH, MARION HAMMETT. "Recollection of Dos." <u>Connecticut
Review</u>, 8 (April), 21-24.
Affectionate recollection of Dos Passos and his wife Katy
and of their summers at Provincetown by Katy's sister-in-
law. Smith feels that Katy was partially responsible for
Dos' move to the political right and his falling out with
Hemingway.

23 STEGNER, WALLACE. <u>The Letters of Bernard De Voto</u>. Garden
City, N.Y.: Doubleday and Co., p. 118.
Feels that the work of Dos Passos and his contemporaries
does not represent "the sum of American experience in the
Twenties."

24 STEINBECK, ELAINE and ROBERT WALLSTEN, ed. <u>Steinbeck: A Life
in Letters</u>. New York: The Viking Press, pp. 566, 570.
Steinbeck writes to his wife from Hawaii and Japan of
the 1957 P.E.N. tour he is making with John Hersey and Dos
Passos.

25 STEINMANN, ELAINE MARIE FRIEDLE. "Adams, Dos Passos, Mailer:
Three Novelists of Democracy." Unpublished doctoral dissertation, University of Michigan.

1976

Comparison of the authors' views on democracy as revealed in Democracy, U.S.A., and Armies of the Night.

26 WILSON, EDMUND. The Twenties. Edited by Leon Edel. New York: Farrar, Straus and Giroux, passim.
Numerous references to Dos Passos from Wilson's notebooks.

27 WOODRESS, JAMES, ed. American Literary Scholarship: An Annual, 1973. Durham, N.C.: Duke University Press, pp. 93, 224, 225, 227, 238, 264, 435.
Reviews Dos Passos criticism of the year.

1976 A   BOOKS

1 PALMER, MICHAEL HAMILTON. "The Dramatic, Literary, and Historical Significance of John Dos Passos' Three Plays and Their Relationship to the Major Works." Unpublished doctoral dissertation, George Peabody College for Teachers.
Views Dos Passos' plays as the workshop in which the "themes, techniques, methods, style, and design" of the later novels, particularly U.S.A., were developed.

2 SORENSON, DALE ARCHIE. "The Pastoral Art of John Dos Passos." Unpublished doctoral dissertation, Bowling Green State University.
Calls for a major reassessment of Dos Passos' work, viewing it in the pastoral tradition.

1976 B   SHORTER WRITINGS

1 ADAMS, LAURA. Existential Battles: The Growth of Norman Mailer. Athens: Ohio University Press, pp. 11, 12, 15, 24, 37, 65n.
Notes the similarities between the Camera Eye sections of U.S.A. and the Time Machine sections of The Naked and the Dead. Thinks that from Steinbeck, Wolfe, Dos Passos, and Farrell, Mailer learned that "when large minds engage great chunks of life, a strong personal style is the catalyst which turns data into art."

2 ANDERSON, DIANNE LUCE. "Faulkner's Grimms: His Use of the Name Before Light in August." Mississippi Quarterly, 29 (Summer), 443.
Takes exception to Don Graham and Barbara Shaw's view (Mississippi Quarterly, 27) that Faulkner borrowed the name Percy Grimm for Light in August from John Dos Passos.

1976

3 BRADBURY, MALCOLM. "The Denuded Place: War and Form in
   Parade's End and U.S.A.," in The First World War in Fiction:
   A Collection of Critical Essays. Edited by Holger Klein.
   London: Macmillan, pp. 193-209.
       Despite the differences between the men and their books,
   Bradbury finds important similarities in their use of
   World War I to examine the complexities of history. Special
   attention to how their differing views of the war and its
   effects on society influenced the structure and style of
   their novels.

4 CAYLOR, RUTH ANITA. "The Modern Spanish Novel of the Multiple
   Protagonist." Unpublished doctoral dissertation, Wayne
   State University.
       Calls Dos Passos the originator of the multiple protago-
   nist in fiction.

5 COOK, SYLVIA JENKINS. From Tobacco Road to Route 66: The
   Southern Poor White in Fiction. Chapel Hill: The University
   of North Carolina Press, pp. 69, 138.
       Notes the influence of Dos Passos on William Rollins, Jr.'s
   1934 proletarian novel, The Shadow Box.

6 DETTELBACK, CYNTHIA GOLOMB. In The Driver's Seat: The
   Automobile in American Literature and Popular Culture.
   Contributions in American Studies. Number 25. Westport,
   Conn.: Greenwood Press, pp. 23, 67, 75-80.
       Cites Dos Passos' ironic use of the automobile as a
   symbol of status for those who own one, as a lack of status
   for those who do not, a symbol which is "often accomplice
   to human lies and deception."

7 EDMISTON, SUSAN and LINDA D. CIRINO. Literary New York: A
   History and a Guide. Boston: Houghton Mifflin Co., pp.
   103, 105, passim.
       Many references to Dos Passos' haunts in New York City.

8 EPSTEIN, JOSEPH. "The Riddle of Dos Passos." Commentary, 61
   (January), 63-66.
       Feels that Dos Passos' artistic decline was not so much
   a result of the political shift from left to right--for
   there have been conspicuous examples of successful novelists
   more conservative than Dos Passos--but that the decline is
   more personal, a growing despair in which Dos Passos could
   no longer summon sympathy for his characters. This, Epstein
   feels, resulted in flat and sterile characterization and,
   as a result, bad art.

9 FARRELL, JAMES T. "How Should We Rate Dos Passos?" in
   Literary Essays: 1954-1974. Edited by Jack Alan Robbins.
   Port Washington, N.Y./London: National University Publica-
   tions, Kennikat Press, pp. 118-121.
       Reprint of 1958.B11.

10 HEYMANN, C. DAVID. Ezra Pound: The Last Power. New York:
    The Viking Press, pp. 55, 250.
        Mentions Dos Passos. Notes his statement advising Pound
    be released from St. Elizabeth's.

11 HILL, ROBERT F. "Dos Passos: A Reassessment." The University
    Bookman, 10 (Winter), 27-39.
        Intelligent summary of the political conflicts beginning
    in the late thirties which affected Dos Passos' writing and
    the critics' perceptions of the writing. Compares Midcentury
    favorably to U.S.A. to show that Dos Passos' artistic powers
    had not significantly declined. Feels that Midcentury is
    successful because its kaleidoscopic technique, which it
    shares with U.S.A., is essential to Dos Passos' art.

12 HOWE, IRVING. "The American Voice--It Begins on a Note of
    Wonder." New York Times Book Review (4 July), pp. 1-3.
        Says in this bicentennial overview of American litera-
    ture that Dos Passos' characters, while "turning leftward
    politically retain more of the Emersonian sensibility than
    they, or, at the time, even he [Dos Passos] can realize."

13 HUGHSON, LOIS. "Narration in the Making of Manhattan Transfer."
    Studies in the Novel, 8 (Summer), 185-198.
        Considers Manhattan Transfer an explosive acceleration
    of the stylistic innovation of Dos Passos' earlier novels.
    Through a close textual reading, Hughson shows how Dos
    Passos developed techniques for capturing the energy and
    emotion of New York.

14 JACKSON, BLYDEN. The Waiting Years: Essays on American Negro
    Literature. Baton Rouge: Louisiana State University Press,
    p. 59.
        Mentions Dos Passos' comment that books may have "two
    kinds of extension, horizontal, through a few years, and
    vertical, through the ages."

15 KATOPES, PETER J. "Wesley Everest in John Dos Passos'
    Nineteen Nineteen." Notes and Queries, 23 (January), 22.
        Notes the probable sources for Dos Passos' portrayal of
    Everest.

1976

16 LARDNER, RING, JR. The Lardners: My Family Remembered. New
    York: Harper and Row, Publishers, p. 225.
        Mentions Lardner and Dos Passos as among the first con-
    tributors to Esquire.

17 LEWIS, KATHLEEN BURFORD. "The Representation of Social Space
    in the Novel: Manhattan Transfer, Naked Year, and Berlin
    Alexanderplatz." Unpublished doctoral dissertation,
    University of Iowa.
        Examines how the structure of Manhattan Transfer em-
    phasizes Dos Passos' theme of the decadence of American
    society.

18 McDOWELL, MARGARET B. Edith Wharton. United States Authors
    Series. New York: Twayne Publishers, p. 114.
        Considers it a mistake to compare Wharton's novel of
    World War I, A Son at the Front, with the war novels of
    Dos Passos and Hemingway, because it "is not a battlefield
    novel . . . it is a novel depicting the social stress and
    strains that the war entailed among the civilian populace
    as a whole."

19 SANDERS, DAVID. "John Dos Passos as Conservative," in A
    Question of Quality: Popularity and Value in Modern Creative
    Writing. Edited by Louis Filler. Bowling Green, Ohio:
    Bowling Green Popular Press, pp. 115-123.
        Compares U.S.A. and Midcentury in an attempt to study
    the relationship between Dos Passos' political conservatism
    and artistic decline.

20 _____. "John Dos Passos Interview," in Writers at Work: The
    Paris Review Interviews. Fourth series. Edited by George
    Plimpton. New York: Viking Press.
        Reprint of 1969.B69.

21 SEELYE, JOHN. "Doctorow's Dissertation." New Republic, 174
    (10 April), 21-22.
        Feels that, in Ragtime, E. L. Doctorow has taken "the
    qualities of Dos Passos' U.S.A. . . . and placed them in a
    compactor, reducing the bulk and hopelessly blurring the
    edges of definition." Nevertheless, the result is "an
    artifact which retains the specific gravity of Dos Passos'
    classic."

22 SHIRER, WILLIAM L. 20th Century Journey: A Memoir of A Life
    and the Times. New York: Simon and Schuster, passim.
        Many brief references to Dos Passos. Shirer considers
    the Veblen sketch to be the best biography of U.S.A.

23 SNYDER, ROBERT E. "The Concept of Demagoguery: Huey Long and
His Literary Critics." <u>Louisiana Studies</u>, 15 (Winter),
61-83.
Describes how <u>Number One</u> and other novels based on Long
have shaped the public's perception of him.

24 SPIEGEL, ALAN. <u>Fiction and the Camera Eye: Visual Consciousness
in Film and the Modern Novel</u>. Charlottesville: University
Press of Virginia, pp. 176-178.
Notes the influence of both Eisenstein and Joyce on Dos
Passos' montage technique in <u>U.S.A.</u> Feels that Dos Passos
"embodies the last resurgence of the bold technical experimentation of the Twenties," but that he softened and diluted
the technique: "Because Joyce's perspectives, even with
their union, strive to maintain their integral distance
from one another, their combined effects are always of
resonance and analogies. The Dos Passos montage operates
essentially on a single level, and no matter how disparate
the juxtaposed perspectives seem to be, they always manage
to come together and merge in one strong, clear gesture of
social protest." Joyce's method is dialectical; Dos Passos'
additional, in the tradition of Melville and Whitman, "the
epic cataloguers and listmakers of American space."

25 TENANT, EMMA. "Boneyard." <u>Listener</u>, 95 (22 January), 102.
Calls E. L. Doctorow's <u>Ragtime</u> a "post-Passos [sic]
pastiche."

26 TOOKER, DAN and ROGER HOFHEINS. "Interview with James Leigh,"
in <u>Fiction! Interviews with Northern California Novelists</u>.
New York: Harcourt Brace Jovanovich, p. 142.
Leigh feels that if there has ever been a Great American
Novel, <u>U.S.A.</u> is it: "It's got everything in it."

27 WAGNER, LINDA WELSHIMER, ed. <u>Interviews with William Carlos
Williams: "Speaking Straight Ahead."</u> New York: New
Directions, pp. xix, 58.
Wagner concludes her introduction: "And for Williams,
his own perfect joy came from the thrill of accurately
catching his people, in their own language, and in a poetry
that opened <u>form</u> and <u>genre</u> to all kinds of experimentation.
It could well be that in the future, Williams will be compared more often with those other great innovators of modern
American literature--Stein, Hemingway, Dos Passos--than
with his fellow 'poets.'"

28 WAGNER, LINDA W. "The Poetry in American Fiction." <u>Prospects</u>,
2 (1976), 513-526.

Examines how Dos Passos and others reshaped poetic con-
vention--particularly the idea of the image--in their
fiction.

29 WESTERHOVEN, JAMES N. "Autobiographical Elements in the
Camera Eye." American Literature, 648 (November), 340-364.
Making use of the biographical materials in The Best
Times, Townsend Ludington's The Fourteenth Chronicle,
Melvin Landsberg's Dos Passos' Path to "U.S.A.," and the
Dos Passos collection at the University of Virginia,
Westerhoven demonstrates the close parallels between the
Camera Eye sections of U.S.A. and the actual events, per-
ceptions, and feelings of Dos Passos' own life.

30 WOLFF, GEOFFREY. Black Sun: The Brief Transit and Violent
Eclipse of Harry Crosby. New York: Random House, pp. 52,
65, 88.
Several references. Epigraph to chapter five is a
quotation from 42nd Parallel.

31 WOODRESS, JAMES, ed. American Literary Scholarship, 1974.
Durham, N.C.: Duke University Press, pp. 68, 133, 143, 227,
242-244, 260, 434, 453.
Reviews Dos Passos criticism of the year.

32 ZAVARZADEH, MAS'UD. The Mythopoeic Reality: The Postwar
American Nonfiction Novel. Urbana: University of Illinois
Press, pp. 72, 98, 158.
Mentions the stylistic influence of Dos Passos on con-
temporary writers of the "nonfiction novel," particularly
Hersey and Mailer.

1977 A BOOKS

1 MARZ, CHARLES HERBERT. "John Dos Passos: The Performing
Voice." Unpublished doctoral dissertation, Brandeis
University, 313pp.
Study of the relationship between "fundamental social
and aesthetic responsibilities," of the tension between
"obligations to the Word and to the World." Believes that
Dos Passos found men who met those obligations in the
Founding Fathers: Washington, Madison, Paine, Williams,
and Jefferson.

2 MIZENER, SHARON FUSSEZMAN. Manhattan Transients. Hicksville,
N.Y.: Exposition Press, 48pp.

Examination of the characterization, use of imagery and symbolism, and, to a lesser extent, the social views of Manhattan Transfer.

1977 B   SHORTER WRITINGS

1   ATLAS, JAMES. Delmore Schwartz: The Life of an American Poet.
    New York: Farrar Straus Giroux, pp. 97, 108, 128, 189, 281.
        Several references to Dos Passos and to Schwartz's essay
    on him which Atlas says "can only be called definitive."

2   BLOODWORTH, WILLIAM A., JR. Upton Sinclair. United States
    Authors Series. Boston: Twayne Publishers, p. 115.
        Calls Dos Passos "the most passionately involved" writer
    in Sacco and Vanzetti's defense. Bloodworth feels that, of
    the at least nine works of fiction based on the case, Dos
    Passos' U.S.A. and Sinclair's Boston are the best.

3   BLOTNER, JOSEPH, ed. Selected Letters of William Faulkner.
    New York: Random House, pp. 134, 251, 409-410.
        Several letters mention Dos Passos. In one, 1940 letter,
    he bemoans the fact that there have appeared no younger
    writers to force himself, Hemingway, and Dos Passos--"the
    veterans now"--to fight "tooth and toenail to hold our
    places. . . . There are no young writers worth a damn that
    I know of."

4   BRANTLEY, JOHN D. "Dos Passos' Conversion from Class Struggle
    to Moral Middle Class Mobility." Lost Generation Journal,
    5 (Spring), 20-21.
        Feels that The Grand Design and Chosen Country represent
    a dramatic change in Dos Passos' portrayal of middle class
    characters. Brantley feels that middle class characters
    had necessarily compromised themselves in Dos Passos' earlier
    fiction, but now it was possible to live within society
    without sacrificing one's morality.

5   DONALDSON, SCOTT. By Force of Will: The Life and Art of Ernest
    Hemingway. New York: Viking Press, pp. 39-41, 104-105,
    216-217, passim.
        Discusses the relationship between Hemingway and Dos
    Passos, their falling out over the Spanish Civil War, and
    other incidents.

6   EZELL, MACEL D. Unequivocal Americanism: Right-Wing Novels
    in the Cold War Era. Metuchen, N.J.: The Scarecrow Press,
    pp. 34-38, passim.

Surveys Dos Passos' later career, noting his generally
enthusiastic reception by conservative critics. Concludes
that his views in this later period were consistent with
earlier ones. Dos Passos still continued to attack injustice, but from different sources.

7 FEUERLICHT, ROBERTA STRAUSS. Justice Crucified: The Story of
Sacco and Vanzetti. New York: McGraw-Hill Co., pp. 92, 93,
351, 381-382.
Notes Dos Passos' opposition to the executions of Sacco
and Vanzetti and his writing of their behalf.

8 HALLOWELL, JOHN. Fact and Fiction: The New Journalism and the
Nonfiction Novel. Chapel Hill: University of North
Carolina Press, pp. 12, 44, 94, 95.
Mentions Dos Passos' influence on the non-fiction
techniques of John Hersey, Dan Wakefield, and Norman
Mailer.

9 HOOPES, JAMES. Van Wyck Brooks: In Search of American Culture.
Amherst: The University of Massachusetts Press, pp. 148,
272, 297.
Brief mention of Dos Passos, stressing Brooks' altruistic
efforts to aid the younger writer's career.

10 KAWIN, BRUCE F. Faulkner and Film. New York: Frederick Ungar
Publishing Co., pp. 5-6, 8, 10-11, 147.
Acknowledges Faulkner's admiration for Dos Passos and
comments on their use of the cinematic technique of montage
in their fiction.

11 KOMAR, KATHLEEN LENORE. "The Multilinear Novel: A Structural
Analysis of Novels by Dos Passos, Doblin, Faulkner, and
Koeppen." Unpublished doctoral dissertation, Princeton
University.
Analysis of the structural texture of Manhattan
Transfer.

12 LEVIN, HARRY. "Being Strong: Edmund Wilson's Letters." The
New York Review of Books, 24 (27 October), 3-4, 6.
Review of Letters on Literature and Politics which notes
Wilson's criticism of Dos Passos' later conservative views
and faults Ludington's collection of Dos Passos' letters
for a paucity of return letters to Wilson from this exchange.

13 LUDINGTON, TOWNSEND. "Life Among the American Rover Boys."
Lost Generation Journal, 5 (Spring), 12-16.

Considers Dos Passos' prep school years at Choate to be
important in forming Dos Passos' sense of alienation from
the American, middle-class Establishment.

14 _____. "The Ordering of the Camera Eye in U.S.A." American
Literature, 44 (November), 443-446.
Feels that Dos Passos attempted to show, in the ordering
of the Camera Eye, "his gradual assimilation into a world
beyond the shelter of his self-conscious imagination."
Finds, in Dos Passos' increasing ability to associate himself with the outsiders and downtrodden, an element of
personal hope at the end of the trilogy.

15 McALEER, JOHN. Rex Stout: A Biography. Boston: Little, Brown
and Co., pp. 196, 198, 208, 224.
Mentions Dos Passos in several contexts.

16 McCONNELL, FRANK D. Four Postwar American Novelists: Bellow,
Mailer, Barth and Pynchon. Chicago: The University of
Chicago Press, p. 71.
Feels that Norman Mailer's "Time Machine" sections in
The Naked and the Dead, owe much to Dos Passos' "Camera
Eye" segments yet remain "distinctively 'Maileresque.'"

17 MAY, KEITH M. Out of the Maelstrom: Psychology and the Novel
in the Twentieth Century. New York: St. Martin's Press,
pp. 89, 90, 97.
Mentions Sartre's praise for Dos Passos, his belief that
"'Dos Passos is the greatest novelist of our time,'" to
demonstrate the international significance of the modern
American novel. May, himself, feels that in Hemingway,
more than Dos Passos, one may discern "an existential view
of men."

18 MOREAU, GENEVIEVE. The Restless Journey of James Agee.
Translated by Miriam Kleiger. New York: William Morrow
and Co., pp. 66, 149.
Mentions Dos Passos as one of the "writers whom Agee
first chose as models."

19 MORSE, JONATHAN. "Dos Passos' U.S.A. and the Illusions of
Memory." Modern Fiction Studies, 23 (Winter, 1977-78),
543-555.
Feels that through the fictional characters of U.S.A.,
Dos Passos reveals his theory of the historical dialectic.
Thinks that while Dos Passos uses Joycean means, he has a
Tolstoyan end of illuminating a theory of history. Calls

1977

U.S.A. essentially a conservative book for "it is an attempt
to re-establish the continuities of history for a nation
which . . . has always tried to drown out the past in the
raucous hallucination of an eternal present."

20 PENKOWER, MONTY NOAM. The Federal Writer's Project: A Study
in Government Patronage of the Arts. Urbana: University of
Illinois Press, pp. 191, 233, 243.
Occasional mention of Dos Passos. Includes a brief
account of the rejection of a suggestion that Dos Passos
head an FWP Advisory Committee "on the ground that the
author was a 'Fascist' and a 'reactionary' because of his
disillusionment with the communists in Spain."

21 PORTER, KATHERINE ANNE. "The Never-Ending Wrong." Atlantic
Monthly, 239 (June), 37-48, 53-64.
Mentions Dos Passos as one of the participants in the
Sacco-Vanzetti defense. Reprinted: 1977.B22.

22 _____. The Never-Ending Wrong. Boston: Little, Brown and
Company, pp. 23, 33, 51.
Reprint of 1977.B21.

23 SCHOLL, PETER A. "Dos Passos, Mailer, and Sloan: Young Men's
Initiations." Lost Generation Journal, 5 (Spring), 2-5,
23.
Concludes that One Man's Initiation--1917, The Naked and
the Dead, and War Games, three war novels from three different wars, each by a young Harvard man, "trace a rough but
graphic picture of America's deepening disillusion with
warfare."

24 SINCLAIR, ANDREW. Jack: A Biography of Jack London. New
York: Harper and Row Publishers, pp. 133, 248.
Credits London, in The Road, with creating a new kind of
American hero, "a sort of knowing Huckleberry Finn," which
"was to inspire Dos Passos" and other modern American
writers.

25 SPILLER, ROBERT E. Milestones in American Literary History.
Contributions in American Studies. Number 27. Westport,
Conn.: Greenwood Press, pp. 37, 40, 70, 72, 93.
Dos Passos is mentioned a number of times in this col-
lection of reviews of major works of American literary
criticism.

26 THORNTON, PATRICIA ELIZABETH. "The Prisoner of Gender: Sexual
Roles in Major American Novels of the 1920's." Unpublished
doctoral dissertation, University of New Brunswick.

Finds Dos Passos similar to other major novelists of his time in his belief that woman's emancipation means man's emasculation.

27 VANDERWERKEN, DAVID. "Manhattan Transfer: Dos Passos' Babel Story." American Literature, 49 (May), 253-267.
    Notes the Old Testament allusions in Manhattan Transfer. Explores in detail "the controlling myth of the Tower of Babel," and how Dos Passos "recasts the ancient materials in an American mode." Concludes that, in Manhattan Transfer, "Dos Passos assumes the role of prophet, a troubler of America like the old troublers of Israel, beseeching us to renew our covenant with the vision that begat us."

28 _____. "U.S.A.: Dos Passos and the 'Old Words.'" Twentieth Century Literature, 23 (May), 195-228.
    Demonstrates how U.S.A. reveals the use of language, by many of its characters, to obscure, falsify, and manipulate.

29 WATTS, EMILY STIPES. The Poetry of American Women from 1632 to 1945. Austin: University of Texas Press, p. 174.
    Notes the stylistic similarities between Muriel Rukeyser's poetry and Dos Passos' fiction.

30 WHIPPLE, ANNE. "Dos Passos and Caldwell Credited Journalism's Contribution." Lost Generation Journal, 5 (Spring), 6-8.
    Summarizes an unpublished Masters thesis--"The Contribution of Journalism to the Creative Writing of John Dos Passos and Erskine Caldwell,"--by Dale Speer which discusses Dos Passos' extensive journalistic writing and argues that much of that writing appears almost unchanged in his fiction.

31 WILSON, EDMUND. Letters on Literature and Politics, 1912-1972. Edited by Elena Wilson. New York: Farrar, Straus and Giroux, passim.
    Many letters to and references to Dos Passos. A rich collection.

32 _____. "Letters to John Dos Passos." New York Review of Books, 24 (3 March), 13-18.
    Eleven letters, written between 1931 and 1964, dealing with literature and politics. Excerpted from Letters on Literature and Politics, 1912-1972.

33 YARDLEY, JONATHAN. Ring: A Biography of Ring Lardner. New York: Random House, pp. 5, 256.
    Mentions Dos Passos.

1978

1978 A BOOKS

  1 COLLEY, IAIN. Dos Passos and the Fiction of Despair. Totowa,
     N.J.: Rowan and Littlefield, 170pp.
       Study of Dos Passos' fiction, primarily the major works:
     Three Soldiers, Manhattan Transfer, U.S.A., District of
     Columbia, and Midcentury. Colley thinks that Dos Passos'
     greatest achievement was in portraying "the sickly futility
     of a life . . . the accumulated detail of daily defeat"
     and how it is "transformed . . . into a destiny." Thinks
     the later fiction less successful because when it "ceases
     to draw energy from a nexus of alienation and doubt it
     loses artistic cohesion. The persona he chose, or grew
     into, was increasingly inimical not simply to his earlier
     purposes as a writer, but to the essential character of
     his literary ability."

1978 B SHORTER WRITINGS

 *1 ARAKELIAN, PAUL G. "Feature Analysis of Metaphor in The Waves
     and Manhattan Transfer." Style, 12 (Summer), 274-285.
       Cited in 1978 MLA International Bibliography. Vol. 1.
     New York: Modern Language Association of America, 1979.

  2 COWLEY, MALCOLM. And I Worked At The Writer's Trade: Chapters
     of Literary History, 1918-1978. New York: The Viking
     Press, pp. 32, 39, 108-110, 128.
       Calls U.S.A. one of "three big novels"--the others are
     The Grapes of Wrath and For Whom the Bell Tolls--which give
     the thirties "clearest expression of the age in its success-
     ive moods of anger, millennialism, and discouragement."
     Thinks U.S.A. represents "what many people besides the
     author felt in those years," but that now it might seem "to
     be an absurdly pessimistic novel."

  3 FOLEY, BARBARA. "From U.S.A. to Ragtime: Notes on the Forms
     of Historical Consciousness in Modern Fiction." American
     Literature, 50 (March), 85-105.
       While noting the similarities between U.S.A. and E. L.
     Doctorow's Ragtime, Foley focuses on the essential differ-
     ence: Dos Passos uses fiction to reveal history which he
     believes to be "knowable, coherent, significant, and in-
     herently moving"; Doctorow uses history to help create a
     mythic fictional past in which the focus is on how the
     fictional characters behave within a highly personalized
     historical frame.

4 LUDINGTON, TOWNSEND. "The Hotel Childhood of John Dos Passos."
   Virginia Quarterly Review, 54 (Spring), 297-313.
       Based on a reading of two unpublished essays which Dos
   Passos wrote while at Harvard, Ludington concludes that
   "the imaginative recreations of his childhood" which appear
   in the novels probably do not exaggerate Dos Passos' loneliness as a child. Calls U.S.A. "a stern yet moving state-
   ment of rebellion against, among many other things, the
   author's early life."

*5 McHALE, BRIAN. "Talking U.S.A.: Interpreting Free Indirect
    Discourse in Dos Passos' U.S.A. Trilogy, Part One."
    Degrés: Revue de Synthèses à Orientation Semiologique, 16.
        Cited in 1978 MLA International Bibliography. Vol. 1.
    New York: Modern Language Association of America, 1979.

6 MORRIS, WILLIE. "A Friendship: Remembering James Jones."
   Atlantic Monthly, 241 (June), 47-53, 58-64.
       Quotes Jones discussing his war trilogy of From Here to
   Eternity, The Thin Red Line, and Whistle: "It was always my
   intention with this trilogy that each novel should stand by
   itself as a work alone. In a way that, for example, John
   Dos Passos' three novels in his fine U.S.A. trilogy do
   not. . . . U.S.A. is one large novel, not a trilogy."

*7 ZARURSKY, Y[ASSEN]. "Dos Passos' Experimental Novel," in 20th
    Century American Literature: A Soviet View. Translated by
    Ronald Uroon. Moscow: Progress Publishers, pp. 331-350.
        Cited in 1978 MLA International Bibliography. Vol. 1.
    New York: Modern Language Association of America, 1979.

1979 A BOOKS

1 WAGNER, LINDA W. Dos Passos: Artist as American. Austin:
   University of Texas Press, 244pp.
       Calls Dos Passos' career a "literary exploration of
   America . . . in search of the national identity and its
   embodiment in a convincing American hero." Wagner gives
   special attention to Dos Passos' poetry, drama, travel
   essays, and historical writing. His experience in these
   various genres helped him shape and expand the themes and
   art of his fiction. Concludes that "Dos Passos' openness
   to the future, to promise, to the life of the imagination
   remained his hallmark, and one finds even in his compara-
   tively dour late years, a continuous curiosity."

Index